REASON, TRUTH, AND REALITY

DAN GOLDSTICK

Reason, Truth, and Reality

UNIVERSITY OF TORONTO PRESS
Toronto Buffalo London

© University of Toronto Press Incorporated 2009
Toronto Buffalo London
www.utppublishing.com
Printed in Canada

ISBN 978-0-8020-9594-7

Printed on acid-free paper

Library and Archives Canada Cataloguing in Publication

Goldstick, D. (Daniel), 1940–
Reason, truth, and reality / D. Goldstick.

ISBN 978-0-8020-9594-7 (bound)

1. Reason. Rationalism. I. Title.

BC177-G64 2008   128'.33   C2008-906538-7

University of Toronto Press acknowledges the financial assistance to its publishing program of the Canada Council for the Arts and the Ontario Arts
Council.

University of Toronto Press acknowledges the financial support for its
publishing activities of the Government of Canada through the Book
Publishing Industry Development Program (BPIDP).

This book has been published with the help of a grant from the Canadian
Federation for the Humanities and Social Sciences, through the Aid to
Scholarly Publications Program, using funds provided by the Social Sciences
and Humanities Research Council of Canada.

Induction is more convincing and clear: it is more readily learnt by the use of the senses, and is applicable generally to the mass of men; but deduction is more forcible and more effective against contradictious people.

Aristotle, *Topics*, Book I, chapter 12 (105a16–19)

Contents

Preface

This book is an essay in pre-Kantian rationalism. At the centre of it is the effort to characterize what *reason* is: not to tell what the *word* 'reason' means, nor yet to tell what brainy facts about humans, other animals, and possible electronic constructions of the future might serve to 'implement' the rational endowment these each to some degree possess or will possess. Rather, the contention will be that to be *rational* is to think – and hence act – on the basis of certain substantive propositions, stating facts about how things are and about how it is incumbent upon one to act. The strategy employed will amount to appealing to the reader's own rationality to agree that all this is so, not merely as far as 'appearances' go, but with respect to things as they are in themselves. The only consistent alternative, it will be argued, amounts to a scepticism which we all know better than to embrace when it comes down to actual practice.

Pretty big claims. It certainly would be surprising if all of them were correct. How much truth there is in the various propositions here advanced will of course be for the reader to decide. Is everything that happens determined by prior causes spatiotemporally linked to its occurrence by a continuous series of intermediate causes? Is there indeed absolutely nothing everlasting – except the undying reality of death itself, the *'mors immortalis'* of which Lucretius wrote? Does the basic difference between what is acceptable and unacceptable morally hinge in truth upon whatever is in the long-term interests of people generally? Can the case for these philosophical positions be made strong enough in a written text to convince any reader sufficiently clear-thinking and honest that they really are inescapable? That must be for you to decide.

As a practical matter, it is hardly possible to thank by name all those who since 1961 have helped me in writing this book. It may, though, be of interest, as a curiosity at least, that earlier drafts of the text were read by A.J. Ayer, John McDowell, Peter Unger, and Calvin Normore. But any reader at all familiar with those thinkers' specific views will certainly know better than to anticipate finding anything like them in the pages that are to follow.

Knowing me as a Marxist, there are readers who will be wondering what all this has to do with dialectical materialism. Those interested are referred to my papers 'Marxism and Epistemological Relativism' (written jointly with Frank Cunningham), *Social Praxis* 6, nos. 3/4 (1979), 237–53; 'Objectivity and Moral Commitment in the World-View of Marx and Engels,' *Science and Society* 47, no. 1 (Spring 1983), 84–91; 'Distributive Justice and Utility,' *Journal of Value Inquiry* 25, no. 1 (January 1991), 65–71; 'Objective Interests,' in *Critical Perspectives on Democracy*, edited by Lyman H. Legters, John P. Burke, and Arthur DiQuattro (Lanham, MD, 1994), 147–64; 'Marxism on Dialectical and Logical *Contradiction*,' *Australian Journal of Philosophy* 73, no. 1 (March 1995), 102–13; 'Out of Engels' Wastebasket, etc.,' *Nature, Society and Thought* 7, no. 4 (1994), 399–414; and 'Dialectics and Metaphysics' (jointly written, from opposing viewpoints, with John Leslie), *Explorations in Knowledge* 6, no. 1 (1989), 1–12. From my contributions to the last-listed item, I have lifted some sentences for use in chapter 16. The words 'give meaning' on page 85, line 4 of the 'Objectivity and Moral Commitment' paper ought to read 'it makes sense.'

PART ONE

Introductory

1 Introduction

Suppose you were given the task of compiling two lists, each of them as full as possible: one a list of truths and (as far as possible) of truths only; the other just listing whatever you believed. And suppose you did compile both lists simultaneously, to the best of your ability. That, in such a case, the two lists would have to contain exactly the same entries as each other is a truism.[1] For it is the very same thing to believe anything consciously (whether more confidently or less confidently) and (whether more confidently or less confidently) to take it to be true.

Indeed, if you simultaneously carried out the 'additional' task, to the best of your ability, of compiling also a list, as full as possible, composed only of listings for things which are at least *probable* (in the most ordinary sense of that word), then the entries on the third list as well would have to coincide exactly with those on the other two. (Just how high a *probability* greater than 50 per cent is it necessary to attribute to something in order to count as considering it *probable*? Whatever the answer, it no doubt corresponds to that degree of confidence in it which it is necessary to have in order to count as believing it.)[2]

---

1 Cf. A.J. Ayer, *The Origins of Pragmatism* (London, 1968), 25–6.
2 There are epistemologists who deny that *any* degree of confidence short of certainty can itself be sufficient for *belief*. This is because they think one has to count as believing any conjunction of one's (conscious) beliefs – or, at least, as doing so if rational. However, where the propositions conjoined are independent of one another, the probability of a conjunction will be *lower* the longer it is. But only fools, insensitive to the consequences of human fallibility, would seriously believe the conjunction of *all* that they (were aware they) believed, I have argued. See D. Goldstick, 'Justified Belief,' *Dialogue* 34, no. 1 (Winter 1995), 104.

This is not at all to say that whatever you believe must be true – for you are not infallible – still less, that whatever is true is already among your current beliefs – for of course you are not omniscient. Whenever you re-examine any belief you hold, or engage in inquiry aimed at answering some question on which you do not yet hold any opinion at all, you show perfectly clearly in practice that you do not regard yourself as being either omniscient or infallible. It is owing to your fallibility, also, that not everything you believe is actually even probable. And likewise, of course, not everything probable is in fact true, for sometimes it is the improbable which actually comes about. All this is common knowledge.

As far as *truth* goes, the truism that consciously believing something is the same thing as considering it *true* imposes a constraint, surely, on any account of what the adjective 'true' can mean, in its most usual sense. Against this, Arne Naess has insisted that it really is possible to believe something without regarding it as true, and without regarding it as even probable.[3] No doubt that is correct where the belief is not conscious. To think of anything as *true* or as *probable* involves adopting a more abstract standpoint than is required merely to believe some-thing without also taking notice of the existence of that belief. Can we not attribute even to a dog, on occasion, the belief that there is some-thing tasty *over there*, without supposing that the dog has any concep-tion of psychological conditions such as *belief*, or has any such abstract conceptions as those of *truth* or *probability*? To make good his denial that believing anything entails regarding it as true, or even probable, Naess proposes a purely 'behavioural' understanding of *belief* – but (somehow) not of *regarding something as true* or *regarding something as probable*. Why not?

At any rate, Naess's philosophical 'scepticism,' as he calls it, express-ly recommends holding beliefs without regarding them as true and without regarding them as even probable. To adopt such a philosophy, and accordingly carry out what it recommends, is presumably to do so *consciously*. So whatever can Naess's meaning be? Perhaps by recom-mending that we *believe* anything only in a 'behavioural' sense, what Naess means is that we should *act as if* we believed it, but without be-lieving it in fact (in the normal sense of 'believing').

But why *should* we act as if we held beliefs which we do not? Naess notes that it is unavoidable, in real life, to act upon various 'beliefs' about

---

3   Arne Naess, *Scepticism* (London, 1968), chap. 2, 36–60.

things. Can this be said, after all, to evince a belief on his part that there are certain ways things *truly* are, which necessitate acting accordingly so as to bring about whatever it is that is needed? Or is he resting his case merely on the *psychological impossibility* of not acting accordingly, at least most of the time? But, in that case, are not the workings of the mind such that what is psychologically impossible is actual belieflessness, and not *merely* the avoidance of ostensibly belief-reflecting behaviour?

David Hume, in his philosophy, stressed the psychological impossibility of belieflessness, adding that an advocate of it

> must acknowledge, if he will acknowledge anything, that all human life must perish, were his principles universally and steadily to prevail. All discourse, all action would immediately cease; and men remain in a total lethargy, till the necessities of nature, unsatisfied, put an end to their miserable existence.[4]

Somehow, this reflection did not stop Hume from advancing theses which, in his own opinion, militated against various propositions psychologically impossible, in full consciousness, to avoid embracing when it came to practice. But when an inquirer is in fact fully convinced of (the truth of) something, how could a conscious refusal to premise it – apart from a temporary refusal under the special conditions of a thought-experiment – ever be squared with self-honesty or serious concern for truth? Where the truth *matters* to us – that is to say, most of the time when it comes to deciding how we shall act – we quickly put aside any philosophizing which purports to place the truth beyond our reach.

If, though, there is no real way to avoid viewing so very many things as *true*, is it actually essential to regard them as being *objectively true*? But what is the contrast intended here? Just what would it be to regard anything as being *true*, without regarding it as being *objectively true*? To accept it, but only with reduced confidence? However, why could not a belief that something is *objectively* the case be held with either a greater or a lesser measure of confidence? Similarly, it is possible consciously to accord belief to something *in general* without regarding it as *completely* true (though perhaps also without being able to specify in what particulars it is not or may not be true; as can happen with good reason, in the

---

4   David Hume, *An Inquiry concerning Human Understanding,* in David Hume, *Enquiries concerning Human Understanding and concerning the Principles of Morals,* ed. L.A. Selby-Bigge, 3rd ed., rev. P.H. Nidditch (Oxford, 1975), 160.

history of science, when a theory starts to break down and show signs of needing to be superseded by a more comprehensive replacement correcting it, but showing why it does hold good in the main). However, why should such qualifications in the way that something is believed prevent the believers from still considering it – to just the extent that they do believe it at all – to be something which is *objectively true*?

Seemingly, the natural contrast with 'objective truth' would be 'subjective truth.' What could it mean for something to be 'true' but only 'subjectively' rather than 'objectively'? The answer which suggests itself in the first instance is that for a belief to be 'subjectively true' is for it to be *true according to the believer*. But, of course, that holds good for any conscious belief whatsoever. The force of anti-objectivism here is to insist that people's beliefs are *only* 'subjectively true.' This would seem to mean that, although they are believed, or believed to be true, there does not exist any more *truth* to them than that: in other words, they, in fact, are *not* true. A line of thought such as this clearly cannot be of help to subjectivists trying to explain how they can believe anything in full consciousness without taking it to be true *objectively*.

This sort of anti-objectivism cannot say, in other words, that by 'subjective truths' what is meant is simply people's beliefs, or their conscious beliefs. On the other hand, surely it is not going to consider the 'subjective truth' of what people believe to be something altogether independent, either, of the fact that they believe it. 'There is nothing either good or bad, but thinking makes it so,' said Hamlet, and we can no doubt understand him here to be insisting on the merely *subjective* as opposed to *objective* 'truth' of all notions about what is good and bad; though, in context, it is not *moral* goodness and badness that Hamlet has in mind. How could something's being true *not* be independent of its being believed? Presumably, in the first place, by its being true *because* it is believed. In the most straightforward understanding of this 'because,' any self-fulfilling expectation would have to fit the description of being true *because* it is believed: for example, when a student's unfounded expectation of failure on an important examination produces an incapacitating mental depression from which failure then does result. But in calling people's beliefs 'only subjectively true,' it cannot be meant that they are all like that. Belief about past facts, for example, cannot possibly *cause* the facts in question, and surely that is not at all what subjectivism means to say if it asserts that people's beliefs are 'true only because they are believed' inasmuch as 'thinking makes it so.'

Let us, then, interpret the 'because' here *logically*, and understand by a belief's being 'subjectively true,' that its truth follows *logically* from its being held. Did Descartes' existence logically follow (as he thought it did) from his believing that he existed? Is it possible to have an un-reasoned belief that you are in pain, and is that logically sufficient for your then *being* in pain (whether psychosomatically or not)? Perhaps there indeed are cases of true belief where the existence of the fact be-lieved is logically necessitated by the existence of the belief. In such cases, if there are any, the fact believed and the fact that it is believed are perhaps not really two different facts. The beliefs in question in such cases must indeed all be 'subjective,' at least in part, in their subject mat-ter: specifically, they must all refer to themselves, at least among other things. This applies at most, though, to only a relatively narrow range of people's beliefs. And so, it cannot be this that anti-objectivism has in mind if it says that people's beliefs can only ever be 'subjectively true.'[5]

What then? Hamlet's dictum about good and bad reminds us that it could be quite sensible to deny that anything can ever be *good-tasting* (or, likewise, ever be *frightening*) 'in itself' – that is, as distinct from how

---

5   Probably the element in the Correspondence Theory of Truth to which philosophical dissenters from it have mainly objected is the idea that the existence of a true belief and the existence of the fact believed are two distinct existences; and the logical indeducibil-ity of either from the other in the commonest sort of case would indeed appear to bear out the Correspondence Theory on that point. To this, the Correspondence Theory only adds that what *truth* amounts to is nothing but a certain sort of matching between those two existents. What sort? The Correspondence Theory itself does not say. However, it does seem trivial that, with any true beliefs, the facts believed are such that, if they were any different, the beliefs too would have to be different *correspondingly* if they were still to be true beliefs: that is to say, for any such differences in how the facts stood, the beliefs in question would have to differ *in the same way* from how they actually are. In other words, the features of the substitute beliefs would have to differ from those of the actual beliefs in the same way as the features of the alternative facts differed from the features of the actual facts. Now, wherever A differs from B in the same way as X differs from Y, A and X will be *alike* in the way that they differ from B and Y. And so, there must then be *some* bona fide resemblance between A and X, between any true belief and the fact believed. But the resemblance involved would not need to be anything more that an *isomorphism*. The philosophical incompleteness of the Correspondence Theory as an account of what *truth* is becomes obvious upon the reflection that *falsehood* too involves a 'correspondence' between beliefs and facts: for, were the facts any different from what they are, the incorrect beliefs which are held would for their part have to be different *in the same way* if they were still to be false beliefs; and so, a sort of resemblance is required between false beliefs and the facts, just as another sort of resemblance is required between true beliefs and the facts. (Cf., Ludwig Wittgenstein, *Tractatus Logico-Philosophicus*, 4.061–4.0621.)

it appears or would appear. Presumably, 'good-tasting' is equivalent to 'pleasant-tasting,' and means or implies 'of such a sort as would please normal tasters under normal conditions' (just as 'frightening' means or implies 'of such a sort as normally would frighten those who are normal'). Whatever the extension of the class of 'normal tasters' (or 'those who are normal') which can be understood as implied here, it surely would in any case necessarily take in the speaker: so that to regard something or other, in full consciousness, as *good-tasting* (or as *frightening*) need not involve believing in the existence of two altogether independent facts: the fact that it really is good-tasting (or frightening), and the fact that it is so regarded, or would be so regarded, especially by oneself. This may be a way in which it is possible after all to consciously regard something as so without taking it to be *objectively true* that it is so. But can somebody's only regarding something as so in that sort of way really count as *believing* that it is so? Just what is a belief?

Surely *beliefs*, at any rate insofar as their subject matter does not make them refer to themselves, are all *objectivity-claiming*, at least implicitly. Consciously to *believe* that something (about a supposedly belief-independent subject matter) is so, is the same thing as believing that it is objectively *true* that it is so – equivalently, that it is an objective *fact* that it is so. In the event of no such fact really existing, the belief will consequently be false (for more on 'factuality,' see chapter 3). Thus a *belief*, properly so called, is a truth-valuable mental condition, one which by its nature is true-or-false: true, in case what is believed is indeed a fact (whether an objective fact or a subjective fact); and false otherwise.[6] It might be objected here that it is not the mental condition of *believing* something which is ever really true or false, but rather only that which thereby is believed. This objection could be readily accommodated by a minor verbal amendment: call *belief* a 'fruth-valuable' sort of mental condition, where a belief's being 'frue' just means that what is believed is *true*. Everything said in this chapter could then, if desired, be rephrased accordingly without any loss to the substantive points being

---

6   Must we call someone's belief to the effect that the present King of France is bald a false belief merely because France is a republic (supposing that the believer in fact does not have some actual individual in mind who really is bald)? If the belief in question is consciously held, it is at the same time a belief that the present King of France being bald is among the truths that there are; so that, if in fact there is no such truth, the belief that there is such a truth will be a false one. For a further defence of 'bivalentism' in the face of the Liar Paradox and 'category mistakes,' see my paper 'Against "Categories,"' *Philosophical Studies* 26, nos. 5/6 (December 1974), 337–56.

made. We shall have to return to the basic conception of *belief* as a truth-valuable mental condition in chapter 3.

Meanwhile, the object has been to urge the untenability of 'metaphysical antirealism,' 'postmodernism,' et cetera, insofar, at any rate, as they are tantamount in practice to comprehensive *scepticism*, in the sense of a philosophy which opposes seriously believing anything.[7] Until the supporters of these positions can explain to us what else they have in mind which is different from this, we are in no position to consider the merits of any such different positions.

For the reasons given, the *truth* of any belief normally must be something quite different from the fact that the belief is held. But must it be different from the fact, if it is one, that holding the belief would be advantageous to the believer(s)? Yes, it must, for it is perfectly possible to hold a belief consciously without at all regarding it as being a belief that is advantageous to hold, even on balance and in the long run. Such may be the position of the persecuted followers of a minority religious conviction which does *not* promise its adherents any special ticket to salvation; or the position (if they are self-aware) of the sort of students mentioned above, whose expectation of failure on an examination, however ill-founded initially, is foreseeably disabling enough in its psychological effects to ensure that they will in fact fail, however much they now remind themselves that their initial pessimism was unwarranted. Similarly, the fact that something is true, if it actually is, cannot be equated with the fact, if it is a fact, that a permanent consensus will eventually be formed in agreement with it, or eventually would be formed among sufficiently scrupulous inquirers if only inquiry into the question were to be carried sufficiently far. For it is perfectly possible to hold an opinion in full consciousness without supposing that such posterity will or would be in agreement with it. Here again, appeal is being made to the truism that consciously believing anything is identical with considering it *true*, as an evident constraint upon accounts of what the word 'true' can mean.

Philosophical 'realism' has sometimes been denied in the name of a semantical doctrine equating anything's *truth* with its eventual conclusive establishability rationally (whether or not, presumedly, its being so

---

7 Naess's 'sceptic' was allowed to 'believe' things but not to *call* them true. Sir Walter Raleigh's 'sceptic,' on the other hand, '... doth neither affirm, neither deny any position; but doubteth of it, and opposeth his reasons against that which is affirmed or denied, to justify his not consenting.' *The Works of Sir Walter Ralegh, Kt.*, vol. 8 (Oxford, 1829), 548.

established were going to get recognized as such, then or later). This doctrine entails, of course, that all truths without exception are establishable conclusively, and, in the second place, it discounts, for these purposes, any considerations but rational ones when it comes to establishing them. But all those who accept the second point to the extent of allowing themselves to be influenced only by rational considerations in determining their beliefs will be inclined to believe anything consciously, and so consider it true, only when they do consider it in fact to be rationally established – and hence, of course, establishable. And so, our truism, that to believe something consciously is to consider it true, will not be violated by such an understanding of *truth* (provided, that is, that the level of confidence deemed requisite for 'belief'can be raised to whatever level of rational support is required before evidence *supports* something 'conclusively;' or, alternatively, the individuals in question regard even tentative belief as rationally warranted only where it may be supposed that fuller inquiry would eventually establish the belief conclusively). We will, however, be turning to a deeper consideration of this 'antirealist' philosophical doctrine in chapter 5.

'Transcendent' or 'dogmatical' realism notoriously was criticized by Immanuel Kant. The idea was to fend off a scepticism supposedly unanswerable otherwise by means of systematically reducing all claims about what can be known.

> ... a complete review of all the powers of reason – and the conviction thereby obtained of the certainty of its claims to a modest territory, as also of the vanity of higher pretensions – puts an end to the conflict, and induces it to rest satisfied with a limited but undisputed patrimony.[8]

This certainly sounds like a proposal to restrict what is considered rationally knowable to a systematically reduced range of subject matter. Notoriously, Kant insisted that only 'phenomena' or 'appearances' are knowable, as opposed to 'things in themselves,' and criticized the 'transcendent' or 'dogmatical' philosophies for claiming to provide knowledge of the latter. But how could any account of anything ever be true and incisive, let alone a piece of anybody's knowledge, except insofar as it characterizes whatever its subject matter is – be it a rock, a society, or even an appearance – as it is *in itself*? Outside of Kantian philosophy,

---

8   Immanuel Kant, *Critique of Pure Reason* (A768=B796), Norman Kemp Smith translation.

and usage influenced by it, the distinction between *appearances* and *things in themselves* serves either to call attention to the fallibility of the way things seem (that is, the way they seem to be *in themselves*) or to mark the difference between truths which are more or less readily apparent but relatively unimportant to a theoretical understanding of the subject matter of an inquiry, and truths, by contrast, which are less obvious but more central to an understanding of that subject matter. In these useful employments, a phrase like 'in itself' has earned an epistemologically honorific force. The trick of Kantian 'Critical Philosophy' is to promise a different, technical meaning to the *appearances/things-in-themselves* distinction, without clearly specifying any, while meantime pointedly withholding the honestly earned honorific force of the phrase 'in itself' when it comes to all that is humanly knowable.

Pre-Kantian rationalism, for instance, asserted as a rational axiom that nothing ever occurs uncaused. But all that is really knowable, Kant insisted, was that this maxim applies to experienceable 'appearances,' in contrast to 'things in themselves.' In the first place, he never did explain why 'things in themselves' had to be unexperienceable. But, beyond that, whatever can be *meant* by the claim that 'Nothing ever occurs uncaused' applies only to experienceable appearances in contrast to things in themselves? Does this mean that it *only appears*, in the course of experience, that nothing ever occurs uncaused (but that this is not or may not be so *in reality*)? Does it mean that nothing which occurs is ever experienceable except *as* (apparently) caused? Or what?

And how ever *can* anything *appear* a certain way to somebody who is not positively of the opinion (whether more confidently held or less confidently held) that it actually *is* that way 'in itself'? Surely this can happen only when *other* appearances or information available to that person conflict with this appearance, resulting in either a contrary opinion or a suspension of all belief on the matter. To raise again a point already suggested, how *could* anything ever *appear* a certain way without appearing to be that way 'in itself'?

If Kantians object that none of this actually captures the special, technical *appearances/things-in-themselves* distinction which is intended, it is up to them to explain what the distinction really is. Surely, until they do, the 'Critical' proposal for restricting knowledge claims must remain without any force.

It is, to be sure, a fact that Kant did not maintain a total silence about where the line between 'appearances' and 'things in themselves' was to be drawn. For, according to his phraseology, all the former and only the former are *objects of possible experience*.

He does expressly deny, for instance, that an absolute first moment of time could be something which any mind experienced (presumably because for that, the experiencing mind would have to be around *before* the beginning of time). He declares both an absolute beginning of time and a lack of any to be alike unexperienceable in principle, and hence humanly unknowable. He calls our attention to the point that to accept that *every event is caused* in a 'dogmatical' spirit, without the critical restriction of such a principle's applicability to *appearances* only, must inevitably lead to denying that there ever was a first moment in time. But he argues that the opposite doctrine, affirming that there was indeed such a first moment, is equally well necessitated by adherence to the rejected 'transcendent' standpoint, since each successive moment would otherwise have to be considered, from such a standpoint, to 'sum up,' as we might put it, or 'complete' an actually infinite series of past events: however, an infinite series cannot ever be coherently thought of as completed in any definite, limited 'sum,' Kant argues in effect – surely unpersuasively (for events *only* express, in a relatively immediate way, what they owe to their more direct causes, bearing traces of any remoter ones only through these).[9] Kant's Critical cure for the 'transcendent' standpoint in philosophy, from which questions such as these arise, appears on examination to be rationally ineffective medicine.[10]

---

9 Kant also argues that, considered 'dogmatically,' there can be no incomposite material atoms, because space necessarily is infinitely divisible; while, equally necessarily, there *must* be some because composition is by its nature inessential, and yet it could not coherently be imagined away without eliminating matter altogether, if everything material were to be composite. However, surely *composition* is not at all inessential to a composite entity, but only to the entity's components. Kant's four 'Antinomies of Pure Reason' include two further such 'conflicts of the transcendental ideas,' each one with a naturalistic 'antithesis' counterposed to a contrary 'thesis,' but the argument for each of these two 'theses' turns out to depend on the supposed necessity of an absolute beginning of time, and so there is no need to deal with them separately. *Critique of Pure Reason*, A426=B454–A461=B489.

10 Is that all there is to be said about Kant's Critical philosophy? Of course not. Indeed, I have myself attempted a somewhat more elaborate criticism in my 'The Kantian Way of Answering Hume,' in Georges J.D. Moyal and Stanley Tweyman, eds., *Early Modern Philosophy* (Delmar, NY, 1985), 177–92. And the reader will certainly be able to notice what is owed to Kant positively throughout this book. Kant's limitation of knowledge to what can or could in principle be experienced reappears, in a

After all this rationalist trumpeting, no reader, perhaps, need be taken by surprise by the information that what is being attempted here is an exercise in pre-Kantian rationalism incompatible also with *empiricism*, interpreted as a philosophy opposing the acceptance of anything – or at least of anything logically contingent – as being *true*, unless it either simply reports experience or else is accepted on account of experiences, on the basis that the experiences would not (or probably would not) be occurring or have occurred if *it* were not true.[11]

This is the thought behind 'Hume's Fork,' classically formulated in the notorious closing paragraph with which David Hume concluded his *Inquiry concerning Human Understanding*:

---

strengthened version, in some forms of the logical empiricist 'Verification Principle,' discussed in chapter 5.

11 This formulation is derived from Carl Hempel's definition of 'empiricism' as the doctrine that all synthetic knowledge is empirical. See Carl G. Hempel, 'Problems and Changes in the Empiricist Criterion of Meaning,' *Revue internationale de Philosophie* 4, no. 11 (January 1950), 41, note 2: 'According to [empiricism], a sentence expresses knowledge only if it is either analytic or corroborated by empirical evidence.' Empirical knowledge is presumedly divisible into knowledge of experiences and knowledge based on inference from experiences. It is important here that the 'inference' in question need not be conscious. For our present purposes, a maximally broad understanding of 'inference' will be in order. Let us say that people believe that p on the basis of 'inference' from the premises that q and that r ... et cetera whenever they believe that p because they both believe that q as well as that r ... et cetera, and are unable to believe that q & r & ... & -p; and let us add that the relation is transitive, so that whatever is believed on the basis of premises in turn believed on the basis of inference from other premises, counts as something for its part believed on the basis of 'inference' from those other premises. Surely, whatever is accepted as true on account of certain experiences, on the basis that those experiences would not (or probably would not) be occurring or have occurred if it were not true, is something that can be described, in this sense, as believed 'on the basis of inference' from those experiences. But just what are 'experiences'? For our purposes, we can say that a mind has 'experiences' at least any time that it comes to believe, without inference, that something is occurring or has occurred, or that something temporal exists or has existed. There is no restriction here on whether the supposed occurrences or existents in question are 'inner,' 'outer,' or 'neutral,' just as the supposed existents can equally well be objects, states, properties, relations, circumstances or the like. And for our purposes, a belief that something exists or has existed can count as a 'belief that something temporal exists or has existed' if and only if what is believed is consistent with the supposed existent ceasing to exist or having ceased to exist. Lastly, a process of inference is an 'inference from experiences,' whether its premises specifically describe these supposed existences or occurrences or (if that is not the same thing) the inceptions of these uninferred beliefs about them.

> When we run over libraries, persuaded of these principles, what havoc must
> we make? If we take in our hand any volume; of divinity or school metaphys-
> ics, for instance; let us ask, *Does it contain any abstract reasoning concerning*
> *quantity or number?* No. *Does it contain any experimental reasoning concerning*
> *matter of fact and existence?* No. Commit it then to the flames: for it can
> contain nothing but sophistry and illusion.[12]

In these words, Hume declares that any purported science which is
not either mathematical or 'experimental' (experiential) is nothing
but 'sophistry and illusion.' He does not, however, say that any (ostensible) assertion which fails the test of some empiricist criterion
must needs on that account be meaningless or otherwise debarred
from being true. He does not actually deny there to be any truths
which are both synthetic – negatable without logical contradiction –
and *a priori* in the sense, let us say, of being both unprovable and
irrefutable by any consistently imaginable experiences. However, if
there are such truths, there is no telling what they are, according to
Hume's Fork.

More than that. According to empiricist philosophy, if ever anything synthetic is believed – even where it actually is something in
principle provable or refutable by consistently imaginable experiences – but that which is believed is neither itself an account of experiences, nor believed on the basis of inference from experiences, that is
going to be a belief which is unwarranted; so that, even if somehow it
should happen to be true, the believer is still going to count as *making*
a mistake in holding it.

The Scottish School of 'common-sense' philosophy founded by
Thomas Reid used to criticize Hume for refusing to accept for philosophical purposes truths like the denial that anything ever occurs uncaused, which he himself agreed it was psychologically impossible to
disbelieve or doubt. Hume had perhaps already anticipated that line of
objection when it came to causal-inductive inference:

> My practice, you say, refutes my doubts. But you mistake the purport of
> my question. As an agent, I am quite satisfied in the point; but as a phil-
> osopher, who has some share of curiosity, I will not say scepticism, I want
> to learn the foundation of this inference.[13]

---

12 Hume, *An Inquiry concerning Human Understanding*, 165. Emphasis in original.
13 Ibid., 38.

There are two different ways of interpreting this response to the objection advanced. According to one of them, Hume thinks that he can be 'quite satisfied' *as an agent* on the question of something's truth, while at the same time *as a philosopher* deliberately refusing to consider it true. Not merely refusing to *call* it true, that is, or refusing to premise or otherwise presuppose its truth for the purposes of developing some particular argument or thought-experiment, but simply, without qualification, *refusing to consider it true* at all, when philosophizing. It would not merely be a neat trick to do that. As we have noted, it is logically impossible to believe anything consciously without considering it to be true. Nor does Hume ever challenge this. And so, according to the second line of interpretation of the words quoted above, what he is saying is that he too agrees fully with the inductive principle, but merely wishes to investigate the *psychology* of inductive inference in human beings and animals. On that interpretation, there is no scepticism about induction in Hume's philosophy. But on that interpretation there is also no place for Hume's Fork; for Hume himself seems to show that (acceptance of) the inductive principle must contravene the Fork. The Scottish philosopher Thomas Brown zeroed in on the sort of issue which is at stake here in this way:

> If, as Mr. Hume confesses, 'none but a fool or a madman' will deny the authority of that principle, he confesses that none but a fool or a madman will deny the just reasonings, which are founded on that principle.[14]

The Scottish School used to make the claim that Hume in fact produced a *reductio ad absurdum* of empiricism, by proving that it led to scepticism. And, indeed, if we for our part are convinced unshakably that, at the very least, it is highly probable that the sun will rise tomorrow (between the Arctic and the Antarctic Circles), then how could we, in our own minds, honestly and consistently withhold assent from any principle of induction on which such a judgment provably depends in order to be warranted, or refrain from rejecting any philosophy that would even by implication disallow the needed principle?[15]

---

14 Thomas Brown, *Inquiry into the Relation of Cause and Effect*, 4th ed. (London, 1835), 378.

15 How could we do so honestly and consistently? But, on the other hand, why be consistent? So at least the objection would run. Devil's-advocating in another connection, Peter van Inwagen speculates in *An Essay on Free Will* (Oxford, 1983): 'Suppose one had a certain belief that one found one couldn't rid oneself of,

In traditional logic texts, an argument was described as 'valid *ad hominem*' if it proceeded validly from something which those to whom it was addressed had admitted themselves, there or elsewhere. And in our own deliberations, addressed just to ourselves, if we ever are unshakably convinced of something, reason surely dictates that we must accept anything which rationally follows from it, as well as whatever is provably requisite for our acceptance of it to count as rationally warranted.

That is the strategy to be followed in this book. The object will be to show that our thinking inextricably depends upon certain principles with very wide implications, which can thus be seen rationally to command assent, and where such assent cannot be squared with the empiricist requirements of Hume's Fork, so much the worse for empiricism. Hume seems not to have noticed that many of the 'sceptical arguments' which he suggests actually presuppose his Fork. Concerning sceptical arguments in general, he himself notoriously declared they '*admit of no answer and produce no conviction. Their only effect is to cause ...* momentary amazement and irresolution and confusion, ...'[16] but he was quite wrong about their unanswerability to the extent that they really depend on an empiricist presupposition which cannot be independently established.

---

however much one tried. And suppose one had indisputable evidence – and regarded it as indisputable evidence – for the falsity of that belief. If it were true that there was something "intrinsically" bad about having contradictory beliefs, then it might well be – depending on how bad it was – that what one should do is to (attempt to) stop having any beliefs that contradict one's "immutable" belief. But if the only thing wrong with having contradictory beliefs is that being in that state ensures believing a falsehood, then there would seem to be no reason to attempt to arrange one's other beliefs in such a way as to avoid conflict with the immutable belief. After all, that belief is *ex hypothesi* in conflict with one's evidence. In all probability, therefore, it is false. If one's other beliefs are supported by one's evidence, then one might as well hold on to them, even though this would ensure that one have at least one false belief, for the immutable belief is very likely false and thus one's having at least one false belief is highly probable in any event. Why give up any *true* beliefs simply to achieve consistency?' (158–9).

Contrary to this, unless one's doxastic attitude towards what a proposition asserts is, overall, more favourable than unfavourable, one cannot count as *believing* it; and if it *is* overall more favourable than unfavourable, one cannot count as *disbelieving* it. So nothing psychological can ever count as any individual's both believing some proposition and simultaneously believing its direct contradictory, let alone doing so deliberately. See my 'When Inconsistency is Logically Impossible,' *Logique et Analyse* 32, nos. 125/126 (March–June 1989), 139–42.

16 Hume, *An Inquiry concerning Human Understanding*, 155.

Consider the set of all cogent reasoning procedures, a set which will be complete only when no good argument is possible that does not exemplify one or more of the procedures belonging to it. For each member of this set, consider the proposition that it actually is a cogent reasoning procedure. Now consider the disjunction of all those propositions. Here, surely, is a true proposition which, being general, does not merely report experiences, and which, moreover, is necessarily a proposition impossible to justify argumentatively without circular reasoning. Unless it can be denied to be true-or-false at all, it must be true *a priori*, in the sense of not being a mere report of experiences, but still warranting acceptance as true independently of any inference from experiences. This conclusion should be altogether unsurprising since one of the disjuncts involved will be the analytic proposition that valid deductive reasoning is cogent. Consider, then, the disjunction of all the other disjuncts. This proposition should not be analytic, but synthetic *a priori*, unless either deduction is the only cogent reasoning procedure, or else one other reasoning procedure can be proved cogent deductively (whether by a trivial or a nontrivial deductive proof). To affirm the first alternative, it will be argued, leads to an untenable scepticism – a scepticism impossible to embrace in practice. To affirm the second alternative is to make a logical claim, and so, as with any logical claim, the burden of proof rests with whoever makes it, and in the absence of any good grounds for accepting it, the claim can be taken to be false.

There are certain deductive, inductive, and ethical principles, it will be argued, which the reader as well as the writer of this book is bound to accept in practice. The inductive and ethical principles, being deniable without logical contradiction, are synthetic rather than analytic. And all of the principles are general propositions which are *a priori* in the sense of warranting acceptance independently of any empirical *evidence*. This does not mean, of course, that they are or could be accepted by any mind prior to any experience. No proposition is even understandable without experience. Without any experience, one could no more understand the *a priori* proposition that any square is four-sided than one could understand the *a posteriori* proposition that water is heavier than ice, for instance, and so one could not rightly be credited with believing such things prior to any experience.[17] But in order to tell if it is true or not that

---

17 Cf. John Locke, *Essay concerning Human Understanding*, Book I, chapter 1, section 5:
    '... it is evident, that all children ... have not the least apprehension or thought of ...
    innate truths ... if these words "to be in the understanding" have any propriety, they

any square is four-sided, no *more* experience is required than such as is needed just to understand the proposition; whereas, even after the proposition that water is heavier than ice is clearly *understood*, additional experience can be needed in order to be able to tell that it is *true*.

Whether analytic or synthetic, not every truth which is *a priori* in the present sense is *obviously* true the way the proposition 'Any square is four-sided' is. Whether analytic or synthetic, any *a priori* truth which is neither obvious nor obviously at least probable will require some sort of argument in order to establish it. Naturally, whatever follows *a priori* from *a priori* truths will likewise have to be true *a priori* in the present sense.

But the present sense of '*a priori*,' in which a general truth is '*a priori*' if acceptance of it is warranted independently of any empirical evidence, is different from the sense of the expression introduced above, in which a proposition is '*a priori*' if and only if it is 'both unprovable and irrefutable by any consistently imaginable experiences.' For, on the one hand, we can at least *conceive* that there might be a truth which not only is unprovable by any consistently imaginable experiences, but is actually impossible ever to be warranted in accepting at all. And, on the other hand, why should there not be general propositions the acceptance of which could be warranted *either* as a result of inference from experience or else, equally well, quite independently of any such inference? Indeed, the claim will be that just this does hold true of the deductive and inductive principles to be discussed, although deductive and inductive inference from empirical evidence cannot be enough to establish any ethical conclusion. That will be the claim. According to (a form of) verificationism, though, what is establishable deductively and what is establishable on the basis of empirical evidence – or even what is establishable on the basis of disparate sorts of empirical evidence – cannot be the very same proposition.

---

signify to be understood. So that to be in the understanding, and not be understood ... is all one as to say anything is and is not in the mind or understanding.' Locke's punning argument here is less convincing, perhaps, than his conclusion that one cannot be credited with having in one's mind anything one could not even understand. Aren't there, for any proposition, certain concepts which it would be logically impossible to believe the proposition without grasping? Could anybody with no inkling of what a square root is, for example, be credited with a belief that two is a square root of four? And don't all concepts, without exception, have to be learned through experience, even those concepts (if there are any) towards which the learning mind has an inborn leaning? There is doubtless no *logical* impossibility in the idea of innate ('hardwired') *understanding* – or, for that matter, in the idea of an innate fluency in Latin, say. But human minds are not like that.

And so, the arguments for verificationism will need to be countered, as well as any other positive arguments for empiricism in general. That is the task undertaken in chapter 5. The contention of this book is that there are indeed some synthetic truths which it is possible to be warranted in believing independently of any experiential verification or confirmation, though some, but not all of these are establishable empirically as well. How shall we classify synthetic truths which it is impossible to be warranted in believing except on the basis of a logical deduction from premises of these sorts in conjunction with truths ascertainable only empirically? And, on the other hand, how shall we classify synthetic truths which are both establishable in that way, and also establishable empirically? Until there is a reason why it matters, there is no need now to invent any special classifying phraseology to cover such cases.

Care has been taken throughout this discussion to avoid any suggestion that an *a priori* truth is always in any sense necessary or true *for certain* (and so a good bet at any odds). Doubtless tautologies are all true for certain, as are also *some* of the synthetic truths which it is possible to be warranted in believing independently of any experiential verification or confirmation. But even a tautology – under another description which does not entail that it is one – can easily fall well short of certainty if it is establishable only by means of a complicated, difficult proof; and this can be so even after the proof has been found, in view of the known fallibility of human beings' deductive powers. By the same token, the history of *a priori* argumentation in philosophy will surely afford ample reason to take nearly everything asserted in this book with rather more than a pinch of suspicion.

The discussion of deductive principles will proceed in chapter 4 as if what they are were unproblematic. As far as inductive and ethical principles go, no such approach is feasible. And, on top of determining what they are, the sort of consequences they have for how the world is and how to act in it will need to be drawn out and defended. Indeed, the defence of the consequences which follow from them is a good part of making the case for them.

They will all only be counterexamples which refute empiricism if they really are synthetic *a priori* truths. Empiricists can object (short of embracing scepticism) that the inductive and ethical principles proposed are really meaningless or otherwise non-truth-valuable, or that they are false, or in any case unwarranted and dispensable, or that they are logically demonstrable tautologies, if not trivial analytic truisms in the first place, or that they are really empirical and not *a priori* truths after all. Each of these alternatives must be effectively rebutted if the anti-empiricism here defended is to be successfully made out, and accordingly different specific chapters in part two (on induction) and part three (on ethics) are devoted to attempting that.

As for the principles of deduction and their consequences – the analytic *a priori* – their *a priori* truth too has been challenged on the grounds that they really are false, 'senseless,' or at any rate, truthvalueless (non-'factual'). That is the challenge which chapter 4 is devoted to meeting. If they can be shown, after all, to be *true* and *fact-stating* (in the same sense in which empirical truths are), the plausibility of the empiricist denial that there can likewise be *a priori* truths which are synthetic will have considerably been weakened.

In the remainder of part one, chapter 2 introduces a special sense of 'self-contradiction' for later use, a sense which includes but is not confined to the (logically contradictory) assertion of something logically impossible. Then chapter 3 concerns what it is, in general, to be *truth-valuable*. Presumably, any datable utterance of an appropriate sentence will be true-or-false only when it is the (honest or dishonest) *expression* of some (purported) mental state or condition on the speaker's part that is capable of being true or false (a *belief*). To the question whether utterances, sentences, propositions, or mental states or conditions are 'the *primary* bearers of truth-values,' no answer is necessary. In chapter 4 (on the principles of deduction) the 'factuality' of analytic truth is defended. Finally, in chapter 5, the philosophy of empiricism is considered and criticized in general.

Part two, as noted above, is on the presuppositions of induction, which rationally requires universal causality, spatiotemporally interconnected, as well as spatiotemporally universal change, it is claimed. Part three, on ethics, argues for a certain version of utilitarianism, the moral philosophy which prescribes that people should care for one another.

The appendixes contain some technical specifications of meaning, at least for present purposes, which it seemed necessary to include, but not in the main text: the 'analytic'/'synthetic' distinction (drawing on an account of 'cognitive synonymity' which I have advanced elsewhere), and 'desire' (in the general sense of a *motivation* of any kind).

Can the present case, in fact, be successfully made out? Can it be made out at least in part? To succeed even in partially advancing the discussion of just some of the topics treated here is still a substantial aspiration.

2 On Moore's Paradox[1]

If I were to say,

'It is not raining outside, but I believe that it is,'

I would commonly be taken to have contradicted myself, although I would not have asserted anything logically impossible.[2] This suggests a wider sense of 'self-contradiction' than the customary technical sense of *logical falsity*.

Just what is the trouble with a locution like this? Clearly, the basis for finding fault with it lies in the fact that it is involved in the meaning of an English declarative sentence like 'It is not raining outside,' that asserting it is a conventional linguistic means of expressing a (conscious) belief that it is not raining outside, and it is logically impossible for such a belief to coexist in the same mind with a belief that it really is raining outside.[3] When I say that making an assertion is a conventional means of linguistically *expressing* a belief in what is asserted, I do not mean that the assertion made necessarily *is* the reflection of any belief, but only that it *purports* to be. The belief will have to be there only if the assertion is *honest*. Lest it be thought that something important is being swept under the carpet here

---

1 Cf. Ludwig Wittgenstein, *Philosophical Investigations*, IIx.

2 That is, I would not have made any statement the denial of which was 'analytic' by the criterion of *analyticity* given in appendix 1.

3 Can one and the same person ever be *literally* 'of two minds?' Presumably not. And so, unless a given person's 'doxastic inclinations' in favour of a proposition outweigh the person's 'doxastic inclinations' in a contrary sense, it is not the case that this person *believes* that proposition. And unless the latter inclinations outweigh the former, it is not the case that the person disbelieves the proposition – that is, believes its logical contradictory. See D. Goldstick, 'When Inconsistency Is Logically Impossible,' *Logique et Analyse* 32, nos. 125/126 (March–June 1989), 139–42.

by the use of terms like these, the relevant point can be brought out sufficiently by means of the following analytic truism:

> If one ever asserts that something is so, either one believes that it is so, or else one wishes to act as if one believed that it were so.

It is not to be thought that the English language is limited to providing English-speakers with conventional linguistic means of expressing their *beliefs*. Equally good examples of 'self-contradiction' as those that arise in connection with beliefs can be obtained in just the same way out of
'Mmm! Yorkshire pudding! I hate it'
or
'Mmm! Yorkshire pudding! Pah!'
or the like. In the English language, 'Mmm!' is a conventional expression of approbation, whereas 'Pah!' or the like is a conventional linguistic expression of the opposite. Here is a general formulation of what it is to 'contradict oneself' in this wider sense which we have been considering:

> One *contradicts oneself* if and only if one says something that either is or logically entails a conventional linguistic expression of a particular state or condition of mind at the same time as one says something that either is or logically entails a conventional linguistic expression of another state or condition of mind whose coexistence in the same mind with the first is logically impossible.

It will be seen that on this definition, the actual asserting of something logically impossible (the making of a *logically contradictory* assertion) will itself count as one important case of *self-contradiction* in this wider sense. At any rate, as far as beliefs are concerned, it is possible to formulate some specific rules for determining when *self-contradiction* occurs.

For example: For any two statements p and q,

(1) If p is logically inconsistent with q, one cannot without self-contradiction assert p and at the same time assert anything which logically entails q.
(2) If p logically entails q, one cannot without self-contradiction assert p and at the same time deny that one believes q, or deny q and assert that one believes p.

(3) If *p* is something that, in view of what one asserts, one cannot then deny without self-contradiction, and *p* and *q* are such that one cannot assert them together without self-contradiction, then *q* is something that one cannot then assert without self-contradiction.

Thus, to illustrate rule (2), if you admit that a particular man is a bachelor, you cannot without contradicting yourself deny that you believe him to be unmarried; and, to illustrate rule (3), if you cannot without contradicting yourself deny that you believe the man to be unmarried, you cannot then without contradicting yourself assert that you have no idea as to his marital status.

On this model, the celebrated negation 'I do not exist' (which René Descartes momentarily entertained only in order to reject) – since 'It is not a truth that I believe I do not exist' validly follows from it – is something nobody could ever utter, with its normal, literal meaning, without *self-contradiction* as here defined. And so, similarly, with many other examples of 'self-refutation.'

In G.E. Moore's honour, let us say that a statement *p* will 'M-imply' any statement *q* whose logical contradictory is impossible to assert without self-contradiction in conjunction with *p*. Thus, whatever something *strictly implies* it will 'M-imply,' but not everything which it 'M-implies' will be something that it *strictly implies* (equivalently, for our purposes: not everything will be something it *logically entails*).

Objection: Could I not, perfectly acceptably, admit that some particular man is unmarried, and yet deny that I believed him to be a bachelor if I simply had not yet learned the meaning of the word 'bachelor'?

Reply: In such a case, you could indeed deny believing that the man was a 'bachelor,' but, in all strictness, you could not correctly deny believing him to be a bachelor (without quotes). Even if you knew no English at all, you could still be correctly reported in English as believing that he was a bachelor so long as you could honestly say that of him in your own language.

Objection: Are we to say, for example, that any mathematician has 'contradicted herself' who admits the truth of some set of axioms, but denies that she has any idea yet as to whether a particular unproved proposition is true or not, whenever the proposition is in fact deducible from those axioms?

Reply: The sense of 'self-contradiction' defined here admittedly is wider than anything we ever use the term for normally. Still, the stock of beliefs of the mathematician imagined in the objection will indeed be a *logically deficient* stock of beliefs, in the sense of being subject to revision on logical grounds alone.

However, if what a person says not only entails but directly is the conventional linguistic expression of a mental state or condition that is logically incapable of coexisting in the same mind with a mental state or condition of which something else the person says not only entails but directly is the conventional linguistic expression, then it follows that the person has made a mistake somewhere and is accordingly obliged to withdraw what has been said, in whole or in part, on pain of a sort of 'self-contradiction' incompatible with good sense. But the facts about people's mental states or conditions, and specifically their beliefs, are facts which it is possible to ascertain empirically. If, then, you, for your part, can be brought to accept on empirical grounds that there are beliefs which you too unshakably hold, you can be thereby rationally disqualified from rejecting the characterization of them as *true*. This was the basic method of the Common Sense School of philosophy. For instance, in his *Inquiry into the Relation of Cause and Effect*[4] (see especially Part 4, section 7), Thomas Brown in effect used reasoning of this sort against the sceptical position associated with the name of David Hume, the fundamental self-contradiction of which might be well summed up in the rationally inadmissible assertion, 'I believe that nature is uniform, but there is no telling whether it is or not' (i.e., *it is completely uncertain whether it is or not*). Similar considerations hold good against John Mackie's early paper, 'A Refutation of Morals,' the first and last sentences of which read as follows:

> We all have moral feelings: all of us find that there are human actions and states of affairs of which we approve and disapprove, and which we therefore try to encourage and develop or to oppose …
>
> … But in any case we have shown that the great mass of what is called moral thought is, not nonsense, but error, the imagining of objective facts and qualities of external things where there exists nothing but our feelings of desire and approval.[5]

---

4 Thomas Brown, *Inquiry into the Relation of Cause and Effect*, 3rd ed. (Edinburgh, 1818).
5 John Mackie, 'A Refutation of Morals,' *The Australasian Journal of Psychology and Philosophy* 24, nos. 1/2 (September 1946), 77, 90. Mackie himself apparently thought he could satisfactorily deflect criticism of this sort by just brandishing the expressions 'first

To make good the Common Sense view on these questions, and then to draw the appropriate conclusions from it, is the purpose of this book.[6]

---

order' and 'second order' here: he speaks of 'first order moral views, positive or negative: the person who adopts either of them is taking a certain practical, normative, stand. By contrast, what I am discussing is a second order view, a view about the status of moral values and the nature of moral valuing, about where and how they fit into the world. These first and second order views are not merely distinct but completely independent.' J.L. Mackie, *Ethics: Inventing Right and Wrong* (Harmondsworth, Middlesex, UK, 1977), 16. Since when, though, will an assertion '...' be consistent with 'It is false that ...,' despite their being first-order and second-order locutions, respectively? The sort of philosophical self-partitioning being recommended here by Mackie (as by many others) is discussed further in chapter 33 of this book.

6 Most of this chapter appeared in print in my 'On Moore's Paradox,' *Mind* 76, no. 302 (April 1967), 275–7.

3 On Factuality

In the years between the two world wars, the Wittgensteinian and logical positivist philosophies assaulted the ears of the traditional-minded by flatly denying there to be any 'fact of the matter' at all (to put it in the idiom of a later generation) on any of the great questions of ethics, 'metaphysics,' theology, and even logic and mathematics. In a straightforward sense, they were denying that any ethical, 'metaphysical,' theological, or even logical or mathematical thesis was ever 'true' in that sense in which it might be correct, in favourable conditions, to call a police officer's testimony 'true' or to call any of the findings of the natural sciences 'true.'

Are there different senses of the word 'true'? (Aside, that is, from the senses it takes in such English phrases as 'true heart,' 'rings true,' and so on.) Empirical semantics always has to proceed from a general presumption of univocity. More than one lexical sense is never to be attributed to a term without a special reason for doing so. In the case of a word like 'cape,' it is, indeed, possible to distinguish two discrete senses, geographical and sartorial; and precisely for that reason it is not a case of two different species of any common genus called 'capes.' The zeugmatic sentence, 'There are geographical and also sartorial capes,' is bad English just because there is no sense for the word 'capes' to take in it.[1] But, without a univocity presumption, there would be no way to bar an objection against practically any sentence whatever as being zeugmatic: thus, 'Some telephones are black and some are green' counts as

---

1 On the other hand, there is nothing linguistically the matter with the second-order sentence, 'There are geographical and also sartorial "capes"' – that is, 'There are geographical and also sartorial things called "capes."'

good English only on condition that the word 'telephones' can be viewed as generic and univocal.

It will be necessary, in succeeding chapters, to consider particular arguments that have been advanced for denying the univocity of 'true,' or for denying that whoever adopts any philosophical position is thereby committed to thinking of it as true. Meanwhile, what is it to *think of something as true*? As was remarked, in effect, in chapter 1, whenever a person thinks of something as true, *what* the person thinks will be false unless it actually is, in fact, true; and so, any linguistic formulation of what the person thinks will have to express something truth-valuable, that is, true-or-false.

This suggests an extremely simple and direct argument against the denial of objective truth in all those areas in which philosophers have claimed that, for 'logical' reasons, it is not to be had. Even if not conclusive, the argument may justifiably be considered onus-shifting: it may establish a warranted *presumption* that any position held in those areas should be considered truth-valuable, until proved not to be.

First, though, a brief consideration is required of the distinction between what a linguistic expression means *literally*, and what context and social convention can permit a speaker to communicate beyond that. When Mark Antony said, 'Brutus is an honourable man,' was he asserting, or was he denying, that Brutus was an honourable man? Using the trope of *irony*, he was, of course, doing both. At the most literal level of meaning, what he said was indeed an assertion that Brutus was an honourable man. But by means of making that literal claim he managed, more tellingly, to assert exactly the opposite. Or consider 'rhetorical questions' – for instance, 'What is the point of it all?' At the most literal level, whoever says this is asking a question, namely, the question what the point of it all is. But, arising out of the literal meaning, the ultimate force of what is said is to assert that there is *no* point to it all. No doubt the speaker achieves this latter communication just because asking where something is to be found can easily reflect doubt about not only where, but whether, it is really to be found.[2] Nevertheless, the assertoric force of

---

2 Cf. John R. Searle, 'Indirect Speech Acts,' in *Syntax and Semantics*, vol. 3, ed. Peter Cole and Jerry L. Morgan (New York, 1975), 59–82: 'In asking *Why not stop here?* as a suggestion to stop here, [the speaker] challenges [the hearer] to provide reasons for not doing something on the tacit assumption that the absence of reasons for not doing something is itself a reason for doing it' (78). Searle's illuminating discussion of the sort of phenomenon considered here is conducted in an Austinian framework, but leaves very little with which to disagree. In place of my example below, 'You

the sentence will nowadays, by long-standing convention, arise out of its interrogative meaning automatically, as a rule, and probably assume much greater prominence than the literal meaning, of which, though, the sentence's indubitably interrogative *form* will still always be there to remind us. In explaining the use of the word 'quality,' J.L. Austin[3] and others have made the point that the term functions as a dummy stand-in for adjectives in general, such as 'red,' 'external,' 'deceitful,' et cetera. Its meaning, on this account, is characterized completely by noting that it is simply the material-mode counterpart of the word 'adjective.'[4] The consequence has somehow not been drawn from this, that, for example, the Kantian type of objection to the Ontological Argument – to the effect that *existence* is not really a quality – must fail then, since 'existent' really is a perfectly good adjective.[5] To the idea that, wherever there is an adjective, there must be a quality, Grelling's Paradox may pose a problem. Consider the adjective 'heterological,' said to apply to adjectives if and only if they are not self-descriptive, as 'short' and 'polysyllabic' are, but 'long' and 'monosyllabic' are not. Is 'heterological' a heterological adjective? Contradiction appears to result from either an affirmative or a negative answer, and from this it has been concluded that there is no such quality *really* as 'heterologicality.'

In any case, Stephen Schiffer has written:

> ... there is a risk that a certain *pleonastic* use of 'property' will precipitately seduce one into thinking that language-independent properties, and thus the propositions they determine, exist. Suppose ... one were concerned to construct a correspondence theory that required that there were facts that were language independent in just the way that propositions are supposed to be. Then one would take no comfort in the utterly pleonastic sense of 'fact' that enabled one to move back and forth between 'Michele is funny' and 'It's a fact that Michele is funny.' Likewise, if one's concern

---

will kindly observe silence while inside the main building,' Searle (65) cites 'Officers will henceforth wear ties at dinner' instead.

3 See J.L. Austin, *Philosophical Papers* (Oxford, 1961), 126.

4 This proposal will have to be amended to incorporate a restriction, at least in English, to *adjectives capable of being predicate adjectives* (unlike 'some,' for instance).

5 Kantians could still argue that existence cannot be a *defining* quality of anything. Kant's point remains impressive that the possibility of asking the question whether something exists or not presupposes that it will be *the same thing* – and, therefore, the same sort of thing – in the event of existing as in the event of not existing. See *Critique of Pure Reason* A600=B628.

were the existence of language-independent properties, one would take no comfort in the pleonastic sense of 'property' that enabled one to move back and forth between 'Michele is funny,' and 'Michele has the property of being funny.'[6]

Presumably, one must find comfort where one can. Stephen Schiffer, meet Sabina Lovibond, who (claiming to base herself on the later Wittgenstein) develops a position according to which:

> ... the only legitimate role for the idea of 'reality' is that in which it is coordinated with ... the metaphysically neutral idea of 'talking about something' ... It follows that 'reference to an objective reality' cannot intelligibly be set up as a target which some propositions – or rather, some utterances couched in the indicative mood – may hit, while others fall short. If something has the grammatical form of a proposition, then it is a proposition ...[7]

Can we take seriously the idea that, wherever a grammatically acceptable declarative sentence has been assertively uttered, there is some actual fact which thereby has been asserted, or else – where the sentence is not true but rather false – has been denied? Let us imagine how the debate would go.

PRO: That is simply what the word 'fact' means. And in essence, the same thing applies equally to the expressions 'state of affairs,' 'reality,' et cetera.

CON: Let us stick to *facts*. You have no right to be so confident about how the word is used. The member of a religious community declares, 'We are firm in the faith of our fathers,' a dissenter objects, 'We are shackled by an outworn creed,' and a commentator observes, 'You are both reporting the same *facts*, but adding different theological value-judgments.' The *factual* content of what the first two speakers said was the same for both, but the remainder of what

---

6 Stephen Schiffer, *Remnants of Meaning* (Cambridge, MA, 1987), 51.

7 Sabina Lovibond, *Realism and Imagination in Ethics* (Oxford, 1983), 25–6. However, Lovibond's *verbal* 'realism' has to be set against her notion (67–8) that the degree of 'objectivity' characterizing any realm of discourse is a matter of 'the scope allowed to intellectual authority' in it by the prevailing social consensus.

each one affirmed was a matter of the differing *meanings* that they
each ascribed to the facts in question.

PRO: And why isn't it a matter of fact what the true *meaning* of something is? Even if it is right that what each of those two speakers
asserted can be divided into a theologically neutral statement
(reporting the present strength of traditional religious beliefs) and
a theologically partisan statement (supporting or opposing those
beliefs), that is no reason for denying that both statements made in
each case are factually true-or-false. There is a way of speaking in
which any true statements that count as answering the same
questions can be said to 'state the same facts' as one another, even
if they are far from equivalent. 'The cat is on the mat,' for instance,
and 'Rasputin is on the doormat' are said, in this way of speaking,
to 'report the same fact' as each other, whenever both are correct
responses to a query about that one particular feline's whereabouts.

CON: Whenever two rival accounts of things are being debated, the
debaters may disagree, as we say, *either* about 'the facts' *or else* about
the proper interpretation to be placed on those facts. It is a common-
place that, even where there is complete agreement about *the facts* –
that is, the empirical data – people may well still disagree about what
those facts *mean*. That is the way we talk. Similarly, in a court action, a
distinction is made between the *facts* of the case and the relevant *law*,
and the lawyers on the two sides may dispute about either. Here again,
the distinction is drawn in non-philosophical discourse between actual
facts, on the one hand – in principle verifiable empirically – and the
concepts people use for *evaluating* such facts, on the other hand.

PRO: But isn't it (for the most part, at least) an empirical matter of fact
what the prevailing law is anywhere? When both sides in a legal
dispute are said to agree about 'the facts' of the case, can't that be
construed in the etymological sense of 'the deeds done?' And what
it is that constitutes *data* for theorizing is a highly relative matter.
One inquiry's conclusions will serve as data for a different inquiry:
for example, the established results of palaeontology are *givens* for
archaeology. On a broader view, *all* are factual in reality.

CON: You claim there is nothing more to what the words 'true' and
'fact' mean than what is expressed by putting a sentence which is to
be uttered in the declarative. But this is to confuse grammatical
form with logical form. Consider a sentence such as 'You will kindly
observe silence while inside the main building' (said, let us assume,
with the same intonation contour as would be normal for 'You will

doubtless observe silence while inside the main building'). Here we have a grammatically declarative sentence whose correct meaning is understood only if it is understood as expressing a *command*, rather than a true-or-false *statement*. To respond to 'You will kindly observe silence while inside the main building' with, 'Yes, that's a fact,' would evince either some sort of misunderstanding, or else, attempted humour. Since a sentence can be declarative in form but imperative in its actual meaning, there must be more to what is *meant* by a locution which does make an explicit or implicit truth-claim than is covered by merely stating its surface grammatical form. Otherwise, 'You will kindly observe silence while inside the main building' would be statement-making after all.

PRO: Yes, it actually is a statement-making sentence. But only literally. Beyond the literal level of meaning, its ultimate communicative force is imperatival. It is a 'rhetorical prediction,' just as 'What is the point of it all?' is a rhetorical question. But it secures its imperatival force only *through* its literal predictive meaning. The characteristic of any words used to address people *imperatively* is that they say what to do, whether by means of an order, an entreaty, a recommendation, et cetera. But the 'rhetorical prediction' form can only be employed for issuing orders, and that is because only persons in authority would normally be able to come up first with the corresponding predictions in the full assurance that they will be fulfilled, so that to use this form of words is to purport to be expressing the commands of someone in authority.

CON: Suppose the imperative mood were to be dropped from the English language, and all commands were expressed in the declarative, on the model of 'You will observe silence while inside the main building.' Surely we do not distinguish between *stating* and *commanding* merely because we have in mind the imperative mood as the today *standard* means of expressing commands, for the statement literally made by a 'rhetorical prediction' would still be distinguishable from the command arising out of it. It still would be true that not all literal predictions had the force of commands. But, if statements can be distinguished from commands independently of the distinction between declaratives and imperatives, then there must, after all, be something more about what it means for a form of words to make a *statement*, something that is not fully conveyed by characterizing the word 'statement' as merely meaning whatever is expressed by a sentence in the declarative.

PRO: If there were no imperative mood and commands were all put in the form of declaratives, it would not, it is true, be impossible to distinguish still between commands and predictions – or rather, between commands and predictions-not-implying-any-command – but the distinction would then just be one between two different subclasses of the class of predictive *statements*.

CON: But what about languages other than English? In present-day English, you say, the meaning of the word 'statement' is fully conveyed by characterizing it as the term for whatever is expressed by a sentence in the declarative. What criterion are we to use for distinguishing, say, between *statements* and *orders* made in other languages?

PRO: The criterion for us to use, as English-speakers, will simply be how the locutions in those languages translate best into English. All those locutions and only those locutions which translate into English sentences in the declarative can correctly be described as expressing 'statements' in the sense which that word has in English.

Enough of this imaginary debate. Can the issue of propositionhood, truth, and factuality really be trivialized as easily as that? Let us distinguish the question whether every grammatically well-formed declarative sentence in English is statement-making in character – that is, fact-alleging – from the question whether it is possible to identify what it means to be *statement-making* without referring back to the declarative sentence *form*. The latter question amounts to asking whether we can identify any particular *meaning* to interpret that form for sentences as standardly conveying. Would it not be quite surprising to have to conclude by denying that any particular non-arbitrary meaning distinction was marked by the difference between the declarative and other forms?

Before returning to this second question, we had better cast a last glance, as far as the present chapter goes, at the philosophical resistance to the thought that every grammatically well-formed declarative sentence has a statement-making sense. During the heyday of the British Ordinary Language Philosophy in the years after the Second World War, a favourite move was to single out different classes of declaratives and deny that they were statement-making. Thus, J.O. Urmson, in his well-known article 'Parenthetical Verbs,' asserted that when you personally have no feelings on the matter at all you can still say, 'Madam, I regret that your son is dead,' without being a hypocrite, 'even within the excusable, conventional, limits of hypocrisy,'[8] and he went on to declare that you can actually say, without describing your feelings, 'I much regret that your son is dead, he was a dear friend.' These extra-ordinary claims about language are just asserted by Urmson, as though obvious, without any argument. The 'I much regret ...' opening, Urmson advises us, is a 'signal ... made for its own sake as an act of sympathy.' But how is the utterance of precisely those words able to serve as an act of sympathy if *not* by means of a suggestion (credible or otherwise) of regret on the part of whoever is speaking? And how do we convey that suggestion by using those words if it is not by *saying* – truly or falsely – that we regret?

An even more famous example of Ordinary Language Philosophy than this was J.L. Austin's discussion of *performatives* from 1955.[9] 'Explicit performatives' were declaratives, like 'I promise to come,' which enable those using them to perform a socially constructed sort of *act*, such as promising to come, by means of *saying* that they perform it. Only, Austin could not himself put it that way, since he made a big point of denying that explicit performatives were statement-making (except for those of the 'I state that ...' pattern). Then, 'implicit performatives,' such as 'I shall come,' when said by way of making a promise to come, were declared to mean the same as the corresponding explicit performatives, and hence to be likewise non-statement-making. That one might be able to make a promise *by* making a prediction apparently did not occur to Austin.[10] However, suppose one says, 'I hereby swear on the Bible,' while actually holding one's hand on a book of Greek recipes. Can't we describe this as a case where one (intentionally or not) has said something false,[11] even though it is not a case of *swearing* falsely

---

8   J.O. Urmson, 'Parenthetical Verbs,' *Mind* 61, no. 244 (October 1952), 484–5.

9   J.L. Austin, *How to Do Things with Words*, 2nd ed. (Cambridge, MA, 1975)

10 Or did it? I am assuming Austin's 'illocutionary force' concept was meant to be a generalization of the ethical noncognitivist distinction drawn between the so-called 'descriptive' and 'evaluative' uses of language. That philosophical move, at any rate, would surely be defeated, if it were admitted that one could *evaluate* an action by means of *describing* it as 'worthy,' or as 'objectionable.'

11 That whoever said this in those circumstances would be saying something false might perhaps be challenged by followers of Keith S. Donnellan, according to whom there is a 'referential' as well as an 'attributive' use of definite descriptions, such that someone can actually be said to have made a wholly true statement in saying, for example, while holding a book of Greek recipes and having it in mind, 'I am now holding the Christian Bible in my hand,' meaning all those words in their ordinary senses, provided that the phrase 'the Christian Bible' in this sentence is here being employed 'referentially' rather than 'attributively.' See his article, 'Reference and

inasmuch as, in the circumstances, no real *oath* (as ecclesiastically understood) has actually been sworn at all? But what else can one have said here that is false if it is not just *that one has sworn on the Bible*? There exists a philosophical opinion to the effect that nothing can be true unless it *could* be false, and so a performative like 'I say no!' might be denied to be truth-valuable (statement-making) on grounds such as that. But it is best to leave this line of thought until the discussion of tautologies and contradictions in chapter 4.

There is no need here to go through any further examples, such as expressions of intention or rule promulgations, which Ordinary Language philosophers at different times denied to be statement-making despite a declarative form. The point is that we can often do something *else* by making a statement of a certain sort, and this can be, and often is, regulated by definite social conventions without the latter having to count among the linguistic conventions that fix literal meanings.

Back to the question whether it is possible or not to identify what it means to be statement-making without referring back to the declarative sentence form. Is there no possibility of independently identifying any *meaning* which the declarative form can be interpreted as standardly communicating? When we discover that languages as different from English as Hungarian, Chinese, and Hidatsa (spoken among the Sioux Indians of North America) in fact have a linguistically distinct declarative form for sentences just as English has, it is time, perhaps, to suspect that there must be some extra-linguistic meaning there. But what is it?

Even if we do say that to utter a declarative sentence in the standard, literal way always implies a truth-claim, how much farther ahead will that take us? For what is a truth-claim? And the point will always remain that, though whatever is true is true, no matter by whom or in what circumstances it is asserted, the same can certainly not be said of declarative sentences. For instance, even without any change in linguistic meaning, 'Today is Tuesday' must have a different truth-value on Tuesday and on Wednesday. Let us go back to the mental state or condition which the declarative sentence form conventionally expresses: namely, belief. Can we identify what it is that distinguishes a mental

---

Definite Descriptions,' *Philosophical Review* 75, no. 3 (July 1966), 281–304. Is it possible to speculate that this doctrine has attracted support much more on the basis of its complexity, on the one hand, and the way it lends itself to logical elaboration, on the other hand, than it has on the basis of any actual empirical adequacy in the light of the positive facts of our usage?

state or condition as being one of *belief*? According to chapter 1, it is being true-or-false. Can we say anything more than that?

Contrary to William James's pragmatism, the class of true statements and beliefs and the class of useful statements and beliefs cannot coincide with each other exactly, since there certainly are some useful falsehoods. Nevertheless, to believe something to be true is thereby to dispose yourself to believe presumptively in the usefulness of such belief. (To believe something 'presumptively' is to either believe it or fail to do so because of being influenced by considerations taken to militate specifically against it. Whoever in full consciousness believes presumptively that something is so can be said, then, to believe it to be 'presumptively' so.) You cannot really believe something, after all, without being disposed to act on that belief, should certain appropriate circumstances arise. And you cannot be consciously disposed to act in a particular way, should certain circumstances arise, without regarding that way of acting as the most useful way of acting in those circumstances.[12] A belief's being true thus M-implies the presumptive utility of holding it. From the point of view of somebody who accepts a belief in full consciousness, the ways of acting which holding it disposes a believer to adopt, in various circumstances, automatically make the belief presumptively useful, and it can fail to be useful in fact only if holding it in addition gives rise to different and undesirable byproducts, and these byproducts are together sufficient to outweigh *both* whatever desirable byproducts it has, *and also* the desirable consequences of choosing the correct course of action should the appropriate circumstances arise. We can say, at any rate, that whenever people have asserted that they believe something, they cannot, without contradicting themselves, deny that they have a presumptive desire to believe it. Accordingly, just as whatever is true is true no matter who asserts it, so also it will be presumptively desirable for anybody whatever to believe it. (To have a 'presumptive' desire for something is to either desire it or fail to desire it only because of being influenced by considerations taken to militate

---

12 See my paper 'Belief,' *American Philosophical Quarterly* 26, no. 3 (July 1989), 231–8. It is a tautology that whatever way of acting you ever do consciously choose you then regard as being the most useful way of acting, in the circumstances, for the furtherance of whatever you desire. If to *believe* something, is not already to have a certain sort of desire, it is to be *disposed* to desire whatever instrumentalities *would* be most useful for furthering your ultimate desires in case that belief and your other beliefs *were* all to be true. See also appendix 2 of this book, defining 'desire' for present purposes.

specifically against its desirability. By 'desirable' here, is 'desirable for the individual in question' what is meant, or 'desirable absolutely' [i.e., ethically]? What is meant is the disjunction.)

This brings out the essentially *social* character of the concept of truth. Just as people who have asserted something cannot then deny without contradicting themselves that anybody who asserted it would (to that extent) be speaking truly, they cannot then without contradicting themselves deny it to be presumptively desirable for anybody whatsoever to believe it, and so, if self-aware, to consider it to be true, as *they* do. But it is not just any kind of mental state or condition that possesses this social character which *belief* has. For example, to say, 'If only Charlie were here!' is indeed to employ a form of words purporting to reflect a particular state of mind (in this case, a wish that Charlie were present); but even on the part of a completely honest speaker no specific attitude, or even presumptive attitude, need be involved as regards whether or not anybody else shares *this* particular state of mind. It is only *belief* which is the right sort of mental state or condition for that. It is only calling something *true* which M-implies a presumptive attitude about anybody whatsoever sharing the thought expressed. Here we have the *meaning* conveyed by the declarative sentence form. That, then, shows what it means to be true-or-false.

4 On the Canons of Deductive Inference[1]

There is a principle in things, about which we cannot be deceived, but must always, on the contrary, recognize the truth – viz. that the same thing cannot at one and the same time be and not be, or admit any other similar pair of opposites. About such matters there is no proof in the full sense, though there is proof *ad hominem*. For it is not possible to infer this truth itself from a more certain principle, yet this is necessary if there is to be a completed proof of it in the full sense.

Aristotle, Metaphysics, trans. W.D. Ross, 1061b34–1062a5

For it is impossible for any one to believe the same thing to be and not to be, as some think Heraclitus says. For what a man says, he does not necessarily believe; and if it is impossible that contrary attributes should belong at the same time to the same subject (the usual qualifications must be presupposed in this premise too), and if an opinion which contradicts another is contrary to it, obviously it is impossible for the same man at the same time to believe the same thing to be and not to be; for if a man were mistaken on this point he would have contrary opinions at the same time.

Aristotle, Metaphysics, trans. W.D. Ross, 1005b23–31

Some indeed demand that even this shall be demonstrated, but this they do through want of education, for not to know of what things one should demand demonstration, and of what one should not, argues want of education.

---

1 Much of this chapter is taken from my paper 'Could God Make a Contradiction True?' *Religious Studies* 26, no. 3 (September 1990), 377–87.

For it is impossible that there should be demonstration of absolutely everything (there would be an infinite regress, so that there would still be no demonstration); but if there are things of which one should not demand demonstration, these persons could say what principle they maintain to be more
self-evident than the present one.

We can, however, demonstrate negatively even that this view is impossible, if our opponent will only say something.

Aristotle, *Metaphysics*, trans. W.D. Ross, 1006a4–14

Thus, then, it is the highest degree evident that neither any one of those who
maintain this view nor any one else is really in this position. For why does a
man walk to Megara and not stay at home, when he thinks he ought to be
walking there? Why does he not walk early some morning into a well or over
a precipice, if one happens to be in his way? Why do we observe him guard-
ing against this, evidently because he does not think that falling in is alike
good and not good? Evidently, then, he judges one thing to be better and another worse. And if this is so, he must also judge one thing to be a man and
another to be not-a-man, one thing to be sweet and another to be not-sweet.
For he does not aim at and judge all things alike, when, thinking it desirable
to drink water or to see a man, he proceeds to aim at these things; yet he *ought*,
if the same thing were alike a man and not-a-man. But, as was said, there is
no one who does not obviously avoid some things and not others.

Aristotle, *Metaphysics*, trans. W.D. Ross, 1008b12–25

Without doubt, the above is a highly selective selection of quotations.
Aristotle certainly did have other things to say as well, as far as the Principle
of Non-contradiction goes, and those other things may have been more
important to his systematic philosophy. But the passages quoted, at any
rate, can perhaps be summarized fairly in the following points:

1 It is impossible to be mistaken as to the truth-value of the Non-
   contradiction Principle. Indeed, to make a claim that anybody both
   believes something and simultaneously believes its contradictory
   too, is to speak inconsistently (to assert a 'logical impossibility,' as
   we would say today).[2]

---

2 It is altogether logically possible, of course – indeed, only too easy – to think
   inconsistent thoughts. But to believe a proposition and also its contradictory –

2 Since nothing is more certain than the Non-contradiction Principle, it is impossible to *demonstrate* it, in the sense of inferring it from something which is more certain than it is.
3 But people professing to question the Principle can be rationally led to accept it, provided they will agree to exchange words at all. Their own behaviour will show that in practice they are committed to it.

Aristotle himself never drew the distinction between a merely physical or psychological impossibility and a logical impossibility. Indeed, for our purposes too, it can be stipulated that whatever it is logically contradictory to assert will *a fortiori* be something physically and psychologically *impossible*. The objection that this cannot but involve a logically inadmissible conflation will be rebutted below. Aristotle claims that disagreeing with the Non-contradiction Principle (except in words only) is psychologically impossible. It is contrary, let us accept, not only to human nature, but to the psychological nature of any mind at all. (In the event that nothing could even *count* as the *thought* of a *mind* without an at least implicit commitment to non-contradiction, this will be true *a fortiori*.) An express recognition of the truth of the Non-contradiction Principle can therefore be elicited from anyone who is honest and intelligent enough by way of a Socratic sort of intellectual midwifery – a 'proof *ad hominem*' – according to Aristotle.

Let us notice, though, that like any other argument, an *ad hominem* argument against professed challenges of the Non-contradiction Principle is *bound* to be question-begging also. For to any argument whatever on the subject we can at least *imagine* the response: 'Yes, that does conclusively prove the truth (or the impossibility of denying) the Non-contradiction Principle; and, what is more, the Principle is in addition quite false as well.' To object that such a response will have to be logically *contradictory* is of course to beg the question right away against any challenge to the Principle of Non-contradiction. That this question-begging feature of any rational argument on the issue need not, apparently, detract from an argument's rational conclusiveness may prompt a re-examination of what we mean by 'circular' reasoning and in what ways such reasoning is objectionable.

---

simultaneously to believe and disbelieve the same proposition – would have to involve agreeing with the proposition on balance and simultaneously disagreeing with the proposition on balance. See my 'When Inconsistency Is Logically Impossible,' *Logique et Analyse* 32, nos. 125/126 (March–June 1989), 139–42.

Let us say that a piece of reasoning *presupposes* a proposition if and only if it would be impossible to be warranted in reasoning that way if it were not independently possible to be warranted in believing that proposition. (Thus, the inference, 'There is water on the roadway; therefore, it has rained,' can be said to *presuppose* that a water-sprinkler truck has not gone by.) Let us call a piece of reasoning *circular* whenever it premises or otherwise presupposes its own conclusion.

What, then, is wrong with circular reasoning? Aristotle's second point, as formulated above, suggests the objection that it could never serve the purpose of increasing our knowledge, but could succeed as reasoning only where it was *unnecessary* in that its conclusion was already, quite independently, just as certain beforehand as all the considerations it advanced were capable of establishing. According to this, people could be influenced by such reasoning only where its circularity was hidden from them, and that would be why circular reasoning was objectionable. This charge against circular reasoning, in effect amounting to one of uselessness-at-best, could scarcely be described as involving the gravest of offenses against reason. And besides, there is a big psychological difference between being rationally committed to something unwittingly and accepting it as true in full consciousness; any process of thought capable of leading a mind rationally from the first condition to the second would not at all be useless, surely. It remains, though, that circular reasoning can only be any good in lending support to its conclusion where it is possible to be warranted in believing that conclusion independently of it. Whatever can be supported by circular reasoning, in other words, must also warrant acceptance even without such reasoning.

Not only is even the most compelling *ad hominem* argumentation necessarily 'circular' in the sense defined. It is also worth emphasizing that its aim – to compel people's assent to a proposition, on pain of irrationality, by citing empirical evidence about what they believe – is something achieved in even the most favourable sort of case *without actually deriving that proposition as a conclusion from this evidence.* For it normally will not at all follow from even the most rationally compelling *ad hominem* argumentation that such evidence probably would not exist if the proposition to which it seeks to compel assent were not true. And in this consideration may be seen a potential line of reasoning in favour of scepticism concerning anything to which assent is compelled by an *ad hominem* argument.

You cannot consciously hold any belief without considering it *apt to be true* – that is to say, in the circumstances in which it is held really likely to be a true belief. If that likelihood did not exist – if your belief, were it to be true, would be so only by chance – this would have to militate against your being warranted in continuing to hold the belief. Thus, any assertion that something is so M-implies the current existence of a belief that it is so on the part of the speaker, but also a further claim that whatever is responsible for this belief would not be giving rise to it, or at any rate sustaining it, in all likelihood, if it were not in fact true. Thus, no matter how firmly a belief is held, it is bound to be rationally undermined by any consideration to the effect that there is no reason why whatever is responsible for it should be particularly likely to be 'reliable' in this respect – that is, unlikely to give rise to, or at any rate sustain, the belief unless it is actually true.

Human nature, it is said, is what is responsible for our belief that the Principle of Non-contradiction is true. Is that all there is to it? In other words, is whatever accounts for human nature such that we would still find the Non-contradiction Principle impossible to doubt even if it were not true?[3] If the answer is yes, then we can hardly be warranted in accepting the Principle and relying on it in our reasoning.[4]

---

3 Here we have a subjective conditional whose protasis introduces a logically contradictory supposition. But, as I argue in 'The Truth-conditions of Counterfactual Conditional Sentences' – published in *Mind* 8, no. 345 (January 1978), 1–21 – that will not at all invalidate the question. Even though everything whatsoever is *strictly implied* by a logically contradictory premise, some subjunctive conditional sentences whose protases introduce logically contradictory suppositions are empirically true, and some are false. 'If 2^3 were equal to 9, a fluorine atom would have 2^3 protons in its nucleus' is true, and 'If 2^3 were equal to 9, a nitrogen atom would have 2^3 protons in its nucleus' is false. (However, the exact formulation given in the cited paper must be amended by changing the words 'true orange sentence' appearing on the top line of page 18 to 'members of S.')

4 It was no doubt a parallel sceptical worry which motivated the following comment of Immanuel Kant on the causal principle and the Common Sense School's *ad hominem* defence of it: 'The concept of cause, for instance, which expresses the necessity of an event under a presupposed condition, would be false if it rested only on an arbitrary subjective necessity, implanted in us, of connecting certain empirical representations according to the rule of casual relation. I would not then be able to say that the effect is connected with the cause in the object, that is to say, necessarily, but only that I am so constituted that I cannot think this representation otherwise than as thus connected. This is exactly what the sceptic most desires. For if this be the situation, all our insight, resting on the supposed objective validity of our judgments, is nothing but sheer illusion ...' (*Critique of Pure Reason* B168, Norman Kemp Smith translation [London, 1933], 175).

   Indeed, unless there really is apt to be something more to causal necessitation than the psychological necessity of *believing* that cause-and-effect connections exist

It may have been this issue that the eleventh-century Islamic theologian Ibn Hazm was raising when he sought to cut down the pretensions of rationalistic philosophy by stressing that Almighty God could always have made us creatures with a different nature, lacking any predisposition to disbelieve what we perceive to be logically contradictory. René Descartes, in his time, insisted that omnipotence gave God the power to make even a logical contradiction true, notwithstanding our actual God-given perception that such a thing's being true is impossible.[5] Descartes appears not to have been sceptical in the least about Non-contradiction himself, but commentators have wondered how compatible his confidence on that score was with this view taken by him about omnipotence. Their point becomes comprehensible perhaps, if viewed in the light of the problem of how we can be assured that whatever is responsible for this predisposition of ours to disbelieve what we see to be logically contradictory would really not still give rise to it, or at any rate sustain it in us the way it does, if the Non-contradiction Principle was not actually true.

Our human nature is what it is as a result of biological evolution by natural selection, supplemented, no doubt, by subsequent social evolution. The psychological disposition not to accord belief simultaneously to contradictories is doubtless genetically inherited by each of us and a result of the biological evolutionary process.[6] (In the event nothing could even count as a *mind* possessing any *beliefs* without having this 'predisposition,' the evolution of such logicality will not then be distinct from the evolution of *mentality* itself, and what is said here will hold good still.) Once it had appeared, this mental disposition was retained by succeeding generations of our ancestors because it had survival value, and it had survival value, surely, because the Principle of Non-contradiction

---

in objects, then such belief will, so far as we can tell, be quite illusory. But the Scottish philosophers of Commonsense, with their habit of appealing to the plan of a loving Creator, were very far from admitting that the causal principle would still be psychologically indubitable even if it were not true. As elsewhere in biology, evolution by natural selection is a process in considerable measure yielding the same outcome here as divine planning would yield.

5 Letter to Denis Mesland of 2 May 1644, in *Œuvres de Descartes*, ed. by Charles Adam and Paul Tannery (Paris, 1972), 118–19.

6 Cf. Charles Darwin in his 'M Notebook': 'Plato ... says in Phaedo that our "*necessary ideas*" arise from the preexistence of the soul, are not derivable from experience. – read monkeys for preexistence.' In Charles Darwin, *Metaphysics, Materialism, and the Evolution of Mind*, ed. Paul H. Barrett (Chicago, 1974), 30.

is actually true. It will be necessary to rebut below the objection that it makes no sense to talk thus about the difference which the truth of the Principle of Non-contradiction makes to the way the world is, ensuring for instance this much about the weather, that it is never both raining and not raining anywhere.[7] Meanwhile, we can see how essentially on the right track those theorists were who used to compare an entire evolving species to an individual experimenter. Our psychological nature leads us to believe the Principle of Non-contradiction because of a long process of evolutionary hit-or-miss, a process which, insofar as it gives rise to a faculty or faculties for believing things, has a tendency towards doing so in such a way that the eventual beliefs ensuing are predominantly true. It is, to be sure, only the *past* survival value of logical consistency among beliefs held that is responsible for our having a psychological nature now which leads us to believe the Principle of Non-contradiction. But that to which the past survival value of such consistency was due, viz., the correspondence of the Non-contradiction Principle to reality in the past, in turn ensures its correspondence to reality in the future also. For its correspondence to reality in the future follows from its correspondence to reality in the past both deductively and inductively. And so, there is no danger that what is responsible for our believing the Non-contradiction Principle would still give rise to such belief, or at any rate sustain it in us, even if the Principle were not true.

Nor need any exception be taken to the employment here of the fact that the Non-contradiction Principle is true in order to defend believing it against the particular line of sceptical objection envisaged. The objection was to the effect that, even if such belief *were* to be true, that would only be by chance. The rebuttal denies this. In any case, to those in no doubt as to the truth of the Principle of Non-contradiction, the need to premise or otherwise presuppose it cannot make any line of reasoning less compelling. But what about the objection that any argument from evolution must needs depend on inductive evidence, which can never render any conclusion as certain as the Principle of Non-contradiction already is, *a*

---

7 'I know nothing about the weather,' said Ludwig Wittgenstein, 'when I know that it is either raining or not raining' (*Tractatus Logico-Philosophicus*, 4.461). But he scarcely advanced any argument for this claim. To be sure, anybody who confined a weather report to the statement merely that it was either raining or not raining would be taking pay under false pretences. But is this not so just because we could never learn from such a report anything *which we did not already know* (provided that we did understand what rain is)? In that practical sense, there is no reason to deny that what a logical axiom states is *uninformative*.

priori and without any argument? In the first place, the evolutionary considerations brought to bear here were not all being advanced as an argument for the truth of the Principle (but merely as a rebuttal, not to any case for its falsity, but only to a certain sceptical argument telling, at most, against the *warrantability* of believing it). Secondly, even if this were to have been an inductive argument for the Principle of Non-contradiction, why should its inability to confer complete certainty on its conclusion be thought to detract at all from its *cogency*, rather than just its *utility*?

But was it overhasty to assert as psychological fact that nobody ever could disbelieve or even doubt the Principle of Non-contradiction? There certainly have been professed deniers of it, as some think Heraclitus was.[8] Many have simply been verbally confused in an obvious way, but the twentieth-century Christian convert Lev Shestov[9] appears to have been exceptionally clear-headed on the subject, if of necessity self-deceived (according to those of us too 'doctrinaire' to accept that he actually believed – instead of just wishing or thinking he believed – the blatant absurdities that he said a true believer had to swallow). According to the way Shestov interpreted Judeo-Christian religious belief, God not only could but did change the past, in spite of its being logically contradictory to say so:

> In order to escape from the nightmare, one must repudiate the 'law' of contradiction upon which all the self-evident truths of waking consciousness are based. One must make an enormous effort – and wake up.[10]

Recapitulating, we can perhaps read these two sentences of Shestov's as saying:

---

8 Indeed, Heraclitus's philosophy did run counter to what for Aristotle was metaphysically inseparable from his Law of Contradiction: the persistence of ingenerable and indestructible essential *natures* of things, and hence of perpetual, fixed species. Aristotle seems to have thought that this is required by our very ability to say what anything is.

9 V.V. Zenkovsky, *A History of Russian Philosophy*, vol. 2, trans. George L. Kline (New York, 1953), 785, gives reasons for the conclusion that Shestov was indeed a Jew who converted. However, James C.S. Wernham, *Two Russian Thinkers: An Essay in Berdyaev and Shestov* (Toronto, 1968), 102, remains unconvinced. See especially Shestov's *Athens and Jerusalem* (Athens, OH, 1966).

10 Leon Shestov, 'In Memory of a Great Philosopher: Edmund Husserl,' trans. George L. Kline, *Philosophy and Phenomenological Research* 22, no. 4 (June 1962), 468.

1 Non-contradiction's being actually borne out in the world is a
  nightmarish prospect.
2 And so an enormous effort is called for in order to repudiate it and
  all the psychological 'self-evidence' based upon it.
3 From which one can emerge disbelieving the Principle instead.
4 And only then will one have the real truth.

Point 2 accepts that repudiating the Non-contradiction Principle does
go against the psychological grain. Did Shestov's 'enormous effort' of
auto-thought-control succeed? Did he succeed in actually 'repudiating'
Non-contradiction in his mental life? When he wanted to go to Megara,
for instance, did he set himself to head (directly or indirectly) towards
Megara? Or – all right, let us say and/or – did he *not* do that? But what
good reason could he have had against choosing the second option,
except the impossibility of simultaneously both going to Megara and
not going to Megara? To be sure, the present line of thought, like any
other, presupposes the Non-contradiction Principle; however, as an *ad
hominem* argument really addressed not to Shestov but to the reader, it
is perhaps no less compelling on that account.

But, at this rate, it should be unsurprising that, despite the text, a
Shestov admirer could be at pains to deny Shestov actually meant to
renounce the Non-contradiction Principle *across the board*, so to speak,
rather than just in some selected cases.[11] What that would mean, presumably, is recognizing the application of deductive reasoning to some
questions but not to others.

Let R be the range of questions to which deductive reasoning is applicable. Can a question both fall within R and not fall within R? Clearly
not, or the restriction will be nugatory, for it will then be possible for
any assertion to be immune from logical criticism, whether the question it answers falls within R or not. Accordingly, the range of questions
to which deductive reasoning is applicable will have to include questions as to what questions fall within R and what questions do not. We
thus can proceed with our discussion in full confidence that the questions being discussed fall within the range of questions R. R, then, is
that range of questions to whose answers the canons of deductive inference are applicable. A proposition may be said to fall within R if it gives
a true or false answer to a question which falls within R. And so it is

---

11 See, for example, Bernard Martin's laudatory introduction to his English translation
   of Shestov's *Athens and Jerusalem*, 37–9.

easy to see that, if a proposition falls within R, its negation will fall within R also. Since it is to the propositions within R that deductive inferability is applicable, we must lay it down that anything deductively following from propositions in R is itself a proposition in R.

We had better narrow our understanding of 'deductively following' for these purposes, however, so as to block the excessively quick inference that all questions fall within R; for from any proposition and its negation answers will *follow deductively* to any question whatever if 'follows deductively from' can simply mean 'is strictly implied by' here, inasmuch as a logically contradictory pair of propositions is said to *strictly imply* everything. Fortunately, there *is* an account of 'following deductively' which will be adequate for our present needs. Borrowing our general idea from T.J. Smiley,[12] we may say that, for the purpose of this paragraph and the next, the statement that a conclusion 'follows deductively' from certain premises will mean that the material implication of that conclusion by the conjunction of those premises is expressible in a material-implication sentence which is an interpretation of a tautological formula of the first-order predicate calculus such that neither the formula's implicate nor the negation of its implicans is itself a tautological formula of the first-order predicate calculus. On this definition, a conclusion will 'follow deductively' only from premises which bear to it a relation which is sufficient for strict implication independently of any inconsistencies in those premises. So defined, the relation 'follows deductively from' will not, however, be transitive – that is to say, not everything which *follows deductively from* what *follows deductively from* given premises will itself *follow deductively from* those premises. At that rate, 'deductive following,' so defined, does diverge from deducibility as usually conceived, but in the present context there is no harm in giving up transitivity in this way. In fact, it is actually an advantage, as will become clear.

Here is a proof that, even with such an understanding of what it is to 'follow deductively,' there cannot be a proposition falling outside the range, R, of propositions to which deductive reasoning is applicable. Let P be any proposition. Then 'P is in R' and 'P is not in R' will both be propositions in R. Let them be represented by 'A' and 'B,' respectively. Since B is a proposition in R, the logical disjunction of B and P, which follows deductively from B, will also be a proposition in R. Since that proposition and A are both in R, P, which follows deductively from

---

12 T.J. Smiley, 'Entailment and Deducibility,' *Proceedings of the Aristotelian Society* 59 (London, 1959), 233–54.

those two premises, will have to be a proposition in R as well. It is true that the 'relevance logic' of Alan Ross Anderson and Nuel D. Belnap specifically rejects inferences of the last sort – 'disjunctive syllogism' inferences[13] – and thus avoids results like this. To their critique of this inference pattern it will therefore be necessary to turn right away. Aside from *such* objections, though, we have seen that, of necessity, any proposition whatsoever will have to be a proposition in R, that is, the range of questions to which the canons of deductive inference are applicable. There is no way to allow deductive inference an application to some questions but not others. From the merest foot in the door, it unstoppably extends its sway without limit.

In appealing right now to the 'disjunctive syllogism' it was, indeed, necessary to note that the 'relevance logicians' A.R. Anderson and N.D. Belnap specifically object to it. But why is it that they object to it? They say it commits a 'fallacy of relevance.'[14] What is that? Explaining their philosophical motivation, they write:

> For more than two millennia logicians have taught that a necessary condition for the validity of an inference from A to B is that A be relevant to B. Virtually every logic book up to the present [twentieth] century has a chapter on fallacies of relevance, and many contemporary elementary texts have followed the same plan. Notice that contemporary writers, in the later and more formal chapters of their books, seem explicitly to contradict the earlier chapters, when they try desperately to bamboozle the students into accepting strict 'implication' as a 'kind' of implication relation, in spite of the fact that this relation countenances fallacies of relevance.[15]

But where is this lack of relevance of premises to conclusion in the disjunctive syllogism? Anderson and Belnap agree there is no fallacy there 'with respect to our ordinary reasonings,' as 'perhaps always when the principle is used in reasoning one has in mind an intensional meaning of "or," where there is relevance between the disjuncts.'[16] But why, then, should a lack of mutual relevance as between the disjuncts of a truth-functional disjunction invalidate a disjunctive syllogism? It is not as though Anderson and Belnap

---

13 Alan Ross Anderson and Nuel D. Belnap Jr., *Entailment, The Logic of Relevance and Necessity*, vol. 1 (Princeton, NJ, 1975), 165–7, 296–300.
14 Ibid., 165.
15 Ibid., 17.
16 Ibid., 165.

disallow truthfunctional disjunctions as genuine propositions capable of figuring in deductive inference.[17] Quite obviously, their objection stems from the derivability from any given inconsistent premises of irrelevant conclusions by strict-implication reasoning *chains* which include a disjunctive syllogism.[18] In contrast with the approach of the last paragraph and the one before it, Anderson and Belnap are taking the transitivity of the relation of *deducibility* for granted. It may be objected, though, that the argument given in the last paragraph really does so too. But does it, in fact? We can say three arguments are found in the last paragraph: an argument from B to the disjunction of B and P; an argument from that disjunction and the proposition A to the conclusion P; and a two-step argument from the proposition that B falls within R to the conclusion (in light of the first argument) that B's disjunction with A falls within R also, and then from that initial conclusion and the proposition that A falls within R to the final conclusion (in the light of the second argument) that P falls within R also. Does even the third of these arguments require inferential transitivity? But even supposing it does, there can be no question of faulting *it* for any lack of relevance between premises and conclusion.

It is really a misconceived move, then, to appeal (unlike Anderson and Belnap themselves) to anything in relevance logic in defence of the view that discourse containing 'localized' inconsistencies can still be entirely correct.[19]

---

17 Ibid.

18 Ibid.

19 In *In Contradiction: A Study of the Transconsistent* (Dordrecht, Netherlands, 1987) and other writings, Graham Priest, too, rejects the universal validity of the disjunctive syllogism (DS), in order to keep logical contradictions localized. But he accepts there that 'it is quite legitimate to use the DS in consistent situations' (138) – meaning situations where (as Priest agrees to be the most usual case) no logical contradiction is, in fact, true. And is not the situation envisaged in the last paragraph genuinely such a situation? In any event, it does often happen in the history of science that theorists are faced with results which are provably inconsistent but also very well substantiated – and certainly superior to any alternative theories available. Their inconsistency shows that they are not absolutely correct, but there is no point in waiting, before using them in scientific practice, until logically purified replacements have been devised that are just as good theoretically. The inconsistent theories can still be seen to be substantially true, even if not absolutely true, and so, surely their acceptance for the time being, thus qualified, is going to be rationally called for at those junctures. Special logics may well be needed then so as to deal with such theories without multiplying paradoxes unduly; and for such purposes disallowing disjunctive syllogism inferences can legitimately present itself as one possible quite appropriate move to make. Nothing in the present chapter should be taken to detract at all from the service to the cause of truth which the work of 'paraconsistent' logicians like Priest can provide.

The truth of the Non-contradiction Principle has to be seen as exceptionless.[20]

At this point the reader may be more than a little impatient, never having questioned standard deductive inference or the unrestricted range of the Non-contradiction Principle in the first place. However, if the truth of such a principle can be a substantive piece of *a priori* knowledge, albeit analytic (undeniable without logical contradiction), will that not undermine the plausibility of empiricism's denial that there likewise can be synthetic *a priori* truths as well? In order to deflect this line of thought, once it has been conceded that the Principle of Non-contradiction is not in the least false it will have to be claimed that the truth of the Principle is really not *a priori* but empirical, or else that really the Principle is somehow not itself true-or-false – not substantive, not really 'about the world.' And some empiricist philosophers have, in fact, been prepared to assert that the canons of deductive inference, and logical and mathematical truths in general, are all knowable only empirically. John Stuart Mill was famous for making such a claim, and, in the twentieth century, P.W. Bridgman[21] and W.V. Quine asserted as much for their part (insisting, in the case of Quine, on a much broader concept of empirical proof than J.S. Mill's somewhat narrow conception of induction). From what has been said above, it will be no surprise that the line to be taken here is going to be that these truths are indeed establishable empirically, by means of

---

20 What about 'the logic of fictions,' then? Is it not true to state that Hamlet died of poisoning in the blood on some day of the month or other, for instance, but yet *not* true to state that Hamlet died on an even numbered date, or true to state that Hamlet died on an odd-numbered date either? This, however, will be perfectly comprehensible if it can be understood that in reporting on a fiction to say, 'Hamlet died of poisoning,' just means something like, 'In the Hamlet-story it was said or implied that Hamlet died of poisoning,' et cetera. At that rate, there will be no breach of non-contradiction or any other logical requirement here. Where a speaker means to leave open the historical or fictional character of an account, it is apparently necessary to add an explicit qualifier such as 'supposedly' before saying, 'Robin Hood lived in Sherwood Forest,' for example, but, where the meaning is clearly one thing or the other, such a qualifier is not required.

21 'Even the statement of the syllogism itself in its most guarded form: "*If* 'a' is 'b' and *if* 'c' is 'a,' then 'c' is 'b'"' does no more, at least as far as my own analysis can find, than sum up in compact form this general description of my past experience: namely, "whenever I have encountered an 'a' which was a 'b' and a 'c' which was an 'a,' then always I have noticed that 'c' was also 'b'"' (P.W. Bridgman, *The Intelligent Individual and Society* [New York, 1938], 65–6). No doubt, if Bridgman had been somewhat more careful, he would rather have written here: 'Whenever I have encountered some *a*'s which were all *b*'s and a *c* which was one of those *a*'s ...'

inductive proofs as conclusive as any inductive proofs are, but circular when it comes to proving propositions such as the Principle of Non-contradiction because, like any arguments whatever, those ones too must already presuppose such principles as Non-contradiction. It is impossible for any argument of any sort to go through successfully unless a non-contradiction requirement can be maintained. Consequently, it will be possible to be warranted in believing the Principle of Non-contradiction on empirical grounds, only if it is likewise possible to be warranted in believing it independently of such grounds. In other words, if the Principle of Non-contradiction is true at all, it is true *a priori*.

But is it really true? Given that it is not at all false, unless it is true it is truthvalueless. And such in fact is the position taken by the conventionalist philosophy of logic and mathematics inspired by the early and the late works of Ludwig Wittgenstein.[22] According to this philosophy, logically contradictory and tautologous sentences do not express anything true-or-false because they are just 'senseless.' All *genuine* propositions, Wittgenstein tells us, say that certain conditions obtain: those conditions, namely, which would in each case obtain if those propositions were each to be true. But logical contradictions are true under no conditions, he adds, while tautologies are 'true' unconditionally (not really *true*, as, if they were, they would have really false denials). But this way of speaking is far from obligatory.

No doubt, whatever is expressed by the words, 'Any barnyard containing seven fowl of the species chicken, five fowl of some other species, and no additional fowl, contains twelve fowl in all,' is demonstrably tautologous (undeniable without logical contradiction). What is to stop us from saying that the condition it asserts to obtain is simply the condition that any barnyard containing seven fowl of the species chicken, five fowl of some other species, and no additional fowl contains twelve fowl in all? What is to stop us from saying similarly that the condition which the logical contradiction '7+5=13' asserts to obtain is simply that of 7+5 equalling 13? The Wittgensteinian answer will be that 7+5 equalling 13 is not really a possible condition. To be sure, it is not among the conditions which are *logically* possible – that is, the conditions that logic is insufficient to rule out. By the same token, though, living forever is not *biologically* possible, in that the laws of biology do suffice to rule its occurrence out; but that doesn't warrant our concluding that

---

22 Ludwig Wittgenstein, *Tractatus Logico-Philosophicus*, 4.461; *Philosophical Investigations* I, 513.

there is *no condition* which a claim of biological immortality asserts to obtain. When Wittgensteinians insist that no condition is even *specifiable* under which 7+5 would equal 13, they must mean 'consistently specifiable' – that is, specifiable without logical contradiction. But what is the independent reason for denying that anything inconsistent can count as a *specification* for these purposes?

Another way of advancing the conventionalist view is to say that whatever is either analytic or logically contradictory will have to be truthvalueless because whether what it says is or is not in order is a matter merely of the linguistic expressions used in formulating it, and not of any other fact standing outside of itself. But why are we unable to say it is a fact that 7+5=12, and that this fact 'stands outside' of the assertion '7+5=12,' just as the fact that ~7+5=13 'stands outside' of the assertion '7+5=13'? The reply will be that what makes '7+5=12' in order (and '7+5=13' not in order) is *merely* the meanings of the symbols used. It will be insisted that, while the truth or falsity of what any assertive sentence says has to depend, of course, on the meanings of the symbols used in formulating it – because it has to depend on what the sentence means – where what a statement-making sentence says is consistent and synthetic, its truth-value will not follow from a statement of those meanings *alone*. In response to this, it must be admitted that the truth-value of logical contradictions or tautologies does follow – logically – from premises which just state what sentences expressing them *mean*. But, equally, from premises stating only that what a certain sentence means (as it is used) is that some animal is immortal, it follows *biologically* that what that sentence (as it is used) says is false.

Wittgensteinians sometimes argue that *truth* and *falsity* are logically correlative notions, so that, where there is no logical room for one, there is no logical room for the other, either. From which the conclusion is drawn that any sentence with assertive *sense* must (as used) state something which is logically capable of being true and logically capable of being false.[23] Parody: '"Consistency" and "inconsistency" are logically correlative notions, so that, where the *consistency* of something somebody has said is logically ruled out, its *inconsistency* is ruled out also; and *vice versa*.'

---

23 Such a line of thought as this is, at any rate, frequently *attributed* to Wittgenstein. See *Philosophical Investigations*, I, 251.

In his book, *Introduction to Logical Theory*,[24] P.F. Strawson in effect argued that 'logical knowledge' is simply language-bound *grammatical knowledge*, although of a more general character than what is usually so called – but still essentially about what turns of phrase are in order and what ones are not. One might have thought that a distinction could be drawn between merely saying something ungrammatical and saying something which is logically contradictory, on the grounds that in the former case, but not the latter, what is said can always be reformulated in acceptable, rule-conforming terms without distorting the speaker's meaning. Mind you, on the Wittgensteinian view, there is no 'sense' there in the first place when something logically contradictory is said (though nevertheless, a logical contradiction somehow is still not 'non-sensical'). It is unclear whether the following, quoted from Strawson, was intended by him as a serious *argument* for his position, or simply as a pedagogically helpful way of formulating it:

> Suppose a man sets out to walk to a certain place; but, when he gets half-way there, turns round and comes back again. This may not be pointless. He may, after all, have wanted only exercise. But, from the point of view of a change of position, it is as if he had never set out. And so a man who contradicts himself may have succeeded in exercising his vocal chords. But from the point of view of imparting information, of communicating facts (or falsehoods) it is as if he had never opened his mouth. He utters words, but does not say anything. Or he might be compared with a man who makes as if to give something away and then takes it back again.[25]

> Variants on 'is inconsistent' are 'is self-contradictory,' 'is logically impossible,' 'is logically false.' Now suppose we deny, or assert the contradictory of, an inconsistent statement. We saw that a man who makes an inconsistent statement says, in a manner, nothing at all. His statement cancels itself. So what is said by a man who denies an inconsistent statement? It seems that he says nothing either: he, too, leaves things where they were.[26]

If Strawson did mean all this to be an argument for his position, presumably the argument would be something like the following: someone who contradicts himself says in one breath what he unsays in

---

24 P.F. Strawson, *Introduction to Logical Theory* (London, 1952).
25 Ibid., 2.
26 Ibid., 21.

another (or even the same) breath; therefore, all in all, the net effect is that he has said nothing, at least as far as asserting something goes. On this account, unsaying something you have said makes it thereupon cease to be something which you assert; it simply restores the *status quo ante* as far as anything's being asserted by you is concerned.

Surely the most that could be said for an argument like this is that it would apply (at best) to those language-users, and those only, that contradict themselves both knowingly and openly. Considerations of this sort *might* lead us to affirm that, for instance, 'It is raining here and it is not raining here,' understood literally, says something alike impossible either to believe or to assert. But, on the other hand, they can by no means compel us to admit the impossibility of disbelieving or denying such a thing. Anything meaningful, in the way of assertions, must have a meaningful negation. But why should it follow that anything believable must have a believable negation or that anything assertible must have an assertible negation?

We may note that to argue for the undeniability of logical principles like the Principle of Non-contradiction from the linguistic *meanings* of the expressions used in formulating them necessarily counts as just another example of *ad hominem* argumentation in philosophy: the attention of those addressed is drawn to what they themselves mean by those expressions, from which the truth of (formulas expressing) a Principle like Non-contradiction does logically follow. But the *circularity* of such argumentation is clear from the imaginability here, as before, of the *verbal* response: 'Yes, in view of what I, too, mean by the expressions used in formulating it, the Principle of Non-contradiction must indeed be undeniably true; and, furthermore, it is false also.' To object that saying this is *inconsistent* with the speaker's own use of 'true' and 'false' as mutually exclusive predicates would, of course, again be question-begging.

But this consideration should not stop us from connecting the undeniability of 'No proposition is both true and false,' say, with the meanings of the words 'true' and 'false' in our language. For 'Every proposition is either true or false' a similar claim of undeniability has been made, and similarly challenged. 'Alternative logics' certainly are constructible, in which familiar formulas expressing rules and axioms are replaced with very different ones. A comment often made is that such alternatives do not really bespeak disagreement on any substantive matter, but only different assignments of *meanings* to the symbols being used. For example, where 'true' and 'false' mean 'provable' and 'disprovable,' 'Every proposition is either true or false' will *not* obviously express a tautology. With regard to that, if it really is psychologically impossible to dissent from what something like the Principle of Non-contradiction asserts, then claims made about 'alternative logics' by logical conventionalism will, to just this extent, be borne out.

Here, however, are two positive arguments against Wittgensteinian conventionalism regarding logic and mathematics.

In the first place, on the Wittgensteinian view, one who has accepted the premises of a valid mathematical demonstration has learned nothing further when brought to accept the conclusion (since, if there were anything which that demonstration did teach the individual, it would at least be the material implication of the conclusion by the conjunction of the premises, and that, being tautologous, is of necessity *uninformative*, according to Wittgenstein's doctrine). It is more than a little paradoxical to say that valid mathematical demonstration cannot teach us anything; that mathematical tautologies say nothing about the real world. If that were right, it would be an insoluble mystery why the tautologies of applied mathematics are so useful to us, even predictively useful. Moreover, they frequently are *prima facie* establishable inductively, as well as *a priori*. Thus, the material implication of Pythagoras' Theorem by the axiom of parallels was discovered by the ancient Egyptians empirically long before Pythagoras and Euclid came along and mathematically *demonstrated* it. To deny that what the Egyptians discovered empirically is the same thing as the Greek mathematicians later demonstrated is to make the obvious connection between the empirical discovery and the mathematical demonstration irremediably mysterious. Where, if not from the inductive finding, did Pythagoras get the idea for the geometrical conclusion which he set out to demonstrate mathematically?[27] Similarly, that the membership of five sextuples, as of six quintuples,

---

27 'Wouldn't this imply that we can't learn anything new about an object in mathematics, since, if we do, it is a new object?

   'This boils down to saying: If I hear a proposition of, say, number theory, but don't know how to prove it, then I don't understand the proposition either. This sounds extremely paradoxical ... when I learn the proof, I learn something *completely new*, and not just the way leading to a goal with which I'm already familiar.

   'But in that case it's unintelligible that I should admit, when I've got the proof, that it's a proof of precisely *this* proposition, ...

   'There can't be two independent proofs of one mathematical proposition.' (Ludwig Wittgenstein, *Philosophical Remarks*, ed. Rush Rhees, trans. from the German by Raymond Hargreaves and Roger White [Oxford, 1975], 183–4.)

always totals thirty, is something very easy to show inductively. The induction in question is fallible, of course, like any induction; and reasoners who know that the same conclusion is also demonstrable *a priori* will be unwilling to accept apparent empirical counter-evidence (unless the evidence seems *very* strong, in which case, if rational, they will be motivated to scrutinize again the apparently valid demonstration). If the conventionalist view of the nature of tautology were correct, though, what the later *a priori* mathematical demonstration would actually establish is simply that the earlier inductive argument did not, in fact, probabilify anything because there was, after all, nothing there to be probabilified; nothing really true-or-false, that is. Wittgenstein's conventionalism labels as strictly senseless much of our use of language which quite obviously is cognitively meaningful.[28]

Secondly, if Wittgenstein's conventionalist philosophy concerning the nature of contradiction were right, the Shestovian thesis discussed above would then be, not merely incorrect, but *senseless*; and it would be equally senseless to contradict it. We could still say that Shestov's above-cited writings, though meant, indeed, to assert the truth, in fact got *something* wrong, but we should have to add that it wasn't anything about God or the world. It would have to be simply a linguistic mistake that Shestov made. What he got wrong, we should have to say, was (neither more nor less than) the rules of his language. Not the English language, mind you, as he did not write in English. But even from the above quotation in English it would have to be possible for us to determine that he must have got his own language's rules wrong. How would it be possible to determine that? The evidence would have to be that the words quoted are contradictory *in English*. Normally when what purports to be a clear rendering of somebody's thoughts into English results in incorrect English – phraseology violating the linguistic rules of English – the conclusion warranted is simply that the translation must be faulty. Here, fidelity to Shestov's thought demands violation of the logical rules. Moreover, his basic thought seems clear as a bell, does it not? The

---

28 But can validly arguing deductive reasoners *really* know more at the end of their reasoning, and thanks to it, than what they knew at the beginning in knowing the premises of the argument if, as is in fact the case, every step in (what goes on psychologically in a mind performing) a fully articulated valid deduction involves merely (at the most) a selective *reorganization* of what the reasoner already knows? Even such a mental process of *reorganization* should be seen as effecting a genuine increase in a reasoner's knowledge, I have argued in my 'Cognitive Synonymy,' *Dialectica* 34, no. 3 (1980), 200–3.

Wittgensteinian position would oblige us to deny that any basic thought of his, whether correct or incorrect, is expressed in the above quotation. For, if it did affirm a real thought of his, correct or incorrect, it would not then be senseless. On the Wittgensteinian view, the quotation above exhibits a linguistic error; and yet not an error of Shestov's, for the only linguistic error the above quotation could exhibit would be an error in English, but Shestov, in writing down his thought, was not making any error in English. Suppose it is said that what Shestov himself wrote must have exhibited a linguistic error *parallel* to the error exhibited by the English version of what he wrote; and that different languages must accordingly have certain *parallel* rules, the violation of any of which is 'contradictory' in some translinguistic sense. What sense? What parallelism? The Wittgensteinian position on the linguistic character of logic and of contradiction makes these questions impossible to answer.

Certainly, to call principles like the Principle of Non-contradiction undeniable is not to overlook that at times words have been uttered whose literal meaning would be to deny them. It is necessary either to take those words otherwise than literally as they are used on such occasions, however, or else to conclude that the persons uttering the words either are being consciously dishonest in speaking the way they do, or else are confused and/or in error as to their own actual opinions.

When it comes to some basic principle(s) of logic, then, it appears we can distinguish three quite different sorts of disagreement. *First*, there is the sort of disagreement which can and does arise between the proponents of divergent 'logics.' The issue in dispute will be apt to turn here upon the *meanings* of the logical symbols employed; most probably, in particular, upon what meanings it is more expedient to attach to those symbols for whatever purposes are in view. In furtherance of such purposes, the only restrictions on the construction of any 'alternative logic' are those dictated by the requirements merely of (meta-)consistency. Whatever rules are devised for the manipulation of logical symbols must be rules that never could turn out to be *both* obeyed and not obeyed in some cases, or *neither* obeyed nor not obeyed, and so forth. The truth of what the last sentence says follows from the meanings which the expressions used in formulating it have in the *English* language, to be sure. But, as what the sentence says is true, that which would be expressed by its translation into any other language employed in explaining the construction of an 'alternative logic' would similarly have to govern all explanations of the construction couched in that language. Even if the construction *could* be carried out in the mind of a logician who was not thinking in any language at all, in effect the same dictates of consistency would have to be respected because of the psychological impossibility of thinking otherwise. That much is well bound up with empirically establishable facts about human nature.

Indeed, it is just those empirical facts to which would-be irrationalist deniers of principles such as the Principle of Non-contradiction can be referred in an *ad hominem* argument aimed at curing them of their ir-rationalism. The cure is not guaranteed to work, since there can be no guarantee of honesty, self-honesty, and clear-headedness. But that is a limitation affecting the persuasiveness of absolutely any argument, however conclusive. It is important to remember here that the use of an *ad hominem* line of argument is not at all limited to debates. Any of us can use it in our private reflections in order to satisfy ourselves on some point to which our ways of thinking can be seen to commit us. What other mode of reasoning did Aristotle employ in order to arrive at the Principle of Non-contradiction? What other discovery procedure is there for ferreting out the basic canons of inference, than to start off empirically noting our own ways of thinking in actual and hypothetical cases? And, in debating with any philosopher like Shestov, this does seem to be the rational way to tackle disagreement of the *second* sort.

There is a *third* sort of case of disagreement, though. Taking up Ibn Hazm's suggestion, let us suppose – maybe *per impossible* – that almighty God did create a race of extraterrestrials whose psychological natures did not incline them to accept any sort of non-contradiction principle, and let us further suppose – contrary to what our Principle of Non-contradiction leads us to believe – that these beings did manage none-theless to survive into the present. Could we communicate with them? We could, if their natures did not positively block their discourse from at least on occasion approaching that degree of consistency found in the discourse of someone like Shestov, for instance. But could we *argue* with them? In one sense, no. Since we are specifically imagining them here as beings not particularly disposed to listen to reason, it follows that there is no line of argument we could advance that we could expect to be per-suasive with them. But such a limitation on the persuasiveness of any argument is not a limitation on how strong it is objectively. In this case, the arguments used could even be logically conclusive: it would not be anything the matter with *them*, considered objectively, if those to whom they were addressed were not psychologically disposed to be influ-enced by them. A common opinion holds that it is not possible to con-sider some answer to a question objectively true, and think and reason accordingly, without supposing or presupposing that there is some neutral criterion or other, in principle, by reference to which the question could at least ideally be settled. But we can see, surely, that any such opinion must be mistaken. In any disagreement over the Principle of Non-contradiction, there could not possibly be something *neutral* to which it would be possible to appeal to settle the issue.[29]

---

29 An objection here has been raised to viewing Non-contradiction 'as foundational, something not adjudicable as correct by any deeper principle [though] arguably it *could* be so adjudicated, e.g., by the conditions on something's being a logic at all.' Indeed, Non-contradiction could be so adjudicated quite legitimately, only not without circular reasoning. For the adjudication could be successful only if the principle(s) of adjudication appealed to were applied *consistently*.

5 Preliminary Assault on the Philosophy of Empiricism

> When we run over libraries, persuaded of these principles, what havoc must we make? If we take in our hand any volume; of divinity or school metaphysics, for instance; let us ask, *Does it contain any abstract reasoning concerning quantity or number?* No. *Does it contain any experimental reasoning concerning matter of fact and existence?* No. Commit it then to the flames: for it can contain nothing but sophistry and illusion.
>
> David Hume[1]

There are, at most, three kinds of beliefs which can pass muster with empiricism. In the first place, something can be believed because, whether directly or on the basis of a deductive proof, it has been perceived to be tautologous. But such a belief, of course, is never *synthetic*. Secondly, there is the sort of case where even the fullest statement of that which is believed only reports what has actually been experienced. But such belief is, of course, never *general*.[2] And thirdly, there is belief

---

1 David Hume, *An Inquiry concerning Human Understanding*, in *Enquiries concerning Human Understanding and concerning the Principles of Morals*, ed. L.A. Selby-Bigge, 3rd ed., rev. P.H. Nidditch (Oxford, 1975), 165. Emphasis in original.
2 If a more precise, technical characterization is wanted, then for our purposes we could (rather restrictively) understand a 'general' belief as one capable of formulation in purely qualitative terms exclusively. Any such formulation would accordingly contain no proper names, no terms with a token-reflexive, or indexical, element in their meanings, and no spatially or temporally locating expressions which locate (or purport to locate) anything absolutely. See my paper 'What Are "Purely Qualitative" Terms,' *American Philosophical Quarterly* 23, no. 1 (January 1986), 71–81. (By such a definition, however, the existence, e.g., of itchiness at some

held on the basis of inference from what has been experienced, whether the inference has been consciously drawn or has not. Accordingly, no *general synthetic* belief can ever pass muster with empiricism unless it is held on the basis of inference from experience.

Against all three of these kinds of beliefs objections have been forthcoming from empiricist-influenced quarters. We already observed in chapter 4 how a philosophical effort has been made to call all tautologies truthvalueless, so that acceptance of them could not then constitute a case of *belief*, strictly speaking, if the argument of chapters 1 and 2 holds good. Against the second of the proposed classes of beliefs it has been objected that any statement whatsoever is at least partly 'interpretative,' and so no statement could 'only report what has actually been experienced.' This, however, will follow only if it can be agreed *either* that an interpretation is not the sort of thing which can ever itself be objectively correct, *or else* that no statement of (any part of) what some individual believed could ever count as 'only reporting what had actually been experienced' by the person unless the person were to be *infallible* in giving credence to what the statement asserted. Otherwise, the obvious psychological fact that what people believe themselves to experience, and indeed what they do experience, are both heavily influenced by other beliefs of theirs, need not detract from the justifiability of claiming there are many beliefs belonging to this second class which on occasion do warrant acceptance as true. This is fortunate, since, if there were no warranted beliefs belonging to the second class, there would be no warranted beliefs belonging to the third class either, as the latter beliefs are all held on the basis of inference from the former. For our purposes, the position of 'empiricism' is not committed to accepting the legitimacy of these three classes of beliefs, but only to a refusal to recognize the legitimacy of any beliefs which do not belong to one or another of these three classes.

---

time or other is arguably a 'general' truth knowable directly in experience, because anyone conscious of being itchy *now* knows this truth already. And, arguably too, a statement of this synthetic truth does not state anything more, in such a case, than just what is being experienced – though it does state less. Accordingly, for the purposes of the present chapter we could rule that what is believed 'on the basis of inference from experience' includes, as a degenerate case, all beliefs validly deducible from a report of what has been experienced, whether the believer has actually gone through any mental process of deduction or not. But, *if not*, there is no reason to suppose, despite this verbal usage, that what will make the belief thus held warranted on any occasion is anything whatever beyond the experience itself, such as the belief's deducibility from experience.)

'Empiricism' is often phrased as a refusal to accept the legitimacy of any synthetic statements which are not in principle capable of being established or refuted empirically. At that rate, there would be no 'empiricist' objection to holding a general synthetic belief groundlessly, as long as it *could* conceivably be established (or refuted!) empirically. But just as it seems plainly unjustifiable to call someone's belief warranted on the grounds that, though not self-evident, what is believed is provably tautologous – except where the believer has spotted this fact – is it not equally unjustifiable to *call* somebody warranted in believing something, by virtue of its inferability from experience, except where the experience in question is *actual* experience – and moreover actual experience of the believer's – and, in addition, the pertinent inference has been *actually drawn* by the believer (whether consciously or not)? Of course it is possible to be warranted in believing things on the basis of other people's experiences and inferences, if we have good empirical grounds for regarding them as apt to be reliable on whatever the subject is, in addition to good empirical grounds for holding that they have indeed claimed to have experiences of the appropriate sort and to have drawn the conclusions in question. But what we believe is then just another example of an inductively inferred conclusion drawn by us from what we ourselves have experienced (in a suitably broad sense of *inductive inference*). For present purposes, though, there will be no need to distinguish here between beliefs held on the basis of the inductive support lent to them by experiences of the believer(s) and beliefs held on the basis of inductive support lent to them by experience in general.

At all events, it does seem as if empiricism is committed to the claim:

(1) No general synthetic belief is warranted unless it is held on the basis of inference from experience.

But, notoriously, a claim like that is itself general and does not *look* to be either analytic or inferable from experience. To avoid self-refutation, therefore, canny empiricists are apt to follow the example of Rudolf Carnap, who wrote in 1937:

It seems to me that it is preferable to formulate the principle of empiricism not in the form of an assertion – 'all knowledge is empirical' or 'all synthetic sentences that we can know are based on (or connected with) experiences' or the like – but rather in the form of a proposal or requirement. As empiricists, we require the language of science to be restricted in a certain way ...[3]

If this is taken literally, it says that Carnap does not deny there to be synthetic propositions which it is possible to be warranted *a priori* in believing. It is just that he favours a policy (language) by the adoption of which synthetic *a priori* truths are never actually to be acknowledged. Carnap was not illiberal, and did not want to prohibit anybody from saying things which violated the proposed empiricist 'requirement'; according to what he says, he is not even going to contradict them. On the basis of the position announced, we could not even take Carnap as denying the view that the above statement (1) is positively false, and that the claims to synthetic *a priori* truth advanced in this book are bona fide counterexamples to it; he merely proposes, he says, to observe a grumpy silence on the whole issue. It is little wonder that in his subsequent writings he did not consistently succeed in conforming fully to this austere self-limitation! In fact, he did persist in considering all belief in synthetic *a priori* truth to be objectively mistaken.

Indeed, it is even going too far to say, as the previous paragraph does, that Carnap's proposed restriction on 'the language of science' would preclude the formulation of any claims to synthetic *a priori* truth in that language. Carnap's interrupted sentence at the end of the above quotation continues, '... we require that descriptive predicates and hence synthetic sentences are not to be admitted unless they have some connection with possible observations, a connection which has to be characterized in a suitable way.' In the paper 'Testability and Meaning,' from which this quotation is taken, and in the subsequent, even more permissive 'The Methodological Character of Theoretical Concepts,'[4] the restriction upon 'the language of science' that is proposed is only a restriction on its vocabulary. There is nothing in any of this to rule out the formulation of synthetic *a priori* truths using descriptive predicates which do have the desired connection with possible observations. As a logical empiricist,

3 Rudolf Carnap, 'Testability and Meaning – *Continued*,' *Philosophy of Science* 4, no. 1 (January 1937), 33.

4 Rudolf Carnap, 'The Methodological Character of Theoretical Concepts,' in Herbert Feigl and Michael Scriven, eds., *Minnesota Studies in the Philosophy of Science*, vol. 1, *The Foundations of Science and the Concepts of Psychology of Psychology and Psychoanalysis* (Minneapolis, 1956), 38–76.

Carnap did not and could not envisage such a possibility. But it is not at all ruled out by *what he says* here.

Let us go back to statement (1), then. It certainly looks like the assertion of a definite proposition, true or false. And, in particular, unless it is analytic or merits belief on empirical grounds, it must either be unworthy of belief or be a falsehood.

It is not as though no one ever has asserted that acceptance of (1) is, in fact, warranted on empirical grounds.[5] But to any inductively derived theory of which (1) is a consequence, propositions such as the synthetic *a priori* truths discussed in this book can always be proposed as refuting counterexamples, and to rule them out in advance because plenty of other synthetic propositions may be cited which do warrant credence just on empirical grounds seems weak in the extreme. Until some better theoretical case for statement (1) is developed and empirically confirmed, to call (1) inductively warranted is surely question-begging.

Is statement (1) analytic, then? That there has been no shortage of professed deniers of (1) is relevant, but not in principle indefeasible evidence against the statement's self-evidence. People are not infallible authorities on the subject of what they mean by the expressions they use, and it could conceivably be that active bias and confusion have enabled it to escape so many that the way they themselves use words altogether precludes the phraseology employed above in formulating (1) from expressing anything but a truth. However, the burden of proof would have to rest with the supporters of statement (1) to show that what it asserts is either a self-evident or a demonstrable analytic truth. For our purposes, it will be unnecessary to distinguish sharply between reasons advanced for the former or the latter conclusion. In any event, the upshot of all these arguments, should they be successful, is to show that what statement (1) asserts is not only a truth but a logically necessary truth, and hence by no means anything which can be called self-refuting.

---

5 A. Cornelius Benjamin, 'Is Empiricism Self-Refuting?' *The Journal of Philosophy* 38, no. 21 (9 October 1941), 571: 'One very obvious kind of knowledge occurs when we make judgments such as "this is red" at the moment when we are seeing red. This seems a clear-cut case of the truth or falsity of a non-tautologous proposition being determined by experience. Hence the empiricist is convinced beyond any reasonable doubt that *some* knowledge is acquired through experience. He then formulates the hypothesis that *all* knowledge is so acquired.' He then adds: 'The hypothesis of empiricism is known in the same way that any hypothesis is known, and is justified by the same sort of procedure' (572).

There has, however, been one sort of move designed to secure that result for free, as it were, and this is to declare that what (1) asserts is analytic 'in an empiricist language.' But once it is accepted that the *English* sentence used in formulating statement (1), above, does not express something which is tautologous, there will be no way of supposing that any sentence in another language might be interpretable as *saying the same thing* as that sentence, unless what it too says is not tautologous. Supporters of W.V. Quine's critique of *synonymity* will be unwilling to accept anything like this as a criterion for admissible translation, but as their position necessarily leads to the rejection of the concept of *analyticity* and, indeed, of apriority generally, their dissent from the views defended here falls rather outside the scope of the present discussion.[6]

This brings us to the specific philosophical arguments which can be seen as giving support, if successful, to the conclusion that (1) is analytic. What the philosophers who developed these arguments had in mind was not so much a defence of statement (1), but rather a *verificationist* position to the effect that grasping the linguistic meaning of any synthetic assertive sentence is grasping what experiences would warrant calling what the sentence says true. No distinction could then be drawn between (consciously) believing what it says and (consciously) believing those experiences to have occurred.

Chronologically, first, perhaps, is the 'phenomenological' line of argument to the effect that there is no difference between imagining

---

6 If two different assertive sentences cannot, in principle, be paired together as having the same sense as each other, then not even such a synonymity as that between 'bachelor' and 'unmarried man' can be cited to back up calling 'Every bachelor is an unmarried man' analytic. Quine's grounds for rejecting synonymity, as normally conceived, are that no behavioural, and hence no scientific, distinction can be drawn between people's habitually using two such noun phrases interchangeably in the appropriate contexts because of *meaning the same* by them, and their doing so because of tacit confidence in the coextensiveness of what the phrases stand for; and, as empirical evidence is indisputably relevant to establish the rationality (pragmatically) of using two expressions interchangeably in the sort of case where what non-Quineans would consider *meaning-rules* are at stake, there can be no Quinean basis for limiting in any way at all the sort of case where empirical evidence is relevant to the attribution of truthvalues to assertive sentences. See W.V. Quine, 'Truth by Convention,' in Otis H. Lee, ed., *Philosophical Essays for Alfred North Whitehead* (New York, 1936), 90–124; 'Two Dogmas of Empiricism,' reprinted in W.V. Quine, *From a Logical Point of View* (Cambridge, MA, 1961), 20–46; and W.V. Quine, *Word and Object* (Cambridge, MA, 1960), chap. 2, 26–79. I propose a rebuttal in D. Goldstick, 'Cognitive Synonymy,' *Dialectica* 34, no. 3 (1980), 183–203.

something and imagining *experiencing* it, and hence all that we can *mean* by asserting some state of affairs exists is that certain experiences have occurred, are occurring or else will occur or under given conditions would occur.[7] Although this line of argument doubtless goes back to Berkeley, it is far from clear that he himself would have agreed with it, emphatic as he was that we indeed can think about, and even know, more than it is possible in principle to experience sensorily (in particular, God's existence). Berkeley writes:

> ... as it is impossible for me to see or feel anything without an actual sensation of that thing, so it is impossible for me to conceive in my thoughts any sensible thing or object distinct from the sensation or perception of it.[8]

Anti-Berkeleians can object that imagining something, even visually, does not need to involve imagining any spectator viewing it, the scene visualized being different in the latter case from (what would otherwise be) the same scene visualized without any spectators in it. Just as the camera is not normally in the scene it photographs, the subject matter about which any particular mind is thinking need not include that thinking mind itself. To this objection Berkeley replied as follows:

> But say you, surely there is nothing easier than to imagine trees, for instance, in a park, or books existing in a closet, and no body by to perceive them. I answer, you may so, there is no difficulty in it: but what is all this, I beseech you, more than framing in your mind certain ideas which you call *books* and *trees*, and at the same time omitting to frame the idea of any one that may perceive them? But do not you your self perceive or think of them all the while? This therefore is nothing to the purpose: it only shows you have the

---

7 'We have to recognize that relativity to consciousness is not only an actual quality of our world, but, from eidetic necessity, the quality of every conceivable world. We may, in a free fancy, vary our actual world, and transmute it to any other which we can imagine, but we are obliged with the world to vary ourselves also, and ourselves we cannot vary except within the limits prescribed to us by the nature of subjectivity. Change worlds as we may, each must ever be a world such as we could experience, prove upon the evidence of our theories and inhabit with our practice.' Edmund Husserl, 'Phenomenology,' *Encyclopedia Britannica*, 14th ed. (London, 1929), vol. 17, 701; reprinted in Roderick M. Chisholm, ed., *Realism and the Background of Phenomenology* (Glencoe, IL, 1960), 125. (Chisholm gives C.V. Solomon as the translator.)

8 George Berkeley, *Principles of Human Knowledge*, I, 5, in *The Works of George Berkeley, Bishop of Cloyne*, vol. 2, ed. A.A. Luce and T.E. Jessop (London, 1949), 43.

power of imagining or forming ideas in your mind; but it doth not shew that
you can conceive it possible, the objects of your thought may exist without
the mind: to make out this, it is necessary that you conceive them existing
unconceived or unthought of, which is a manifest repugnancy.[9]

This much is certainly true: you cannot think of something without
thinking of it; whatever you think of is going to be something thought
of by you. But does it follow that you can only think of anything *as*
something-being-thought-of? No, for 'It is impossible to think of something which is unthought-of' is ambiguous as between a 'referentially
transparent' and a 'referentially opaque' meaning.[10] In the latter way of
speaking to call what is thought of *thought of* is not at all trivial, but
describes *how* the thinking mind thinks of it (as being). And so, as far as
this argument goes at least, it has not been proved logically impossible
to think there to be realities answering the description of being *unthinkable* even, let alone answering the description: *impossible to establish
through any experience*, sensory or otherwise.

Undoubtedly, C.S. Peirce was a genuine verificationist. But neither
he, nor those taking their lead from him, seem to have noticed that the
following behaviourally based argument, from his famous paper 'How
to Make Our Ideas Clear,' is not in fact an argument for verificationism,
strictly speaking.

---

9 Berkeley, *Principles*, I, 23, ibid., 50. Emphasis in original.
10 The terminology comes from Quine. To adapt his example, we can see the ambiguity
there is in a sentence like 'Jane wants a cottage.' For on a 'referentially transparent'
interpretation it is definitely conveyed that Jane has some particular cottage in
mind. While on a 'referentially opaque' interpretation the meaning is merely that
she deplores her cottagelessness. The idea is that in the former case, but not the
latter, it is (given enough information) 'transparent' to what actually existing thing
the phrase 'a cottage' refers here. In the latter case, 'Jane wants a cottage' just
characterizes Jane's wants. Similarly, 'Phil is looking for the mayor' is ambiguous as
between one interpretation, on which Phil is looking for somebody in particular,
whether or not Phil knows that person to be the mayor, and another interpretation,
on which what Phil wants is simply to find whoever-is-mayor. Only on the first
interpretation is the speaker committed to there even being any mayor at all.
Similarly, 'It is impossible to think of an F' is ambiguous as between a referentially
opaque reading, on which it is merely a *kind of thought* that is said to be impossible,
and a referentially transparent reading, on which some class of actual items is identified – namely, F's – and it is denied that any thought could ever be about any of
them. Naturally, no particular member of the class of unthought-of entities ever gets
thought of. But that doesn't make the existence of such a (nonnull) class of entities
unthinkable as a possibility in general.

... the whole function of thought is to produce habits of action; and ... whatever there is connected with a thought, but irrelevant to its purpose, is an accretion to it, but no part of it. If there be a unity among our sensations which has no reference to how we shall act on a given occasion, as when we listen to a piece of music, why we do not call that thinking. To develop its meaning, we have, therefore, simply to determine what habits it produces, for what a thing means is simply what habits it involves. Now, the identity of a habit depends on how it might lead us to act, not merely under such circumstances as are likely to arise, but under such as might possibly occur, no matter how improbable they may be. What the habit is depends on when and how it causes us to act. As for the when, every stimulus to action is derived from perception; as for the how, every purpose of action is to produce some sensible result. Thus, we come down to what is tangible and practical, as the root of every real distinction of thought, no matter how subtle it may be; and there is no distinction of meaning so fine as to consist in anything but a possible difference of practice.[11]

Doubtless it is not necessarily the case that 'every purpose of action is to produce some sensible result.' (Think of the very last sentient being in the universe, devoid of any belief in a hereafter, using what it full well knows to be its dying breath to press a button ensuring the continuance of at least plant life.)[12] Nevertheless, we can accept that a *proximate* result which believing anything produces whenever believers act on what they believe is invariably some sense-perceptible behaviour (allowing people's uninferred self-awareness of their own *mental* behaviour to count as 'sense-perception' also, for present purposes: though here, in Kant's phrase, it is just their 'inner sense' which they are exercising). Let us, then, try reformulating Peirce's argument as follows. It is impossible for one belief to differ from another without differing as regards what sense-perceptible behaviour it would produce on its holder's part under what experiential conditions (other beliefs being the same, presumably). Therefore, two beliefs cannot really differ from each other without *differing empirically*. Accordingly, if what is supposed to be a truth-valuable

---

11 C.J.W. Kloesel, ed., *Writings of Charles S. Peirce*, vol. 3 (Bloomington, 1986), 265.

12 Or is even this result 'sensible,' after all, in that nothing in *it* (that is, in the continuance of plant life) precludes sentient beings from perceiving it. Compare 'This car can do 100 kilometres-per-hour,' and 'This car can't do 100 kilometres-per-hour, or *any* speed, as it has no driver.' On the other hand, if this does really count as a case of something sense-perceptible, then so do many things often not classified that way.

statement and its 'negation' do not differ from each other empirically, they cannot really state differing potential beliefs, and so they are not really going to be contradictory propositions: consequently, they will not really be true-or-false *propositions* at all.

However, the trouble with this as an argument for empiricism is the gap between showing that two beliefs cannot really differ from each other without 'differing empirically' in the sense in which that arguably is or can be established, and showing that two beliefs cannot really differ from each other without differing in the type of experiences which would (be taken by the believer to) *conclusively prove* the propositions believed. The observable behaviour to which a belief prompts its holder will not normally form any part of the observational evidence on the basis of which the belief could warrantably be held.

Consider the following two sentences: 'It was wrong of you to have deliberately performed that abortion' and 'It was not wrong of you to have deliberately performed that abortion.' These two sentences certainly seem to express differing opinions. And it certainly seems that people who held the differing opinions would be apt to behave quite differently in certain identical circumstances: for, as will be argued in chapter 19, to regard any sort of action as morally wrong is to be somewhat motivated (even if not on balance motivated) to refrain from ever performing such an action. But, when it comes to the empirical evidence required before either of these assertions could warrantably be made, many would say that *on that score* there is no difference between what the two sentences express. At any rate, it is not obviously inconsistent to say that, while at the same time accepting the indicated behavioural difference between what the two sentences express. Even granting Peirce's behavioural view of *belief*, then, one is not obviously compelled by that to accept any sort of empiricist verifiability requirement for the meaningfulness of assertions. But we will have to return to behavioural-type grounds for verificationism shortly.

Meanwhile, let us look first at Ludwig Wittgenstein's case against the possibility of *a priori* truth in his *Tractatus Logico-Philosophicus*:

2.221 What a picture represents is its sense.

2.222 The agreement or disagreement of its sense with reality constitutes its truth or falsity.

2.223 In order to tell whether a picture is true or false we must compare it with reality.

2.224 It is impossible to tell from the picture alone whether it is true or false.

2.225 There are no pictures that are true a priori.[13]

Let us concede to Wittgenstein that the truth or falsity of any assertion is a matter of how what it means *compares* to reality (2.222). It does not follow that it has to be possible for somebody to *make* the comparison in order for the assertion to *be* true or be false. For it has not been shown there is any logical contradiction in the supposition of some assertion having an in-principle-unascertainable truth-value. Still less does it follow at all that empirical verification is the only real way of making the comparison (ascertaining an assertion's actual truth-value), or that it cannot sometimes be done on the basis of a consideration of just the assertion itself – 'the picture alone.'

But maybe it is a mistaken interpretation to suppose Wittgenstein intended these sentences as any kind of *argument* for his position. In that case, so much the worse for his position!

Next we have Moritz Schlick's advocacy of logical empiricism to consider. Schlick notes that, directly and indirectly, all meanings are taught ostensively, that is, empirically, and he uses this fact to proceed from

... whenever we ask about a sentence, 'What does it mean?', what we expect is instruction as to the circumstances in which the sentence is to be used; we want a description of the conditions under which the sentence will form a true proposition, and of those which will make it false.[14]

to

... the meaning of a proposition can be given only by giving the rules of its verification in experience.[15]

In what circumstances, then, is 'It was wrong of you to have deliberately performed that abortion' to be used? The answer which immediately suggests itself is: the proposition expressed will be a true one in just those

---

13 Ludwig Wittgenstein, *Tractatus Logico-Philosophicus*, trans. D.F. Pears and B.F. McGuinness (London, 1961), 19.

14 Moritz Schlick, 'Meaning and Verification,' *The Philosophical Review* 45, no. 4 (July 1936), 341.

15 Ibid., 342.

cases where an abortion has been deliberately performed by the person(s) addressed and such action was morally wrong. Although the meaning of the expression 'morally wrong' is learned empirically, it does not follow that the meaning rules so learned are rules specifying what sort of empirical evidence is necessary and sufficient to establish that something 'morally wrong' has, or has not, been done. In general, the premise that it is an empirical fact what people mean by the expressions they employ is insufficient to show that *what* they mean by any assertion they make is some proposition establishable empirically, and only empirically.

In *An Analysis of Knowledge and Valuation*, C.I. Lewis wrote:

> Leaving aside any question of Kant and the correct interpretation of his doctrines, we may see the essential consideration which suggests the impossibility of synthetic judgments a priori. Any character in the absence of which we should refuse to apply a term, is of the essence. It is included in the signification of the term ...[16]

Can we say that *immorality* is a characteristic in the absence of which users of the expression 'morally wrong' would refuse to apply the expression? Could we legitimately make at least the amended claim that immorality is a characteristic in the *supposed* absence of which users of the expression 'morally wrong' would, *if honest*, refuse to apply it? Obviously the claim will not be correct without those amendments, but doubtless it is, with them, a correct claim, as *immorality* is indeed included in the signification of 'morally wrong.'

But must we include in the signification of any adjectival expression absolutely *every* characteristic in the supposed absence of which users of the expression would, if honest, refuse to apply it? Only, surely, if the sole considerations capable of motivating such a refusal were considerations of linguistic meaning. What if the users of the expression 'morally wrong' firmly *believed* that whatever was morally wrong was divinely forbidden (or hedonically suboptimal, or whatever)? In that case they would, if honest, refuse to apply the expression 'morally wrong' in the supposed absence of any divine prohibition (or hedonic suboptimality, or whatever). Does it necessarily follow that *divinely forbidden* (or *hedonically suboptimal*, or whatever) is included right in the signification of 'morally

---

16 Clarence Irving Lewis, *An Analysis of Knowledge and Valuation* (La Salle, IL, 1946), 163.

wrong,' in their parlance?[17] Only if anything which is firmly enough believed is, by virtue of that, a tautology; that is, only if the verbal expression of any sufficiently firm belief has to be analytic. Just how firm would a belief have to be to be sufficiently firm here?

The amended Lewis position will presumably be that the characteristic of being F is part of the signification of any adjectival expression, '...', whose users would, if honest, refuse to apply the expression in the supposed absence of F-ness *provided that the refusal were not due to a belief that whatever was ... was F* – unless the 'belief' in question were *so* firm that 'holding' it was merely a matter of the senses in which the 'believer' habitually used certain linguistic expressions: that is, unless the trivial truth of the 'belief' followed immediately from the habitual meanings the 'believer' attached to such expressions as would be employed in straightforwardly formulating it: in other words, unless what was 'believed' was actually something logically impossible to disbelieve or doubt (doubt of the truth of the *sentence* expressing it then having to be, not doubt of *it*, but only doubt as to whether the sentence's meaning really was such as to make the sentence express *it*).

At that rate, Lewis's argument for 'the impossibility of synthetic judgments *a priori*' becomes merely an argument for the analyticity of whatever it is logically impossible to disbelieve or doubt. At least, it is only thus reformulated that the argument could be defensible. But which proponents of synthetic judgments *a priori* ever supposed them *logically* impossible to disbelieve or doubt? Not even every analytic judgment is logically indubitable in that sense. At all events, there is no intention to suggest any of the synthetic *a priori* propositions which will be proposed in this book possess such *logical* indubitability. Lewis's critical fire appears to miss the target.

An argument due to Henryk Mehlberg's *The Reach of Science*[18] infers something entailing statement (1) from considerations about linguistic vagueness. Mehlberg's argument has the virtue that it does not deny the *meaningfulness* of consistent synthetic declarative sentences which fail to assert anything empirically verifiable, but only denies their possession of any unique truth-value. A second virtue of the argument, for defenders of the positivistic interpretation of quantum

---

17 Whether it follows or not, this sort of meaning analysis for moral vocabulary is considered on its own terms in chapter 19.

18 Henryk Mehlberg, *The Reach of Science* (Toronto, 1958).

mechanics, would be its denial of any unique truth-value not just to whatever it is *logically* impossible to verify, but even to whatever it is *empirically* impossible (contrary to empirically establishable natural laws) to verify. Like other writers, Mehlberg stresses that it is only by public, empirical methods that meanings can ever be communicated to language-learners, but he does not try to claim that is sufficient to provide him with his conclusion. His central emphasis is on how the vagueness of some component expression's meaning can keep what an assertive sentence states from possessing any unique truth-value at all. For example, 'The number of trees in Toronto is even' will have a particular unique truth-value only if what it states holds good for *all* geographical delimitations of what the word 'Toronto' signifies, or else for *none* of them. That will be a matter of how the statement checks out *empirically* on each of these different construals, it is said, in effect. And from that, it does follow that a consistent synthetic statement will always be too vague to have any definite truth-value unless it is theoretically possible to ascertain what truth-value it has by empirical means.

But why could it not be the case that some consistent synthetic sentence had the same unique truth-value for the whole range of alternative construals of every vague expression it contained, even though there was no method of finding that out, even theoretically? Secondly, even if the meanings of any sentence's constituent expressions do have to be communicable by empirical means, why must it be by empirical means only that the truth or falsity of any consistent synthetic assertive sentence can be checked out for all possible alternative construals?

Anthony Quinton's argument for verificationism in 'The *A Priori* and the Analytic' does not really hinge on any erroneous etymology of the word 'contingent' as originally meaning *dependent*:

> The idea of the empirical is a development or elucidation of the idea of the contingent. It aims to explain how a statement can owe its truth to something else, what conditions the something else must satisfy if it is to confer truth on a statement. To require it to be experience is to say that unless it is something of whose existence we can in principle become aware then the form of words involved has not made out its claim to be a statement. No limit is set here to the possible forms of experience or awareness, in particular no equation of experience and sense-experience is implied. For a form of words to be understood as a statement we must know what its

truth-conditions are and to know this is to be able to recognize them when they occur, to know what it would be like to experience them.[19]

Just why does Quinton think a form of words has not made out its claim to make a statement unless that which it claims to be actual (that on which its truth depends) 'is something of whose existence we can in principle become aware'? His answer is that to know what any statement asserts it is necessary to have the capacity in principle to become aware of the actual realization of that which the statement asserts. And furthermore, he thinks it is necessary to know in advance 'what it would be like' for that awareness to come into being. But why? Why is it impossible to know what a statement's truth conditions are without having the capacity to recognize cases where they are fulfilled, let alone knowing in advance by what marks their fulfillment would be recognizable?

Quinton's argument, then, both requires, and yet fails to do more than affirm, an unqualified identification of *the conditions on which the truth of a statement is dependent* and *the conditions on which the ascertainment of the truth of a statement is dependent*. Over the years, a very popular line of argument for bridging this gap has indeed turned upon the experiential processes of first-language learning. It is claimed that even just to grasp any statement couched in (language ultimately understood in terms of) phraseology so learned must involve an appreciation of what would count as justifying the assertion of that statement, or at least its logical consequences. In the words of Michael Dummett summing up the reasons which have led philosophers to this view of what it is to understand such a statement:

> In the very nature of the case, we could not possibly have come to understand what it would be for the statement to be true independently of that which we have learned to treat as establishing its truth: there simply was no means by which we could be shown this.[20]

Given a purely learning-theory approach to the psychology of mother-tongue acquisition, such a line of argumentation as this does readily

---

19 Anthony Quinton, 'The *A Priori* and the Analytic,' *Proceedings of the Aristotelian Society*, n.s., 64 (1964), 34.

20 Michael Dummett, 'The Reality of the Past,' *Proceedings of the Aristotelian Society*, n.s., 69 (1969), 244; reprinted in Michael Dummett, *Truth and Other Enigmas* (Cambridge, MA, 1978), 362.

open the door to empiricist theorizing. It is argued that non-logical semantic primitives are first learned ostensively, through a conditioning process pairing them with various different sensory stimulations, and then the meanings of other non-logical terms are learned directly or indirectly from explanations in terms of those 'observational' primitives. So that, according to this view, any description of a state of affairs which human beings are capable of articulating is ultimately a statement to the effect that certain directly observable conditions were, are, or will be realized.

However, an alternative view of the initial language-learning process conceives the learners as proto-scientifically hypothesizing, even if not consciously, the existence of psychological states or conditions more or less analogous to their own in order to explain the speech and other behaviour of the language-users they encounter in their environment.[21] The fact that quite informal processes are nonetheless demonstrably sufficient for complicated learning achievements far beyond what the learners are capable of articulating should be enough to overcome inhibitions against imputing to juvenile language-learners the development of an explanatory theory of their elders' speech behaviour which in principle distinguishes, if only implicitly, between what would be counted by those speakers as conclusively *justifying* the assertions they utter and what would be counted as making the assertions *true*.

But the Dummettian case for verificationism need not be conceived to rest exclusively on considerations about first-language learning. Linguistic competence must be something capable of public manifestation, if its existence can be detected and communicated at all. In the words of Crispin Wright,

> Knowledge of use is not essentially verbalisable knowledge. So if knowledge of declarative sentence meaning is to be knowledge of truth-conditions we should not construe the latter as essentially articulate. Rather it must be

---

21 Quine has of course argued, in effect, that the apparent distinction between these two accounts of a child's initial language-learning cannot be sustained. (See, in particular, chapters 1 and 2 of *Word and Object*, cited in footnote 6 of this chapter.) It is on those very grounds that he denies the distinction between a language user's habit of employing two predicates interchangeably (in appropriate contexts) because of a sufficiently firm synthetic *belief* in their coextensiveness, and a language user's habit of employing the terms interchangeably because of *meaning the same* by them. (My proposed rebuttal to such a denial of *synonymity*, as normally conceived, is given in the paper 'Cognitive Synonymy,' cited in footnote 6.)

recognitional capacity: the ability to recognise, if appropriately placed, circumstances which do, or do not, fulfil the truth-conditions of a sentence and to be prepared accordingly to assent to, or withhold assent to, its assertion. There is no hiatus between this ability and knowledge of the sentence's meaning;

... Grasp of the sense of a sentence cannot be displayed in response to unrecognisable conditions; nor, if we take seriously the connexion between meaning and use, can such grasp go any further than its capacity to be displayed ...

... a practice involving recognition-transcendent objectives is not as such a *communicable* practice; for it will not matter if someone misunderstands an objective of this sort providing he grasps aright the circumstances under which the claim that it is realised may legitimately be made.[22]

Is *detecting immorality* a 'recognition-transcendent objective'? Suppose two different people use differing criteria to 'recognize immorality.' Does it follow that they must *mean* different things from each other by the word 'immorality' (or the word 'recognize')? If it does follow, then there is no point of substantive disagreement between the two of them on this score; for it can only mark a disagreement between two people that one of them calls 'immoral' what the other one denies to be 'immoral' if they *mean the same* as each other by that word. But if they do mean the same as each other by 'immoral,' then *detecting immorality* is indeed a recognition-transcendent objective. Why should that make the practice of trying to detect immorality (or trying to abstain from immorality) an unteachable or otherwise *incommunicable* practice? From the fact that *you* recognize certain criteria for immorality it does not follow that you cannot judge others to be trying to detect immorality (or trying to abstain from immorality) unless they use the same criteria and call immoral all the same sorts of behaviour as you call immoral. You can accept that the way they act manifests a complete grasp of the *concept* of immorality on their part even if they do lack what *you* regard as a full capacity to recognize actual cases of immorality. And so, you must accept that there actually is a hiatus between knowledge of what 'That is an immoral action' means and the ability to recognize, if appropriately placed, actions which are, and which are not, immoral.

---

22 Crispin Wright, 'Truth Conditions and Criteria,' *Proceedings of the Aristotelian Society*, supplementary vol. 50 (1976), 224–5, 232–3.

Imagine a community whose members could be convinced that an 'immoral action' had been performed simply by showing them that a deliberate abortion had been performed. Imagine someone learning this community's language who comes to think that in that language 'is an immoral action' means something disjunctive, with 'is a deliberate abortion' one of the disjuncts. As far as the conceivable objective of *detecting immorality* goes, such a learner perhaps 'grasps aright the circumstances under which the claim that it is realized may legitimately be made' in the eyes of the community; but still, such a learner need not have understood the concept of *immorality* at all. In particular, the point could have been completely missed that the community *disapproves* of whatever it considers 'immoral.'

Claims of the sort made about the word 'immoral' in the two preceding paragraphs do not go uncontested, and we will be returning to the debate in chapters 19, 21, and 24. But for now it is sufficient that nothing in Wright's Dummettian argument refutes these claims. Grasp of linguistic meanings does indeed need to be publicly manifestable. But it has not been shown that the *only* behaviour capable of manifesting the comprehension of what some predicate in a language means is that of systematically applying it and withholding it in all those cases where the members of the community which speaks the language normally regard it as sufficiently evident that the predicate does really apply, or not apply.

So much for arguments aimed at showing that statement (1) either is analytic or warrants credence on the basis of inference from experience. It does seem to follow that, if the statement is a true one, it does not warrant credence; and, hence, that it must either be a false statement or else be unworthy of credence.

But is this perhaps overhasty? Defending the logical empiricist Verification Principle against a parallel objection, J.L. Evans wrote:

> One of the commonest arguments ... is to the effect that the Verification
> Principle can be shown to be nugatory simply by asking whether the state-
> ment of the principle is itself either a tautology or an empirical statement,
> the only types of statement which the principle allows to be meaningful ...
> But the question fails to appreciate the nature of the verificationist thesis. To
> use an analogy: consider the two statements, 'the chair collapsed because
> John sat on it' and 'every event has a cause.' If we describe the first as a
> causal statement, then we cannot describe the second in the same way. The
> Principle of Causation cannot itself be a causal statement co-ordinate with
> statements which exemplify it; indeed to call it a principle is to intimate that
> it is not a statement at all. In a similar way, we should not expect the Principle

of Verification itself to be subject to the criteria which it lays down governing meaningful statements. We do not expect a weighing-machine to weigh itself.[23]

Normally, to be sure, scales cannot weigh themselves. But we do not expect them to be weightless either. If we take seriously Evans's suggestion that the Principle of Verification perhaps 'is not a statement at all,' then we must class the sort of verificationism he would take it to express, like Rudolf Carnap's, as not actually *denying* any of the claims made in this book.

However, maybe the sort of empiricism envisaged is best understood in terms of an amendment to statement (1), aimed at saving (most of) what the statement says from self-refutation, in some such way as the following:

(2) No general synthetic belief is warranted unless it is held on the basis of inference from experience *or* is about the conditions under which alone a general synthetic belief is warranted.

This version, though no longer self-refuting, surely does have more than an air of the *ad hoc* about it. Would it be possible to secure plausibility by invoking here an analogue of some sort of theory of logical types? How about:

(3) No *first-order* general synthetic belief is warranted unless it is held on the basis of inference from experience?

For these purposes a 'first-order' belief could be understood to be a belief other than a belief about beliefs, or other than a belief about the conditions under which alone a general synthetic belief is warranted. Under the latter interpretation of 'first-order' (3) is only a 'notational variant' of (2), and under the former interpretation (3) looks only slightly less *ad hoc* than (2). But there was supposed to be an independent philosophical rationale for distinguishing 'orders' in this sort of way; namely, a general logical taboo against self-reference, a taboo motivated by the notorious 'semantical paradoxes' such as the Liar. At that rate, it is a question here of *sentences'* assertive meaningfulness supposedly being forfeited in case of self-reference. This suggests:

---

23 J.L. Evans, 'On Meaning and Verification,' *Mind* 62, no. 245 (January 1953), 3.

(4) No one is ever warranted in believing what a first-order general
     synthetic sentence states except on the basis of inference from
     experience.

Here we have a sentence asserting something which it is not self-refuting to believe, as the sentence here is itself not 'first-order' (where a 'first-order' sentence means a sentence other than one which makes reference to any sentence(s)). The plausibility of this move, however, must rest upon the philosophical plausibility of the general logical taboo against self-reference. But does the sentence, 'No sentence is assertively meaningful which refers to itself,' refer to itself or not? If it does refer to itself, it must be either assertively meaningless or else false. If it does not, then it is not a *blanket* ban that it imposes: there is a class of sentences, including itself, which *it* does not, after all, deny to be both self-referring and still assertively meaningful. This sort of difficulty is well known. Logicians who find the distinction between 'first-order languages' and 'higher-order languages' expedient for their purposes take care to make their formal constructions 'semantically open,' and, whatever logical principles of construction they employ in devising any 'formal languages' or systems of 'formal languages,' they do not attempt to formulate these principles *in* the 'languages' so constructed. This way of proceeding can be entirely unobjectionable for their purposes, but we for our part appear to be left without any general logical basis for a ban on self-reference such as could provide independent philosophical grounds for reformulating (1) as (4).

That leaves us with the non-self-refuting but patently *ad hoc* (2). All those believing statement (2) would seemingly have to admit that this belief of theirs was itself a synthetic general belief warranted *a priori*. For empiricism on those terms, how many genuine takers could there be?

It would appear that all the preceding does amount to a fairly strong preliminary case against the position of empiricism.

PART TWO

On the Canons of Induction

6 Preliminary Considerations

According to the traditional account of the history of philosophy, David Hume propounded a Problem of Induction. He maintained that, if forecasts of the future are to have any chance of being rational, they must be based 'inductively' (to use a word he did not) – that is, they must be based upon the identification of some pattern in what has been observed, and the anticipation that this pattern will continue on. Such a procedure presupposes, Hume thought, the proposition that 'the course of nature continues always uniformly the same' or that 'the future will resemble the past' (to employ two turns of phrase Hume did use).[1] But what justifies the presupposed proposition? It is not establishable by unaided deductive reasoning, being deniable without contradiction; nor would it be impossible to remain consistent in denying it, while at the same time acknowledging any report, however extensive, of what has been so far observed. On the other hand, though, the proposition is not justifiable inductively either, since any such inference, on account of presupposing, like all inductive inference, this very proposition, would be a case of circular reasoning. 'This therefore is a point, which can admit of no proof at all, and which we take for granted without any proof,' Hume concluded.[2]

So runs the traditional (and arguably accurate) account of Hume's sceptical reasoning here. If such an account is correct, it is perhaps

---

1 David Hume, *A Treatise of Human Nature*, ed. L.A. Selby-Bigge, rev. P.H. Nidditch (Oxford, 1978), 89, and David Hume, *An Inquiry concerning Human Understanding*, in *Enquiries concerning Human Understanding and concerning the Principles of Morals*, ed. L.A. Selby-Bigge, 3rd ed., rev. P.H. Nidditch (Oxford, 1975), 37.
2 David Hume, *An Abstract of A Treatise of Human Nature*, appended to the Nidditch revised edition of the *Treatise of Human Nature*, 652.

remarkable that Hume failed to consider that this famous inductive presupposition, which he said that 'we' take for granted, could not but be a counterexample to his own empiricist doctrine that whatever could not be justified by any combination of observation, deduction, and induction would have to be 'nothing but sophistry and illusion.'[3] Or would Hume claim to be able to take for granted something which he himself considered to be nothing but sophistry and illusion?[4]

For our purposes, of course, Hume exegesis does not matter. More important is the philosophical problem raised and its stated subject matter, inductive inference. Or *is* there really any problem here? Or even, indeed, is there really any such mode of inference – or any such rationally acceptable mode of inference – as 'induction' is said to be? There is controversy on each point.

Up until about 1960, at any rate, quite a lot of philosophical attention was devoted to the traditional Problem of Induction. And philosophers' various strategies for solving – or 'dissolving' – the problem filled much of the literature. But, although each of these was generally considered unsatisfactory, a consensus tended to develop anyway in English-speaking philosophy in favour of the reassuring conclusion that empiricism had nothing to worry about here: the consensus was able to be all the stronger because after about 1960 much less philosophical attention was directed to the specifics of the argument; and also because from about the late 1970s on, anti-realist or fideist philosophies were increasingly influential in denying the necessity – or possibility – of objectively rational answers to such questions in any case.

Those concerned to take the issues raised by the Problem of Induction seriously would have reason to use an expanded conception of 'inductive' inference which did not restrict its attention to extrapolations of immediately apparent patterns in phenomena from the observed to the not-yet-observed. Twentieth-century discussions of the Problem of Induction have generally also included, under the 'inductive' heading, scientific (or everyday) inferences to the best causal explanations for observed phenomena. After all, whenever such explanatory hypotheses

---

3 Hume, *An Inquiry concerning Human Understanding*, 165.

4 In another connection, Hume claimed to 'rely entirely' on 'carelessness and in-attention' to fend off sceptical doubt (*A Treatise of Human Nature*, 218). But surely *not* in this inductive connection at the time when he was penning that very claim in the confident expectation that to the path described by the point of his pen there would indeed correspond a permanent mark spelling out just those words and not, say, any different, contradictory phrases.

are brought in to support predictions, the Humean point can always be urged, that this presupposes the same proposition about the future resembling the past or the course of nature continuing uniformly the same; so that, if the problem Hume identified really does arise in the simpler, extrapolative case, it equally arises here, too.

There are, it is true, philosophers who deny that any one topic-neutral 'inductive method' is specifiable for use across the board in natural sciences ranging from astronomy to zoology, let alone also in the conduct of our daily lives and in the understandings we develop as a basis for predicting human beings' actions. And, indeed, the diversity of the different modes of reasoning and judgment found in these different spheres is certainly impressive. Where the predictive reliability of any such mode of thinking is not evident or probable *a priori*, or acceptable as an article of faith, specific observational evidence will be required to back it up. Any rational support which those previously made observations provide for the according of credence to predictions generated by such a mode of thinking will arguably depend on the Humean presupposition of the 'uniformity' of the course of nature, or the future's resemblance to the past: at least, it arguably will depend on a presupposition of that kind in any one such sphere if it does in any other. It is reasoning like this which tends to justify regarding 'induction' (in some suitably broad sense) as a single methodological subject matter.

The advocates of induction standardly claim that our reliance upon it is indispensable if we are going to be rational in forming any expectations – including all our conditional-expectations about what outcomes will be likelier to ensue if we take particular steps. In practice there is surely no way to duck the pressing question whether induction is or is not to be employed in the interests of, as far as possible, forming correct expectations and avoiding ones which are not correct. If the answer to that pointed question is no, this will have to be because induction is dispensable, or else because it is positively deceptive, or else because it is just not, in fact, reliable at all as a guide to truth. But if the answer to the question is yes, then any considerations supporting such an affirmative answer will, of course, be either inductive ones or logical ones, or else considerations of some other sort – if, indeed, any particular supporting considerations at all are required.

The foregoing alternatives give rise, thus, to the meta-inductive philosophical positions of sensationalism, nihilism, scepticism, inductivism, 'naturalism,' and synthetic-apriorism, respectively.

But what *is* induction? Elucidation of the answer to this question is, of course, what ought to emerge from the whole of part two, and in particular from chapter 15: but something undoubtedly should be said in advance to indicate just what I am talking about. The following are all things which I *believe* to hold true of the mode of reasoning outlined in chapter 15:

(1) Inductive reasoning is indispensable in the conduct of daily life.

(2) Inductive reasoning is indispensable to every empirical science.

(3) Inductive reasoning is indispensable for knowing what events will occur in the future, wherever this is not something which is known without any reasoning at all, or logically deducible from general truths which are known without any reasoning at all in conjunction with observational data, or premises.

(4) A piece of inductive reasoning whose conclusion does not follow logically from the data, or premises, on which that reasoning is based, is not necessarily a bad inference by inductive standards of reasoning.

(5) Where statements of the data, or premises, upon which inductive reasoning is based are value-neutral propositions, the conclusions of that inductive reasoning, if they have been derived properly, must also be value-neutral propositions.

(6) Wherever one fact, or a set of facts, lends inductive support to another fact, it does so on the basis that it itself would not be an actual fact, or set of facts, but for the existence of that other fact to which it thus lends inductive support.

(7) A reasoner is, in many cases, sanctioned by inductive standards of inference to conclude from the prevalence of something up to the present its probable prevalence in the near future also.

(8) It is by induction alone that one is ever entitled non-deductively to argue as such from effects to causes or from causes to effects.

(9) It is by induction alone that one is ever entitled to infer from the comparative simplicity of a theory its probable truth.

It will be convenient for purposes of exposition to regard (5), (6), (7), and (9) as constituting jointly our preliminary definition of the concept 'inductive reasoning.'

7 Sensationalism

Has any philosopher ever dared to maintain that sense-experience by itself is *so* 'theory-laden,' or empirical theories so useless, as to make all inductive inference unnecessary? Is there anyone around who really views induction as being completely dispensable? There are people who seem to say that but turn out to mean by 'induction' some specific, more narrowly defined sort of inference than we are discussing here.

It was, indeed, a different story with Karl Popper, who always insisted on the dispensability of induction in *science*, from which he apparently excluded *applied science*, since he was willing to speak in *The Logic of Scientific Discovery* of '... the metaphysical faith in the existence of regularities in our world (a faith which I share, and without which practical action is hardly conceivable).'[1] It seems that 'science' for Popper was a game of conjectures and refutations and *not*, even in part, a way of telling what is going to happen in the future. Even in his late work, *Objective Knowledge*, it is possible to argue that he could only see his way clear to calling it 'rational' to prefer the most thoroughly tested scientific theories as a basis for practical action in this sense of 'rational': a lot of scientific *reasoning* would have gone into the process leading up to the situation in which those theories were the most thoroughly tested ones; which evidently is a different matter from whether at least the approximate truth of those

---

1 Karl R. Popper, *The Logic of Scientific Discovery*, trans. K.R. Popper, with the assistance of Julius Freed and Lan Freed, 3rd ed. (New York, 1965), 252.

theories or the truth of predictions derived from them would be a *good bet* at all.[2]

Most people will agree that *in a sense* there certainly are good ways of telling what is going to happen other than reasoning inductively: turning to proved authorities or reliable instrumentation, for instance. But it is common to base reliance upon authorities or instrumentation on the *inductive* case for their reliability. This applies even when it comes to reliance upon seers, Ouija boards or holy books to foretell the future. There are, to be sure, (secular or religious) *fideists*, who rather repose confidence in prophecies from such sources through a conscious act of faith, or say they do. But in most cases they themselves must admit that only a small (even if supremely important) part of what they need to know about the future is covered by such prophecies, making induction indispensable for all the rest: indeed, generally even for understanding what it is that the holy books prophesy, or, even for understanding what their inspired interpreters are *saying* they prophesy.

It does not appear, though, as if anybody maintains that *all* we can know about the future vicissitudes of anything can be learned just by

---

2 Karl R. Popper, *Objective Knowledge* (Oxford, 1979), 22 (emphasis in original):

> ... since we *have* to choose, it will be 'rational' to choose the best-tested theory. This will be 'rational' in the most obvious sense of the word known to me: the best-tested theory is the one which, in the light of our *critical discussion*, appears to be the best so far, and I do not know of anything more 'rational' than a well-conducted critical discussion.

> ... this choice is *not* 'rational' in the sense that it is based upon *good reasons* for expecting that it will in practice be a successful choice: *there can be no good reasons* in this sense, and this is precisely Hume's result.

A theory's survival of testing-grounded critical discussion better than any of its rivals will make preferring it as a basis for action 'rational,' Popper says, though this cannot qualify as a *good reason* for expecting predictions based on the theory to come true. At that rate, the theory's appearing 'best' cannot mean its appearing aptest to be at least approximately true. Its appearing 'best' must just mean that it has most fully met the Popperian criterion for scientific acceptability: survival of testing-grounded critical discussion. The 'rationality' of preferring theories that have best survived such a process apparently derives, for Popper, from the 'rationality' of the process of such critical discussion; and the 'rationality' of the critical discussion seemingly derives, for Popper, from the property it has of incorporating so much *reasoning* of the sort which Popper approves for 'scientific' purposes: but Popper does not approve of that sort of reasoning with any thought that theories which can best survive discussion incorporating it will thereby be rendered apt to be at least approximately true in their predictions.

directly observing it without setting ourselves to draw any inductive inferences from what we observe.

Some things can, indeed, be known thus. For example, we are very frequently able simply to look at something and with no further conscious ado *see* that it is about to fall. But since some knowledge of the future is not thus derived, the Problem of Induction will remain for such knowledge as is not. Moreover, having analysed induction in these latter cases, it will be possible to give an account on the same basis of psychologically real inferences, even if not conscious ones, underlying the feeling of relative certainty (or likelihood) that we are apt to have on such occasions.

An exception must be allowed, I think, in the case of the mind's normal self-consciousness of its own current volitions. To notice yourself deciding to raise your right hand, say, (I mean, to be aware of such a decision as it is made) involves recognizing that that hand now is apt to rise, other things being equal; but such recognition will commonly *not* be based merely on the recollection (conscious or otherwise) that, in the past, mental events like this have usually had that sort of bodily sequel; still less is it based, in the commonest case, on any idea whatever of the causal mechanism whereby the decision gets executed. The position is rather different, however, with the perception of external causal transactions. With them, it is necessary to *learn* to perceive what happens as exemplifying a specific causal relationship.

The phenomenological psychologist A. Michotte has contended otherwise.[3] And in their philosophical book *Causal Powers*,[4] R. Harré and E.H. Madden argue for treating this sort of experience as 'immediate' and non-inferential:

> To the objection that one is never aware of inferences in such cases, the unconvincing reply ... comes that such inferences are automatic, telescoped, non-discursive and unconscious. To an unprejudiced eye, that is equivalent to saying that they are not inferences at all. (60)

Being 'unprejudiced,' apparently, involves sharing the 'generally accepted' view that 'in human experience ... one cannot be thinking *about*

---

3 A. Michotte, *The Perception of Causality*, trans. T.R. Miles and Elaine Miles (London, 1963).

4 R. Harré and E.H. Madden, *Causal Powers* (Oxford, 1975).

something without being aware that one is thinking about that thing.'[5] In my view, on the other hand, the weatherwise codger who 'sees' that it is going to rain, for instance, immediately upon looking at the clouds, without being able to specify any actual features of the clouds' appearance that have served as *cues* for this judgment, should nonetheless be considered to have *inferred* the imminence of rain from such features, even though not consciously; for otherwise, 'precognition' would not only be a quite familiar everyday occurrence, it would not even be 'extrasensory' perception, but rather, in a case like this, straightforwardly *ocular* and *visual*.

A further consideration of the psychology of *the direct experience as of causality* ('the causal impression') will be found in chapter 17.[6] It is good enough, however, for our purposes here to note the obvious untenability of any 'sensationalist' claim that induction is dispensable, thanks to the sufficiency of unsupplemented sense-experience for telling what is going to happen.

---

5 Ibid., 59.

6 Sometimes (case I), it is possible, by using one's sense-organs, to acquire quite directly – i.e., without any conscious inference – an awareness of some (contemporaneous or non-contemporaneous) causal transaction – that is, an awareness of something causing something. On the other hand (case II), sometimes what goes on in one's consciousness is just the same as what goes on in case I except for either or both of these two differences: (a) the causal transaction in question does not actually occur (or, if the transaction does occur, does not actually cause one's experience, at any rate not in the right way to make that experience a *perception* of it); and/or (b) one does not actually believe that the transaction has occurred. It is to the sort of mental process common to both case I and case II here that I intend the phrase 'the direct experience as of causality' to refer.

8 Naturalism

Is it *necessary* that beliefs formed in accordance with our ordinary inductive practices have warrant? I think not. There could be creatures who did
not follow the sort of inductive policies we follow; such creatures might be
such that their practice was not encapsulable in a rule at all, or such that
while encapsulable, it was not encapsulable in anything like the Straight
Rule. Further, creatures who reasoned in this way could be cognitively
successful (in worlds quite different from ours); ... God could have created
the world in such a way that inductive (Straight Rule) policies would be
unsuccessful; he could have created creatures such that when their faculties functioned properly, they did not reason in accord with the straight
rule but in some other way; and he could have adjusted their mode of
reasoning to the world in such a way that it would yield truth. Had such
creatures, by way of some cognitive accident, begun to form beliefs in *our*
inductive way, those beliefs would not have had warrant.

Alvin Plantinga[1]

By inductive 'naturalism' I mean the view that it is possible using
deductive reasoning alone to derive expectations for the future, for
example, from information about the past and present only. The philosophical objection to any such deduction should call to mind the parallel claim in meta-ethics (see chapter 21) that any attempt to deduce

---

1 *Warrant and Proper Function* (New York, 1993), 127–8. (According to the 'Straight
  Rule,' as it is called, the relative frequency of any characteristic in a whole population can be expected to approximate its relative frequency in that portion of the
  population sampled so far.)

a moral judgment from morally neutral premises will necessarily involve a 'naturalistic fallacy.' Of course, whatever premises actually did entail a moral judgment would not then be morally neutral; but what morally neutral propositions are there? In particular, are empirical propositions all morally neutral, as the opponents of ethical naturalism claim?

Our parallel problem here is whether a sufficiently full account of the past and present would not be enough to entail positive consequences concerning the future. But what sort of information belongs in 'an account of the past and present,' and what counts as a 'positive' consequence concerning the future? Trivially, one can indeed validly deduce the outbreak of war in August 1914, for instance, from information nominally all 'about' the period up to August 1914 if

'The period up to August 1914 was an immediately prewar period'
is allowed to count as giving (only) such information. But a long tradition in philosophy does treat the causal powers or propensities of things as facts about how they are *now* from which what future outcome will ensue or be apt to ensue can be seen as following logically. According to the thinking of Averroes and Spinoza, for example, whatever were genuinely to *cause* anything would have to necessitate it logically. And Leibniz probably held that the conjunction of *everything* about the antecedents of any event would be enough to entail its occurrence, though actually to draw the inference would be (frequently) beyond the capacity of minds like ours, possessed of only finite capacity.[2]

According to a likewise venerable opposing tradition in philosophy, however, 'all beings in the universe, consider'd in themselves, appear entirely loose and independent of each other,' as David Hume strikingly expressed the idea.[3] A Humean will deny the 'immediately pre-war state'

---

2 'In the case of a contingent truth, even though the predicate is really in the subject, yet one never arrives at a demonstration or an identity, even though the resolution of each term is continued indefinitely. In such cases it is only God, who comprehends the infinite at once, who can see how the one is in the other, and can understand *a priori* the perfect reason for contingency; in creatures this is supplied *a posteriori*, by experience.' G.W. Leibniz, *Philosophical Writings*, ed. G.H.R. Parkinson, trans. Mary Morris and G.H.R. Parkinson (Totowa, NJ, 1975), 97. For Leibniz's original Latin, see Louis Couturat, ed., *Opuscules et fragments inédits de Leibniz* (Hildesheim, 1966), 17.

3 David Hume, *A Treatise of Human Nature*, Book III, Part I, section 1, ed. L.A. Selby-Bigge, 2nd ed., rev. P.H. Nidditch (Oxford, 1978), 466. Cf. William of Ockham, 'God can separate every distinct thing ['*omne absolutum distinctum*'] from any other and keep it in being without that other,' *Quodlibet* VI, q1.

of Europe just before August 1914 to have been something genuinely about Europe 'considered in itself' right then – unless what 'Europe's pre-war state' means is just something expressly concerning strategic commitments made, ultimatums, mobilizations, and so on, facts of such a sort, Humeans claim, that no report of them, however full, could suffice to *entail* the subsequent outbreak of war. According to this view, if 'Europe was in a prewar state' does mean something which entails the ensuing outbreak of war, then this in fact is not a statement exclusively about conditions prior to August 1914, after all; and any statement which does report such conditions exclusively can entail nothing at all about what happened later.

The idea evidently is that, for any point in time, there are facts about conditions and occurrences up to and including that time, and facts about conditions and occurrences after that time, such that no statement of any facts of the former sort entails any statement of facts of the latter sort, and any statement of fact whatever is entailed by the conjunction of a statement of facts of the former sort with a statement of facts of the latter sort. Put like this, such a thesis is hard to gainsay just because, apart from there being anything real at all up to the time in question, the thesis does not actually commit itself to there being any other facts whatsoever which are genuinely 'about conditions and occurrences up to and including that time.'[4] However, the opponents of inductive naturalism claim that there actually are plenty of such facts. Indeed, they are apt to claim that absolutely all facts knowable empirically without any inference, conscious or otherwise, up to the time in question are examples of such facts. And they claim as well that many things which are not knowable thus but which can be of critical importance for planning future courses of action and inaction are 'facts about conditions and occurrences after that time,' facts of such a sort that no statement of any of them is validly deducible from a statement of facts of the former sort.

What grounds are there for this indeducibility claim? Is it sufficient that no deduction of the required kind has been found? A.C. Ewing

---

4   That 2+2=4 is a statement of fact which, as it is entailed by any premise, will be entailed also by a conjunction of the kind described. But what about the fact, if it is one, that the infliction of suffering upon people is to be avoided if possible, other things being equal? If there is such a fact, and if a statement of it nevertheless is not entailed by any empirical premises, there will be no harm in our counting that fact, for our present purpose, as a 'fact about conditions after the time' in question. The same thing will hold for any other logically contingent facts there might be that either are impossible to know empirically or are knowable non-empirically.

argued in 1934 that even without being apparent to us a logical connection between cause and effect *could* still exist:

> An Egyptian thinker of three thousand years ago would have no doubt denied any *a priori* connection between the different properties of triangles on the ground that he could see none. Inability to detect the presence of a connection cannot prove its absence.[5]

However, as suggested in chapter 5 in connection with the alleged analyticity of the empiricist principle, there surely is a strong basis for a burden-of-proof rule here. In the absence of an apparently valid deduction or any specific indication that one likely could be constructed, surely a (defeasible) *presumption* of logical indeducibility will be in order. After all, actual demonstrations of indeducibility (such as the celebrated proofs of Lobachevsky and Gödel) are relatively scarce even in relation to the sorts of questions on which valid demonstrative argumentation commonly is possible. Where the unsuccessful search for a valid deductive inference has been prolonged, diligent, skilful, and imaginative, the presumption of indeducibility warranted will surely be all the stronger.

In any case, for an *ad hominem* argument here as powerful as possible, let the reader call to mind some extremely imminent future certainty or near-certainty such as (to cite the traditional example) tomorrow's sunrise. Imagine some millenarian sect, however misguided, flatly denying that this will occur, and denying likewise, of course, that this will probably occur, in view of a wholesale end-of-the-world held to be more imminent still. However strong the empirical evidence for predicting instead that which you, rather, expect as confidently as you do, unlike the members of this sect, would it really have to be not just irrational but in fact *logically inconsistent* on their part to acknowledge all that evidence while still persisting in their denial? Would they have to be contradicting *themselves* in taking the position here imputed to them? Surely not. In the case of tomorrow's sunrise, for instance, the evidence in favour of predicting its occurrence is of two sorts: the observation that the sun has regularly risen so often up till now; and all the observations made to date that lend support to the astronomical theory from which tomorrow's sunrise follows (for the torrid and temperate zones). In

---

5   A.C. Ewing, *Idealism: A Critical Survey*, 3rd ed. (London, 1961), 175.

either case the prediction of such an occurrence tomorrow will depend, as Hume saw, upon the supposition that the course of nature can be expected to continue on the same as in the observed past (at least in relevant respects, at least for the near future, we may add by way of qualification). If the reader will admit that there is not going to be any *logical inconsistency* in rejecting this supposition – whatever irrationality otherwise there may be – that looks like enough to settle the question decisively against inductive naturalism.

But the inductive naturalists have not been idle, and positive arguments against this conclusion have indeed been forthcoming. As mentioned above, one line of argument has involved attributing causal properties or propensities to things as they are *now* from which what future outcomes will ensue or be apt to ensue could be seen to follow logically. But the objection to this is that, where the logical inference does follow validly, the possession of those causal properties or propensities will no more really be facts about the condition of their possessors *now* than being a 'pre-war' period was really a fact about the period leading up to August 1914, rather than a fact actually about what happened after that period, phrased only nominally in terms of the earlier time.

Rather than accept the insufficiency of any deductive reasoning to justify drawing inferences about the future on the basis of observations made up to now, a more popular way of opposing such a conclusion in recent times has been to argue that the inductive mode of reasoning, though itself non-deductive, is nonetheless justifiable deductively. Sometimes the conclusion of the deductive argument advanced is just that, no matter what actually will happen or be apt to happen in the future in fact, the advantageous course to take now is to proceed *as if* the inductively supported predictions were (at least predominantly) going to come true. This line of argument is treated under the heading of inductive 'Pragmatism' in chapter 10.

But through the last century, the most popular way of arguing, in effect, that inductive inference is justifiable deductively has probably been to maintain that a forecast's 'justification,' for instance, can simply be *defined* in terms of inductive support, thus making the 'justification of induction' tautological. After all, didn't Ludwig Wittgenstein himself say something like this?

All testing, all confirmation and disconfirmation of a hypothesis takes place already within a system. And this system is not a more or less arbitrary and doubtful point of departure for all our arguments: no, it belongs to the essence of what we call an argument. The system is not so much the point of departure, as the element in which arguments have their life.[6]

In accordance with this, P.F. Strawson in 1952 offered the following syllogism:

It is an analytic proposition that it is reasonable to have a degree of belief in a statement which is proportional to the strength of the evidence in its favour; and it is an analytic proposition, though not a proposition of mathematics, that, other things being equal, the evidence for a generalization is strong in proportion as the number of favourable instances, and the variety of circumstances in which they are found, is great. So to ask whether it is reasonable to place reliance on inductive procedures is like asking whether it is reasonable to proportion the degree of one's convictions to the strength of the evidence. Doing this is what 'being reasonable' *means* in such a context.[7]

Here is a medieval parody:

It is an analytic proposition that it is reasonable to have a degree of belief in a statement which is proportional to the magnitude of the authority behind it; and it is an analytic proposition, though not a proposition of mathematics, that the authority behind a statement is unequalled if that authority is a Book of the Bible. The Books of the Holy Bible are just the sort of thing we *mean* by authority. So to ask whether it is reasonable to place reliance on the statements in the Bible is like asking whether it is reasonable to proportion the degree of one's convictions to the magnitude of the authority for them. Doing this is what 'being reasonable' *means* in such a context.[8]

If, contrary to this, a modern Bible scholar were to be so verbally inept (or waggish) as to call it an error to take everything stated in the Books of Matthew, Mark, Luke, and John as gospel, we would know what the

---

6 Ludwig Wittgenstein, *On Certainty*, ed. G.E.M. Anscombe and G.H. von Wright, trans. Denis Paul and G.E.M. Anscombe (Oxford, 1969), 16e.

7 P.F. Strawson, *Introduction to Logical Theory* (London, 1952), 256–7.

8 To be sure, observational evidence is needed to establish just what statements are made in the Bible. But that needn't be thought to detract from the Bible's authoritativeness. To be an *absolute* authority, the Bible would not have to be the *only* authority there is, but just untrumpable as far as whatever it does state goes.

scholar *meant*, and recognize it as a self-consistent standpoint, even if poorly (or drolly) expressed. In place of the Bible here, Aristotle or the Koran could substitute equally well. It is easy to see how Wittgensteinianism of this sort leads to relativism. But, in so far as it does, of course, it does not *justify* inductive inference as against alternative ways of foretelling the future, like consulting the Bible. However, in any case, Wittgenstein and Strawson are wrong about empirical linguistics. The word 'argument' and the phrase 'being reasonable' do not in fact mean what Wittgenstein and Strawson said that they do. Not only is it perfectly possible to *understand* the outlook of people who profess a somewhat different view from one's own on what a good argument is or what it is to be reasonable – and to do this without any equivocation in the sense of 'argument' or the sense of 'reasonable' employed. Using the word 'argument' and the word 'reasonable' univocally, it is perfectly possible to report a disagreement over what a good argument is and a disagreement over what it is to be reasonable. But such a report would be impossible unless there were univocal meanings of the terms in question shared by both sides of the disagreement; or, at least, unless both sides had concepts expressible in terms of such univocal phraseology. Where one person calls something 'reasonable' and another one denies it to be 'reasonable,' they have genuinely disagreed with each other only if they both mean the same thing as each other by 'reasonable.'

In opposition to those who think predictive reliance upon induction presupposes something about the world such as the course of nature's aptness to continue on the same, Strawson argues strenuously (with some recourse to the inductive pragmatist line of argument) that induction and induction alone would remain the way to make whatever forecasts were possible no matter how things were in the world.[9] Here he differs from the view of Alvin Plantinga quoted in the epigraph to the present chapter.

In order to probe this disagreement more deeply (and so defend Plantinga's side of it), let us start with an only medium-sized departure from complete predictive reliance upon induction. No doubt a 'fundamentalist' can be defined as somebody who holds that the Christian Bible in its entirety is literally true (at any rate, except where the language is poetic overtly). And we may define a 'fideist' fundamentalist as someone who avowedly takes such a position by a 'leap of faith' rather than on the basis of any argumentative grounds. Certainly, there

---

9   Strawson, *Introduction to Logical Theory*, 258–63.

are such people. It isn't that they make no use of induction. But for them the conclusions of inductive inference are always trumped by the say-so of the Bible in any cases of conflict. How is this avowed position of theirs either self-inconsistent or in any way inconsistent with a full acknowledgment of all those observational facts inductively relied on by their opponents to predict future developments at odds with the Bible's say-so? Surely, there need not be any logical inconsistency here.

Let us now proceed, in the spirit of Plantinga, to imagine a deity purposely fashioning creatures whose psychological make-up disposed them to worship Him/Her/It and to accept and act upon whatever expectations came to them when in that devout state of mind, but never or seldom to remember having done so previously; and let us further imagine this deity creating a universe in which such expectations normally came true, whether inductively supported or not, but where inductively based expectations normally did not come true if formed otherwise than in a genuinely devout state of mind. In the circumstances imagined, wouldn't these creatures be thinking in the *right* way if they proceeded in accordance with their devout mental predispositions when forming expectations for the future? And wouldn't any lapses from that into inductive thinking in an undevout frame of mind amount to actual *error* on their part (even in those exceptional circumstances where the expectations so formed did come true)?[10]

Up to this point not a word has been said about mathematical probability theory. The probability calculus certainly is a deductive system, so it is only natural to think of it in connection with the inductive naturalist project of deducing at least what will probably take place in the future from information about the present and past. The standing objection to this is that any application of mathematics to actual goings-on in the world has to depend on a partitioning of possibilities into a finite set of mutually exclusive and jointly exhaustive alternative cases

---

10 Nor does the 'right' way of thinking here have to mean merely the way apt to be advantageous. It is not only inductive naturalists who can accept that in some cases it's an *erroneous* way of thinking that is apt to be advantageous to the thinker. For instance – to cite William James's famous example, though not in support of his conclusion – it may well on occasion be necessary for a mountain climber to irrationally underestimate the difficulty in successfully leaping over some chasm in order to be able to muster the courage requisite to make the necessary leap and survive. See James's famous essay, 'The Sentiment of Rationality,' in William James, *Essays in Pragmatism*, ed. Alburey Castell (NY, 1948), 27.

of equal initial probability, or at least an initial comparative ordering of the possibilities of different cases. In practice, this can often be done empirically by observing the relative frequencies of different cases up to the present and drawing inductive conclusions from that, or else by recourse to inductively supported theories that have statistical or probabilistic consequences for the future as well as the past and present. But the inductive naturalist program could derive no assistance from methods that would require the results of inductive reasoning as premises for any mathematical deduction.[11]

There are people, sometimes calling themselves 'Bayesians' (though the label, perhaps, does not need to mean that), who claim they can sidestep the problem by showing mathematically how new evidence is able to raise the probability of a hypothesis in any case. The idea is that, no matter *how* subjectively they were made, from almost any

---

11 Can Christopher Peacocke's discussion of enumerative induction in *The Realm of Reason* (Oxford, 2004) be faulted on grounds such as this? Perhaps not. In certain circumstances, he says, the fact that all the observed possessors of one characteristic, F, also share another characteristic, G, will entitle a reasoner to conclude from this that all Fs are Gs. 'My thesis is that the explanation of the existence of this entitlement is that in the given circumstances ... it is reasonable to think that the easiest way for all of the singular propositions ... to hold ... is for some condition C to hold which explains why all Fs are Gs' (137). What makes one way for something to come about 'easier' than another way? 'One way is an easier way than a second for a certain state of affairs to come about if the first way is exemplified in a wider range of initial conditions that could bring about the state of affairs – where this "could" is empirical (rather than being the "could" of pure metaphysical possibility)' (83–4). 'Which ways are the easier ways is largely an empirical matter' (83). 'Largely,' Peacocke says. If it were *always* at least a partly empirical matter, that would classify his position under the *inductive justification of induction* heading, the topic of chapter 9. Only if at least some enumerative inductions could be justified entirely *a priori* would his position rest on the supposition that the more different *a priori* possibilities there are for something to occur, the greater the probability of its occurrence will be. Is that supposition itself for Peacocke an *a priori* truth? 'According to [a theory of apriority proposed by Peacocke], in using an a priori way of coming to judge that *p* a thinker is using a method which guarantees, as a result of the very nature of *p* and the way in which its truth-condition is determined, that the thinker judges that *p* only if it is the case that *p*' (173). Could anything which falls short of making the truth of the proposition that *p* a logical necessity ever provide the required guarantee? Only in a trivial sense. Wherever the proposition that *p* is in fact true, of course, any 'method' of coming to judge that *p* will indeed, trivially, bring it about that it is judged that *p* only if *p*. And whenever the statement that *p* has a truthvalue at all, the 'method,' for example, of *correctly guessing* the answer to the question whether or not *p* will likewise, trivially, guarantee that it is judged that *p* only if *p*.

sufficiently comprehensive initial assignments of probabilities to different possibilities, it will follow mathematically that evidence to the effect that certain of these possibilities have been realized can raise or lower the ensuing probability of a given hypothesis. Now Bayes' Theorem does show the way in which an eventuality's coming to pass can raise or lower the probability of a hypothesis, depending on the prior probability of the hypothesis and of the eventuality and the likelihood of the eventuality given the truth of the hypothesis (provided that the prior probability of the hypothesis is greater than zero and less than one hundred percent). But, except for evidence so 'complete' that a report of it would entail the truth of a hypothesis, for no evidence, however extensive, does it follow from Bayes' Theorem alone that such evidence would be sufficient to raise the probability of the hypothesis over 50 per cent.

This brings us back to the issue of how, in any particular case, to go about partitioning all possibilities into 'equiprobable' alternatives. Appeal is sometimes made here to a 'Principle of Indifference,' stating that, if there is insufficient reason to give more credence to one alternative than another, the two then are equally probable. For purposes of furthering the inductive naturalist program, the Principle of Indifference would have to be analytic; but is it even true? In one way such a principle, or something like it, is indeed not merely true but analytically true. That the probabilities of two alternatives are equal does just mean that there is no more reason to give credence to one of them than to the other. But, if the effect any piece of evidence will have on the probability of anything is dependent upon the probabilities of different things prior to any empirical evidence whatever, can it be said that the members of *any* set of mutually exclusive and jointly exhaustive alternatives, prior to any empirical evidence whatever, are necessarily all equally probable? Surely not.

Bertrand's Paradox has proved especially persuasive on this point with the mathematically inclined. Given only that a chord has been drawn in some circle, what is the probability that the chord is longer than the side of an equilateral triangle inscribed in the circle? The different geometrical 'proofs' that yield conflicting answers can be shown to rest on differing equiprobability assumptions. (For example, that the chord of the circle is equally likely to intersect the diameter perpendicular to it in any equally long segment of that line between its two ends; or that, if either end of the chord lies at one vertex of an equilateral triangle inscribed in the circle, the other end of the chord is equally likely to fall in any of the three equally long arcs connecting each pair of the triangle's vertices).[12]

For a simple illustration of the same logical point, consider the toss of a coin. Is it equally likely to land heads-up and to land tails-up, in the absence of *any* relevant empirical evidence? Why aren't the following five alternatives equally probable *a priori* instead: heads-up, facing north; heads-up, facing east; heads-up, facing south; heads-up, facing west; tails-up? A conceivable objection might be raised on the grounds that, even when a coin has landed heads-down, that head will still be facing north, east, south, or west. So isn't it arbitrary, the objection will run, to partition heads outcomes but not tails outcomes? Consider, then, a roulette wheel which stops at a red sector, at a black sector, or at a green sector of its spinning circle. Since any sector of a circle can be mapped on to any other sector or amalgam of sectors, why aren't these three alternatives – or even just two, red and not-red – equally probable *a priori*, irrespective of differences in area? To state that such differences in area or in arc-lengths here have an *a priori* bearing on the relative probabilities of different outcomes once the wheel is set spinning, at any rate does not appear to be stating a tautology.[13]

But what about the Law of Large Numbers, Bernoulli's Law? This theorem can be seen as specifically relevant to sampling, but inductive reasonings always can be construed in that way, the occasions on which observations have been made being taken as a sample out of all past, present, and future occasions – or, conceivably instead, out of all past, present, and future occasions less than a certain finite time-interval away from the present. It follows from Bernoulli's Law, given one proviso, that the larger the size of any sample relative to the size of the population sampled, the likelier it is that the sample will be at least approximately representative of that population (for any specified margin of approximation), and that this likelihood can be increased to any specified degree by taking a big enough sample. The requisite proviso, however is that

12 See William Kneale, *Probability and Induction* (Oxford, 1949), 184–5; Martin Gardner, *More Mathematical Puzzles and Diversions* (Harmondsworth, Middlesex, UK, 1966), 173–5; Jerzy Neyman, *Lectures and Conferences on Mathematical Statistics and Probability*, 2nd ed. (Washington, 1952), 15–18.

13 George N. Schlesinger, in *The Sweep of Probability* (Notre Dame, IN, 1991), exerts himself doughtily to defend the Principle of Indifference against objections parallel to these, conceding only that *where* 'equally reasonably looking [equiprobability] assumptions lead to different results ... the principle will be of no use' (191). But where, in the complete absence of all empirical evidence, will this not be the case?

any member of the population is *equally likely* to get to included in the sample taken.

The synthetic character of such an equiprobability posit seems fatal to the argument of inductive naturalists like Donald Williams[14] who would base themselves on the 'statistical syllogism' (e.g., 'Most As are Bs. This is an A. Therefore, this is probably a B.'). Thus, Williams might reason:

> The majority of (big enough) samples out of a population are samples which are at least approximately representative of the population sampled.
> This is a (big enough) sample out of a population.
> Therefore, this will probably be a sample which is at least approximately representative of the population sampled.

The trouble here is with the first premise of this syllogism. It is easy to prove that the majority of (big enough) *subclasses* of any population are going to be at least approximately representative of it (for any given margin of approximation). But are the members belonging to any one subclass as likely as the members of any other to enter our database and so become jointly a *sample*? Any members of the population that are still in the future will obviously not have entered our database yet. So the present equiprobability posit would have to imply that somehow none of them was any likelier than any other member of the population to have its occurrence in the future – whatever that might mean! In any case, the posit will surely not be a tautology.

---

14 Donald Williams, *The Ground of Induction* (Cambridge, MA, 1947). It is true that Williams does, on page 137, issue the following explicit disclaimer: '... a probability conclusion is not of the form of *It is probable that the sun will rise*, related by a demonstrative implication to its premise; it is of the form of *The sun will rise*, related by a probability implication to its premise. (See page 46.)' On page 46, this is justified by reference to the fact that the probability of a proposition in relation to one body of evidence can differ from its probability in relation to another body of evidence. However, on page 44 we read: 'What we call "the" credibility or "the" probability of a proposition is its credibility or probability in relation to the propositions which we happen, at the moment the statement is made, to know to be true ...' Now, in this sense 'the' probability of a sunrise tomorrow *will* be deducible from facts about the past on Williams's account, provided only that the facts as to what propositions about the past we have come to know are included among the facts about the past to be taken into consideration in making the deduction.

Last of all we come to the ingenious inductive naturalism of Roy Harrod,[15] who insists quite strenuously that he requires no appeal to the Principle of Indifference. His strategy is first to justify deductively a very modest form of induction – expecting the prolongation into at least the near future of long-standing 'continuities' experienced up to now – and then on that basis to justify anticipating the continued efficacy of more specific inductive methods found to have been successful predictors in the past.

> Consider a journey by ... a nescient man along a continuity ... Let a conclusion be proposed that this continuity will continue for a length constituting at least one-tenth of the length for which it has already proceeded. In more general terms we may suppose a belief in a continuance for at least $1/x$ of the length for which it has already proceeded. If we entertain the belief of at least one-tenth, which is the conclusion of our argument, continuously from the beginning to the end of the journey, it is quite certain that we shall be right ten times for every once that we are wrong. We shall be right during the first ten-elevenths of the journey and wrong during the last eleventh. If we entertain the belief of continuance for at least $1/x$, it is quite certain we shall be right x times for every once that we are wrong. This, in accordance with the traditional notation, gives a probability of being correct of $x/x+1$ ...[16]

Harrod thinks that this argument is enough to justify (as being bound to prove true most of the time) a belief in the further continuance of the imagined traveller's path along the continuity for at least one-tenth (or $1/x$th) of the distance already traversed. This belief Harrod wants the traveller to 'entertain ... continuously.' At each point in the traveller's progress along the path in question, the prediction about the path's further continuance which holding it would prompt the traveller to make will be a different prediction, of course. In effect, Harrod wants the intervals between predictions to 'be made as small as possible.'[17] But why? Isn't it only at finite,

---

15 Roy Harrod, *Foundations of Inductive Logic* (London, 1956).
16 Ibid., 52–3.
17 Ibid., 57. Harrod in effect admits that if the first prediction is only made after nine-tenths (or $\frac{x-1}{x}$) of the path has been traversed, *no* predictions made will end up being correct (58). But with the interval between predictions 'as small as possible,' Harrod evidently thinks it safe to say at least half the predictions will be correct as long as the actual total length of the path exceeds three times a 'minimum sensibile' (58–9).

commonly irregular intervals that *it matters to us* to predict the future? *If* every point along the path traversed was *equally likely* to be a point where a prediction got made, each prediction which was made would then be likelier than not to be one of those ones that were going to come true. Which would then bring us back to an equiprobability posit.

But perhaps it can be argued that really *continuously* holding a belief of the sort Harrod envisages isn't altogether an absurd conception, after all. Can we imagine a driver who manages to retain a standing expectation that the road will continue on ahead for at least one-tenth of the distance covered so far? Or, alternatively, can we conceive of a rather clever fly crawling along a coloured stripe and availing itself of Harrodian considerations to justify continuously retaining an expectation that this stripe of colour will continue on for at least one-tenth of the distance already crawled? Could not the motorist and the fly derive some comfort from the reflection that it was mathematically demonstrable that there would continuously be at least ten chances out of eleven of their expectation being correct?

Rather than pursue this interesting line of thought any further, it is time to offer instead a general objection telling against any attempt, including Harrod's, to justify sheer unqualified extrapolative induction at all. The point is that such a forecasting method, unqualified, just cannot be justified even as a starting strategy.

The argument to be offered is inspired by Nelson Goodman, but in contrast to his treatment in *Fact, Fiction and Forecast*, it has no recourse to any but purely qualitative predicates.[18] Let 'checker' be a colour predicate which applies to sections of paths. Then, when the letter 'd' designates some particular distance, calling any section of a path 'checker' will mean that such parts of it as are wholly between nd and (nd-d) away from the path's starting point, for any odd value of n, are red all over, and such parts of it as are wholly between md and (md-d) away from the path's starting point, for any even values of m, are black all over. Here we are to imagine our clever fly crawling along a red continuity, which may or may not lie on a checkerboard. The fly has

---

18 In contrast, that is, to 'positional' or other predicates requiring to be understood in terms of particular spatial or temporal locations, proper names, or phraseology in general with an 'indexical' or 'token-reflexive' element in its meaning. See Nelson Goodman, *Fact, Fiction, and Forecast* (London, 1954), 73–83, 85–6; and Dan Goldstick, 'What Are "Purely Qualitative" Terms?' *American Philosophical Quarterly* 23, no. 1 (January 1986), 71–81.

crawled a distance of d so far. Should it predict that the path directly ahead will continue to be red, or should it predict that the path directly ahead will continue to be checker – in which latter case the path ahead will have to immediately turn black. Unqualified, the rule which Harrod's argument purports to justify would sanction predicting that it will continue on red for a further distance of at least one-tenth d, and also predicting that it will continue on checker for a further distance of at least one-tenth d. These two predictions, being incompatible with each other, cannot really both be warranted by the same body of evidence; and therefore any deductive argument which purports to justify a rule like Harrod's for making predictions must be invalid.

The key to the matter, in fact, is the superior *simplicity* of the hypothesis that the path will continue red as compared to the hypothesis that it will continue checker; for to continue red, it would not have to change colour, but to continue checker, it would.[19] However, since Harrod's argument, like any other argument for an inductive method unqualified by a simplicity rule, is lacking in this essential respect, it cannot possibly justify a single inductive inference.

19 The point is that change always requires an explanation; and no matter what explanans is postulated – or even if no *particular* explanans is postulated at all – any theory requiring such explanatory supplementation is on that account more complex than it would otherwise be. (See chapter 14.) It is necessary to notice at this point that it is not a sufficient condition of something's *changing* that it cease to be characterized by a property which it has formerly possessed; if that were sufficient, then ceasing to be checker would of necessity no less constitute a change than would ceasing to be red. The point is that because our colour terms are the *classificatory* expressions that they are, it is logically necessary on the one hand, that any two 'red' objects will to that extent resemble each other and, on the other hand, that any 'red' object will to that extent differ qualitatively from any 'black' object. The proposition that two checker things differ in spatiotemporal location to a certain extent will have to logically imply that they are not wholly alike in the visual effects that they would produce. However, no such logical implication can be carried by the proposition that two red things differ spatiotemporally to any extent. (But, it may be objected, what account can be given of *resemblance* other than in terms of the sharing of a common property? It is analytic, it must be admitted, that there cannot be a case of resemblance which does not consist in the sharing of some common property; and it must be admitted likewise, with respect to every property in the sharing of which a resemblance can consist, that the resemblance in question will follow in each case as a logical consequence of the proposition that the property is in fact shared. Nevertheless, what the example of 'checker' shows is that it is not logically necessary and not even true that every case of the sharing of a common property will to that extent be a case of mutual resemblance. If this fact really does stand in the way of the desired 'account' of *resemblance*, then it will be necessary to be satisfied with some other 'account,' or with none.)

9 Inductivism

Is it possible to justify induction inductively? There can be no question about the favourable tendency of the available empirical data. Very, very often in the past, and certainly far more often than not, inductive methods have proved to yield correct predictions, which (from all inductive indications) have been and will continue to be absolutely essential for human survival. But is there, as David Hume thought, necessarily a vicious circularity in reasoning like this? To say no, one must either deny, like J.S. Mill, that the reasoning required has to be circular,[1]

1 J.S. Mill, *Collected Works of John Stuart Mill*, vol. 7, *A System of Logic*, ed. J.M. Robson (Toronto, 1973): '... there is a principle implied in the very statement of what Induction is; an assumption with regard to the course of nature and the order of the universe; namely, that there are such things in nature as parallel cases; that what happens once, will, under a sufficient degree of similarity of circumstances, happen again, and not only again, but as often as the same circumstances recur. This, I say, is an assumption, involved in every case of induction. And, if we consult the actual course of nature, we find that the assumption is warranted.' (Book III, chapter 3, 306).

In chapter 21, however, concerned to rebut the charge of circular reasoning, Mill is at pains to insist that in fact no such general principle does need to be presupposed by humanity's very earliest inductions. 'The induction, Fire burns, does not require for its validity that all nature should observe uniform laws, but only that there should be uniformity in one particular class of natural phenomena ...' (568, note at *). From myriad cases of such *departmental* uniformity in nature, Mill envisages a grand induction to the uniformity of nature overall. But (1) why wouldn't even a past-to-future departmental inductive inference presuppose at any rate a principle of the uniformity of that department of nature? just what would warrant even that limited, departmental presupposition? and (2) wouldn't a grand inductive inference concerning nature overall presuppose the uniformity of nature in general, and what would warrant making that general presupposition?

or else insist, like R.B. Braithwaite, that, even if it is circular, this need not be a fatal objection.[2]

What, then, is 'circularity' in reasoning and what grounds might there be for objecting to such reasoning? The same sort of answers should be given here as were given in chapter 4. In the same spirit, we can for our purposes too define a 'circular' piece of reasoning as one that premises or otherwise presupposes its own conclusion, where a piece of reasoning can be said to 'presuppose' some given proposition whenever it would be a mistake to believe the conclusion of that reasoning on the basis of that reasoning unless it independently were the case that to believe the given proposition would not be to make a mistake. (It should go without saying here that relative to the end of believing what is true on a given question rather than what isn't, a belief which, in particular circumstances, it is a 'mistake' to hold may happen to be true in fact, and a belief which it is no 'mistake' to hold may in fact be false. For example, it does sometimes occur that a patient is diagnosed correctly as a result of faulty reasoning.)[3]

All inductive justifications of induction will necessarily fall into two classes. Either they will argue directly for induction's predictive reliability now and in the future on the evidence of its observed reliability in the past; or else they will infer its general reliability henceforth from a claim about the way things have been and will be which is advanced as the best explanation for some previously observed facts. In either case the final conclusion – that induction is generally reliable – would indeed appear to be inferred by means of reasoning which presupposes that very proposition.

But is the circularity *vicious*? What might it be anyway, which would make such circular reasoning faulty? As I asked in chapter 4, what is wrong with reasoning that presupposes its own conclusion?

Consider the fideist fundamentalists, mentioned in chapter 8, who favour accepting only such inductively supported conclusions as do

---

2 'I do not wish to deny that there is a sort of circularity involved ... but it is a peculiar sort of circularity whose viciousness is by no means obvious,' R.B. Braithwaite, *Scientific Explanation* (New York, 1953), 277. However, although Braithwaite does think that inductive evidence is necessary to make belief in the predictive effectiveness of induction 'reasonable,' he also leans towards *ad hominem* considerations in his view, for example, regarding '*e*' (the proposition that a policy of inferring inductively is an effective one), that 'a belief in *e* is self-rationalizing – not, of course, in the sense that believing *e* makes this belief itself reasonable, but in the sense that believing *e* carries along with it a belief that this belief in *e* is reasonable' (291).
3 Cf. footnote 10 of chapter 8, above.

not contradict the statements made in the Bible. Any *consistent* adherents of this position would be unmoved by inductive arguments for relying on induction even in opposition to statements made in the Bible, because their principle of evidence would lead them to give weight to inductive evidence only in support of conclusions that were consistent with everything said in the Bible. But are there really any consistent adherents of fideist fundamentalism? Whether there are or not, it plainly is just minds already disposed inductively that could ever be convinced by inductive evidence for anything, including evidence for the reliability of induction. So are circular arguments, such as inductive justifications of induction, bound then at least to be *useless*, incapable of convincing people of anything they do not already accept?

Not necessarily. We previously looked into an issue parallel to this in chapter 4. In order to be convinced of something by inductive evidence it is not necessary to already accept the reliability of induction *consciously*. And, in the mind of someone properly disposed, the inductive evidence for induction's reliability can indeed end up producing a fully conscious acceptance of such a conclusion. Must the reasoner then draw back from reaching that conclusion this way because the reasoning involved is circular? Why can't the reply be given that, if inductive inference ever has rational force, it must have it, on the same basis, in this case also?

Arguably, the most that can be said against inductive justifications of induction is that they can only lend rational support to their conclusion because this proposition is already worthy of credence independently of all empirical evidence. And so we can say that, if this proposition is to count as establishable empirically, what it states must be something already warranted *a priori*.

10 Pragmatism

In our planning for the future, we all rely heavily on inductively based predictions, and we therefore by and large have a strong interest in those being, as far as possible, predictions which will come true. The inductive pragmatists' aim is the rational vindication of our reliance on induction, but, as committed empiricists (with no place in their philosophy for anything synthetic *a priori*), they undertake to achieve this using deductive reasoning only. Nevertheless, it is perhaps best not to classify them as inductive naturalists, because they make a point of stressing that no conclusion about the future, not even a qualified and guarded one, can ever be validly deduced from premises exclusively about the present and past.

C.S. Peirce[1] asks us, in effect, to regard our observational data as a sample out of a population extending without limit into the future. Inductive canons, he suggests, will tell us to estimate the proportional distribution of different phenomena in the entire population as approximating their relative frequency in the sample. On this basis, what is the *probability* (assuming no other evidence bearing on it is available) that the next occasion to be encountered out of the total population of all observable occasions (or, better, all occasions ever actually observed or to be observed) will conform to something that has been found up to now to hold good in p% of all instances observed? The best estimate, Peircian inductivism tells us, will be a probability of p%. The Peircian case for favouring this method of arriving at predictions rests upon a frequency interpretation of *probability*, according to which the 'probability' of a sort

---

1 See his 'The Doctrine of Necessity Examined,' in *Collected Papers of Charles Sanders Peirce*, ed. Charles Hartshorne and Paul Weiss, vol. 6 (Cambridge, MA, 1935), 31–5.

of occurrence taking place next time (in the absence of any other relevant considerations) will equal the ratio of occurrences of that sort to past, present, and future times overall, and this ratio is equal to the mathematical limit (if any) to which the ratio of occurrences to times converges over the series of all relevant past, present, and future times taken together. Peirce stresses that it is only times at which actual observations have been or will be made that are relevant for his purposes.

Whatever the actual probability (so conceived) of any sort of thing occurring – provided only that there is some value or other for this probability – Peirce's point here is that, carried sufficiently far with new observational data continually coming in, the inductive method, as he conceives it, is bound to yield estimates of the probability of this sort of thing's occurrence which will eventually converge to that actual value. For there being an actual value for such an occurrence's probability just *means* that there is a value to which the ratio of such occurrences to times will converge if the series is extended without limit. Insofar as the instances actually observed up to any point form an unrepresentative sample of all instance, Peirce notes, the inductively based estimate of any sort of occurrence's probability will be incorrect; but, in that case, new observations will necessarily lead sooner or later to a revised estimate, and the series of such revised estimates of the probability in question will have to converge eventually to the actual probability, if there is any actual probability.

What does this argument prove? It proves that continued use of the Peircian inductive method to estimate the probability of any sort of occurrence will indeed yield something like the correct answer, if there is one, in the long run. But, as John Maynard Keynes notoriously observed, in the long run we'll all be dead.[2] What this argument does not

---

2 In 'The Doctrine of Chances,' reprinted in *Writings of Charles S. Peirce: A Chronological Edition*, vol. 3, ed. Christian J.W. Kloesel (Bloomington, 1986) 283–4, Peirce himself writes: '… death makes the number of our risks, of our inferences, finite, and so makes their mean result uncertain. The very idea of probability and of reasoning rests on the assumption that this number is indefinitely great … logicality inexorably requires that our interests shall *not* be limited. They must not stop at our own fate, but must embrace the whole community. This community, again, must not be limited, but must extend to all races of beings with whom we can come into immediate or mediate intellectual relation.'
   The important thing, says Peirce, is the predictive success in the long run of 'the whole community.' But will that *community*, however broadly defined, still be around in the long run – i.e., forever? Peirce says that the guiding consideration should be what would ensue if inquiry *were* to go on forever – see his *Collected*

establish is that the Peircian inductive method is at all likely to yield anything like the correct answer soon enough to be of positive use to us. Nor does it establish that induction is any apter to yield an approximately correct answer than different methods which would now yield a prediction conflicting with the predictions that receive inductive support: methods, that is, involving reliance on holy books, oracles, crystal balls, Ouija boards, and so on and so on.

In replying to this, Hans Reichenbach makes the point that induction does have the provable advantage as a method for accurate forecasting that it is bound to be effective if any method is; for, if any method of foretelling the future is at all effective, it will prove itself in use and so come to receive inductive support for the forecast that its predictions will tend to come true; and then induction, too, will be able to get at least that much right. Some clairvoyant, for instance, conceivably *might* actually have the knack of prophesying correctly. But:

> The indications of the clairvoyant can differ, if they are true, only in the beginning of the series, from those given by the inductive principle. In the end there must be an asymptotical convergence between the indications of the clairvoyant and those of the inductive principle. This follows from the definition of the limit.[3]

Is that a reason to favour inductively based predictions right now, for practical purposes, over the predictions of any claimed clairvoyant, say, given that the predictions conflict? That, after all, is what a *pragmatic* vindication of induction must justify. But Reichenbach insists that it's by induction that the predictive abilities claimed for a clairvoyant or

---

Papers, vol. 2 (Cambridge, MA, 1932), 405 (2.661) – but *why* should that be so? Suppose we grant Peirce, at least for the sake of argument, that *the community* will indeed last forever, and that it makes sense to consider it as if it really were a single, composite inquirer. Even granting all this, why should we 'embrace' it in making *our* shorter-term forecasts. (Here Peirce cites an ethical imperative; but why isn't making the truest prediction we can *now* the best way of serving even the longest-run interests of inquiry-in-general?) Is it going to be argued that any single forecast made will be likelier than not to (roughly) match the degree of success of the overall majority of forecasts in a total population of forecasts arrived at in the same sort of way? In that event, the whole argument here would rest, after all, on the 'statistical syllogism' discussed in chapter 8.

3 Hans Reichenbach, *Experience and Prediction* (Chicago, 1938), 353–4.

soothsayer are to be tested, because it is induction that can be *demonstrated* to be predictively effective if any method of predictions is.[4]

> We would ask the soothsayer to predict as much as he could, and see whether his predictions finally converged sufficiently with the frequency observed in the continuation of the sequence. Then we would count his success rate. If the latter were sufficiently high, we would infer by the rule of induction that it would remain so, and thus conclude that the man was an able prophet. If the success rate were low, we would refuse to consult him further.[5]

But remember, what Reichenbach has to justify is reliance on inductively supported predictions *now* in preference to the conflicting predictions of the soothsayer. Three problems suggest themselves.

In the first place, Reichenbach writes as if there were no difficulty in ascertaining a soothsayer's predictive success rate in the past. But suppose inductive methods indicate that his success rate has been low, while he himself claims a high success rate. Isn't it unwarrantly begging the question in favour of induction and against him to discredit his say-so in such a case? After all, this was supposed to be a purely deductive argument in vindication of induction. On the other hand, it must be admitted that not absolutely everything we claim to know about the past is known on inductive grounds alone. For memory does not function by inference at all, not even in the broadest sense. To be sure, it is only on inductive grounds that we are ever warranted in trusting the claims other people make about what they remember. And even one's own apparent recollections can be assessed in the light of inductive canons; where they pass the test, it will be because the actual occurrence of what one now seems to recall turns out in the circumstances to be the best causal explanation of the apparent-recollection experiences that one has. Still, purported individual memories ostensibly are a source of information about the past independent alike of induction and the soothsayer. Is that enough, though, to entitle such experiences to trump the authority claimed by the soothsayer? No one denies that memory is fallible. Would inductive pragmatism have gained much by shifting its problem from that of rationally justifying

---

4   Ibid., 354.
5   Hans Reichenbach, *The Theory of Probability*, trans. Ernest H. Hutten and Maria Reichenbach, 2nd ed. (Berkeley, 1949), 476.

reliance on induction, over to that of rationally justifying reliance on induction-cum-memory?

But, even if that line of objection is waived, the Reichenbachian argument faces a second difficulty. For every soothsayer with a low predictive success rate to date there are always any number of other soothsayers (or other conceivable methods for predicting the future) which are as yet empirically untested. What is the non-question-begging basis for dismissing predictions from these sources in favour of such inductively supported predictions as conflict with them? A course of action (or inaction) needs to be decided on now. Why should inductively supported predictions be preferred now to conflicting predictions from other sources merely because whatever of those other sources actually are any good predictively will foreseeably come to secure induction's eventual backing, when it is too late?

Lastly, what if the supporters of some method for foretelling the future admit that their method has not been particularly effective in the past but insist that it will be from now on? Wouldn't it be unacceptably question-begging, in this context, to dismiss their claims just on inductive grounds?[6] Where his past success rate has been low, Reichenbach says,

> ... the soothsayer may refer us to the future, declaring that on continuation of the sequence his prediction of a limit may still come true. Although clairvoyants favor such an attitude, finally even the most ardent believer no longer places any faith in them. In the end the believer submits his judgment to the rule of induction. He must do so because the rule of induction is a method *of which he knows that it will lead to the aim* if the aim is attainable, whereas *he does not know anything* about the oracle and the clairvoyant.[7]

Now, surely Reichenbach has pointed to a real psychological fact about human nature here. People in fact cannot bring themselves to put any reliance on a way of predicting the future which they themselves agree has been ineffective in the past. (Where they see something as having changed so as to turn what was an ineffective into a henceforth effective forecasting technique, it will not be simply that technique on which they are relying.) But a fact about human nature isn't sufficient for Reichenbach's purpose of vindicating predictive

---

6 Cf. Max Black, '"Pragmatic" Justifications of Induction,' *Problems of Analysis* (Ithaca, NY, 1954), 177–8.

7 Reichenbach, *The Theory of Probability*, 476. Emphases in original.

reliance on induction by means of a purely logical argument. The believer in inductively unsupported ways of foretelling the future, Reichenbach declares, 'must' in the end submit to the authority of induction. And why? Because says Reichenbach, 'he knows' – that is, it is logically provable – that in the quest to ascertain a limiting frequency induction carried sufficiently far will eventually yield something like the right answer if there is one, whereas 'he does not know anything about the oracle and the clairvoyant.' But why *must* the supporters of an oracle or clairvoyant admit that they know nothing of the seer's predictive abilities henceforth merely because they have neither inductive grounds for their trust in the seer nor a deductive argument like Reichenbach's for the conclusion that the seer will eventually come to back any other way of making predictions which is effective? Of course, whoever were to place real *faith* in a seer would by no means admit to 'knowing nothing' of the seer's predictive abilities.[8]

If the foregoing case against inductive pragmatism holds good, there is no need to probe Reichenbach's claim that induction 'is the only method *of which we know* that it represents a method of approximation.'[9] The case for inductive pragmatism fails even if induction really is the only internally coherent forecasting method of which it can be logically proved that, whatever the actual probability (if there is one) of any given sort of occurrence taking place, the results which are yielded by that forecasting method, carried sufficiently far, will arrive eventually at an approximation of this actual probability.

---

8 To be sure, the word 'faith' is sometimes used, even by its champions, in contrast to 'knowledge.' But even believers reposing 'faith' in a seer's predictive abilities feel assured that their confidence does have a reliable foundation, and that is what matters for present purposes.

9 Reichenbach, *The Theory of Probability*, 477.

11 Nihilism, Scepticism, and Decisionism

... observing that all this nature is in motion, and thinking that nothing is true of that which changes, they came to the belief that nothing indeed may be truly said of that which changes altogether and in every way ... Cratylus ... finally thought that nothing should be spoken but only moved his finger ...

Aristotle[1]

The sceptic doth neither affirm, neither deny any position; but doubteth of it, and opposeth his reasons against that which is affirmed or denied, to justify his not consenting.

Sir Walter Raleigh, 'The Sceptic'[2]

decisionism *n*. the view that in a given area ... there are no ultimate object- ive grounds for reaching a decision.

The Blackwell *Dictionary of Philosophy*[3]

If Cratylus actually held what Aristotle says he did, he denied the truth of anything whatever that would assume the world's continuing on as in the past. A partial inductive nihilist, on the other hand, such as the

---

1 *Metaphysics*, Book IV, chapter 5, 1010a7-13, trans. Hippocrates G. Apostle (Blooming-ton, 1966), 66–7.
2 *The Works of Sir Walter Ralegh, Kt.*, vol. 8 (Oxford, 1829), 548.
3 Thomas Mautner, ed., *A Dictionary of Philosophy* (Cambridge, MA, 1996), 93.

sort of fideist fundamentalist discussed in chapter 8, would only assert the falsity of *some* inductively supported statements. It is noteworthy that almost all actual fundamentalists really maintain, rather, that the weight of the inductive evidence does in fact tell in favour of their claim that everything the Bible states is literally true. Indeed, even avowed fideists and irrationalists usually turn out to be basing their understanding of themselves as 'going beyond reason' upon a rather narrow conception of what 'reason' is. Usually they think (for example) that they have had a profound personal experience of such a character that nothing short of Divine causation could explain it – a straightforwardly *inductive* consideration, as that term is being employed here – though they will freely admit that their evidence falls short when it comes to public communicability, repeatability, et cetera. To be sure, there exist some philosophically trained intellectuals who consciously avoid taking any such line as that, no doubt without the least intentional dishonesty, and still proclaim their dissent from what they admit to be on balance supported by the inductive evidence. *Do* they know their own minds? Perhaps there is enough empirical evidence overall to say of them, as of the professed deniers of the Law of Noncontradiction discussed in chapter 4, that self-deception and imperfect introspection otherwise, as well as unrecognized vagueness in their thinking, together with a certain measure of outright mental confusion, can sufficiently explain why they say what they do without requiring us to infer the existence of any psychological limitation in how inductively disposed they actually are in fact.

These inductive considerations are certainly no refutation of nihilism: but perhaps they do have *ad hominem* force. Perhaps they can prompt pertinent reflections in the reader: reflections sufficient to make clear to one the untenability of even partial inductive nihilism. That which (as a matter of psychological fact) you *cannot* clearheadedly and honestly believe, you do not, if clearheaded and honest, believe. *Ad hominem* argumentation at its most cogent does not try at all to prove something, but it can still succeed in rationally compelling assent to it on the part of whoever before was committed to it only implicitly. Arguably, that does apply to the falsity of even partial inductive nihilism. And it should in the same way apply to inductive scepticism also. As we saw in chapter 2, 'That man is a bachelor, but I have no idea what his marital status is' and 'I believe that nature is uniform, but there is no telling whether it is or not' are both 'self-contradictory' statements, in a relevant sense. So, too, is 'Psychologically, I myself am inductively-disposed when it comes to forecasting the future, but there is no telling whether induction is in reality any good as a way of fore-casting the future.'

To understand that you yourself right now are inductively disposed when it comes to forecasting the future is to hold right now the con-scious belief that induction is a good way of forecasting the future. For what psychological difference could there be between your state of mind in the one case and in the other? We at least are entitled to main-tain this much: the proposition that you consciously believe induction is a good way of forecasting the future entails and is entailed by the proposition that you are aware of being inductively disposed when it comes to foretelling the future.[4]

Satisfied that inductive scepticism is untenable, one still may wonder who, if anybody, has ever embraced this famous philosophical position. David Hume, in particular, never did embrace it, though he did (I would contend) describe arguments for it which he said were un-answerable. However that may be, there are grounds for calling Karl Popper an inductive sceptic.

> My own view is that the various difficulties of inductive logic here sketched
> are insurmountable. So also, I fear, are those inherent in the doctrine, so
> widely current today, that inductive inference, although not 'strictly valid,'
> *can attain some degree of 'reliability' or of 'probability.'*[5]

> Our science is not knowledge (*epistēmē*): it can never claim to have attained
> truth, or even a substitute for it, such as probability.[6]

How paradoxical that Popper built his reputation in philosophy as a champion of science and the scientific mentality.

Something similar might be said of even such a profound philosopher as Rudolf Carnap, whose 'decisionism,' as we may call it, on the subject of induction gives every indication of being consciously modelled on his

---

4   To be sure, all this will not hold good if consciously *believing* something just means,
    for instance, being disposed to voice assent to a declarative sentence expressing it.
    But that must surely be wrong, if only in view of our all-too-real potential for being
    dishonest, not to mention motives like shyness, and so on. My sketchy remarks
    about belief in chapter 3, I seek to amplify as far as non-normative *belief* goes in my
    'Belief,' *American Philosophical Quarterly* 26, no. 3 (July 1989), 231–8. The claims made
    here will stand up if that analysis holds good.
5   Karl Popper, *The Logic of Scientific Discovery* (New York, 1965), 29. Emphases in original.
6   Ibid., 278.

non-cognitivism in meta-ethics.[7] In his view, to endorse an inductive method was not to assert anything true or false, but just to express a (more free or less free) choice in favour of it, one that would find reflection in a readiness to form, modify, retain, and discard particular beliefs in accordance with it, beliefs that could for their part be true or false, but the inductive attitude so taken up would not itself be any such true-or-false belief. To call something 'probable,' Carnap liked to say, (unless the reference were to some sort of thing's statistical frequency) was just such a truthvalueless endorsation of a readiness to bet on it – or else it was a statement, in relation to a certain body of evidence and a certain inductive method, of what odds that method sanctioned offering on it from that evidence – something which Carnap considered would have to follow deductively given that evidence and that inductive method.

In the most common meaning of the word 'probable,' it is impossible to regard a proposition as 'probable' without *believing* it, whether more confidently or less confidently. In just this sense, though, if inductive decisionism is correct, that a proposition is probable isn't something capable of ever being *believed* because it isn't something capable of being true or false. Whoever calls a proposition probable, to any degree, endorses that degree of confidence in it, to be sure. However, the favourable attitude so expressed (honestly or otherwise) cannot be itself a belief, from the point of view of inductive decisionism, given that whatever is *believed* is indeed something which is capable of being true or false. But even the sketchy remarks on *belief* in chapter 3 are sufficient, I think, to make it possible to see that such a favourable attitude to a degree of confidence in a proposition really is a *belief* itself, and that a thing's being probable to a particular degree therefore is something capable of being true or false. A really determined objector might be tempted to reply that, in that case, as there really are no objective probabilities in fact, in the relevant sense, all such beliefs must of necessity be false beliefs. Any objector seriously taking that position, though, would clearly no longer be a decisionist any more, but a sort of nihilist,

---

7   Rudolf Carnap, *The Continuum of Inductive Methods* (Chicago, 1952), 53: '... the question arises as to which of the available methods a man X ought to choose if he wants to determine degrees of confirmation and estimates on the basis of his observational results. This is fundamentally not a theoretical question. A possible answer to a theoretical question is an assertion; as such it can be judged as true or false, and, if it is true, it demands the assent of all. Here, however, the answer consists in a practical decision to be made by X.' And see 'The Philosopher Replies,' in P.A. Schilpp, ed., *The Philosophy of Rudolf Carnap* (La Salle, IL, 1963), 982.

a complete one at that. And what is clearer than the untenability of inductive nihilism?

It is possible, however, to imagine a reader reacting somewhat less than favourably to intellectual bludgeoning like this. That induction is generally reliable, I have argued, is a proposition which must be agreed to by anyone clearheaded and honest who is disposed as we human beings are to rely on it. No one can consciously accept any proposition, I dare say, without regarding such acceptance as not just correct but *justified*, in some relevant sense.[8] However, even so, a belief's being correct and its being justified are not the same thing. That our belief in induction is psychologically grounded in our human nature has often seemed to commentators, indeed, a reason actually for doubting or denying that it is an objectively justified belief. The idea must be that in that case the belief's being true, should it even be true, could only be so through some lucky chance. Even when a belief is true, if what makes it true has nothing to do with what makes it believed, the belief cannot be a *justified* belief, in the pertinent sense.[9]

What is it, then, that makes us believe in induction's reliability? Something innate in our psychology, no doubt. Something deep-seated in the genetic inheritance of our species – and not just our species. How did it get to be genetically embedded in our animal ancestors? No doubt the trait has been perpetuated down through so many generations and bequeathed to us because it has had 'survival value.' And no doubt reliance on induction has had survival value because of induction's actual reliability. So that what makes us hold the belief that induction is reliable does indeed have something to do with what makes the belief true. Its being true is not, then, a matter of chance. To be sure, it is only the past reliability of induction which figures in explaining our existing belief in its reliability for the future. But from its past reliability, its reliability for the future does rationally follow – inductively, of course.

There is no vicious circularity in arguing that our belief in induction's reliability is a case of *justified* belief given the premise that this belief is

---

8   See my 'Justified Belief,' *Dialogue* 34, no. 1 (Winter 1995), 99–111.

9   Why not? Because, when what is responsible for a belief being held has nothing to do with what would make it true, if it were to be true, then such a belief only could be true by chance: it wouldn't be particularly *apt* to be true; but it surely is impossible to hold a belief consciously without regarding it as indeed apt to be true. See my papers 'A Contribution Towards the Development of the Causal Theory of Knowledge,' *Australasian Journal of Philosophy* 50, no. 3 (December 1972), 238–48, and 'Justified Belief,' cited in note 8.

true. And for the *truth* of the belief that induction is reliable no argument is required. Amongst us – the writer and readers of this book – induction's reliability is a point on which (provided only that we are clearheaded and honest) we already are completely agreed.

But what is the significance of this point? What must be true for induction to be reliable? That is the issue which will have to occupy us next.

12 Possibility, Probability, Negation, and Change

... actual scientific research has thus far shown the need to analyse nature in terms of a series of concepts that involve the recognition of the existence of more and more kinds of things; and the development of such new concepts has never yet shown any signs of coming to an end. Up to the present, the various kinds of things existing in nature have, at least as far as investigations in the field of physics are concerned, been found to be organized into levels. Each level enters into the substructure of the higher levels, while, vice versa, its characteristics depend on general conditions in a background determined in part in other levels both higher and lower, and in part in the same level. It is quite possible, of course, that further studies will disclose a still more general pattern of organization of things. In any case, it is clear that the results of scientific research to date strongly support the notion that nature is inexhaustible in the qualities and properties that it can have or develop.

David Bohm [1]

Just what does necessity add to *de facto* universality? Uncontroversially, that holds good necessarily which both holds good in all actual instances, past, present, and future, and would hold good as well in any additional instances if there were to be any. But just what does it mean to say that something *would* hold good if a certain condition were to obtain? In a paper entitled 'The Truth-Conditions of Counterfactual Conditional Sentences,' I argued for an epistemic interpretation, in general, of the statement that if A were to be the case then C would be the case: that is,

---

1 *Causality and Chance in Modern Physics* (London, 1957), 140.

for an interpretation of such a statement as in effect asserting the *infer-ability* of C's being the case from A's being the case in conjunction with background information. Where the background information can include C's being the case (in fact) in all relevant instances of A's being the case, the inference is even deductively valid.[2] (In practice, what an assertion of 'necessity' adds to a recognition of something's being the case in all instances known so far is a fully *confident* claim that it will also be the case in any additional instances there might be.)

Where it is possible to tell that something holds good in absolutely all instances given any empirical evidence whatever, no matter how skimpy, its holding good can then count as an '*a priori*' necessity. For example, whenever something's holding good in absolutely all instances is a logical necessity, it is going to be an *a priori* necessity, likewise.[3]

More contentious than *a priori* necessity, I am sure, will be *a priori* probability. Can it ever be possible to tell that something (logically contingent) is a *good bet* even where no empirical evidence at all is available? It must be possible to do this, if empirical evidence can ever make anything probable. Let 'h' abbreviate an assertion of something which is, in fact, probable, thanks to a body of evidence reported in a sentence abbreviated by 'e.' If 'e' reports *all* the evidence bearing on the probability of what 'h' asserts, then it will have to be possible to tell *a priori* that what 'e' states, if itself sufficiently warranted, will render what 'h' states probable. (In such a case, of course, the evidence 'e' reports will have to include evidence sufficient to show that any other relevant evidence is either unavailable or, if available, unlikely to outweigh the case in favour of what 'h' states.) For, if it were only empirically that it was possible to tell that

---

2   'The Truth-Conditions of Counterfactual Conditional Sentences,' *Mind* 87, no. 345 (January 1978), 1–21. I argue in that paper that Nelson Goodman gave up too soon the sort of general line of approach which I am following in his groundbreaking 1946 'The Problem of Counterfactual Conditionals,' reprinted in Nelson Goodman, *Fact, Fiction and Forecast* (London, 1954), 13–34. A further way in which my paper diverges from the treatment of the question by Goodman and others is the argument advanced there that *any* fact(s), however 'accidental,' can ground counterfactual conditional claims in general, and not just (as Goodman maintains) some 'counteridentical' subclass of counterfactuals. (Since writing 'The Truth-Conditions of Counterfactual Conditional Sentences,' however, it has been shown to me that the formulation given there is faulty in one way. As noted in footnote 3 of chapter 4, the words 'true orange sentence' appearing on the top line of page 18 needs to be amended to 'member of S.')

3   However, an exception must be acknowledged in the case of the sort of indemonstrable logical truths which appendix 1 argues for recognizing.

the fact that e (if itself sufficiently established)[4] made it probable that h, then the statement that e, would be incomplete as far as reporting all the evidence which contributed to making it probable that h was concerned.[5] But it could be possible to tell *a priori* that its being the case that e (if sufficiently established itself) would make it probable that h, only where it was possible to tell *a priori* that it wasn't the case that it was both true that e and false that h. In other words, wherever it were to be probable that h thanks to evidence to the effect that e, it would have to be possible to tell *a priori* that it was probable that e⊃h.[6]

We see thus that *probabilities* are so thoroughly 'evidence-relative' that even the 'absolute' *a priori* probability of anything is just a matter of that value which its probability *would* still have in the event no empirical evidence were available – or, rather, more strictly, in the event none were available apart from (second-order) evidence establishing that no relevant (first-order) empirical evidence was available.[7] The 'availability' in question does mean availability to some individual or group, but the

---

4 Let us, for these purposes, count it as a (degenerate) case of a fact's being 'sufficiently established' that it not require *any* reasoning to back it up in the circumstances obtaining. (To avoid misunderstanding, it should be noted here that there is no intent whatsoever to suggest that all 'evidence' must necessarily be empirical evidence.)

5 It is surely absurd that there should be a set of conceivable observations such that it would be possible to tell only after making them whether or not they were observations of such a sort as to contribute, if made, towards justifying the conclusion that probably h. (Bas C. van Fraassen, who specifically rejects any conception at all of objective probabilities apart from statistical frequencies, is not really denying this point on page 174 of his book *Laws and Symmetry* [Oxford, 1989]. David Lewis, he says, 'asserts: A rational person who envisages the different possible episodes that further experience may bring him will also know [if we abstract from practical limitations] what he will believe in each case, at the end.' Van Fraassen objects, 'What of the person who says: "I can envisage all of these possible episodes, one and only one of which will come to pass – I do not know now exactly what opinions and expectations I will form in response..." – is he not rational?' Of course, it is not necessarily irrational to resist making any prediction now as to how new evidence will affect one's opinions. But, if there are specific [even though not perfectly precise] answers to the question how certain possible pieces of new evidence ought to affect the estimates to be made of the probabilities attaching to different conceivable contingencies, surely those specifics should be no less knowable now than after obtaining the new evidence in question.)

6 See my paper 'A Little-Noticed Feature of *A Priori* Truth,' *The Personalist* 58, no. 2 (April 1977), 131–3.

7 Any empirical evidence *against* the proposition that e⊃h would have to include evidence that e. But, since, by hypothesis, 'e' is a statement of evidence including evidence sufficient to warrant the conclusion that no further (relevant) empirical

'available' evidence need not be limited at all to the evidence currently in their possession. For, on the one hand, we are able at times quite consistently to say that something improbable has manifestly happened, and we can often quite consistently say, on the other hand, that researchers are still seeking out evidence so as to be able to tell how probable something is. What evidence is *available* can depend on how much time and also resources, mental as well as material, are available to track it down, and that can depend in turn upon how *important* it is to answer the question on which the evidence gathered would bear, relative to the importance of whatever competing demands there are on the time and resources of those concerned. How long or hard to search for evidence is a question the answer to which is, of course, always going to depend on the human purposes motivating the search. But it will still be an objective matter what the right answer is, because it will not be dependent on what an inquirer – or anybody – feels or thinks it to be.[8]

We have already in chapter 8 met with the so-called *statistical syllogism*, by which the probability of something's being a certain way is inferred from its membership in a 'reference class' most of whose members are that way. No one will endorse such an inference without qualification when the membership of that reference class isn't all the relevant empirical evidence available. But suppose it is. Suppose the only available empirical evidence about something is its membership in a class, most of whose members have a certain characteristic, either intrinsic or relational. Is it in order, then, to infer that probably it, too, will have that characteristic – is its possession of that characteristic a *good bet* under those conditions? How could it fail to be? On the other hand, though, what logical contradiction is there in *denying* that, other things being equal, for something to share a characteristic possessed by the majority of members in a class to which it belongs is a good bet? Admittedly, if this principle of inductive method is an example of a synthetic *a priori* truth, it is not a very impressive example. Nonetheless, the principle seems an indispensable one, and we shall be returning to it. If information is available to the effect that something is an *a*, and

---

evidence is available, if such evidence were to be available, that would count *against* 'e' and hence *in favour* of 'e⊃h.'

8   See my 'Three Epistemic Senses of *Probability*,' *Philosophical Studies* 101, no. 1 (October 2000), 73, note 2. The three senses of 'probability' referred to in the title of that paper are a (long-run) frequency sense, a 'credibility' sense (explained in terms of advisable betting odds), and a sense combining both frequency and credibility considerations (think of bets placed on alternative shorter-run frequencies).

that *a*s are mostly *b*s and that no further relevant information is available,[9] then the something in question is for its part likely to be a *b*. And, if information is available to the effect that something is an *a*, that exactly half of all *a*s are *b*s, and that no further information is available, then the something in question isn't any likelier to be a *b* than not to be one. In general, if information is available to the effect that something is an *a*, that exactly the same proportion of *a*s are *b*s as are *c*s, and that no further relevant information is available, then the something in question is equally likely to be a *b* and to be a *c*.

I use the term 'something' here, of course, so as to cover – well, *everything*. The word 'event' though, I wish to employ in a narrower sense, that of a 'type-event,' involving change from one specific condition to another, describable wholly in purely qualitative terms.[10] In this sense, a single *event* can occur any number of times over, and two or more different *events* can occur together at the same place and time. An event in this sense can be either cyclical or noncyclical. In a *cyclical* event, the change brought about in the first phase of its occurrence is later reversed, so that the condition which initially was changed returns, and at the end of the event's occurrence, conditions are the same as at the beginning in whatever respects it was in which the event's occurrence was the occurrence of a change.

Any (specific) non-cyclical event is *a priori* improbable given a long enough future. The reason for this is that before any event can begin to occur again at the spot where it last occurred, or at least where its last occurrence ended, there must be a reverse change restoring the initial

---

9 Where information bearing upon something's probability is available to the effect that p, and the proposition that q follows *a priori* from the proposition that p, need we count the proposition that q as providing 'further information,' in the relevant sense, whenever the proposition that p&q 'says more' than the proposition that q does? No, we need not, for present purposes, provided the proposition that q has no bearing, distinct from that of the proposition that p, upon the probability which is in question. (This last proviso is meant to avoid the kind of problem posed by Bertrand's Paradox, discussed in chapter 8.)

10 That is, terms with no 'indexical' or 'token-reflexive' element in their meaning, phraseology free, therefore, of any names, first- and second-person personal pronouns, demonstratives, and expressions of all sorts which (correctly or otherwise) spatiotemporally locate whatever they apply to *absolutely*, and so on. See my 'What are "Purely Qualitative" Terms?' *American Philosophical Quarterly* 23, no. 1 (January 1986), 71–81.

condition which its occurrence had altered.[11] Where change from F to G counts as one event, any change from G back to F will be a case of the nonoccurrence of that event. But the F-to-G event can't recur until a G-to-F event has first taken place. So it is by just one occurrence at most that F-to-G occurrences can outnumber G-to-F occurrences in any sequence of occurrences so generated; and even there the frequency of F-to-G occurrences would have to converge to equality with the frequency of G-to-F occurrences as the sequence were extended without limit. Hence, in such a sequence (sufficiently extended), the frequency of F-to-G occurrences couldn't possibly exceed 50 per cent at the most. Thus the *a priori* probability of F-to-G change occurring on any single occasion couldn't in any case exceed 50 per cent. But, in addition to change from F to G and change from G to F, there are also all the possibilities for an interval of no change at all in the relevant respect(s): for example, the possibility of F persisting throughout the interval or the possibility of G or some other condition persisting instead. It will hardly strike anyone as outlandish to assert that all these comparatively static alternatives together must jointly have a finite (i.e., more-than-infinitesimal) *a priori* probability value, even if not a particular definite value, and in any case this conclusion will emerge from the argument of chapters 13 to 16. The consequence is then that, given a long enough future, the occurrence of any (specific) noncyclical event on any single occasion will be something improbable *a priori*.

And the same thing holds good of any (specific) cyclical events as well. For, in place of counterposing to the possibility of a change from F to G the possibility of a change instead from G to F and the additional possibility of there being no change in the relevant respect(s) during the time interval in question, we can here counterpose to the possibility of an F-G-F change the possibility instead of a G-F-G change and the additional possibility also of no relevant change occurring through that interval of time.

---

11 Descartes and others have claimed that some events which occur do not occur at any (precise) spot or series of spots at all. However, rather than a complete jumble of all the events of this sort which occur at any time, Descartes, at least, asserted the existence of a plurality of distinct beings for these occurrences severally to befall. In any case, unless the spatially unlocated occurrences of events which take place at any one time are all occurrences within a single and undivided existent, there must be something analogous to or connected with the spatial location of bodies to distinguish different series of occurrences from one another. At that rate, what the present text asserts will still stand, *mutatis mutandis*, even if not all events that occur do always occur in space.

It is necessary to notice what the preceding considerations do not establish. They do not establish that an interval of change in any particular respect is ever less probable *a priori* than a static interval. So it has not been established, given some initial condition as existing, that this condition is ever *a priori* likelier to persist than to alter. As far as the preceding considerations go, it is merely that in the absence of available evidence as to what the initial condition is on any single occasion, the occurrence of any *specific* change thereupon will be less likely *a priori* than its nonoccurrence. This is a highly limited conclusion.

Nor does the *a priori* improbability of any event, in this sense, give rise to the possibility of drawing any distinction in principle between 'positive' and 'negative' contingencies ontologically: not, at any rate, as far as the *a priori* probability of any 'negative' contingency being greater than that of its 'positive' logical alternative is concerned. As we saw, discussing the 'Principle of Indifference' in chapter 8, the pie of logical possibility can be sliced in any number of different ways. Is something's being the case 'positive' and its not being the case 'negative'? But the former alternative, for its part, is just the failure of the latter to be realized. Each is the logical alternative of the other, and there is no *a priori* basis, in general, for treating one as 'positive' and the other as 'negative.' *In our environment*, non-plants do indeed vastly outnumber plants, for example: and that empirical fact makes it expedient to use a linguistically positive expression for plants and a linguistically negative expression for everything else. But the non-existence of any plant somewhere just is the existence of one or more non-plants there. (If an absolute vacuum can be located somewhere, count that as another sort of 'existent' there.)[12] Even in the limited case of *events*, as that term is being employed here, there is no basis in any of this for considering the *a priori* probability of an event's non-occurrence ever to be more than finitely many times greater than the *a priori* probability of its occurrence. So far, however, discussion has been confined to possibilities of limited specificity. Insofar as it is possible (and why not?) to speak also about possibilities of unlimitedly detailed specificity, the case will arguably be different when it comes to them. The realization of any one of *these* possibilities anywhere would logically necessitate the occurrence there of anything and everything which was logically compatible at all with the occurrence there of

---

12 But see, contrariwise, my 'Why Is There Something Rather than Nothing?' *Philosophy and Phenomenological Research* 40, no. 2 (December 1979), 265–71, which argues against even the logical possibility of a bounded vacuum.

that possibility's realization. Would the *a priori* probability of that possibility's non-realization be only finitely many times greater than the *a priori* probability of its realization? In chapter 13 we will find a reason to answer that question in the negative.

The presumption is that what exists contingently has at least the logical potentiality for unlimited complexity. The quotation that opens this chapter maintains that this potentiality actually is realized in nature. Chapter 16 will advance an *a priori* case for that, to supplement the empirical grounds cited by the quotation's author. The argument here, however, will limit itself just to the logical potentiality claim.

Chapter 8 argued for the logical independence from each other of the conditions occurring at different times. Mustn't the same thing hold for the conditions obtaining simultaneously at different places? Consider any region of space[13] as containing an infinite series of concentric 'shells' with the thickness of each shell at any point being equal to, say, one-third of the distance between the shell's outer boundary at that point and some centre common to all the shells in the entire region, the distance being measured along a path lying wholly within that outer boundary. This will divide the region up into infinitely many subregions, with the conditions in each such subregion logically independent of the conditions in the others. Not that this shows that there may not be some finite set of finitely complex descriptions which together completely describe conditions in the entire larger region. But it does show that, even if so, there would have to be also some infinite set of logically independent descriptions to whose conjunction the conjunction of the first set would be logically equivalent – or, at least, there would have to be an endless series of ever longer conjunctions of logically independent descriptions such that each member of this series of conjunctions was logically equivalent to the conjunction of that first set of descriptions.

---

13 I mean here a continuous region with convex boundaries as approached from the outside, and with no internal 'holes': a region such that the shortest route between any two spots within it lies entirely within it. Any differently shaped region will of course be subdivisible without remainder into regions like this, or else expandable into a region like this.

13 Causality and Impermanence

... we may believe that whenever a thing of precisely the same kind is placed in precisely the same circumstances as another, it will behave in precisely the same way; nor is more required by the principle of the Uniformity of Nature; and yet we may doubt whether such precise repetition ever occurs.

H.W.B. Joseph[1]

Consider a knife slicing through a potato. Why are we apter to think of the knife, not the potato, as 'causative' of the result which ensues? After all, *each* of them, given the other, is both necessary and sufficient in the circumstances for the production of that result. Of course, we are apt to think of the knife as 'active' and the potato as 'passive' here. For, anyway, what contribution does the potato make to the end result beyond just being there at the required time? Whereas the knife, on the other hand, contributes by virtue of its own process of *change* – that is, its change of place – which has begun prior to any contact with the potato. Moreover, the interaction that takes place certainly does produce a drastic and permanent alteration in the potato, though not in the knife. But so what?

The 'active'/'passive' contrast has, however, long been treated as deeply meaningful in the thinking of our culture – and not just in its book-learning. 'Active' and 'passive' have long been associated, for example, with *male* and *female* in people's thinking. For its part, the Western philosophical tradition has got into considerable trouble before now on

---

1 *An Introduction to Logic* (Oxford, 1906), 372.

account of this. We, at any rate, are able to see all this now as problematic, but even a genius like Aristotle was sufficiently smug about it to think, for example, that animals inherited their organic design entirely from their male parents, while 'the female is as it were a male deformed.'[2]

In spite of all that, might we not be justified still, perhaps, in trying to salvage at least one thought from Aristotle's concept of an 'efficient' cause, which was, in his conception, what actually *moved* matters along towards the result, by contrast with a passive 'material' cause, which, in his conception, was that which whatever happened, happened *to*: might we not be justified in retaining at least the thought that to cause a process of change in anything the actual occurrence of some prior change is necessary, in addition to (comparatively) unchanging background conditions?

Thomas Aquinas, who specifically denied that whatever acted as the (efficient) cause of anything necessarily had to be prior to it in time, cited the example of *illumination* to support his point.[3] We, of course, consider that the lighting-up of a spot at any distance from a source of light does take time. But why did Aquinas, who thought it didn't, still consider fire as the cause in this example and lighting up the spot as effect, rather than vice versa? Mustn't it have been something like *this*? – Fire and light do indeed come together, but to produce fire-and-light what is required is to do something first at that location where the fire is going to be,[4] and to remove any obstruction in the space between that location and the spot which is to be lit-up. If this is right, it illustrates the

---

2 *On the Generation of Animals*, Book II, chapter 3, 737a26–27 (*Aristotle's De Partibus Animalium I and De Generatione Animalium I, with passages from II.1–3*), translated by D.M. Balme (Oxford, 1972), 65. Later in the same work, Aristotle is led by this mode of thinking to write, for example, '... for the most part males take after their father – and females after their mother,' Book IV, chapter 3, 768a24, Aristotle, *On the Generation of Animals*, with an English translation by A.L. Peck (Cambridge, MA, 1963), 407. G.E.R. Lloyd, *Science, Folklore and Ideology* (Cambridge, 1983), 94–105, gives the details of how Aristotle's preconceived idea of male superiority led him astray in comparative zoology.

3 Thomas Aquinas, *De Aeternitate Mundi*, 4, and *Summa Theologiae*, Part I, Question XLVI, Article 2, Reply to Objection 1. In St Thomas Aquinas, Siger of Brabant, St Bonaventure, *On the Eternity of the World*, trans. from the Latin by Cyril Vollert, Lottie H. Kendzierski, and Paul M. Byrne (Milwaukee, 1964), 21, 66.

4 Compare the way an increase, for instance, in infant mortality is said to 'cause' a rise in the death rate, and not vice versa. (Precisely because these two things do occur simultaneously in the sort of case envisaged, this is not going to count as an example of *causation* in the sense defined here.)

power of the conception that causality can operate upon locations at any distance away only via operating at nearer ones.

As in chapter 12, the concept of an 'event' employed here is the concept of a *type* of change, capable of occurring at different times and places, and capable of occurring together with another, different event taking place at the same time and place. And the terms 'condition' and 'circumstance' are being employed here, synonymously with each other, in a type sense also.[5] Chapter 12 advanced the case for the logical independence of the various occurrences taking place at different locations in space just as at different times. Accordingly, nothing will count as an 'event,' a 'condition,' or a 'circumstance,' in the usage here employed, unless it is fully specifiable in phraseology of such a sort that any events and other conditions at different times and places which are each fully describable in such phraseology will all have to be logically independent of one another.

I don't know who first formulated the idea of a 'cause' of anything as being a nonredundant member of a set of jointly sufficient preconditions for it.[6] Consistently with the definition of 'necessity' in chapter 12, let us say that a *sufficient* precondition of anything is something which wouldn't fail to be followed by it. And a *nonredundant* member of a set of jointly sufficient preconditions for something will be a condition in the absence of which those other preconditions *are not* jointly sufficient for that sequel. Thus, for example, several different combinations of conditions are alternatively sufficient to produce a lighting-up effect. In at least one such set the use of a match is nonredundant because all the other members of that set of conditions are jointly still insufficient for the production of the lighting-up result as long as they are not combined with the use of a match.

Do all the occurrences of events that are causes or effects of other events' occurrences take place at locations in space? At any rate, the statement that they all do does not appear to be an analytic proposition. Had we been able to consider it analytic, the definition of 'cause' for present purposes would be easier to formulate. Where an I is the

---

5 That is to say, any 'condition' or 'circumstance,' in the present sense, will be specifiable in a phrase couched in purely qualitative terms exclusively. (See above, chapter 12, footnote 10.)

6 See, for instance, Michael Scriven, 'Causes, Connections and Conditions in History,' in *Philosophical Analysis and History*, ed. William H. Dray (New York, 1966), 238–64; and J.L. Mackie, *The Cement of the Universe* (Oxford, 1974).

direction-and-length of some (type of) path through space and time, type-event E could be said under conditions C to 'cause' type-event F if and only if, for some direction-and-length-of-path I, (1) whenever E occurs under conditions C there is a path through space and time of direction-and-length I with that occurrence of E at its starting-point and with an occurrence of F at the end of it, and (2), whenever F occurs at the end of a path through space and time of direction-and-length I with conditions C occurring at the path's starting-point, E occurs at that starting-point also. And token event-occurrence e could be said to 'cause' token event-occurrence f if and only if, for some E, some F, some C and some I, e has taken place, is taking place, or will take place under conditions C followed by f after an interval of direction-and-length I such that, under C, E causes F to ensue at the end of an interval of direction-and-length I, and e and f respectively are occurrences of E and F.

With its heavy cultural overlay (at the very least), the concept of *causation* we have is manifestly pluriform; and any definition of 'cause' likely to be useful for philosophical purposes is going to have to incorporate certain elements of the existing concept, therefore, at the expense of others. But causation at a spatial (or temporal) distance and causal transactions involving occurrences of events that are unlocated spatially have both been heavily discussed in the literature, so that to attempt at this stage to rule them out by mere definitional fiat does look objectionable, even if they are due to be expressly ruled out *a priori* later on. Regarding the merits of the latter move (in chapter 17) the reader, of course, will be the eventual judge.

Meanwhile, we can say for now that, if and only if two events, E and F, are so related that, for some length of time T and some combination of circumstances C,

(a) all sufficiently long sequences of event-occurrences containing occurrences of E contain occurrences also of F after a time-interval of length T and at the same spatial distance (if any) in the same direction away from E's occurrence – where the circumstances C obtain at the time and place (if any) of the occurrence of E and at the very same distance (if any) and in the same direction away from the place identified in the preceding as the place for F's occurrence (provided that F does occur at a place) –

and (b) all sufficiently long sequences of event-occurrences containing
         F contain also E at a time-interval of length T prior to F's
         occurrence and at the very same spatial distance (if any) away
         from it which is referred to in (a) as separating the occurrences
         of E and F, but in the reverse direction – where an occurrence
         of the circumstances C by a time-interval of length T precedes
         the occurrence of F and takes place at the very same spatial
         distance (if any) and in the same direction away from it which
         is referred to in (a) as separating the place (if any) where F
         occurs from the place (if any) where C occur –

then, in circumstances C, E is a *cause* of F. (The phrase 'sufficiently long'
in (a) means long enough for at least a time-interval of length T after the
occurrence of E; in (b) 'sufficiently long' means long enough to go on
for at least a time-interval of length T before the occurrence of F.)

In any of the sequences of occurrences mentioned in (a) and (b), the occurrence of E may be called a 'cause' of the occurrence of F. A 'cause' of an
event on any particular occasion means a cause of its occurrence then.

But what about 'overdetermination'? What about the sort of case in
which the occurrence of an event X is causally producible, in the circumstances obtaining, either by a prior occurrence of event Y or by a
prior occurrence of event Z a certain length of time earlier, but in fact X
occurs preceded by the occurrence, that much earlier, of Y and Z both?
For our purposes we can treat X's occurrence as *caused* on that occasion
by the earlier occurrence of the event Y-or-Z. According to Special
Relativity theory, the length of time as well as the spatial distance separating two occurrences can vary from one 'inertial frame' to another.
And it is even possible to *imagine* a physics according to which what
occurred earlier than something from one time-standpoint occurred
later than it from another time-standpoint. At that rate, what was 'cause'
and what was 'caused' would vary from one time-standpoint to another. But this would not stand in the way of the objective specification
for each such standpoint, just as for each relativistic 'frame,' of just
which occurrences are causes of which, and by just what intervals of
time and space they are separated.

Here now is a two-point formulation, for our purposes, of the philosophical thesis of determinism.

I. No event ever occurs uncaused, and no event ever occurs
    without any effect (Principle of Universal Causation).

II. Between the occurrence of any event and the occurrence of any
of its causes there is a continuous path in space and time such
that in any interval on that path there is located an occurrence
which is caused by the latter and is a cause of the former
(Principle of Contiguity).

If determinism is true, (1) the occurrence of events will continue on in
the future forever and has been going on now for longer than any finite
length of time, and (2) the occurrence of any event takes place somewhere in space. These two claims need to be defended.

In the first place, the finitude of time either forwards or backwards
from the present, if it *were* possible given determinism, would require a
cause-and-effect series of occurrences converging to a temporal limit in
the future or in the past, such that, although there was no last occurrence
or first occurrence, as all occurrences had both successors and predeces-
sors, nevertheless nothing occurred after a certain time, or nothing occurred before a certain time. But what about the end of all change, or the
beginning of it? Why wouldn't that qualify itself as the occurrence of a
change – an 'event' – and, therefore, given determinism, require both
prior causes and subsequent effects? Or is an absolute beginning of
change not to count as itself the occurrence of any change on account of
not being preceded by any temporally prior condition which it alters?
Which way of construing things is most in keeping with the spirit of
determinism? It is surely best to interpret Universal Causation as applying to 'events' in the more inclusive sense of that word. Surely any sudden lurching into action, or cessation, of all process whatsoever, without
any cause or without any effect, is quite contrary to what Universal
Causation means. And consider the following unexpected consequence.

Suppose there were going to be events occurring at any time prior to
midnight on A.D. 31 December 3000 but no occurrences thereafter. In
that case, the thirty-first century A.D. would begin but would only last
for one year, the year 3000. In fact, that year and that century would
turn out to be the same period of time. Having to admit the possibility
of something like this would be the price of accepting the applicability
of universal causation only to 'events' in the less inclusive sense of the
term. But whether Universal Causation should be accepted in any form
at all still remains to be considered, of course.

In conjunction with Universal Causation, the Contiguity Principle certainly does rule out any spatially unlocated occurrence of an event, because there could hardly be a path through space and time from or to that
occurrence unless that occurrence had some location in space as well as

time. However, it is possible to imagine an argument against construing determinism this way on account of modalities. Suppose that at noon on Monday there is a possibility of rain in Toronto on Wednesday, but that by Tuesday this possibility has ceased. A change has surely occurred between Monday and Tuesday. Is this an example of an event occurring without occurring anywhere in particular? On the other hand, few will accept that a possibility of this sort can ever come into existence or cease to exist without a contemporaneous change in any *actuality* – where an 'actuality' means something for the realization of which possibilities alone are (logically) insufficient. For our purposes, we can *identify* the coming-into-existence or the cessation of any such possibility of this sort with whatever contemporaneous change in actualities is involved. Something similar can be said as well about the coming-into-existence and cessation of conditional impossibilities and necessities. When an electromagnet is switched on, it is impossible for light enough pieces of metal to be brought into its vicinity without beginning to move towards it, if unimpeded. And, when the electromagnet is switched off, that is no longer the case. However, to identify the coming-into-being and cessation of impossibilities and necessities of this transient sort with contemporaneous changes in *actualities*, we must for these purposes define 'actualities' in a more general way, as realities fully specifiable in nonmodal terms which do not demand semantical unpacking even in part in subjunctive conditional terms.[7]

We see, then, what determinism entails. According to it, the occurrence of any event whatever takes place somewhere in space and is

---

7 It is worth noting that, when a given turn of phrase is said to 'demand semantical unpacking' in terms of a certain sort (at any rate, in the sense in which I am using the phrase), there is not necessarily any suggestion at all of a philosophical doctrine of 'logical priority' or translinguistic semantical 'primitiveness.' In learning how to use the English subjunctive conditional or anything else with the same semantic force there is something *common* which must be grasped in each case – unless it is understood already – before the learners can be credited with having succeeded in their learning-task. (Saying this, of course, is only saying that to have the same semantical force it is necessary to have *something* in common, to be to some extent similar.) There is, then, something of which one must have a grasp in order to know how to use either the English subjunctive conditional or anything else with the same semantical force. Anyone lacking such a grasp would, as a result, be unable to understand the meaning of certain specific turns of phrase 'which demand semantical unpacking at least in part in subjunctive conditional terms' in the sense intended here.

The preceding paragraph is a slightly amended reproduction of the closing parenthesis on page 21 of my paper 'The Truth-Conditions of Counterfactual Conditional Sentences,' *Mind* 87, no. 345 (January 1978), 1–21.

preceded by a continuous series of earlier occurrences of events stretching back in time without limit, such that any earlier occurrence in this series is sufficient, under the conditions in which it takes place, for the ensuing of that event, while *its* occurrence, in turn, in the conditions under which *it* takes place, is sufficient for the ensuing of any event that occurs in a continuous series of occurrences of events stretching forward in time without limit. Thus, given determinism, the occurrence of any event which ever takes place is determined by the conditions occurring at any earlier time. Of course, any condition which ever obtains either lasts forever or else commences or ceases to obtain at some time or times. In the former case, given determinism, the condition's prevalence at any time would be uniquely determined by its prevalence at any earlier time. In the latter case, the condition's commencement or cessation, given determinism, would be an *event*, the occurrence of which was determined by conditions earlier on, so that this condition's prevalence for as long as it did ever prevail would be determined by those earlier conditions also. Such are the implications of determinism, as here formulated.

* * *

That nothing lasts forever is certainly not a new idea. And there is nothing novel about pushing the thesis of universal impermanence to the point of denying that any genuine possibility's non-realization ever lasts forever either. Arthur Lovejoy referred scornfully to such a conception back in 1933 as 'the Principle of Plenitude,'[8] but in fact, in one form or other, it found its way into the philosophies of such sober thinkers as Aristotle,[9] Spinoza,[10] and Carnap.[11]

---

8 Arthur O. Lovejoy, *The Great Chain of Being* (Cambridge, MA, 1936). The book is an expansion of his 1933 William James Lectures delivered at Harvard University.

9 For example, *De Caelo*, Book I, chapter 12 (281a29–30): 'If there are things capable both of being and of not being, there must be some definite maximum time of their being and not being ...' Aristotle advances what looks like a (fallacious) attempt to prove this proposition at 281a34–b1 and 281b18–25.

10 Benedict Spinoza, *Ethics*, Part I, Proposition 35: 'Whatever we conceive to be in God's power necessarily exists.'

11 Rudolf Carnap, *Logical Foundations of Probability* (Chicago, 1950), and *The Continuum of Inductive Methods* (Chicago, 1952). Summing up the point with unsurprising disapproval, A.J. Ayer writes: '... it is a somewhat startling feature of Carnap's system that the probability that a universal hypothesis holds in a universe with an infinite number of individuals, no matter what the evidence, is always 0. This has the strange consequence that a kind of ontological argument is valid in the system.

Is it incoherent to affirm the transitoriness of absolutely everything except transitoriness itself? We are perhaps on the track of a satisfactory answer to such a charge of incoherence if we reflect that saying no possibility will go unrealized forever doesn't imply that any *impossibilities* will ever come to pass. But what would 'possibilities' and 'impossibilities' be, for these purposes? Surely *logical impossibilities* could not count as 'possibilities' here, on just about any showing. Pairs of pairs of anything would never cease to compose quadruples, whatever the world's flux. And are there, perhaps, some sorts of *change* whose occurrence would be logically impossible even though either the before-state or the after-state would be possible enough in itself? Could space possibly *change* from being three-dimensional to being four-dimensional, for instance? *Perhaps* not. Then, could universal impermanence for its part be another case of something whose holding good ever *entails* its holding good forever? Maybe not, for where's the *logical impossibility* in the cessation eventually of anything contingent prevailing prior to a certain time, but with the prevalence ever after of certain conditions that commence only from then on?

However that may be, the 'conditions' in different spatiotemporal regions, which we have noted in chapter 12 must be logically independent of each other, could not, in any case, include things like two-times-two equalling four, or universal impermanence. The universal impermanence principle will thus be in itself coherent enough, surely. It will

---

If we take any non-contradictory predicate which it contains, whether simple or compound, then, provided that the number of individuals is infinite, we can demonstrate that the universal hypothesis that all of them lack the property for which the predicate stands has the probability 0; and from this it will follow that the existential hypothesis that at least one of them has this property has the probability 1.' A.J. Ayer, *Probability and Evidence* (London, 1972), 38. This is a fair criticism of Carnap to the extent that he without doubt wouldn't have wished actually to affirm universal impermanence. He may have regarded it as a necessary 'legal fiction' embedded implicitly in the scientific method. Even the 'ontological argument' jibe may be legitimate. Carnap's logical positivism, of course, obliged him to consider anything foundational in methodology (as it could not be established empirically without circular reasoning) to be analytic. But what was analytic he considered to be a mere matter of linguistic convention. Regarding (what in his system amounts to) the assignment of *a priori* probability values for different properties' chances of instantiation, Carnap writes: 'The use of these values ... is simply the use of a certain mathematical concept; therefore it is merely a question of convenience. To object to this is like objecting to the use of imaginary numbers in physical laws, as beginners sometimes do and presumably some philosophers did in the beginning.' *The Philosophy of Rudolf Carnap*, ed. P.A. Schilpp (La Salle, IL, 1963), 990–1.

amount to the denial that any sort of spacetime region occupancy does hold good of absolutely every sufficiently extensive space-time region. The phrase 'sufficiently extensive' is essential here because, trivially enough, not every space-time region *could*, for example, contain (phases of) a fully grown elephant, since some will be too small spatially to contain more than a toe of even the smallest possible fully grown elephant.

Universal impermanence *is* a radical thesis, however. For one thing, it entails that there are no 'laws of nature' of the sort to which certain philosophies of science have been attached, but only 'laws' in a decidedly more modest sense, contingent regularities prevailing throughout certain finite regions of space-time. If determinism is true, each such regularity, when and where it does prevail, will be a condition whose prevalence then and there will be determined by prior circumstances, since these events and other conditions must causally explain both the beginning and the end of that prevalence. Given the unlimited duration of the past and the future which determinism entails, universal impermanence allows no room even for any contingent 'frequentist' *probability* – at any rate in the classic sense of a definite limiting value for all time to the frequency of some type of occurrence. That no space-time region of more than a certain extent will *ever* contain instances of anything in greater (or lesser) profusion than some such limiting value is certainly ruled out by universal impermanence. For many, considerations of this sort would have to tell heavily against accepting the universal impermanence principle. Not to mention common sense, which doesn't just deny that any cow will ever jump over the moon, but equally cannot countenance the idea that any bovine-like animal will *ever*, in however distant a future, succeed in jumping over a lunar-like planetary satellite.[12]

On the other hand – more in keeping with common sense – if determinism and the universal impermanence principle should both be true, then no exact recurrence of all the same conditions will ever take place. For, if that did happen, if (token-)conditions were ever exactly alike on two different occasions merely a finite length of time apart, the result would be the same each time: an unvarying cycle running through

---

12 The point of the adjectives 'bovine-like' and 'lunar-like' here is to capture the logical implication of the universal impermanence principle that *any* purely qualitatively expressible descriptions, in however extensive finite detail, to which some cow and the moon now answer, will describe an animal and a planetary satellite over which such an animal will *eventually* jump (as long as the descriptions are insufficient to rule the feat out *a priori*).

exactly the same stages to return eternally to each of them. At that rate, some out of the infinite set of *a priori* possibilities would never occur, since there would not be sufficient time in any such cycle of merely finite duration. Some possible events, indeed, would individually take longer to occur than that entire length of time.

This result lends support to the present chapter's epigraph to the extent that it suggests the innocuous 'vacuity' of the determinist thesis (where 'All Fs are Gs,' for instance, counts as 'vacuously' true whenever there are, in fact, no Fs). If determinism and the universal impermanence principle are both true, and the conditions occurring at two different times are never exactly alike, then every total state of affairs uniquely determines everything occurring earlier no less than it does everything occurring later. For not only do determinism and universal impermanence rule out any exact recurrence of the very same conditions with differing sequels on two different occasions, they equally rule out any exact recurrence of the very same conditions on two different occasions with even slightly differing antecedents. Just as there would not be even slightly differing sequels without at least slightly differing antecedents, so likewise there would not be even slightly differing antecedents without at least slightly differing sequels. No exact recurrences ever take place, and so the total state of affairs at any time uniquely determines the total state of affairs at any other time, earlier or later.

14 Simplicity

... the physicist's ... predilection for the simple law is so strong that he will retain it, even when it does not fit the observations exactly, in spite of the existence of complex laws that do fit them exactly ...

The actual behaviour of physicists in always choosing in practice the simplest law that fits the observed facts therefore corresponds exactly to what would be expected if they regarded the probability of making correct inferences as the chief determining factor in selecting a definite law out of an infinite number that would satisfy the observations, and if they considered the simplest law as having far the greatest prior probability.

Harold Jeffreys[1]

From universal impermanence to a principle of (relative) permanence. As has often been observed, in effect, the essence of the Simplicity Principle is the presumption of (relative) local homogeneity through time and space in any single respect. When it comes to the passage of time anywhere, this is a presumption against the occurrence there of any significant change during that time in any given respect(s).[2] Other things being equal as between two conflicting accounts of the same

---

1 *Scientific Inference* (Cambridge, 1931), 40–1.
2 Cf. Elliott Sober, *Simplicity* (Oxford, 1975), 38: 'A frequently expressed intuition about the role of simplicity in hypothesis choice is that hypotheses that predict a change in the world are less simple than hypotheses that predict no change. An allied intuition is that hypotheses which say that a given class of individuals is uniform and homogeneous are simpler than those which say that the class is nonuniform and heterogeneous. These two intuitions are closely related; change hypotheses express a special, temporal, kind of heterogeneity.'

time period somewhere, the less 'eventful' of the two accounts will be the *simpler* one, in the relevant sense, and hence the likelier one to be true.

It is, of course, type-'events,' in the sense specified in chapter 12, that are in question here. The requirement that any such 'event' involve change specifiable entirely in purely qualitative terms is sufficient to rule out any recourse here to 'ill-believed predicates' of the sort Nelson Goodman has made famous.[3] For instance (to simplify Goodman's own example), consider the predicate 'grue,' applying before midnight on 31 December 2009 to such things and only such things as are green and after that time to such things and only such things as are blue. Plainly, for an object to remain 'grue' from one day to the next it would have to stop being green at midnight on 31 December 2009, just as in order to remain green it would have to stop being 'grue' at that time. Which exemplifies greater permanence, the sceptical objector then triumphantly asks, a thing's remaining *green* or remaining *grue*? The answer must be that to remain 'grue' is to *change*, whereas to remain green isn't. Goodman's objection to the dismissal of a term like 'grue' as not being *purely qualitative* rests on his rejection of the *analytic/synthetic* distinction and the concept of *synonymity*, I have argued, so that for those of us who disagree with him on that score the objection can have no force.[4]

But what about the case of a purely qualitative predicate like 'checker,' brought up in chapter 8? When the letter 'd' designates some particular distance, it will be recalled, describing any section of a path as 'checker' means that such parts of it as are wholly between nd and (nd-d) away from the path's starting-point, for any odd values of n, are red all over, and such parts of it as are wholly between md and (md-d) away from the path's starting-point, for any even values of m, are black all over. Where a stretch of some path of length d has been so far traversed and found to be red – and hence, by definition, also 'checker' – I asserted in chapter 8 that for the path to continue on being *red* for the stretch ahead, it would not have to change colour, but to continue on being *checker*, it would. The point being that, because our colour terms are the *classificatory* expressions they are, it is logically necessary that any two 'red' objects to that extent resemble each other, whereas the same thing does not hold – but sometimes just the reverse – of any two 'checker' objects.

The above has all been for the purpose of spelling out what (relative) permanence, or homogeneity through time, involves: the point is to

3 Nelson Goodman, *Fact, Fiction, and Forecast* (London, 1954), 73–80.

4 D. Goldstick, 'The Meaning of "Grue,"' *Erkenntnis* 31, no. 1 (July 1989), 139–41.

theorize in such a way as, other things being equal, to minimize the postulation of change. But, even excluding all recourse to any predicates like 'grue' and 'checker,' don't we still have a problem here when it comes to comparatively assessing different amounts of change? We're looking here for an *a priori* canon of inductive method. But isn't it only empirically that we can tell that an alteration of colour, say, is *less of a change* than a metamorphosis from caterpillar to moth; or even that warming up from 20° to 21°, say, is *less of a change* than warming up from 21° to 90°? What we need is an *a priori* principle to enable induction to get started. After that, inductive findings can give theoretical grounding to comparative judgments of *similarity*, and hence of relative homogeneity through a stretch of time (i.e., relative changelessness) as well as throughout a given extent of space.

No matter what empirical evidence there is or isn't, won't red have to count as *more similar* to orange than to yellow; and won't a temperature of 20° have to count as *more similar* to a temperature of 22° than to a temperature of 23°? This is because, in an intuitively obvious sense, it is true *a priori* that orange is *intermediate* between red and yellow,[5] and a temperature of 22° is *intermediate* between a temperature of 20° and a temperature of 23°. Barry O'Neill and I sought to explain this concept of *intermediacy* a little further in a joint paper we wrote on (objective) *relative truth*. There logically can be no more continuous, direct way of changing from red to yellow or from 20° to 23°, we maintain in effect, than a way which involves passing through an orange stage or a 22° stage at some time between the beginning and the end of the process.[6] On that basis, a (continuous, direct) change from red to orange or from 20° to 22° is *less* of a change than a (continuous, direct) change from red to yellow, or a (continuous, direct) change from 20° to 23°. The (application of) the Simplicity Principle will therefore treat changes from red to orange or from 20° to 22° as likelier, other things being equal, than changes from red to yellow, or from 20° to 23°.

---

5 The colour terms 'red,' 'orange,' and 'yellow' being the classificatory expressions that they are, their linguistic meanings are such that to call something *orange* is thereby to classify it as intermediate between something just like it otherwise but *red* and something just like it otherwise but *yellow*; that is, it is involved right in what it means to be 'red,' to be 'orange,' and to be 'yellow' that being coloured *red* is being coloured in a way more similar to being coloured *orange* than to being coloured *yellow*, and so on.

6 D. Goldstick and B. O'Neill, '"Truer,"' *Philosophy of Science* 55, no. 4 (December 1988), 589–91.

At this point, though, if not before, a critical reader will be asking what reason there is – at any rate, what *a priori* reason there could be – for methodologically favouring in this manner the postulation of a minimum of change, even subject to the 'other things equal' qualification. And to another critic the suspicion is going to occur that any reason given will have to be less convincing than the need for a simplicity presumption is on its own. About that, readers will have to judge for themselves from the sequel. In any case, though, whoever finds the methodological need for a simplicity presumption convincing *a priori* has already given up the scarcely uninfluential philosophy of empiricism; and that result is already significant in itself.[7]

According to the Principle of Causality introduced in chapter 13, the occurrence of a given change at any time, in the circumstances obtaining at that time, requires the occurrence of a specific (type of) causative event earlier on, what specific (type of) event is causally required being dependent on the conditions prevailing at that earlier time. However, the point was made in chapter 12 that any specific (type of) event is less likely *a priori* to occur than not to occur; and so the occurrence of the causation required, in the circumstances, for the production of the later change in question will be improbable *a priori*, and consequently the nonoccurrence of that change will be probable *a priori*. (It will be recalled

---

7 Contrary to this, in 'How to Tell When Simpler, More Unified, or Less *Ad Hoc* Theories Will Provide More Accurate Predictions,' *British Journal for the Philosophy of Science* 45, no. 1 (March 1994), Malcolm Forster and Elliott Sober cite Hirotugu Akaike's 1974 theorem on the curve-fitting problem and comment: 'In the past, the curve fitting problem has posed a dilemma: Either accept a realist interpretation of science at the price of viewing simplicity as an irreducible and *a prioristic* sign of truth and thereby eschew empiricism, or embrace some form of antirealism. Akaike's solution to the curve fitting problem dismantles the dilemma. It now is possible to be a realist and an empiricist at the same time.' (28). However (using the term 'likelihood' in the technical sense of *the probability of data given the truth of a hypothesis*) Forster and Sober are candid enough to acknowledge: 'There are three kinds of assumption behind the proof of Akaike's Theorem. First, there is a 'uniformity of nature' assumption that says that the true curve, whatever it is, remains the same for both the old and the new data sets considered in the definition of predictive accuracy. The second kind of assumption consists of mathematically formulated conditions that ensure the 'asymptotic normality' of the likelihood function (*viz.* the likelihood viewed as a function of parameter values) ... The final assumption is that the sample size (the amount of data) is large enough to ensure that the likelihood function will approximate its asymptotic properties.' (29). So here are two empiricists helping themselves to *both* a 'uniformity of nature' postulate *and* a kind of 'fair sampling' postulate as far as observational errors go!

from chapter 12 that something's being 'probable *a priori*' means its being probable in the absence of any available empirical evidence against it.)

So much for the presumption in favour of homogeneity over time. Now consider a very fast trip taken through space by any human or other animal, vegetable, or mineral body. If the trip were fast enough, the space around the 'traveller' would form a region in which conditions changed less or more, in the course of the trip, according as the conditions in the larger region travelled through were more or were less homogeneous. (Even if the trip were somewhat slower, the *a priori* presumption against very much change taking place in the course of it would *tend* to support the same conclusion.) So the postulation of heterogeneity in space is to be minimized also.

The presumption against change over time evidently amounts to (more or less) the same thing as 'the supposition that the future will be conformable to the past,' upon which proceed all inductions concerning what is yet to come, according to Hume.[8] And then, just as an unfailing concomitance or sequence observed in the past can on this basis be projected into the future, so can an observed statistical *tendency*. It minimizes the expectation of change to suppose that, if something has been the case a certain proportion of the time in our past experience, the same thing will hold good in our future experience as well. And the presumption in favour of local homogeneity in space in the same way sanctions *sampling*: for, insofar as any spatially dispersed but finite 'population' can be presumed homogeneous, the statistical distribution of characteristics observed in the part of the population which has been sampled can be expected, other things being equal, to prevail over the whole of the region it occupies.

Why is a smooth curve or band on a graph 'simpler' (and hence scientifically a better bet) than a comparatively bumpy one? That is because, no matter what in nature (or in human affairs) the different points on that curve or in that band stand for, there will be more similarity among the facts they represent according as whatever pattern in things the graph depicts is appropriately expressible in a comparatively smooth curve or band. To be sure, it is always possible to change any comparatively smooth curve into a comparatively bumpy one, or vice versa, merely by manipulating the axes or the scales of representation

---

8 David Hume, *Inquiry concerning Human Understanding*, Section IV, Part II, in David Hume, *Enquiries concerning Human Understanding and concerning the Principles of Morals*, ed. L.A. Selby-Bigge, 3rd ed., rev. P.H. Nidditch (Oxford, 1975), 35.

employed. For that very reason the coordinate system chosen for representing the different quantities whose variations are to be plotted will be appropriate in this connection only to the degree that patterns in the world which really are comparatively regular ones get represented by comparatively smooth curves or bands on the resulting graph.

Why does a linear equation count as 'simpler' than a quadratic equation, or, in general, an equation of lower degree and its corresponding curve, by comparison with an equation of higher degree and its corresponding curve, other things being equal? The answer is that, other things being equal, the lower the degree of a continuous polynomial, the simpler it is, because the nth derivative is necessarily going to be constant for any equations of degree n or lower.

The Simplicity Principle is often thought to mandate minimizing the number of 'independent postulates' in developing a scientific theory. On the present showing, this is on the right track, insofar as the more 'independent postulates' a theory requires, the more distinct 'cases' there will be in the fluctuations of the theory's subject matter, should the theory be true, and hence the more heterogeneity there will be there.

The methodological Simplicity Principle with which we are concerned here, is a rational norm governing the choice among conflicting explanatory hypotheses to account for a given body of observed facts. Even the precept 'Entities should not be multiplied beyond necessity' has a place here, to the extent that the non-existence of a given sort of thing in any region will make what does exist there all the more homogeneous.[9] Of course, the precept is often invoked in *prima facie* quite different connections, for example, as a quasi-aesthetic demand regarding the choice among alternative modes of expressing what amounts to the same mathematical information. To minimize the number of 'entities' for which undefined nouns stand is to 'simplify' the notation in a sense: indeed, such notational simplification could prove, in the end, to make theoretical simplification of the sort discussed here psychologically easier ('simpler') to think through.

But there can be no place for notational considerations in the basic canons of inductive method themselves. Given the *analytic/synthetic* distinction, we can insist that the language of science must be in principle immaterial to its actual content. Newton theorized in Latin and

---

9 Cf. Sober, *Simplicity*, 42: '... eliminating an existential hypothesis opens the door for introducing a uniformity hypothesis (i.e., for the denial of the eliminated existential claim).'

Einstein in German. Their different vocabularies may have assisted or hindered their thinking in various ways, but any comparison of their rival theories on the score of simplicity – or even any comparison sufficient just to establish the theories' logical incompatibility – must be carried out independently of all particular modes of linguistic expression. (And if a pair of theories cannot be so compared, in what way could they be *rivals* to each other? What would stop anyone from happily subscribing to both of them?)

In quest of notational simplicity, one might be led to consider that the ascription to something of a single property, expressible by means of a one-place predicate, would at least on that score yield a 'simpler' theory than any alternative not so constructed. But any theory whatsoever is expressible conjunctively as 'Something is such that ...' which does qualify grammatically as a bare property-ascribing formula. (If only properties expressible in purely qualitative terms are to be allowed for these purposes, let an ordered n-tuple be formed of whatever particulars are mentioned in any statement of the theory, and the theory can then be re-expressed as the ascription of a single property of the required sort to that one entity.)

It was a much more full-blooded standard of simplicity than anything relative to a linguistic form of expression that Isaac Newton appealed to in the first two of his four 'Rules of Reasoning in Philosophy' at the beginning of Book III of his *Principia Mathematica*:

Rule I: *We are to admit no more causes of natural things than such as are both true and sufficient to explain their appearances.*
To this purpose the philosophers say that Nature does nothing in vain, and more is vain when less will serve; for Nature is pleased with simplicity, and affects not the pomp of superfluous causes.

Rule II: *Therefore to the same natural effects we must, as far as possible, assign the same causes.*
As to respiration in a man and in a beast; the descent of stones in *Europe* and in *America*; the light of our culinary fire and of the sun; the reflection of light in the earth, and in the planets.[10]

His Protestant appeal to frugality aside, what Newton has in mind here does seem to be much the same as what the present chapter has

---

10 *Sir Isaac Newton's Mathematical Principles of Natural Philosophy and his System of the World*, trans. Andrew Motte and Florian Cajoli, ed. Florian Cajoli (Berkeley, 1966), 398.

been outlining. In methodological discussions nowadays, the simplicity of theories is often treated as a positive feature standing alongside comprehensiveness in scope, considered as a different and distinct positive feature. But in fact, as Newton tells us, these are really not two distinct methodological considerations. Where the choice is between accounting for different sets of facts by separate, unrelated explanations and accounting for them all by a (not overcomplex) single explanation, surely the latter alternative is the clear winner as far as simplicity – comparative homogeneity – goes. As was clearly seen by Newton, the homogeneity presumption is quite indispensable for even the most rudimentary scientific theorizing.

But more sophisticated theorizing can turn on an appeal to simplicity also. One of the most famous examples in the history of science is the choice of Kepler's (and later Newton's) heliocentrism over Ptolemy's geocentrism. To oversimplify somewhat, both theories had things moving about in closed paths in the heavens, but the Ptolemaic theory required more of such movements than the theory of Kepler. Anyone committed to the physical reality of the Ptolemaic model of the heavens was committed to holding that *some* real process or other corresponded to the revolution of the centre of an epicycle about the approximate centre of the universe, but Kepler's model, otherwise just as good, at least, as the Ptolemaic model,[11] was in no need of epicycles, and hence on that count alone was theoretically superior and more deserving of scientific acceptance. To mention just one more example, William Harvey (1578–1657), the discoverer of the circulation of the blood, had to choose between the continuous manufacture and destruction of vast quantities of blood at all the respective extremities of the veins and arteries, or else, alternatively, the passage of blood from the arteries to the veins by a process too minute to be detected by the naked eye. That there was *some* such movement beyond the visible blood vessels was certain, and there was no reason at all to suppose that what was causing the blood to flow part of the way in this direction (namely, the heart's pumping) could not

---

11 Or is this unfair because a circular orbit is *simpler* than an elliptical one, since all arcs of a circle retain a constant curvature? But the actual paths of the heavenly bodies to which Ptolemy attributed epicyclic motion were very far from being circular, according to his theory, and certainly they were far bumpier than Kepler's elliptical orbits. Perhaps, if there had been positive evidence of any actual physical reality corresponding to Ptolemy's 'epicycles,' his theory could have enjoyed a genuine comparative advantage over Kepler's on account of the superior simplicity of circular as compared to elliptical motion.

equally well cause it to flow the whole way around. Harvey was led accordingly to postulate an unobservable movement of blood from the arteries to the veins through either 'an anastomosis of vessels [linking capillaries] or else the porosities of the flesh and solid parts'[12] to complete the circuit of the body's blood. Only later did Harvey's hypothesis, which had already won general acceptance, secure conclusive confirmation through use of the microscope and other means.[13]

Apropos of such examples, it is worth pointing out that at any stage in the history of science when a previously accepted theory is being challenged on the grounds of apparent empirical disconfirmation, it is always open to the theory's defenders to attempt to save the greater part of it by so reformulating what it asserts as to take the new data into account in an either more or less *ad hoc* fashion. Such a process of revision is certainly legitimate, as long as the new theory so formed is still less complex than any available alternative (sufficiently) compatible with the data. But, past that point, such hypothesis-saving is a theoretical sin, and marks those who engage in it as unscientific or, in a more general phrase, irrational.

To cling to some conviction despite any and all empirical evidence, when done in a way that is both irrational and socially abnormal in a high degree, that is the sort of behaviour which can be called *insane*. A feature of many paranoia cases, we are told, is the insistence upon imagining all manner of possible ways in which others are out to get the patient, and placing sinister interpretations on the most ordinary

---

12 Quoted from page 179 of his *Excertatio anatomica de motu cordis et sanguinis animalibus* (page 75 of the English translation: *Movement of the Heart and Blood in Animals, an Anatomical Essay*) in Yehuda Elkana and June Goodfield, 'Harvey and the Problem of the "Capillaries,"' part 1, *Isis* 59, no. 196 (Spring 1968), 67.

13 Like Newton, Harvey too derived *simplicity* teleologically: 'All the works of God and Nature are perfect, therefore there is nothing wanting and nothing redundant, nor anything without a purpose ... Nature does nothing by many things that can be done by fewer ...' (William Harvey, *De Motu Locali Animalium* [1627], trans. Gweneth Whitteridge [Cambridge, 1959], 127.)

For a later example from the history of science, consider Antoine-Laurent Lavoisier's boast in 1783 that on the basis of his 1777 postulation of *oxygen* 'all the phenomena were explained with an astonishing simplicity.' 'But if everything in chemistry is explained in a satisfactory manner without the aid of phlogiston, it is from that alone infinitely probable that this principle does not exist; that it is a hypothetical being, a gratuitous supposition; and, indeed, it is given in the principles of good logic not to multiply beings without necessity.' (*Oeuvres de Lavoisier*, vol. 2 [Paris, 1862], 623.)

occurrences. The patient's beliefs need not be internally contradictory or formally inconsistent with the data they are supposed to explain. But such beliefs *are* irrational and unlikely to be true, inasmuch as they are needlessly complex.

Karl Popper based his career as a philosopher of science on the justifiable insight that hypothesis-saving in defiance of sufficient observational counterevidence is unscientific. Only, he omitted the necessary qualifier 'sufficient,' as used in the preceding sentence. Harold Jeffreys has not been the only one to note that actual researchers – reasonably enough – are prepared to bet on simplicity to the extent of oftentimes discounting ostensible counterevidence – at any rate, up to a point. Up to what point? Up to the point where the hypothesis of 'experimental error' (or misrecollection, fraud, etc.) ceases to be simpler than any alternative hypothesis, I suggest. Short of that point, simplicity does dictate discounting apparent counterevidence. What counts as observed fact here need not include every apparent observation but can take in instead, rather, only the fact *that* such-and-such an observation *appears* to have been made. However, when apparent counterevidence builds up past a certain point, depending on circumstances, continuing to discount it then ceases to be the simpler, saner alternative.

In actual scientific – and everyday – practice, it must be said, the inquirer is often confronted with competing hypotheses which cannot be directly compared with each other on the score of simplicity, for it is only a certain part of each hypothesis belonging to such a competing pair that can be directly compared for simplicity with a part of the other hypothesis. That is to say, the two hypotheses are otherwise impossible to compare for simplicity, but each one entails a subhypothesis, as we can call it, which is comparable to the subhypothesis entailed by the other one. Where each subhypothesis *would not be true* unless the governing hypothesis which entails it were true,[14] that hypothesis which entails the simpler of the two subhypotheses can be judged the simpler one, and hence the more probable of the two overall. (Naturally, what is meant to be included in a 'hypothesis' or 'subhypothesis' here is not confined to what would be asserted in the statement of some candidate for natural law status. Anything in the way of initial conditions, observations, or

---

14 Let me refer the reader to my discussion of the subjunctive conditional construction in my paper 'The Truth-conditions of Counterfactual Conditional Sentences,' *Mind* 87, no. 345 (January 1978), 1–21. (However, the words 'true orange sentence,' appearing on the top line of page 18 of that paper, should be amended to 'member of S.')

whatever else could be pertinent is meant to be included as well in what a potential 'hypothesis' or 'subhypothesis' in the present sense states.) When one hypothesis comes out simpler and hence more probable than another one overall, thanks only to comparable subhypotheses which they each entail, the uncompared remainder of each such hypothesis can unobjectionably be deemed 'equiprobable' to the uncompared remainder of the other hypothesis for these purposes. Accordingly, *equiprobability*, even *a priori*, only needs to enter the picture as, so to speak, an accounting device for dealing with parts of what is asserted by theses which are *unequally* probable *a priori* overall, and so there is no need to seek out some ultimate unit possibilities that would somehow be equiprobable *a priori* in any absolute fashion.

* * *

Where, then, do we stand at this point? What sort of world are we talking about? In chapter 12 we noted that there are unlimitedly many logically possible variations in the conditions obtaining at any one time. As for the total state of affairs obtaining at any time, absolutely specific in every detail, no such state of affairs ever recurs in the course of any finite temporal period, however long, according to the principles of chapter 13. But, according to those same principles, every possible combination of conditions specifiable in a description of only finite complexity *is* going to recur any number of times in different spatial locations at finite, sometimes irregular, temporal intervals. Every concomitant of that combination of conditions which is possible *a priori* and specifiable in a description of only finite complexity will likewise occur together with it any number of times in different spatial locations at finite, sometimes irregular, temporal intervals. And, similarly, the logical alternative to this concomitant condition – its non-realization – will likewise, if such is possible *a priori*, occur in conjunction with that combination of conditions any number of times in different spatial locations at finite, sometimes irregular, temporal intervals. Does this mean that the greater the specificity of any such combination of conditions – the more detail it takes in – the less frequently it will occur in time and space? Not necessarily, in any finite region of space-time; and, even over the whole of space in the long run of time, as we have seen, any specific limiting frequency for the occurrences of anything would run counter to the principles of chapter 13. But the relative frequency of (any given degree of) change in any specific respect, on the one hand, and no change (that great) in that respect, on the other hand, will be a different matter. For on any single occasion the event necessary to produce that much change in that respect, given the principles of chapter 13, will necessarily occur less often than fail to occur, on account of all the possible alternatives to its occurrence – each of which will individually have to come up any number of times in the long run – because these alternatives to its occurrence will include, but will not be confined to, the occurrence of the reverse change in the same respect, and, even if that reverse change had been the sole alternative to its occurrence, the frequency of the event's occurrence could still, not even then, exceed 50 per cent overall.

From this it follows that any condition which ever prevails anywhere will, more often than not, go on prevailing there for a while, and will more often than not, prevail in neighbouring regions of space as well. In this generality, actual observation, on the whole, surely bears such a proposition out. That does constitute stability to a degree. Is it 'cosmos,' or is it 'chaos'? Those are terms favoured by many writers attracted to a Design Argument for deity. They often argue that all life, and certainly successful inductive reasoning, would be impossible without a degree of stability in the world around us, a degree of stability which can consistently be at least imagined not to exist. Should its actual existence be considered surprising, or surprising in the absence of a supernatural Designer? To the argument that it shouldn't be surprising to us, since we wouldn't be around to notice the stability if it didn't exist, the objection is justifiably urged that the lucky survivor of a firing-squad barrage has got sufficient reason to be surprised. One Design Argument thinker has written, in effect, that if we thought it really was just by chance that the universe now exhibits the orderliness we see around us, we would

> have reason to believe ... that its orderliness would shortly be lost: compare how a monkey who has just typed a sonnet is unlikely to maintain his high standard for long, no matter how many sonnets he produces over infinite time. In short we could not trust Induction.[15]

Observing the world around us, we do find some stability and some instability in it. Is the stability greater than we should expect just on general principles? Not if the principles are those of chapter 13. On the whole, the empirical evidence (as a matter of logically contingent fact) does bear the Principle of Simplicity out. It is no detraction from the inductive case for the Principle's correctness that such reasoning is of

---

15 John Leslie, 'Anthropic Principle, World Ensemble, Design,' *American Philosophical Quarterly* 19, no. 2 (April 1982), 149.

necessity circular since, like all inductions, this one too presupposes the Simplicity Principle. This induction must be warranted if any others are, since it presupposes nothing more than they do. All that will follow here, since the Principle of Simplicity must independently be defensible if inductions in general are warranted – and they are – is that assent to the Simplicity Principle stands in no need of any empirical backup to render it warranted. It is warranted *a priori*.

15 How to Reason Inductively

> If, as Mr. Hume confesses, 'none but a fool or a madman' will deny the authority of that principle, he confesses that none but a fool or a madman will deny the just reasonings, which are founded on that principle.
>
> Thomas Brown (1778–1820)[1]

Like speaking one's native tongue, reasoning inductively is something which comes easily. Indeed, induction may be even easier than speech if Hume is right that non-human animals do it too.[2] Perhaps it is better, though, to reserve talk of 'reasoning capacity' only for something more sophisticated than bare conditionability, even if that psychological trait does contain the germ of all our inductive reasoning. And, certainly, even with human beings, to say that it is easy to do something isn't at all to say that it's easy to do it well. To be able to reason inductively at all, however, clearly is not difficult for us humans. But, as with speech, what can indeed be complicated is to spell out just what the competence involves.

David Hume made a point of claiming, of course, that we all 'take for granted' some general proposition(s) about the way the world is in

---

1 *Inquiry into the Relation of Cause and Effect*, 4th ed. (London, 1835), 378.
2 David Hume, *Treatise of Human Nature*, Book I, Part III, section XVI, ed. L.A. Selby-Bigge, 2nd ed., rev. P.H. Nidditch (Oxford, 1978); David Hume, *Inquiry concerning Human Understanding*, section IX, in David Hume, *Enquiries concerning Human Understanding and concerning the Principles of Morals*, ed. L.A. Selby-Bigge, 3rd ed., rev. P.H. Nidditch (Oxford, 1975).

reasoning inductively.[3] As for the specific propositions he mentioned, Hume himself raised the question how rational it was actually to consider them to be true. Nor has there been a lack of philosophers prepared to say straight out that they are not. Meanwhile, other philosophical critics have insisted at any rate that they are not really necessary to render inductive reasoning warranted, and also, or alternatively, insisted – fairly convincingly – that they are not even sufficient. The present chapter is concerned only to continue the argument of chapter 14 for the sufficiency of the *a priori* principles being proposed: determinism and universal impermanence.

When it comes to our processes of conscious reasoning, doubtless the psychological disposition closest to the conditionability we share with other animals is the tendency to presume that the future will be apt to resemble the past; or, in general, to adopt the default supposition of homogeneity in the absence of definite evidence to the contrary. Here is Isaac Newton again, invoking what amounts to the Simplicity Principle in the defence of every well-grounded induction against imaginable counter-hypotheses. The quotation is again from the Rules of Reasoning in Philosophy at the beginning of Book III of his *Principia Mathematica*:

Rule IV: *In experimental philosophy we are to look upon propositions inferred by general induction from phenomena as accurately or very nearly true, notwithstanding any contrary hypotheses that may be imagined, till such time as other phenomena occur, by which they may either be made more accurate, or liable to exceptions.*
This rule we must follow, that the argument of induction may not be evaded by hypotheses.[4]

Without a precaution of this sort, it's obvious that even the most straightforward induction could be blocked frivolously.

However, when we come to think of it, what seems to justify the projection of any regularity into the future is just the consideration that whatever causes accounted for its holding in previously observed cases will be most likely to continue in operation, other things being equal.

---

3 David Hume, *An Abstract of a Treatise of Human Nature* (1740), in Hume, *A Treatise of Human Nature*, 652.

4 *Sir Isaac Newton's Mathematical Principles of Natural Philosophy and His System of the World*, trans. Andrew Motte and Florian Cajoli, ed. Florian Cajoli (Berkeley, 1966), 400.

Explicitly or implicitly, I wish to argue, any acceptable application of the Simplicity Principle is for choosing among alternative hypotheses about causation. What is apt to strike us as most probably just a coincidental pseudo-regularity within our observation, undeserving therefore of inductive projection into the future, is any pattern of occurrences which seem unlikely to be causally connected to one another and to deeper causes by a sufficiently simple intervening mechanism of the sort required by the Principle of Contiguity. Apparently, research chemical engineers get more or less gently derided by other researchers for being altogether too empirical in their thinking: 'Why, they would even correlate sunspots with cracks in the pavement!' At any time, of course, there are bound to be some such accidental correlations observable, but, lacking causal connections, they would never continue on into the future except by chance. Where the empirical evidence for a correlation is strong enough, though, that can compensate for the difficulty of seeing how the correlation could be causally explained, especially where the correlated occurrences are in rough spatial proximity to each other.

Indeed, given the principles of chapter 13, whatever causal process is ever in operation over any stretch of space and time will of necessity be knowable only incompletely. For between any two stages of the process at all separated by space and time, there will either be no known causal mechanism connecting them, or else that mechanism will itself be a process of which the same thing can be said: that is, between any pair of spatiotemporally separated stages of *it* there will either be no known connecting mechanism, or else that mechanism will for its part be a causal process of which again the same thing can be said; and so on. But the capacity of the human intellect doesn't extend to grasping anything of more than finite complexity. And so, there is no possibility of completely getting away from any reliance on 'induction by simple enumeration,' the straightforward generalization of constant conjunctions known from observation.

Indeed, even in natural science, 'enumerative' inductive generalization can in fact take us a considerable distance in conjunction, at any rate, with a canon of simplicity. What the simplicity criterion is for, on the account given here, is choosing among competing causal hypotheses. And what makes them competitors is the fact, due to the Principle of Contiguity, that in light of everything else which is known or appears to be known, these hypotheses concretely involve alternative stories in conflict with one another about the actual occupancy of particular regions of space-time. In any event, once reflection has narrowed down the possibly relevant factors in the causation of whatever is under investigation to an experimentally or conceptually manageable range, something like Mill's inductive methods and hypothetico-deductive testing can then be used to find out which factors really are causally relevant.

The task of distinguishing the causally relevant factors in situations which arise from those factors, by comparison, that do not have any major effects in the respects which count in the given context – this task is often one of identifying the different *natural kinds* of phenomena that are pertinent to the attaining of a rational understanding of processes at work in those situations. Over quite extensive stretches of time and space, at any rate, the diversity which phenomena manifest is not unlimited, but rather the relational and nonrelational features of things noticeably cluster in such a way that, in the presence of certain characteristics, certain other characteristics are or are not (normally) found.[5] Once natural kinds are identified, their features will then provide a new criterion for comparatively assessing degrees of similarity and dissimilarity in order to apply the relative homogeneity presumption of the Simplicity Principle. The dissimilarity between different chemical substances (elements or compounds) can be taken to exceed the dissimilarity between the liquid state and the solid state of a single substance, for instance. And the difference between a caterpillar and a moth of the same species can be given less weight than the difference between two moths with sufficiently differing DNA.[6] Empirically substantiated natural-kind

---

5   This observation reminds us of Keynes's proposed 'assumption that the objects in the field, over which our generalizations extend, do not have an infinite number of independent qualities; that, in other words, their characteristics, however numerous, cohere together in groups of invariable connection, which are finite in number.' See John Maynard Keynes, *A Treatise on Probability* (London, 1921), 256. The difference, however, is that the statement made in the present text – expressing a proposition which is an inductive *conclusion* as well as a working *assumption* for the conduct of further inductive inquiry – in no way states that the independently varying characteristics of things, even within a given restricted range of cases and instances, are going to be only finitely numerous; it just says that their variability is limited in such a manner that many combinations of characteristics possible *a priori* will not occur in fact.

6   'What matters ... for Aristotle, is not animal species' differences as such ... but rather those differences which point to their causal relations with one another ... one must isolate that attribute or set of attributes which make the thing the thing it is; and these attributes will be causal of the other features of the animal in question.' R.J. Hankinson on Aristotle's Philosophy of Science in Jonathan Barnes, ed., *The Cambridge Companion to Aristotle* (Cambridge, 1995), 124–5, 126.

information accordingly functions, so to speak, as a *relative 'a priori'* basis for new empirical inquiries. And thus (fallibly and corrigibly) the inductive process goes on.

The empirical *basis* of the process still remains the observation of positive instances (and the non-observation of negative instances) of whatever generalization is in question. The wider the variety of circumstances in which it has been observed to hold good, the likelier it will be on a subsequent occasion to be borne out then also, because the greater the probability will be that the variation from occasion to occasion has no relevant effect on the facts with which the generalization is concerned under the conditions prevailing throughout. While any particular condition(s) prevailing earlier can be presumed to go on prevailing in the absence of evidence to the contrary, no two occasions will ever be exactly alike, according to the principles of chapter 13, and so some variation in conditions from one occasion to another, even if it is unknown what it is, can always be presumed, and there will always be a finite (non-infinitesimal) probability of some variation in any one respect in the relevant vicinity. That is why even the sheer number of observed instances in which a generalization has been borne out carries some weight as evidence supporting it, provided that no instances have been definitely observed which are contrary to it.

The support which is lent to a generalization by any fixed body of empirical evidence will be stronger, of course, the narrower and more modest the scope of the generalization thus supported; and the broader any such generalization's scope is, by the same token, the weaker the support that fixed body of evidence will lend to it. For the wider the range of cases and instances to which a generalization is to apply, the more chance there is that the variations in conditions as among the different cases and instances will make a difference causally in the facts relevant to the generalization's holding good or not. Again and again in the history of science, an initially crude generalization has been refined by tracing the facts it reports to a deeper law from which it follows that only a restricted form of the generalization really holds good. The tendency to absolutize initial inductive generalizations from limited evidence is only human, of course, but some antidote to unwarrantable absolutization may be obtained from reflection on the history of science, and on the fact that, in any case, the support which any given body of empirical evidence can lend to a natural law statement must be less the wider the range of cases and instances to which the law is to apply.

According to the present account (and most others), whether or not any *total* body of observational data lends support to a hypothesis, and if so how much, has to be dependent on the observational data and the hypothesis alone. Why then should it matter when the hypothesis was first enunciated, whether *before* or *after* the observations were made? Why should the fact of 'predesignation' make the case for the hypothesis any more impressive? This is because it lends support to the supposition that the hypothesis had something to recommend it, with a measure of reliability, even before those observations were made, something by which the initial proponents of the hypothesis were already influenced; for what else, apart from (improbable) luck, would explain their success in predicting that just those observations would be made? At that rate, 'predesignation' is an empirical fact worthy of inclusion in the total body of relevant data.

This explanation of why theoretical 'boldness' can be scientifically creditable certainly differs from Karl Popper's. According to him, a scientific theory is 'corroborated' – not *supported* – to the extent that it 'went out on a limb' when initially proposed, and has survived 'severe' (serious, prolonged, energetic, imaginative?) testing subsequently. Ridiculous as it seems, for Popper, a theory's scientific worth is in considerable measure dependent on the personal worthiness of the scientists concerned – though not in ways which reflect on the authority of any of them, and consequently on the credibility of such theories as they accept. For Popper theoretical boldness just *is* scientifically meritorious – or, at any rate, it is meritorious because it increases the informativeness the theories proposed will have in case they are true, even though by the same token it diminishes their likelihood of being true. A more sensible account of the scientific virtues, surely, will identify them as traits rendering scientific results more apt to be, not just informative if true, but actually (substantially) true and not false. When all is said and done, 'Heads I win, tails you lose' is objectionable for different reasons from those which justify finding fault with unscientific thinking. Popperian 'falsifiability' is nothing but a methodological red herring.

To return to the comparatively cruder though indispensable sorts of inductive methods, inferring what a whole class's membership will probably be like from the characteristics of a sampled subclass's members or, vice versa, inferring the probable character of the members of a subclass or of a single member from what most of the larger class's membership is like, is being treated philosophically here as justified – when it is – only on the basis of a more deep-going account of what inductive inference is and why it works. This helps to avoid some of the standard problems which beset shallower treatments of inductive reasoning. For instance, the problem of identifying the appropriate 'reference class.' Everything whatsoever has characteristics which place it in a variety of different classes, and the features predominantly shared by the members of one of these classes may well differ from the features predominantly shared by the members of another. So which of two such classes' memberships will a common member of both be likely to resemble more closely? The minimization of heterogeneity, of course, will favour a closer resemblance to the members of the smaller class as providing the more probable alternative, other things being equal. And the overlap class will, of course, be the smallest class of all these three. Nora, for example, is a Norwegian, and it is known that most Norwegians are not Roman Catholics. But Nora, as well, made a pilgrimage to Lourdes, and it is known that most of those who have made pilgrimages to Lourdes are Roman Catholics. Here our knowledge of the world enables us to be confident that the majority of Norwegians who have made a pilgrimage to Lourdes are Roman Catholics. Where there is no independent information about the members of the overlap class, we can still see heterogeneity as minimized by a closer resemblance of most of them to the members of either the smaller overlapping class or the overlapping class with the stronger majority as far as possession or non-possession of the relevant feature goes.

Another standard inductive problem avoided by basing the present treatment of the subject on a philosophically more deep-going account is that of a the so-called 'paradoxes of confirmation.'[7] If
    'Any ravens there are, are black'
is 'confirmed' by any sighting of a black raven (with no other birds in view) and
    'Whatever is not black isn't a raven'
is 'confirmed' by any observation of a white bedsheet (with no birds in view), then the logical equivalence of
    'Any ravens there are, are black'
and
    'Whatever isn't black isn't a raven'
suggests that white bedsheet observations can 'confirm' the stated generalization about ravens. Moreover, 'Every location is unoccupied by any raven coloured otherwise than black,' is also logically equivalent to 'Any

---

7 Carl G. Hempel, 'Studies in the Logic of Confirmation,' *Mind* 104, no. 213 (January 1945), 1–26; no. 214 (April 1945), 97–121.

ravens there are, are black,' so that the observation of a black rock too (with no birds in sight) would seem likewise to 'confirm' the generalization that any ravens there are, are black. But even if we do retain this way of speaking, we do not have to accept that all these observations 'confirm' the generalization in question to an equal degree. For, as we have already noted, more homogeneity is secured through something's resemblance to most members of a smaller class it belongs to than through its resemblance to most members of a larger class it belongs to, other things being equal. The class of all things which are not black is certainly much more numerous than the class of ravens, and so is the class of all locations. If we do retain this way of speaking, we should perhaps take an observation to *support* a hypothesis only if it 'confirms' it *more* than it 'confirms' any contrary hypothesis. A black rock observation, for instance, might be agreed, strictly speaking, to 'confirm' the generalization, 'Every location is unoccupied by any raven coloured otherwise than black,' and therefore to 'confirm' the generalization, 'Any ravens there are, are black,' but it also will 'confirm' in the same way the generalization, 'Nothing black is a raven,' and therefore the generalization, 'No ravens are black.'

To the extent that everything is causally interconnected with everything else, it is not too much, as far as evidence goes, to see anything whatsoever as having some bearing on anything else, even if only slight. The imperative to base inductive conclusions on as much evidence as possible – hence to take into account as many 'reference classes' as possible – only stands to reason. Naturally, in real life conclusions nearly always have to be drawn, at least tentatively, *before* all data conceivably available has been gathered, and how much data actually to gather in each instance will have to depend on the specific circumstances of that case, above all on the time, energy, and other resources available, and the relative weight of whatever considerations make it important to answer the question(s) being investigated in comparison to competing claims on those resources.

The inquirer has to bear all of these considerations in mind, and act on them. Reaching a conclusion on the question(s) being investigated will, besides this, commonly involve taking into account a wide variety of different facts and inferences more directly bearing on the question(s), and weighing them all against one another. And very commonly, it is only up to a point that much precision is either possible or necessary, and so the best course is just to mull over the various relevant considerations mentally and then *see* what conclusion comes to seem most attractive. Questions of which this tends to be true are called matters of *judgment*, and individuals with a marked capacity to judge correctly on such questions are said to be persons who have *good judgment*. It is well known that experience in any field tends to improve a person's judgment in that field, as does general intelligence, good mental health, and so forth. By the same token, of course, lack of experience, lack of intelligence, lack of good mental health, and so forth, have the reverse tendency. The inquirers themselves can take these considerations into account, and should, in deciding how much confidence to place in the conclusions they reach. Once again, the way to take into account these considerations too may just be to direct attention to them and *see* how they influence the convictions which result. What reason is there to suppose that the process of arriving at inductive conclusions in this general way is any different from the comparatively conscious thought processes more readily susceptible of being reduced to explicit formulation?

In the following sceptical passage from Book I, Part IV, section I of Hume's *Treatise of Human Nature*, the relevant thought processes are all imagined to be fully conscious and explicit, and to call something 'probable,' in the sense which Hume means here, is simply to call it *worthy of belief* (so that something lacking any 'probability' in this sense will be unworthy of belief, but need not just on that account be worthy of actual disbelief, let alone completely confident disbelief):

> In every judgment, which we can form concerning probability, as well as concerning knowledge, we ought always to correct the first judgment, deriv'd from the nature of the object, by another judgment, deriv'd from the nature of the understanding. 'Tis certain a man of solid sense and long experience ought to have, and usually has, a greater assurance in his opinions, than one that is foolish and ignorant, and that our sentiments have different degrees of authority, even with ourselves, in proportion to the degrees of our reason and experience. In the man of the best sense and longest experience, this authority is never entire; since even such-a-one must be conscious of many errors in the past, and must still dread the like for the future. Here then arises a new species of probability to correct and regulate the first, and fix its just standard and proportion. As demonstration is subject to the controul of probability, so is probability liable to a new correction by a reflex act of the mind, wherein the nature of our understanding, and our reasoning from the first probability become our objects.
>
> Having thus found in every probability, beside the original uncertainty inherent in the subject, a new uncertainty deriv'd from the weakness of that faculty, which judges, and having adjusted these two together, we are oblig'd by our reason to add a new doubt deriv'd from the possibility of error in the estimation we make of the truth and fidelity of our faculties.

This is a doubt, which immediately occurs to us, and of which, if we wou'd closely pursue our reason, we cannot avoid giving a decision. But this decision, tho' it shou'd be favourable to our preceding judgment, being founded only on probability, must weaken still further our first evidence, and must itself be weaken'd by a fourth doubt of the same kind, and so on *in infinitum*; till at last there remain nothing of the original probability, however great we may suppose it to have been, and however small the diminution by every new uncertainty.[8]

The point of quoting this argument at length here is *not* that the conclusion drawn really follows. Since the sceptical conclusion is obviously mistaken, we are in a position to see that all the argument can prove is that the successive diminutions in question must form an infinite series which converges to nothing in such a way that there is some positive degree of (worthiness of) confidence low enough that no matter how far the process of repeated diminution is carried, what remains will never get reduced down as far as that.

Similar considerations to those which apply to reasonings apply also to the data on which reasonings are based, and certain epistemologists have been led to suppose, in consequence, that to avoid absolute scepticism it is necessary to maintain that the series of successive regresses to data for the purpose of certifying the accuracy of other putative data must be a finite series and must terminate in a species of data which is absolutely certain. But there is no reason why the same answer as applies in the case of our reasoning cannot apply also in the case of the data on which it is based. And, indeed, such conclusions are supported by our actual practice. For the further we carry the process of rechecking a piece of reasoning, and then our reasons for thinking it cogent, and then our reason for thinking those reasons cogent, and so on, or of reinvestigating the data on which the reasoning was based, and then the data by means of which the accuracy of that data can be certified, and so on – the further such a process is carried, the smaller is the effect that each successive stage of it has on our assessment of the actual overall likelihood of the original conclusion. The human mind is not capable of going through more than a finite process of thought in order to reach this limiting value of the overall probability of an inferred belief. Accordingly, perceptual data (usually) come to us with a less than complete degree of conviction right from the start, just what degree of conviction it is depending upon all sorts of factors that we could scarcely

---

8 Hume, *Treatise of Human Nature*, 181–2.

begin to take consciously into account, such as our state of health at the time, the ordinariness of the situation, and so on. And, when we reason, the confidence we place in our own conclusions also varies according to innumerable details of which we are not consciously aware, reflecting on the reliability of our reasoning processes at the time. Individuals whose confidence in their own conclusions varies in this way in a markedly reliable manner are said to be persons who have *good judgment* in this regard.

16 The Case for Universal Impermanence

Suppose we ask an engineer who is building a bridge why he has chosen the particular design. He will refer to certain physical laws and tell us that he regards them as 'very reliable,' 'well founded,' 'amply confirmed by numerous experiences.' What do these phrases mean? ... Here the evidence *e* is obviously the relevant observational knowledge. But what is to serve as the hypothesis *h*? One might perhaps think at first that *h* is the law in question, hence a universal sentence *l* of the form: 'For every space-time point *x*, if such and such conditions are fulfilled at *x*, then such and such is the case at *x*.' I think, however, that the engineer is chiefly interested not in this sentence *l*, which speaks about an immense number, perhaps an infinite number, of instances dispersed through all time and space, but rather in one instance of *l* or a relatively small number of instances. When he says that the law is very reliable, he does not mean to say that he is willing to bet that among the billion of billions, or an infinite number, of instances to which the law applies there is not one counterinstance, but merely that this bridge will not be a counterinstance, or that among all bridges which he will construct during his lifetime there will be no counterinstance.

Rudolf Carnap [1]

That all things pass is, as previously remarked, no novel observation about the ways of the world. The fact of transience is so manifest that, in the tradition, any exemption from mortality was reserved for the gods, or at any rate the divine order; and, indeed, such an order was touted expressly on that account.

---

1 *Logical Foundations of Probability* (Chicago, 1950), 571–2.

Early natural science tended quite consciously to see discovering laws of nature as a way of contributing to the comprehension of that divine order: no wonder scientists imputed reality to such laws. But the actual historical path of science is littered thickly with the whitened bones of once-accepted 'eternal laws,' as we know. And what reason could there be to consider current scientific claims of any depth and generality immune from that historical process? From this, sceptical commentators have jumped in to conclude that, whatever science does, it does not tell us the truth about the world.

But, on closer study, such a conclusion is overhasty. Even in disciplines like physics, superseded scientific theories are often not so much *discarded* as *deepened*, their main claims shown – in virtue of more general regularities of nature – to hold good, if not exactly universally, at least approximately under commonly experienced conditions. The deeper regularities are found to explain the real, if limited, prevalence in nature of the old laws – which thus are actually *vindicated* scientifically as much as *supplanted*. And so, scepticism about science is not really a rational conclusion to draw here.

Nor can these reflections ever justify in any way qualifying the formal statement of current scientific results. It is one thing to expect any law of nature, as currently stated, to prove subsequently to hold good under certain conditions only. To build any specific restriction into the statement of the law now would require foreseeing future scientific discoveries not yet made. To add an *unspecific* qualification to the effect that the law holds good at any rate 'under certain conditions' would make the resulting law-statement not just empirically untestable, thanks to its lack of any definite observational consequences, but totally useless: impossible to apply when it comes to predicting and harnessing natural phenomena for human purposes. (The alternative at least *suggested* by Rudolf Carnap in the epigraph to the present chapter – 'This will hold good for bridges constructed during my lifetime,' and so on – is hardly a viable option for the *community* of applied and 'pure' scientists.) The upshot is that, in some key fields at any rate, scientific laws have got to be formulated in universal terms, even if the better part of wisdom, historically informed, does clearly counsel against giving such laws any unqualified *credence* as far as the scope of their application is concerned.

The foregoing is the empirical case for universal impermanence. The empirical case on the other side is both scientific and commonsensical. In the first place, a science like physics does at the present time, as at any time when knowledge is progressing, bring to light ostensibly universal patterns in nature. In the second place, common sense, for its part, is adamant (as chapter 13 noted), not just in denying that any cow will ever jump over the moon but even in denying that any bovine-like *type* of ruminant will ever jump over any lunar-like planetary satellite at any future time whatsoever, no matter how remote from now. In both cases, the grounds on which such positions rest are entirely inductive.

I'd argue that the empirical evidence for universal impermanence, including in its scope as it does all that humankind has ever experienced and thought, cannot but outweigh the current empirical case on the other side. The voice of common sense and the voice of (incautious) scientists alike have never ceased proclaiming absolutes: things said to hold good everywhere and always, or nowhere and never. But *what* absolutes they've proclaimed has never ceased altering over time; and this, too, is a natural process.

There is a self-refutation objection that admittedly does suggest itself here – of a different sort, though, from the one discussed in chapter 13. That objection argued that the Universal Impermanence Principle is a logically inconsistent claim (because it in effect affirms, as an eternal truth, that there are no eternal truths). The present objection, while conceding logical consistency, argues that the entire tendency of the Principle, if it is accepted, must be to discredit the empirical case for any universal claim whatsoever, and therefore to discredit the empirical case for itself as well. To this objection there are two distinct lines of rebuttal. One of them notes that to embrace the Universal Impermanence Principle does not even require that we in any way qualify the formal statement (for example) of the laws of physics which we accept and apply. Among conceivable reflections on the strength or weakness of the empirical case for Universal Impermanence, it couldn't be a very strong objection which was insufficient even to rule out accepting the Principle as being something quite as well established empirically as the currently best established laws of physics! The other line of rebuttal to the present self-refutation objection is to supplement the empirical case in favour of universal impermanence with an *a priori* argument. To this we can turn as soon as we have taken note, first, of the *a priori* case against absolutely any inductive argument for a universal claim.

Since the entire case against the Universal Impermanence Principle, whether based on common sense or natural science, is of an entirely inductive character, the upshot of discrediting the inductive case for any conclusion having universal scope will be to leave the door open for an *a priori* argument favourable to universal impermanence. We already saw in chapter 15 that any given finite body of empirical evidence will give weaker inductive support to a proposition the more extensive the range of cases and instances about which the proposition makes any claim, other things being equal. It is only natural to wonder how a claim of absolutely unlimited scope could receive any inductive support whatsoever from a fixed body of empirical data like that.[2]

Plainly, there is only one way that this could be the case. It would be required that, as the scope of such a claim's application were successively extended to cover wider and wider ranges of cases and instances, the successive reductions in inductive support which that data lent to the claim would have to converge to nothing in such a way that the series of successive *remainders* left after each such reduction converged to a limit greater than no support, so that the original finite body of data could still lend *some* inductive support even to a claim of absolutely unlimited scope. But surely, far from diminishing, the actual tendency of the series of successive reductions in inductive support will rather be to increase, if anything, for surely, no matter what the range of cases and instances covered in the data base, the *remoter* from them the range of new cases and instances to which the applicability of any generalization is to be extended, the *greater* will the reduction be, if anything, in the rational support lent by that fixed body of data to the newly expanded generalization.

Let us take a temporal example. Consider the scientific inference from a certain finite body of empirical data, drawn from the relatively recent past, to the inductive conclusion that a certain relationship among phenomena has held good and will hold good at least from 100,000 BC to AD 100,000. Reformulating that hypothesis so as to extend its scope to include also the one-hundred-and-first millennium AD will, of course, occasion a reduction in the support lent to it by the given data.[3] And further extending the applicability of the hypothesis to include also the one-hundred-and-second millennium AD as well will naturally occasion yet another reduction in the support conferred on it.

---

2 Cf. C.D. Broad, 'On the Relation between Induction and Probability (Part 1),' *Mind*, n.s., 28, no. 108 (October 1918), 396–7.
3 It would not contradict this statement to allow the possibility of an absolute end to the passage of time at or before the end of the one-hundredth millennium AD. Only if that possibility were a certainty would the likelihood of something's prevalence (at least) at all times prior to the end of the one-hundredth millennium AD fail to exceed the likelihood of its prevalence (at least) at all times prior to the end of the one-hundred-and-first millennium AD.

Will the second reduction be less than the first? On the contrary, it will, if anything, be greater, since the one-hundred-and-second millennium is still more remote from the instances reported in the data base than the one-hundred-and-first millennium is. The farther and farther away in time the instances covered by an inductive conclusion are from the instances reported in the current empirical data base, the less certainty that empirical evidence can confer upon any definite conclusion about what those instances in the ever more remote future will be like. Accordingly, the series of successive reductions in the support lent to any definite inductive conclusion as its temporal scope is indefinitely expanded will not be a diminishing series but, if anything, just the reverse, and so the series of successive remainders here will not really converge to a *positive* limit. Therefore, the degree of inductive support lent to a truly universal natural law statement, applicable to all time whatsoever, by a given finite body of empirical data can only be: no positive support at all.

I see that it is necessary to add a proviso here to the effect that nothing in the evidence *specifically* concerns one part of the remote future rather than another – as, for instance, would happen with regard to the past if the evidence were to include records recording the prevalence of whatever regularity among phenomena were in question throughout the day before yesterday while remaining completely silent about yesterday. The required proviso will be (let us say) that, for some point in time t prior to AD 99,999 and later than AD 60,000, any subsequent temporal interval i is such that, for every temporal interval i* containing i, starting later than AD 50,000, and extending for an equal length of time before and after i, the average probability of the regularity in question's prevalence during a year in i* is equal to the average probability of the regularity in question's prevalence during a year in i.

Given this proviso, it is surely clear that the inductive support any regularity's prevalence during at least the one-hundred-and-first millennium AD will receive from a finite body of observational data drawn from the relatively recent past must, if anything, *exceed* the inductive support its prevalence during at least the one-hundred-and-second millennium AD will receive from the same data. This is because, although the two hypotheses compared here are alike in that each one posits the prevalence of a certain regularity throughout a millennium very remote from the times at which the relevant observations were made while remaining silent about all the intervening times, the millennium with which the first hypothesis is concerned is *less* remote from those times than the millennium with which the second hypothesis is concerned.

Consider, then, the following six time periods, the first five of them continuous, the sixth discontinuous:

A. the time from AD 100,000 to (the beginning of) AD 101,000
B. the time from AD 101,000 to (the beginning of) AD 102,000
C. the time from 100,000 BC to (the beginning of) AD 100,000
D. the time from 100,000 BC to (the beginning of) AD 101,000
E. the time from 100,000 BC to (the beginning of) AD 102,000
F. the time from 100,000 BC to (the beginning of) AD 100,000 *together with* the time from AD 101,000 to (the beginning of) AD 102,000

We have just seen that, whatever inductive support a given finite body of empirical evidence drawn from the relatively recent past lends to a hypothesis asserting the prevalence of some regularity (at least) through-out all of period A, that evidence must lend *less* inductive support to the hypothesis asserting the prevalence of the same regularity (at least) throughout all of period B. And it is presumably agreed that, whatever inductive support that evidence lends to the hypothesis that the regular-ity in question prevails (at least) throughout period C, it will inevitably lend *less* inductive support to the hypothesis that the regularity prevails (at least) throughout period D. Further, given the same fixed body of evidence, it presumably will be agreed that the E-hypothesis will receive still less inductive support from that evidence than the D-hypothesis does, and also, I take it, that the F-hypothesis will for its part receive less inductive support from that evidence than the C-hypothesis does. But how will the F-hypothesis compare with the D-hypothesis? Both differ from the C-hypothesis in boldly including an *additional* millennium within the time period for which they predict the prevalence of the regu-larity in question. But – like the B-hypothesis as compared to the A-hypothesis – the F-hypothesis adds a millennium which is still more remote from the evidence facts and the known and unknown circum-stances surrounding them than the millennium which the D-hypothesis adds. Accordingly, the inductive support which the evidence lends to the F-hypothesis will surely be no greater than the inductive support which it lends to the D-hypothesis. If anything, that inductive evidence will fail to support the F-hypothesis as strongly as it does the D-hypothesis. By the same token, I maintain, the degree to which the E-hypothesis is inductively less well-supported by this evidence than the D-hypothesis should, if anything, *exceed* the degree to which the D-hypothesis is in-ductively less well-supported by it than the C-hypothesis. At any rate, the loss of inductive support occasioned by passing from the C-hypothesis to the D-hypothesis *should not be any greater* than the loss of inductive support occasioned by passing from the D-hypothesis to the E-hypothesis. And this conclusion is all that the argument requires.[4]

Accordingly, no finite body of empirical evidence can lend any in-ductive support whatever to an absolutely universal claim applying to all time without restriction. Viewed in this light, the case against the Principle of Universal Impermanence, being entirely inductive, can have no rational weight whatever.

It is now time for the promised *a priori* considerations telling in favour of universal impermanence. It will be best to start with a fairly simple pair of premises, which can be subjected to critical examination subsequently:

(1) If one sort of thing is more probable than another, it occurs more frequently (i.e., a greater proportion of the time).

(2) Any conjunction has a lower probability than either one of its con-juncts, unless the other conjunct follows a priori from that conjunct.

Given these premises, the line of argument that can be developed is straightforward enough. If the probability of one conjunct in some con-junction necessarily exceeds that of the whole conjunction, then so also will its frequency. Hence, there must be actual instances of that conjunct holding good, but not the whole conjunction, and therefore not the other conjunct. Consequently, no matter what the other conjunct is, if it is not an *a priori* necessity, there will be something from which it does not follow *a priori*, and so there will be actual instances in which it does not hold good.

---

4 If there were strong enough empirical evidence for the likelihood of an absolute end of time by date x converging to certainty for later and later values of x – beyond the value represented by a certain specific date, precise or approximate – perhaps, then, the successive reductions in inductive support for claims extending ever farther into the future would indeed form a diminishing series converging to nothing in such a way as to leave a certain specific degree of support always remaining. However, ultra-shaky cosmological speculations aside, who will advance any such specific date, precise or approximate, as today supported by strong enough empirical evidence? Admittedly, though, if there were such a date strongly enough supported empirically, it would be an example of just the sort of thing the proviso formulated in the last paragraph but one excludes.

The conclusion will then be that nothing of the required kind which is not an *a priori* necessity can hold good everywhere forever.

It is necessary here to explain the need for the phrase 'of the required kind' in the last sentence. The point is that, as formulated above, premises (1) and (2) do not *obviously* mesh with each other. The second premise seems to be concerned with the probability of conjunctions and their conjuncts, while the first premise speaks about the probability of different 'sorts of things.' Just what 'sorts of things'? For the conjuncts and conjunction mentioned in (2) to be capable of holding good only in some instances but not in others, they will need to be something more in the nature of propositional functions rather than particular propositions; for, corresponding to something's 'holding good in certain instances but not in others' is the way in which a propositional function can have truths as certain of its values but not others. For our purposes here we can understand a 'thing' as any space-time region occupant whatever. The logical independence of any two or more such regions' occupancy was noted in chapter 12. In summary, every non-evaluative true characterization of conditions in such a region is logically equivalent to a conjunction of any number of logically independent conjuncts, each one of which characterizes conditions in one part of the region. (By a 'non-evaluative' characterization of conditions is meant a proposition which entails no assessment, whether positive or negative, of anything's merits, either absolutely or instrumentally.) In this chapter and the next the occurrences of any 'conditions,' including any 'events' in any such region, will only include facts that can be reported in non-evaluative propositions expressible wholly in purely qualitative terms[5] (apart from those specifying the particular region concerned) and logically independent of all propositions (merely) reporting the 'conditions' existing in other regions. Any of the conjuncts mentioned in premise (2) will be propositional functions expressible in sentences of the form: 'Space-time region x of shape S is and/or was and/or will be occupied by a thing of type T.' The capital 'S' and capital 'T' here are intended to stand in for specific descriptions, the shape description abbreviatable as 'S' in each case including likewise a determinate specification of the spatial and temporal *dimensions* of the space-time region x. The lower-case letter 'x' is intended here for a variable whose values will be particular spatiotemporal regions having the shape S. (No suggestion is

---

5 See my paper 'What Are "Purely Qualitative" Terms?' *American Philosophical Quarterly* 23, no. 1 (January 1986), 71–81.

intended, of course, that two such regions cannot overlap.) Every propositional value of the conjunction mentioned in premise (2) will be expressible in a conjunctive formula in which the 'x' will be replaced both times by a single expression designating some particular spatiotemporal region. In any such conjunctive formula, each conjunct will describe some value of the 'x' as being a certain sort of space-time region occupant, and we can understand the phrase 'sort of thing' in premise (1) as referring exclusively to *sorts of things* so describable.

Interpreted thus, our two premises now do, I think it must be conceded, validly generate the conclusion that absolutely no condition whatsoever obtains everywhere and forever. To resist the conclusion consistently, it would be necessary therefore not to accept the conjunction of these two premises. Yet both of them seen intuitively so indisputable.

Instead of directly attacking either premise (1) or premise (2) then, our objector will attack their conjunction. 'While premise (1) is true on the frequency theory of probability,' the objector will say, 'premise (2) is true on the *a priori* theory of probability.' Granted. But this need not in itself prevent either of the premises from being true unqualifiedly. The objection must be couched as a charge of equivocation. It must be argued that *only* in the frequentist or statistical sense of the word 'probable' will (1) be true and that *only* in some other sense of the word will (2) be true. Thus phrased, the objection is, I admit, a formidable one, which can only be met by recasting the entire argument. While premise (2) can be retained as it stands, premise (1) must be replaced by a much more modest claim indeed. However, the pair of premises which result from this revision will still, I contend, be sufficient to yield a conclusion favourable to universal impermanence. To ensure the genuine indisputability of the two premises, the sense of the word 'probable,' which it will need to be interpreted as taking both in (2) and in the watered-down replacement for (1) is the 'credibility' sense of the word – that is, the sense of the word 'probable' in which alone the sentence, 'Whatever people believe to be probable they believe,'[6] is analytic.

---

6 And also the sentence, 'Whenever people believe one thing to be more probable than another, they either disbelieve both, but disbelieve the second more confidently than the first, or else believe the first one but not the second, or else disbelieve the second one but not the first, or else believe both, but believe the first one more confidently than the second.' See my 'Three Epistemic Senses of *Probability*,' *Philosophical Studies* 101, no. 1 (October 2000), 59–64 .

It does seem clear that, in this sense of the word 'probable,' premise (2) is indeed indisputable. How could it be denied that the *more* one asserts the more *risk* one takes of asserting something false? And this is just another way of saying that, in the required sense, one's assertion is then that much less certain to be true, its 'probability' is just that much lower. Thus, the basis of premise (2) is simply the intuitive principle that a logical conjunction is always a riskier assertion to make than is either individual conjunct (unless one of these conjuncts is such that the other one follows from it *a priori*).

What is required now is a replacement for premise (1), a replacement specified in such a way as to be weak enough to be incontestable, yet strong enough to yield in conjunction with premise (2), a conclusion sufficient for our purposes. The principle to be relied on here is the following *a priori* proposition, mentioned in chapter 12 (in practice quite indispensable in inductive reasoning): If evidence is available to the effect that the proportion of as that are bs is equal to the proportion of as that are cs, *and* no additional evidence is available that bears on the relative probabilities of a particular individual a's being a b and being a c, then it is no more probable that the a in question is a b than that it is a c (in the 'credibility' sense of the word 'probable'). Now let Z be a particular individual known to be an a. Given this, it will follow from the principle cited, by a simple logical transformation, that if evidence is available as to whether the same proportion of as are bs as are cs, and no evidence is available relevant to the relative probabilities of Z's being a b and Z's being a c *other than* evidence as to whether or not the same proportion of as are bs as are cs, and if, in those circumstances, it *is* more probable that Z is a b than a c, then it must be that evidence is available to the effect that it is *not* true that the proportion of as which are bs is equal to the proportion which are cs.

Consider now the case of an arbitrary spatiotemporal region X which is of such a shape, S', that it can be seen to be possible *a priori* for an S'-shaped spatiotemporal region to be occupied either by an F and not by a G, or else, equally well, to be occupied by both an F *and* a G, where F and G are any two sorts of things whatever.[7] We know that the probability

---

7 How does it ever happen that something 'can be seen to be possible *a priori*'? The failure, after serious inquiry, to find any *a priori* grounds for denying something's possibility can often (defeasibly) suffice to establish its *a priori* possibility. See my paper 'Analytic A Posteriori Truth?' *Philosophy and Phenomenological Research* 32, no. 4 (June 1972), 531–4.

here of X's being occupied by an F must, by premise (2), be greater than the probability of its being occupied by both an F and a G. Let us suppose, further, that there is no evidence available which is relevant to the relative probabilities of X's being an F-occupied spatiotemporal region of shape S' and X's being an F-and-G-occupied spatiotemporal region of shape S' *other than* evidence as to whether or not the proportion of F-occupied and F-and-G-occupied S'-shaped spatiotemporal regions is the same. In that case, we are entitled to conclude, in virtue of the principle cited, that there *is* evidence available as to whether or not it is the case that the proportion of S'-shaped spatiotemporal regions which are F-occupied and the proportion of those which are F-and-G-occupied are just the same – this evidence being, in fact, evidence to the effect that it is *not* the case that the proportion of F-occupied and of F-and-G-occupied regions of that shape are the same.

(Just what is this evidence? It is the evidence provided by the fact that, while F-and-G-occupancy without F-occupancy is impossible *a priori*, F-occupancy without F-and-G-occupancy is *not* impossible *a priori*.).

Since every F-and-G-occupied spatiotemporal region has to be F-occupied, it follows then that the claim asserting that there are some F-occupied spatiotemporal regions of shape S' which are not F-and-G-occupied is a warranted claim, for otherwise the proportion which were F-occupied and the proportion which were F-and-G-occupied *would* be equal. Thus we cannot but accept that there are S'-shaped spatiotemporal regions which are G-less; so that, no matter what sort of thing G is, it cannot be something that is ubiquitous and sempiternal.

Have we assumed anything in this proof other than our two *a priori* premises? Only this: we envisaged, in the above, a case where there was no evidence available that was relevant to the relative probabilities of the S'-shaped spatiotemporal region X's being occupied by an F, and its being occupied by both an F and a G, other than evidence as to whether or not the same proportion of S'-shaped spatiotemporal regions were F-occupied as were F-and-G-occupied. And so, to make this argument apply unconditionally, all that is required is that, for any sort of things which is possible *a priori*, and any shape of spatiotemporal region logically capable of accommodating a thing of that sort, there be at least one region of space-time of that shape with respect to which – aside from evidence as to its spatiotemporal location and shape (and whatever follows *a priori* therefrom) – no evidence whatsoever is at all times universally available; universal availability at a particular time entailing not merely availability than to any *actual* inductive reasoners, but also to any that are at all possible *a priori*, occupying any spatial positions whatever or none.

Since the amount of information available to any reasoners varies directly with their intellectual acuity, to which there is no *a priori* lower limit short of none-at-all, it follows that for *any* degree of proximity of a spatiotemporal region, however great, some inductive reasoners will be possible *a priori* to whom, even within that degree of proximity, no information will be available concerning that space-time region (apart from such information as follows *a priori* from the definite description under which the region is identified in that reasoner's thought – information specifying its spatiotemporal position and shape, let us say). Then, on the other hand, we can see that the magnitude of a space-time region need pose no special problem either. The correct use of the expression 'space-time region' is such that it is a logically sufficient condition of any 'space-time region' existing that some part of it exist: thus, even if everything did begin in the year n BC, for example, it would still be possible to make true statements about what happened in the period from n+5 BC to n-5 BC. So that the only empirical assumption (if even it really is one) that the argument requires to supplement the two *a priori* premises relied upon is the assumption of the existence of *something* spatiotemporal.

We can conclude, therefore, with the proposition, regarding any thing whatever, that it really does not exist everlastingly in all places. As we saw in chapter 13, universal impermanence entails for its part that no sort of thing which is possible *a priori* can be everlastingly absent from all places, and hence that any sort of thing possible *a priori* does somewhere at some time exist.

17 That Determinism Is Incontrovertible

But though animals learn many parts of their knowledge from observation, there are also many parts of it, which they derive from the original hand of nature; which much exceed the share of capacity they possess on ordinary occasions; and in which they improve, little or nothing, by the longest practice and experience. These we denominate Instincts, and are so apt to admire as something very extraordinary, and inexplicable by all the disquisitions of human understanding. But our wonder will, perhaps, cease or diminish, when we consider, that the experimental reasoning itself, which we possess in common with beasts, and on which the whole conduct of life depends, is nothing but a species of instinct or mechanical power, that acts in us unknown to ourselves; and in its chief operations, is not directed by any such relations or comparisons of ideas, as are the proper objects of our intellectual faculties. Though the instinct be different, yet still it is an instinct, which teaches a man to avoid the fire; as much as that, which teaches a bird, which with such exactness, the art of incubation, and the whole economy and order of its nursery.

David Hume[1]

That ... one body may act upon another at a distance through a vacuum, without the mediation of any thing else, by and through which their action and force may be conveyed from one to another, is to me so great an

---

1 *An Inquiry concerning Human Understanding*, section IV, Part II, in *Enquiries concerning Human Understanding and concerning the Principles of Morals*, ed. L.A. Selby-Bigge, 3rd ed., rev. P.H. Nidditch (Oxford 1975), 108.

absurdity, that I believe no man, who has in philosophical matters a competent faculty of thinking, can ever fall into it.

Isaac Newton[2]

I think wide agreement could be obtained on the following six points as necessary conditions of the warrantability of inductive inference. (Not that these are supposed to be all logically independent of one another.)

i   Where an event x has been observed to occur followed by an event or state y after lapse of time t without any occasion having been observed on which event x was not followed by event or state y after lapse of time t, it is in consequence more probable than it would otherwise be, on the occasion of any additional occurrence of event x,[3] that this occurrence will be followed by the occurrence of event or state y after lapse of time t. (Included here among the admissible specifications of the sort of state or event y is, are the spatial relations, if any, that its location, or point of occurrence, bears to the point of occurrence of event x.)

ii   The more occasions on which event x has been observed to occur followed by event or state y after lapse of time t without any occasions having been observed on which event x was not followed by event or state y after lapse of time t, the greater is the probability, on the occasion of an additional occurrence of event x, that this occurrence will be followed by the occurrence of event or state y after lapse of time t.

iii   There is no degree, short of complete certainty, to which this probability cannot be increased on any occasion by appropriate additions to the body of available observational data regarding antecedents (the 'appropriateness' of such additions to the data meaning in the present context that, *if* made, the additions in question *would* increase the occurrence's probability in the required degree).

iv   Among conflicting hypotheses alike consistent logically with all the available observational data, the simplest hypothesis, other things being equal, is the likeliest to be true.

---

2   Letter of Newton's quoted in Florian Cajori's appendix to his edition of *Sir Isaac Newton's Mathematical Principles of Natural Philosophy and His System of the World*, vol. 2 (Berkeley, 1934), 634.

3   At no more than a finite spatial or temporal remove, needless to say.

v   The probability of any logical conjunction is lower than the probability of either individual conjunct, except in the case of a conjunct from which the other one follows *a priori*.

vi Where evidence is available to the effect that the proportion of *a*s that are *b*s is equal to the proportion of *a*s that are *c*s and no additional evidence is available that is relevant to the relative probabilities of some particular individual I being a *b* and being a *c*, given that I is an *a*, then it is not more probable that individual I is a *b*, given that I is an *a*, than it is that individual I is a *c*, given that I is an *a*.

(In all of the above it is, of course, the 'credibility' sense of 'probability' that is being employed, as it is, indeed, throughout this chapter.)[4]

Now, let e be any event which, on the occasions where observations have been made, has usually been followed event or state r after a lapse of time t. We may suppose that r has been observed p% of the time to follow event e after a temporal interval of t, and that n is the total number of occasions on which observations have been made of the sequels to occurrences of event e. Then, by (i), those observations have in themselves made it more probable than it would otherwise be, on any subsequent occasion where there is begun a series of observations of n separate instances of the occurrence of event e and the subsequent occurrence or non-occurrence of r after lapse of time t, that by the time that series of observations is completed, e will have been followed by r after lapse of time t in approximately p% of the instances observed, p being by hypothesis greater than 50. Thus, the inductive projection of merely *frequent* sequences into the future can be treated as a special case of the inductive projection of invariant sequences, just as, more obviously, the reverse can also be done. Accordingly, we may conclude that, the initial series of observations having been made, the occurrence of event e on any new occasion will, other things being equal, increase the probability of the subsequent occurrence of r after lapse of time t.

Now, let f be any logically independent event or state which, on the occasions where observations have been made, has usually not been

---

4   This is the sense of the word 'probable' in which 'Whatever people (consciously) believe they consider to be (at least) probable; and whatever people consider to be (at least) probable they believe,' and 'The more confidently people believe something (consciously) the more probable they consider it to be; and the more probable people consider something to be the more confidently they believe it' are both analytic. An explicit definition is proposed in my 'Three Epistemic Senses of Probability,' *Philosophical Studies* 101, no. 1 (October 2000), 59–64.

followed by r after lapse of time t. Then the compound event or state ef either has or has not usually been followed by r after lapse of time t. Let us consider the latter case (and the former case can be dealt with equally well by considering event or state f and the usual *non*-occurrence of r at the end of lapse of time t). In this latter case, as stated, ef has not usually been followed by r after lapse of time t. Consequently, it must be the case that event or state r has followed event e after lapse of time t proportionally less often than r has followed event e in the absence of event or state f after lapse of time t. Therefore we can say, in accordance with (i) and (ii) above, that the occurrence of e on any additional occasion provides a basis for predicting the subsequent occurrence of r after lapse of time t with less probability than does the occurrence of event e in the absence of f.

Thus, the greater the degree of specification of the antecedents in respect of conditions like f, the greater the degree of probability which attaches to the subsequent occurrence (or non-occurrence, as the case may be) of r after lapse of time t. If the degree of probability of the occurrence of r after lapse of time t on any occasion is to have an upper limit fixed in principle and short of complete certainty, then this must be either because there is only a finite amount of specification of the antecedents in respect of occurrences like that of f that it is possible in principle to keep adding on, or else because on any occasion the series of increments so produced in the degree of probability of the occurrence of r after lapse of time t converges to a limit fixed in principle short of complete certainty.

At any rate, this is what a strong version of the thesis of acausality requires. It requires, that is, that there be at least some events or states in respect of which there is fixed short of total certainty an upper limit to the degree of probability which can be lent to the occurrence or non-occurrence of the events or states in question by *any* information as to antecedents at a given earlier time. This runs clearly contrary to (iii) above. (At any time, after all, *past* regularities can only count as inductive support for the prediction of any future occurrence on the basis of *present* evidence for them.[5] So that, insofar as any conclusion concerning the future is ever inductively warranted, it is warranted by evidence as

---

5 A qualification: What about things known now directly, through memory, to have occurred in the past? But they can serve as inductive evidence for anything in the future, surely, only insofar as the relevant memories' reliability is duly supported, on balance, by the presently available evidence.

to conditions in the present.) Consequently, we may say that inductive inference implies the assumption that any actual occurrence, whether of a state or an event, has for any particular earlier time a sufficient precondition, a logically and in general *a priori* possible condition, that is, which, should it have occurred at that earlier time, could not but have been followed by that state or event at the time of the actual occurrence later on. And by an exactly parallel argument, couched in terms of retrodiction rather than prediction, we can prove that any particular actual occurrence, whether a state or event, has for any subsequent time a sufficient postcondition, an *a priori* possible condition that is, which cannot take place at that subsequent time without having been preceded by the state or event in question taking place at *its* time of occurrence earlier on.

Now, let A be any state or event actually occurring at time t_1. Let X be a sufficient precondition at earlier time t_0 of A's occurrence at t_1. Let B at time t_1 be a sufficient postcondition of X at time t_0 and let Y at time t_0 be a sufficient precondition of B's occurrence at t_1. Let complex event-or-state H be the occurrence of X followed, after a temporal interval of $(t_1 - t_0)$, by the non-occurrence of A. And let complex event-or-state H' be the occurrence of X and Y together followed, after a temporal interval of $(t_1 - t_0)$ by the non-occurrence of A.

A, thus, is something which *actually* occurs at time t_1. Should B occur, its occurrence will be at time t_1 also. And, should either X or Y occur, the occurrence(s) will be at time t_0. Lastly, should either H or H' occur, the occurrence(s) will extend from time t_0 to time t_1. The occurrence of H and the occurrence of H' will alike be logically sufficient for the nonoccurrence of A. And the occurrence of H' will be logically sufficient for the occurrence of H. Moreover,

X (should it occur) will be a sufficient precondition of A,
B (should it occur) will be a sufficient postcondition of X,
and
Y (should it occur) will be a sufficient precondition of B.

It follows from (v) above that, unless the occurrence of H' follows *a priori* from the occurrence of H, the occurrence of H' will have a lower probability than the occurrence of H on any particular occasion. But, in the same sort of way as we saw in chapter 16, (vi) commits us to the proposition that it is impossible for the occurrence of one such contingency to be less probable than that of another one where no other pertinent evidence is available besides evidence to the effect that the two are equally frequent, in the sense that the proportion of the time that one of them occurs is equal to the proportion of the time that the other one occurs. (And there will always be standpoints from which no other pertinent evidence *is* available. Let us here assume such a standpoint.) Accordingly, unless the occurrence of H' follows *a priori* from the occurrence of H, H' and H must be denied to be of equally frequent occurrence. But, if H' and H are denied to be equally frequent, then, from the specification by which 'H'' and 'H' were introduced, it will follow that there are some actual instances of X occurring in the absence of Y without being followed, after a temporal interval of (t_1-t_0), by an occurrence of A. However, given the specification by which 'X' was introduced, it is impossible for X to occur without being followed, after a temporal interval of (t_1-t_0), by an occurrence of A. Therefore, it must be the case that the occurrence of H' does follow *a priori* from the occurrence of H, and hence that the (contemporaneous) occurrence of Y follows *a priori* from the occurrence of X. Thus, since Y has been expressly specified as a sufficient precondition of B, X must likewise be a sufficient precondition for the occurrence of B after a temporal interval of (t_1-t_0). But B has been specified as a sufficient postcondition of X. Therefore, X must be also a necessary precondition for the occurrence of B after a temporal interval of (t_1-t_0).

Since B has been specified as a sufficient postcondition of X, and X, in turn, as a sufficient precondition of A, B must be a sufficient contemporaneous-condition – or 'simul-condition' – of A. It follows, thus, that for any actual occurrence whatsoever and any earlier time, there will always be an *a priori* possible condition the occurrence of which on the one hand would be a sufficient simul-condition of that actual occurrence and on the other hand would have to be preceded at that earlier time by a necessary and sufficient precondition for itself.

Now let 'R' represent the set of respects in which, should A and B actually occur together at t_1 the state of affairs would be different from what it actually is at that time. (There is no suggestion here, of course, that R has to be non-null, that is, that A and B cannot occur together at time t_1.) Now let 'R'' represent the set of respects in which the state of affairs at t_1 would be the *same* as it actually is in the event of the joint occurrence of A and B then. Let C be the condition the assertion of whose existence at t_1 describes the way things actually are at that time, in the respects belonging to R and R'. That true assertion, in other words, is the proposition which reports the occurrence at t_1 of everything which falls under the heading of R' and the non-occurrence of everything which falls under the heading of R. (The proposition asserting the joint occurrence at t_1 of everything which falls under the heading of R' and also everything which falls under the heading of R is a proposition logically entailing the joint occurrence at t_1 of A and B together.) As it has been specified, the condition C will of course have to be a logically sufficient simul-condition of A.

Now let D be a sufficient simul-condition of C, having a necessary and sufficient precondition for its occurrence after a temporal interval of (t_1-t_0), and let S' be the set of respects wherein the state of affairs at t_1 would be different in the event of C and D's joint occurrence from what it actually is, and let S' be the set of respects wherein it would be the same. And let E be the condition the assertion of whose existence at t_1 describes the way things actually are at that time in the respects belonging to S and S'. It is clear that, as specified, E also will be a logically sufficient simul-condition of A.

We could, in the same spirit, go on to specify F as a sufficient simul-condition of D, having a necessary and sufficient precondition for its occurrence after a temporal interval of (t_1-t_0). And we could specify T as the set of respects wherein the state of affairs at t_1 would be different in the event of D and F's joint occurrence from what it actually is, and, similarly, T' could be the set of respects wherein it would be just the same. And G would be the condition the assertion of whose existence at t_1 would describe the way conditions actually are at that time in the respects belonging to T and T'. G, of course, like C and E, would have to be a logically sufficient condition of A.

To run through this series of conditions, it is clear that one could go on adding letters like this without limit (though the alphabet's finitude would swiftly necessitate recourse to more complex *symbols*). What we have, starting with A, is a series of conditions such that every even-numbered member of the series is a sufficient simul-condition of its predecessor in the series, and every odd-numbered member of the series after the first is a condition the assertion of whose existence character-izes the way conditions actually are at the time t_1 in the respects in which the joint occurrence of its predecessor and its predecessor's predecessor in the series would correspond to the way things actually are at that time and the respects in which their joint occurrence would be at variance from the way things actually are at that time; with the proviso that every even-numbered member of the series has a necessary and sufficient pre-condition for its occurrence after a temporal interval of (t_1-t_0). Every odd-numbered member of the series is a condition actually occurring at time t_1 and each of them has a sufficient simul-condition of its occurrence ap-pearing as an even-numbered member (the next member) of our series.

Let K be the set of all even-numbered members of the whole series; and let U be the set of respects wherein conditions at time t_1 would be different from what they actually are at that time in the event of the joint occurrence then of A and every member of K; and let U' be the set of respects wherein conditions at t_1 would be the same as they actually are at that time in the event of the joint occurrence then of A and every member of K. Let V be the condition the assertion of whose occurrence at t_1 describes the way conditions actually are at that time in the respects belonging to U and to U'. That true assertion, then, is a proposition reporting the joint occurrence at time t_1 of all the odd-numbered members of our series.

It is clear from the way it has been specified that V will be a logically sufficient simul-condition of A. Let W be a sufficient simul-condition of V satisfying the following two requirements: (1) that it have a necessary and sufficient precondition for its occurrence after a temporal interval of (t_1-t_0) – let us use the letter 'Z' to represent this necessary and sufficient precondition of W; and (2) that it itself be a condition the assertion of whose occurrence at t_1 logically entails nothing that is not logically entailed by the assertion of the occurrence at t_1 of one or more of the even-numbered members of the series of conditions we have described. These two requirements can be jointly fulfilled because every condition whose occurrence at t_1 is entailed by (the assertion of the occurrence then of) V will have a sufficient simul-condition in some even-numbered member of the series, for the occurrence of which following a temporal interval of (t_1-t_0) there will be a sufficient precondition in turn.

Because it satisfies requirement (2), it is clear that W cannot be a condition the assertion of whose occurrence at t_1 logically entails any characterization of the state of affairs at t_1 which is not a characterization of it in one or more of the respects belonging to U and to U'. But V, as it has been specified, is the condition the (true) assertion of whose occurrence at t_1 describes the way things actually are at that time in the respects belonging to U and U'. Hence V is a condition the assertion of whose occurrence at t_1 logically entails the occurrence or else the non-occurrence of W at t_1. But, since W has been specified as an *a priori* possible sufficient simul-condition of V, the coexistence of V and W cannot be logically impossible. Hence V is a logically sufficient simul-condition of W; and thus V is a sufficient postcondition of Z, which was specified as a necessary precondition of W; and Z will also be a sufficient precondition of V since Z is by specification a sufficient precondition of W, which is specified as a sufficient simul-condition of V.

Thus we see that for any actual occurrence, and for any earlier time, there will be conditions existing at the time of that actual occurrence which, jointly with it, are necessary and sufficient for the occurrence of certain preconditions at that earlier time. So that for any occurrence which actually takes place, and for any time earlier than its time of occurrence, there have been in existence at that earlier time conditions jointly sufficient for the production of that occurrence after a lapse of time equal to the interval between the two times in question. And by an exactly parallel argument, we can show that for any occurrence which actually takes place, and for any time later than its time of occurrence, there will be in existence at that later time conditions whose production requires *its* prior occurrence, earlier by an interval equal to the length of time between the two times in question; and that there will always be in existence at the time of any such occurrence circumstances which, together with it, are jointly necessary and sufficient for the production, after a lapse of time equal to that interval, of the subsequent conditions in question, in the precise circumstances in which those conditions do occur. In other words, all events are caused and all events are causes; and the state of affairs obtaining at any time is uniquely determined by the state obtaining at any other time, earlier or later. So much for the Principle of Universal Causation, as spelled out above in chapter 13.

To establish complete determinism all that remains, then, is to prove that there cannot be any causality at a spatial distance. This conclusion follows from a consideration of point (iv) above, the Principle of Simplicity, which would otherwise, in conjunction with the Principle of Universal Causation, preclude the inference from any data whatever of even the *improbability* of the operation of causality among all the occurrences which are referred to in a report of the data without any intervening causal mechanisms whatsoever.[6] It is clear that such inferences

---

6   C.f. Bertrand Russell, *Our Knowledge of the External World*, 2nd ed. (London, 1926), 110–12, et cetera. Actually, I have put the point rather too weakly here. The Simplicity Principle, as derived in chapter 14, tells us *a priori* that the occurrence of any spatiotemporal event whatever is presumptively improbable. Hence, without the Principle of Contiguity we should actually be entitled to infer from any data at all the *probable* operation of causality amongst all the occurrences referred to in a report of that data without the operation of any intervening causal mechanism at all. Only a phenomenalistic philosophy of space would suppose that it is possible thus to abandon belief in the epistemological realist ontology without thereby giving up all legitimate grounds for the whole range of predictions obtained by induction in its normal employment. Against any such phenomenalism I have argued, in effect,

will sometimes be warranted in fact, and, therefore, that the Principle of Contiguity as well as the Principle of Universal Causation should be accepted, in the form given in chapter 13, as necessary conditions of the warrantability of inductive inference.[7]

We have seen in chapter 15 that determinism thus formulated, in conjunction with the Principle of Universal Impermanence, is also a *sufficient* condition of the warrantability of inductive inference. All of us, of course, make inductive inferences and accord belief to their conclusions, and thus all of us are arguably committed to agreeing that whatever the necessary and sufficient conditions of warranted inductive inferences are must be correct. It is not surprising, therefore, that in the history of philosophy determinism should frequently have seemed so psychologically self-evident and necessary to any interpretation of our experience.

That has, indeed, traditionally been the rationalist argument from *inconceivability*. The inconceivability of indeterminism was the essential point of the maxim, '*Ex nihilo nihil fit et in nihil nil potest reverti*,'[8] where the '*ex*' and the '*in*' are taken in both their temporal and their spatial senses, respectively corresponding to the principles of universal causation and of contiguity.

It is fair to say, though, that in not a few philosophical quarters appeals to inconceivability have tended to fall into some disrepute in recent times. Critics have not been slow about flatly denying many a traditional inconceivability claim. And at the same time they often have embraced the alternative of challenging such a claim's philosophical *relevance*. And, indeed, what bearing *should* anything's inconceivability have (supposing it really is inconceivable) upon our consideration of the truth-value of a proposition which claims it to be an objective impossibility?

---

in my 'Laws of Nature and Physical Existents,' *International Studies in the Philosophy of Science* 7, no. 3 (1993), 260–1. (The operative point here is that, without confusion or dishonesty, whether conscious or otherwise, it is psychologically impossible to deny as inductive nihilism does the legitimacy of the whole range of predictions obtained by induction in its normal employment. See chapter 11.)

7 If the argument up to this point is not thought adequate to preclude the possibility of an absolute beginning or ending of spatiotemporal events, it may be reflected that in the absence of such an *a priori* preclusion the methodological presumption against the occurrence of any change would stand in the way of inferring even the *probability* of any specific developments whatsoever before or after the occurrence of the conditions described in a report of the data.

8 'From ['*ex*'] nothing nothing comes, and into ['*in*'] nothing nothing can revert back.'

Argumentation about *inconceivability*, then, is something that does call for a measure of caution. One way to be philosophically cautious, of course, is to draw distinctions. In what follows, I shall be distinguishing three different ways, or kinds of ways, in which an appeal to inconceivability might be employed philosophically, and, after that, three different types of inconceivability claim, varying in their relative degree of strength. One distinction on which I will not rest any weight is the distinction between what it is logically impossible to conceive and what it is *merely* psychologically impossible to conceive. If the line of argument developed in chapters 3 and 4 has been successful, it should be accepted that a fact is a fact, whether it is a logically necessary fact, an empirical fact, or whatever.

In the early-modern heyday of European rationalism, the appeal to inconceivability was often an appeal to the trustworthiness of an all-knowing and veracious Creator. If He had made us incapable of conceiving something, it was reasoned, that something must be an impossibility in actual fact. Could a Darwinian successor to such an argument be formulated, premising – perhaps debatably – that it is only an incapability of conceiving genuine impossibilities which would be apt to have 'survival value' for a species like ours? In any event, the argument might be objected to as unacceptably circular in this context, since it does rely on causality-and-induction to vindicate reliance on causality-and-induction.

In recent years, epistemological 'coherentists' have advanced a conception of the cognitive enterprise as one of modifying our existing beliefs, where necessary, with a view to as far as possible taking in new purported-information from the senses with minimum psychological disruption. The philosophy would be more aptly called 'methodological conservatism,' I have argued,[9] because the essence of this position is the *presumption* in favour of whatever is currently believed (independently of any empirical case for the believers' relative authoritativeness). Such a presumption is insisted on in conjunction with an insistence also, in the name of 'antifoundationalism,' that no belief is ever warranted unless there are (good) inferential *grounds* for it. At that rate, if it really can count as a good reason for considering something to be so that you already believe it to be so, your inability even to conceive of its failing to be so might be arguably an even better reason. In any case, however, isn't it preposterous to suppose that any initially unwarranted belief of

---

9 D. Goldstick, 'Methodological Conservatism,' *American Philosophical Quarterly* 8, no. 2 (April 1971), 186–91.

yours could *become* warranted thanks merely to your noticing or coming to recognize the fact that you hold it? How could that change a bad bet into a good bet?

This brings us, then, to *ad hominem* argumentation of the sort discussed in chapters 1, 4, and 11. What you cannot conceive otherwise you cannot doubt to be so. And what you cannot doubt you do not doubt. Accordingly, if you think of it at all, you do so with nothing short of full, confident belief. How then could there be any philosophical debate on such a point? Dishonesty. Confusion. Imperfect self-awareness. But in their simplest form diagnoses such as these probably fit the case of resistance to a logical principle like the Law of Noncontradiction rather better than they fit philosophical opposition to determinism. In the latter case it will be necessary to take a deeper look, and this is what will call for distinguishing three different types of *inconceivability*. First, though, let us remember how an *ad hominem* argument of the pertinent sort works. It can base itself just on psychological facts about those addressed; but, where rationally successful, it leads them – provided they are attentive, clear-headed, and self-aware – to a conscious acceptance of propositions which need not be at all restricted to psychological subject-matters. A rebuttal was offered in chapter 1 to the Kantian 'transcendental' move of imposing a mind-related restriction on the import of such propositions as Universal Causation in a context like the present one. Still less would there be any justification for a specifically language-related restriction.

Types of *inconceivability*. The first type has to do with meaninglessness. Where nothing whatsoever has been meant by some verbiage that has been used, there is naturally no possibility of *conceiving* what has been meant. Consider the sentence: 'In the spirit media are vested all experience and knowledge of all vibrations which are thoughts, and its vibrations of infinite velocity are expressed in the media of graduated molecularity at reduced speeds.'[10] The writer of this sentence just possibly did mean something definite – or even indefinite – by it. Alternatively, though, the writer may rather have meant only to *befuddle* and *impress* as many as possible of the readers. To attempt to grasp what was meant by the sentence is to take on a *conceiving* task, but the effort will be doomed to failure if, in fact, nothing at all was really meant by it. In such a case (in contrast, arguably, to the sort of discourse logical positivism attacked), we are brought face-to-face with genuine meaninglessness, and certainly

---

10 Quoted by Robert H. Thouless, *Straight and Crooked Thinking*, 2nd ed. (London, 1953), 106.

a type of *inconceivability*; but not one relevant to our present purposes. As Wittgenstein liked to stress, in literal *nonsense* there is neither truth nor falsity.

Just to grasp a meaning does involve being able to *conceive* something, in a sense. But what do we mean when we say that a round square, or even a quadrilateral with only three angles, is *inconceivable*? In spite of Wittgenstein, it is not a matter of actual literal *senselessness* here. We can understand what is in question here perfectly well and have no difficulty in determining the truth-value of claims about the existence or non-existence of the relevant sorts of objects. Doubtless nobody ever has believed in the literal existence of any round square, though possibly some may have thought they did, or thought something else which they *misexpressed* in such terms. This is an example of the second type of *inconceivability*. The case of the quadrilateral with only three angles is arguably a different matter, however. Somebody might, in fact, successfully grasp this idea perfectly well but, not being very thoughtful, actually believe that there are things like that. But such an unthoughtful belief could not survive real attention being paid to the point, not *sufficient* real attention at any rate. Let us say that such an inattentive thinker as this is able to form an *abstract* conception of a quadrilateral with only three angles but not really to conceive it *concretely*. If a round square isn't even conceivable in the abstract, a quadrilateral with no more than three angles is only impossible to conceive *concretely*. This is our third type of *inconceivability*.

A quadrilateral having just three angles is *almost* inconceivable even in the abstract. It requires *very little* thought to see that such a thing cannot be. However, properly to satisfy yourself, by means of paying attention only, that $17 \times 31 = 527$ and not, say, 537 requires much lengthier thought processes. But those thought processes will simply work out in detail the particular relations among sets of items that any *concrete* case of 17×31 equalling 537, say, would involve, until finally such a thing is found to be inconceivable, and the contrary conclusion is drawn. The arithmetical example is useful also in making it clear that the *concrete conceivability* which is at issue here is by no means the same thing, necessarily, as visual picturability, or sensuous imaginability otherwise. Sensuous imagination is only one way of rendering a conception more concrete.

Before proceeding further, we ought to give consideration here to the objection based on non-Euclidean geometry. Isn't non-Euclidean geometry both inconceivable psychologically and yet also, in one form, in light of the evidence supporting General Relativity, quite believable enough and, indeed, possibly true? Well, *is* Riemannian geometry inconceivable? Is it really psychologically impossible to conceive of a flat surface with a straight line and a point on it, the point off the line, such that through that point on that surface *no* straight line can be traced which will not intersect the first line? *Must* there be an intermediate case, as far as we can conceive, between lines through the point so tilted as to intersect the first line on one side of the point, and lines through the point so tilted as to intersect the first line on the other side of the point: the intermediate case, namely, of a line through that point *parallel* to the first line? Such an intermediate case certainly seems conceivable. What are we trying to conceive when we try to conceive the opposite? It is a question, perhaps, of trying to conceive a situation where no alteration in the tilt of a straight line through the point, however slight, will yield that intermediate case of a line parallel to the first line: a situation where the line's tilt can be altered so as to move the intersection farther and farther away from the original point until, finally, that intersection jumps over to the other side of the point, no less far away from it in the opposite direction. Is this psychologically impossible to conceive? It is doubtless natural to *believe* the contrary, but that is a different matter. The belief isn't unshakable.

Is it similarly possible to conceive concretely what indeterminism postulates? What would it be for 'Ex *nihilo nihil fit et in nihil nil potest reverti*' to be false? For something to come out of nothing it would have to occur as the necessary consequence of no particular event, or there would have to be no event preceding it such that any other event could not have preceded it just as well; one might as well say, no preceding events at all would be needed; and the same goes for its environment; one might well say, no environment at all would be needed.

Try conceiving this concretely. What is required is a concrete, *indvidual* conception of a particular event occurring under those specific conditions. And not just a conception of an event occurring where its causes are not visible but actually where they are visibly absent, or, at least, where there is no notion, however indistinct or unparticularized, of their presence in any form. This would involve the conception of a sequence of two moments in time with nothing occurring at the earlier moment being relevant to the causal determination of something at the later. It would not be enough just to conceive the two moments one before the other. They would have to be conceived as *being* one before the other. To conceive one moment as prior to another it is not sufficient, or even necessary, merely to conceive it prior to conceiving the other. The only way to conceive one moment *as* prior to another is to envisage elements in the situation obtaining at the earlier moment as being *causally* prior to elements in the situation obtaining at the later moment. And you cannot envisage happenings at some earlier time as being causally responsible for occurrences at a later time without envisaging them both as spatiotemporally connected by a mechanism of intermediate causes all along the line. This is how we think of time. There is no way apart from causality to distinguish mentally between two successive occurrences and two simultaneous occurrences.

(Nor will it do here to have recourse to *independent* means of imaginatively dating the two occurrences relative to each other, any more than it will do to imagine the independent verification of the two sides of the equation '25 sheep together with 25 other sheep = 49 sheep.' This will merely push the problem back. If two moments are to be imagined as temporally related *via* their temporal relations with another moment, or other moments, then causal relations must be imagined as holding amongst the events of all three, or all four. And, wherever an occurrence *causes* each of two other occurrences of which one is earlier than the other, then by our definition of 'causality' the first of these latter two also counts as being a *cause* of the second.)[11]

Just because you cannot conceive of one state of affairs as occurring earlier than another without conceiving of something in the former as causally operative in bringing about something in the latter, and doing so by means of a causal mechanism in the spatiotemporal interval between

---

11   See chapter 13. Whenever X 'causes' both Y and Z, with Y preceding Z, there will be circumstances C at the time of X such that in those circumstances X is both a necessary and a sufficient precondition of the occurrence of Y and likewise both a necessary and sufficient precondition of the occurrence of Z. Hence Y is a necessary and sufficient postcondition of X's occurrence, given the existence of the circumstances C at the earliest of the three times in question, and therefore Y is in such a situation a necessary and sufficient precondition of Z's occurrence (owing to the transitivity of the *necessary and sufficient condition* relation). In other words, any sequence starting at the earliest of the three times in question with the existence of the circumstances C and ending with the occurrence of Y at the intermediate time in question will be a sufficient precondition for the subsequent occurrence of Z, and, in fact, a sufficient precondition for Z of which Y's occurrence will be a non-redundant part. (Technically speaking, what has been shown to be a 'cause' of Z here is not Y itself, but is rather any change sequence starting at the time of X and ending with the occurrence of Y. It is quite immaterial, however, what the sequence contains prior to Y; anything at all will do, however exiguous. And so the statement in the text can stand for all intents and purposes.)

them, it does not follow that you have to conceive what the earlier occurrence that is causally operative in bringing about the latter one specifically is, or what the intervening causal mechanism specifically is. The sense of continuity and necessity, that is to say, *repeatability*, which is what conceiving the presence of causal relations comes to, can be fully felt without having any idea as to what it is in particular that accounts for the repeatability in the instance under consideration.

See whether you can form the conception of a ship moving down a stream. The conception will have to be one of a ship successively at several different points along the length of the stream. How can this conception be distinguished from a conception of several similar ships *simultaneously* spaced out at different points along the length of the stream? Only by the fact that in the former conception, the conception of a ship that is really moving down the stream, there are causal relations conceived as obtaining between the different ship-positions conceived.[12] It is by such introspective verification as this that you can discover how your way of conceiving the passage of time involves causal determinism. In the words of Kant,

> If then, we experience that something happens, we in so doing always presuppose that something precedes it, on which it follows according to a rule. Otherwise I should not say of the object that it follows. For mere succession in my apprehension, if there be no rule determining the succession in relation to something that precedes, does not justify me in assuming any succession in the object.[13]

---

12 Instead of a ship moving down a stream, it could just as easily be a rat moving through a maze. In order to conceive of some of the rat-positions as being earlier than others it would be necessary to conceive of a causal relationship between them, that is, it would be requisite to conceive of the earlier rat-positions, not merely as *necessary* conditions of the later ones, but rather as non-redundant members of sets of jointly *sufficient* preconditions of them. This, I think, suffices to answer 'emergent evolutionists' and others who have sought to recognize the inconceivability of a passage of time where the earlier states of affairs weren't *necessary* for the later ones while denying that by the same token these temporal antecedents would also have to be *sufficient* conditions of their sequels.

13 Immanuel Kant, *The Critique of Pure Reason*, A195=B240, the 'Second Analogy of Experience,' 223, Norman Kemp Smith translation (London, 1933, second impression). If this interpretation is not really what Kant meant, it does not matter.

18 The Pitfall of Metaphysics

To us, the cosmic process seems to be evolutionary in character: the universe is expanding (it may be assumed), or matter is being transmuted into energy. The process seems to be temporal-formal in character: non-repetitive and irreversible. But this appearance may be an illusion due to our infinitesimally brief span of observation. Were it longer, sufficiently longer, the cosmic process might reveal itself as a repetitive one: a period of contraction might follow expansion, and so on, in an endless series of pulsations; matter may be transmuted into energy and re-congealed into matter, an endless vibration of a cosmic pendulum. So, to a creature which, compared with us, had an infinitesimally brief span of observation, the repetitive and rhythmic character of respiration or the heart beat or the rusting of iron would appear to be evolutionary in character, for seeing only a minute part of the process, neither the beginning nor the end, he would observe only a temporal alteration of form, and might declare it to be a non-repetitive process. And he would be correct too, for the *process* which he observes *is* non-repetitive, just as the dying star and the decomposing radium represent non- repetitive processes to us. Thus, whether a process be labelled repetitive or evolutionary depends upon the unit of measurement. Any repetitive process is made up of a sequence of events which in themselves are non-repetitive. Conversely, any repetitive process is but a segment of a larger one which is evolutionary in character.

Leslie A. White[1]

---

1 'Science Is *Sciencing*,' *Philosophy of Science* 5, no. 4 (October 1938), 378, note 14.

It isn't like fifty years ago, when it would have been possible to count on an unfriendly reaction to the word 'metaphysics' from readers not only of more advanced but of moderate views also. Positivists, pragmatists, existentialists, Marxists all deprecated, disparaged and dissociated themselves from 'metaphysics' in no uncertain terms, even if they did give differing accounts of what the nub of the offence was.[2] To brand an idea, claim, or outlook 'metaphysical' then was not a bad way to relegate it as pretty hopelessly unintelligent – provided, of course, the label could be made to stick convincingly. Today in academic philosophy there is only the residue of this odium to fuel a *persuasive definition* here. A rhetorical exercise of that nature, it will be recalled, had been identified in 1944 by Charles Stevenson:

In any 'persuasive definition' the term defined is a familiar one, whose meaning is both descriptive and strongly emotive. The purport of the definition is to alter the descriptive meaning of the term, usually by giving it greater precision within the boundaries of its customary vagueness; but the definition does *not* make any substantial change in the term's emotive meaning. And the definition is used, consciously or unconsciously, in an effort to secure, by this interplay between emotive and descriptive meaning, a redirection of people's attitudes.[3]

---

2 In the interests of historical accuracy, I have to qualify this statement as far as the pragmatists and existentialists go. In fact, they didn't all deprecate 'metaphysics' all the time in no uncertain terms. But even the friendliest treatments of 'metaphysics' by pragmatists and existentialists did tend to convey an unmistakable sense of *reserve* about it, a reserve which through time, could deepen into something more like rejection. For example, John Dewey in *Logic: The Theory of Inquiry* (New York, 1938), 66: 'The separation and opposition of scientific subject-matter to that of common sense, when it is taken to be final, generates those controversial problems of epistemology and metaphysics that still dog the course of philosophy. When scientific subject-matter is seen to bear genetic and functional relation to the subject-matter of common sense, these problems disappear.' And even as early as 1939 Martin Heidegger could write, 'The fulfilment of metaphysics, that is, the erection and entrenchment of consummate meaninglessness, thus remains nothing else than ultimate submission to the end of metaphysics ...' (Martin Heidegger, *Nietzsche*, vol. 3, trans. Joan Stambaugh, David Farrell Krell, and Frank A. Capuzzi (San Francisco, 1987), 176. As far as the Marxists go, see, for instance, Engels in *Socialism: Utopian and Scientific*: 'Hegel had freed history from metaphysics – he had made it dialectic ...' in Karl Marx Frederick Engels, *Collected Works*, trans. here by Edward Aveling, vol. 24 (New York, 1989), 304.
3 Charles L. Stevenson, *Ethics and Language* (New Haven, CT, 1944), 210.

What I want to urge now is that the odium was not undeserved, and that the label 'metaphysics' still sufficiently fits something that merits our rejection today. To show that the label does fit is what will necessitate a glance, at least, at the term's intellectual history.

Everyone agrees that the word 'metaphysics' first arose in the Aristotelian school of philosophy to cover what Aristotle had called 'first philosophy' or 'theology' – the systematic study of things eternal, or of 'being *qua* being': how it is necessary to be in order even just to *be*, at all. *Metaphysicians*, in short, were theorists offering a completely general account of what-is. Thus viewed non-methodologically, then, even experimental physics has obviously not been free of metaphysics. With the opposite of any kind of pejorative intent, G.W. Leibniz set out the following definition in *The Principles of Nature and Grace, Founded on Reason*:

> Thus far we have spoken merely as pure *physicists*; now we must rise to *metaphysics*, making use of the *great principle*, usually little employed, which affirms that *nothing takes place without sufficient reason*, that is to say, that nothing happens without its being possible for one who should know things sufficiently, to give a reason which is sufficient to determine why things are so and not otherwise. This principle being laid down, the first question we are entitled to put will be – *Why does something exist rather than nothing*? For 'nothing' is simpler and easier than 'something.' Further, granting that things must exist, we must be able to give a reason *why they should exist thus* and not otherwise.[4]

Here a teleological element has evidently been added to the understanding of what *metaphysics* is. In Leibniz's view – and certainly not in his view alone – it was the *merits* of anything which accounted for its existence; and the *why*-questions which he posed called for answers explaining what the *good* of there being something rather than nothing was, and what the *good* was of things being just the way they are. According to a contrary view, on the other hand, literal purposiveness is found in only a minute fraction of what nature has produced: people and other animals have purposes, but *their* doings aside, everything else requires non-purposive explanation.

Why is there something rather than nothing? The question has to be construed (and was, indeed, by Leibniz) as concerning, not *a priori*

---

4 G.W. Leibniz, *The Monadology and Other Philosophical Writings*, trans. Robert Latta (London, 1898), 414–15. Emphasis in original.

necessities, such as the four prime numbers that 'there are' between ten and twenty, but rather just *temporal* existents. Leibniz was after a teleological account, but even if the demand for purposive explanation is given up, or not insisted on, anyone asking this question does want a general answer, and won't be satisfied to be told that whatever there is at any time exists on account of all that has existed previously. Does this display narrow-mindedness? In any event, I myself have argued in favour of the radical answer to the question, 'Why is there something rather than nothing?' that there simply isn't (logically) any alternative. Every determination is a negation, according to a saying (wrongly) attributed to Spinoza.[5] Could there really be a *pure* negation, which was in no way a positive determination of how things are? Not if, like existence, what non-existence for its part always amounts to is just the non-existence of something specific – and therefore the existence of *something else* instead.[6]

Why, then, are things in fact just *the way they are*, and not otherwise? This is not a question about why things are as they are *now*. On Leibniz's account of time, *now* just is the time when things are this way; and in light of Relativity Theory we can agree with this, given that no exact recurrences ever do take place. The question, 'Why are things the way they are?' is actually asking for an explanation of why things are *in general* the way they are. Well, what way is that? Spatiotemporality aside, there is no way that things are in general, according to the Universal Impermanence Principle.[7] Since, as we have already seen, the question here just concerns what is temporal, the only remaining issue is why everything whatever which (in the relevant sense) exists is located in space.

---

5 By Hegel. See G.W.F. Hegel, *The Encyclopedia Logic*, trans. T.F. Geraets, W.A. Suchting, and H.S. Harris (Indianapolis, 1991), 147. Hegel presumably read Spinoza's Epistle 50 – 'Since, then, figure is nothing but limitation and limitation is negation ['*et determinatio negatio est*'], therefore ... it can be nothing but negation' – and misrecalled both the thought, and even Spinoza's words, as '*omnis determinatio est negatio*' (see Geraets, Suchting, and Harris, note 15 on page 326; see also *The Correspondence of Spinoza*, trans. and ed. A. Wolf [London, 1928], 270).

6 See my paper 'Why Is There Something Rather than Nothing?' *Philosophy and Phenomenological Research* 40, no. 2 (December 1979), 265–71.

7 Is the limitation of space to three dimensions something which actually is so, which is not a necessity *a priori*, and which nevertheless is logically incapable of changing? Contemporary scientific thinking does not *automatically* agree with this, but, should it be true, it perhaps will be a bona fide residual case of *metaphysical* truth, unexplainable, an arbitrary 'brute fact.' (Don't metaphysicians claim, though, to be the arch-enemies of any and all universal-scope 'brute facts'? Contrariwise, whatever is used to explain *everything* must itself go unexplained. Who or what made God?)

But that is a necessary condition of everything which exists being made up of differentiated parts. Anything existent which were not composed of such parts would be only finitely complex, so that it could be described exhaustively in a definitive formula (of finite length) which would be sufficient to entail everything true about its intrinsic character.[8] The denial that anything can be exhaustively summed up in that way is not metaphysical, but anti-metaphysical. The metaphysician is the theorist who wants to put definitive labels on things which will explain everything significant about them. The recognition that nothing in existence can be summed up completely, and that just about everything (logically contingent) that can be said in general terms is only a conditional approximation of the truth, this is the direct negation of metaphysics.

Was that a reasonably persuasive definition?

---

8 Suppose there could be something which were both spatially unlocated and infinitely complex. Its infinity of logically independent aspects would have to be, at any given time, causally related to one another *somehow*, or they could not all be aspects of one single thing. But, where any causal interrelation obtains, such a relation can be a *mediate* one between (among) the relata only if intermediate causes spatially intervene between (among) them. Whatever, thus, were to coexist with any one of them would have to be causally related with it immediately, or not at all. Accordingly, either there will be nothing whatever to unite all these spatially unlocated 'aspects' with one another and set them apart from everything else as aspects of any one separate thing, or else that thing will have to be altogether causally unrelated to anything else whatsoever. What sort of 'existent' would that be?

PART THREE

On the Canons of Morality

19 Preliminary Considerations

Can Reason, which completes its function in seeing things as they are, transform them into what they had better be? Can its stately and placid neutrality command that wild inward world, and, like Neptune's head emerging from the deep, silence the winds and allay the waves by the look of an eye? As well might you commission an academy of sciences to quell a rebellion. Truth has no executive; and to achieve any readjustment of the affections, to expel a traitor, to face a captive, to chain a tyrant *there*, appeal must be made to a faculty that can *cause something*, instead of merely *understanding everything* ...

James Martineau (1886)[1]

Contrary to the views expressed in the quoted epigraph, ethical rationalists have endeavoured to maintain that in the field of morality, at any rate, truth does 'have an executive'; or at least that the *recognition* of truth – like its erroneous misrecognition – is something inherently motivating. Their opponents have commonly agreed that moral convictions are psychologically motivating, but on that very account have denied that they can ever, in so far, qualify as being *true* in the way 'factual' opinions can. This accordingly poses the question with some urgency as to what *moral convictions* are. A question, you might think, of social-scientific taxonomy.

Part two of this book opened with a provisional definition of 'induction' to enable the inquiry to get started. But 'induction' is a

---

1 *Types of Ethical Theory*, vol. 2, 2nd ed. (Oxford, 1886), 482–3. Emphasis in original.

philosophical term of art, though it stands for something endemic to the whole human race – as well, indeed, as other animals in a possibly extended sense. 'Morality,' on the other hand, is an everyday word for a concern confined to our species, though universal or nearly universal there. The taxonomic issues involved in defining *morality* cannot all be fully addressed until chapter 26 is reached. But it is possible to deal with certain issues right away: *are* 'moral convictions' inherently motivating? are moral claims distinguishable or indistinguishable from claims about non-moral matters of fact? is ethical rationalism or isn't it by nature politically dangerous – inimical to freedom of speech?

We had better, also, consider how to demarcate the different possible positions in the field of meta-ethics. Moral claims either are all truthvalueless, or else not. The former, *non-cognitivist* position will be considered under the heading of moral 'decisionism' in chapter 24. In the alternative, if some moral claims are actually true or false, they are either all false, or not. The all-false position, moral 'nihilism,' will also be discussed in chapter 24. Then there is the view that there's *no telling* whether there are any moral truths, or at any rate what they are. That is the position of moral 'scepticism,' treated in chapter 24 as well. If, in the alternative, it really is possible, at least sometimes, to tell that certain moral claims are true, this then will be or will not be possible at least sometimes by sense-experience unaided by any reasoning. The former position I call moral 'sensationalism,' the topic of chapter 20. (Does 'sense-experience' here include the experiences of any 'moral sense'? It does if there is any.) On the other hand, however, if it is sometimes possible, though not by unaided sense-experience, to tell that certain moral claims are true, then this must be either by means of deductive reasoning, employing only analytic or empirical premises, or alternatively by means of inductive reasoning, or else in some other way. The first of these three positions is ethical 'naturalism,' considered in chapter 21. The second is ethical 'inductivism,' the topic of chapter 22. And the third position is the viewpoint which I shall here be defending against all these alternatives. An important school of thought, which I call that of moral 'pragmatism,' seeks to defend committing oneself to morality by means of arguing deductively and/or inductively that that is in one's interests. Though, strictly speaking, such argumentation would come under the heading of 'naturalism' or 'inductivism,' it seems appropriate to devote a separate discussion to moral 'pragmatism' in chapter 23. I wish to argue in this book that morality is a distinct subject matter, and our commitment to it just as much a part of human reason as our basic deductive and inductive mental capacities. Finally, I wish to defend and to prove a particular ethic – a form of utilitarianism – by showing that any moral position at variance with it will have to be internally inconsistent.

Let's come back to the question whether moral convictions are inherently motivating. David O. Brink answers the question with an emphatic no: 'Some people (e.g., certain sociopaths) do not care about what they regard as moral considerations ... the amoralist is someone who recognizes the existence of moral considerations and remains unmoved.'[2] Brink explains that the kind of 'amoralist' he particularly has in mind is not merely one who *on balance* isn't moved to action by acknowledged moral demands but who in fact is *'completely indifferent'* to them.[3] And this 'amoralist,' he insists, really does consider the demanded behaviour to be morally required, and not merely 'morally' required (required according to generally accepted moral norms).[4]

> It is simply unclear why we should assume that the person who professes indifference to what she insists are moral requirements is confusedly using moral language in inverted commas or mistaken about what morality requires. We can imagine someone who regards what we take to be moral demands as moral demands – and not simply as conventional moral demands – and yet remains unmoved ... We may ... think that such a person is merely possible and has never existed and will never exist (although I think this thought is wrong). But we do think that such a person is possible ...[5]

This is what 'we' think, Brink says. Do we? At least it is 'unclear why we should assume' the opposite, he insists. He's right that the burden of proof does rest with the denier of such a thing's logical possibility. To bear that burden, it will be necessary first of all to take up briefly the psychiatric disorder of sociopathy which he mentions, though this topic will need more discussion in chapter 27. Sociopaths, or 'psychopaths,' are often said to be conscienceless, and they are indeed notable for the lack of compunction with which they lie, cheat, physically and verbally abuse innocent people, including all who love them, and casually ride roughshod over the concerns and interests of others (and their own long-term interests as well: characteristically they are anything but prudent

---

2 David O. Brink, *Moral Realism and the Foundations of Ethics* (Cambridge, 1989), 46.
3 Ibid., 48.
4 Ibid., 46.
5 Ibid., 47–8.

individuals). Considering them conscienceless, many a commentator has *expressed* this by saying that, in fact, sociopaths *lack any views* on moral questions.[6] That they often *voice* strong views is another matter. They are characteristically excellent, shameless liars. Brink, however, prefers a linguistic usage that wouldn't make lack of any *moral* convictions directly deducible from consciencelessness.

Or, rather, he imputes such a usage, in effect, to 'us.' But how do we really use moral vocabulary? Could we seriously consider people to view behaviour as 'reprehensible' which we knew they had no honest tendency to *reprehend*, even tacitly? Just what is the supposed psychological difference between *morally disapproving* of something and regarding it as 'immoral'? It is, admittedly, quite possible to have negative moral-type *feelings* about something without, all things considered, regarding it as immoral *or* morally disapproving of it. For instance, that is the state of mind of many who have (as they themselves see it) emancipated themselves from former moral prejudices rooted in their upbringing. Presumedly, Brink will accept that any positive or negative *feelings*, including feelings of reprehension and disapproval, *are* inherently motivating. (Even if such motivations are always potentially capable of being outweighed by stronger countermotivations: what is called 'temptation.')[7]

Imagine a people whose society and language our anthropologists have only encountered for the first time. Suppose there are no bilinguals who can translate this society's language into any tongue accessible to

---

6 For instance, Hervey Cleckley, *The Mask of Sanity*, 3rd ed. (St Louis, 1955), 425, footnote: 'In contrast with all the various diversities of viewpoint and degrees of conviction found among ordinary people, the so-called psychopath holds no real viewpoint at all and is free of any sincere conviction in what might be called either good or evil.'

7 Michael Stoker, however, writes: 'Through spiritual or physical tiredness, through accidie, through weakness of body, through illness, through general apathy, through despair, through inability to concentrate, through a feeling of uselessness or futility, and so on, one may feel less and less motivated to seek what is good. One's lessened desire need not signal, much less be the product of, the fact that, or one's belief that, there is less good to be obtained or produced, as in the case of a universal Weltschmertz. Indeed, a frequent added defect of being in such "depressions" is that one sees all the good to be won or saved and one lacks the will, interest, desire, or strength'. 'Desiring the Bad: An Essay in Moral Psychology,' *Journal of Philosophy* 76, no. 2 (December 1979), 744. Presumably Stocker is using the word 'desire' here in the occurrent sense of a felt *impulse* in favour of what is 'desired.' In the sense defined in appendix 2, though, it is perfectly possible for something to be 'desired' by an individual who feels no such impulse to take action for its sake owing to a feeling of weakness, futility or the like.

our anthropologists. The anthropologists will have to begin by settling down to learn this language the hard way, though perhaps somewhat faster than they originally learned their own native tongue because of what they have learned from the science of linguistics. Clearly, the anthropologists will not have completed their study of this people's language and culture before they can identify what term or terms in that language (if any) mean 'immoral,' for example. Surely any term, '* * *,' in that language would be correctly translatable as 'immoral' in English, only if the meaning of the term were such that no person totally indifferent to something could ever be correctly said in that language to regard it as something which was '* * *.' Isn't this sort of tie-in with motivation a *criterion* for considering any vocabulary in a language to be part of the *moral* vocabulary of that language? To the more specific taxonomic criteria of any people's *moral* utterances, attitudes and institutions we will be returning in chapter 26.

But what if Brink, or those agreeing with his ideas, remain still unconvinced? Perhaps the following reasoning *should* be found sufficient. Whether or not I am right about the meaning of English expressions like the word 'moral,' it is certainly possible to consistently *imagine* a language resembling English in all other ways, but in which the term 'moral' did have the sort of meaning for which I have been arguing. Of course, the English word 'moral' would not correctly translate the word 'moral' in that language unless what I and so many others have claimed about the English language is correct. Without prejudging that question, we can certainly introduce a new term into the English language that *will* accurately translate the word 'moral' in the language imagined, and to symbolize this new term typographically it will be convenient to write it, say, as '*moral.' The question to be raised now is why the field of moral philosophy exists at all. Given its existence, no doubt some could be attracted to it for a variety of motives, historical, careerist, and so forth. But can there be any doubt that the prime reason why there is such a branch of philosophy is interest in answering the question what behaviour is *moral* and what isn't? It certainly is not philosophy alone which addresses that question, but if people weren't concerned with that question at all, it's clear moral philosophy would scarcely exist as any sort of field of inquiry. Why, then, are people concerned with the question of what behaviour is *moral* and what isn't? Surely the answer to that, too, is obvious. A fuss is made about what behaviour is *moral* and what isn't primarily because of concerns about the issue of *how to act* in different situations. So the question of what is *moral* and what isn't concerns people above all because of concern about what is *moral and what isn't. In other words, interest in moral philosophy derives, in the main, from interest in *moral* questions. As this term has been introduced, to answer a *moral* question in any particular way (honestly) is logically incompatible with an attitude of complete indifference. So it is really *moral questions, in the main, which lie at the root of moral philosophy. Thus, to determine what is right and what is wrong *morally in any specific situation or in general is to answer the main question or type of question basically underlying moral philosophy as a field of inquiry. In the last resort, it is only the answer to *moral questions which are of much interest, essentially, in this particular field of inquiry.

That should surely be sufficient justification for employing the word 'moral' to mean '*moral' in the remainder of this book. And so similarly for related terms like 'immoral,' 'upright,' and so on.

Some writers have insistently maintained that a culture could apply its vocabulary of moral epithets straightforwardly to convey empirical information (or misinformation).[8] Just what information could that be? What empirical facts could a truthful speaker be reporting in calling some deed 'immoral,' say? Only two sorts of empirical facts could be said universally to attend all instances of anybody calling a deed *immoral*: (1) the speaker morally disapproves of the deed, or professes to; and (2) the deed contravenes, or allegedly contravenes, some moral norm to which the speaker appeals.

(1) But if 'That is immoral' really meant or even just entailed, 'That is disapproved of by me,' then 'Such is my fallibility that it's certain some things which really are immoral are not things of which I morally disapprove' would be a logically contradictory thing to assert. Who, though, would seriously hesitate to assert it? And who would hesitate to assert, equally consistently surely, 'Without question there are some immoral things of which I neither morally disapprove now nor ever shall, unfortunately, until the day I die'?

(2) In pre-1945 Japan, nearly everyone adhered to Shintoism and morally approved of ritual hara-kiri. We can take it that people were ready to make or accept statements such as, 'Hara-kiri sono Shinto no seisin ni motozuita kagiri wa iikoto de aru,' which would normally be translated, 'Hara-kiri carried out in the Shinto spirit is a good thing.' The Japanese word 'iikoto' is normally translated as *goodness* or *good*

---

8 For instance, Alasdair MacIntyre, *A Short History of Ethics* (New York, 1966), 6–7.

thing. It comes from the word 'yoi,' normally translated as *good*. However, if the understanding of moral epithets here under considera-tion were to be adopted, then 'yoi' would really have to be interpreted as meaning *in the Shinto spirit*, or the like, in pre-war Japanese, and it would have to be theorized that 'Hara-kiri sono Shinto no seisin ni motozuita kagiri wa iikoto de aru,' was analytic and really meant some-thing like, 'Hara-kiri carried out in the Shinto spirit is in the Shinto spir-it,' a true proposition from which nobody at all would ever have dreamed of dissenting – not even, for example, the members of the anti-hara-kiri Christian minority in pre-war Japan. But clearly, any such understanding of this sentence in pre-war Japanese would be a *mis*-understanding of it, and any such translation a mistranslation.

(The foregoing reasoning is inspired, of course, by the so-called open question argument: for example, '"Good" cannot mean "..." because, if it did, then "Is ... good?" would not, in that case, be the open question which it is.' However, it is sufficiently possible to be ignorant or con-fused about one's own use of language to the extent that one considers, 'Is *** really ...?' to be an open question even when '***' does just *mean* '...' in one's own parlance.)

In 1964 John Searle argued it was tautological that promising to do something created an obligation to do it.

> ... promising is, by definition, an act of placing oneself under an obliga-tion. No analysis of the concept of promising will be complete which does not include the feature of the promiser placing himself under or undertak-ing or accepting or recognizing an obligation to the promisee, to perform some future course of action ...[9]

It would seem closer to the mark, however, to say that *promising* is, by definition, an act of placing oneself under an 'obligation' (that is, pur-posely acquiring a *putative* obligation: an obligation according to accepted norms). By way of a parallel, the very concept of 'swearing an oath' is of such a nature as to make 'To swear an oath is to commit oneself in relation to certain definite theological tenets' tautological. The social institution of oath-taking could not be understood in isolation from theology. But present-day historians, for instance, who report the oaths which a medi-eval knight once swore, are not committing *themselves* theologically in

---

9 John R. Searle, 'How to Derive "Ought" from "Is",' *Philosophical Review* 73, no. 1 (January 1964), 45.

reporting what occurred then. By the same token, suppose that the sense of moral obligation to keep promises once they are made were to die out completely – and with it, of course, the practice of making promises as well (for undoubtedly making a promise will serve no purpose where it is known that the promisee cannot expect the promise-maker to feel any particular obligation to do what has been promised). *Imaginably* organized society just might manage to continue on, thanks to the legal sanctions backing up formal contractual 'obligations.' Under those conditions, what would prevent historians of that future epoch from reporting the promises made back in the present? Such reports surely would not commit these historians to morally blaming whoever broke any of those present-day promises without an excuse. And so, the empirical fact that a promise has been made really does not commit anyone reporting it 'by definition' to the existence on the part of the promise-maker of any moral obligation – or even any moral obligation *other things being equal* – to do that which was promised.

More recent attempts to conceive moral evaluation as inextricable from reports of empirical facts have not been based on analyticity claims but have still continued to focus on what Bernard Williams calls 'thick ethical concepts.'[10] In addition to *promise*, he instances such concepts as those of *treachery*, *coward*, *brutality* and *gratitude*. A given culture's distinction between the sort of behaviour which is and the sort of behaviour which is not *cowardly*, for example, cannot be formulated in normatively neutral terms, he maintains, though 'an insightful observer can indeed come to understand and anticipate the use of the concept without actually sharing the values of the people who use it.'[11] To possess the 'insight' of which Williams speaks here, doubtless no amount of value-free empirical or logical information is going to be sufficient, as he conceives the matter. Apparently going still further in this direction, John McDowell seems, in all seriousness, to take the imaginative sympathy required in order just to understand anything in a society's value-system, in his conception, to fall little short of complete agreement with the value-system at any rate on that point.[12] On such a view, any part of learning a community's

---

10 Bernard Williams, *Ethics and the Limits of Philosophy* (Cambridge, MA, 1985), 128–42. The quoted phrase occurs on page 140.

11 Ibid., 141–2.

12 John McDowell, 'Non-cognitivism and Rule-following,' in Steven H. Holtzman and Christopher M. Leich, eds., *Wittgenstein: To Follow a Rule* (London, 1981), 141–62. But see John McDowell, 'Values and Secondary Qualities,' in Ted Honderich, ed., *Morality and Objectivity* (London, 1985), 120 and 127, note 35.

language, learning how to apply its concepts, necessitates participatory observation: it is really an initiation process whereby the successful learner 'cottons on to a practice'[13] that cannot be described in terms free of commitment to that practice. This insistence of McDowell on 'uncodifiability'[14] does not lead him to resist the proposition that in any single instance the correctness of any given moral characterization, from the standpoint of the concepts involved, must 'supervene' upon facts statable in value-neutral terms. However,

> It does not follow ... that the set of items to which a supervening term is correctly applied need constitute a kind recognizable as such at the level supervened upon. ... however long a list we give of items to which a supervening term applies, described in terms of the level supervened upon, there may be no way, expressible at the level supervened upon, of grouping just such items together.[15]

However that may be, all talk of 'thick ethical concepts' indivisibly combining the evaluative and the non-evaluatively descriptive is going to be open here to the same pointed question. Whenever people apply any of these concepts properly to approve or to disapprove of something, how do they *tell* that the concept really fits? Is their verdict a direct – that is, unreasoned – upshot of the sensory stimulation they experience? This is the position of sensationalism. Is it derived by deductive and/or inductive reasoning from any of the (non-evaluatively statable) empirical facts of the case? Those are the positions of naturalism and inductivism. Is the verdict reached through some further sort of reasoning, whether conscious or otherwise? This is in line with ethical rationalism, the position defended in the present text. It is well known that any general principle can be recast as an inference rule: that is to say, for any general principle there is an inference rule such

---

13 John McDowell, 'Virtue and Reason,' *The Monist* 62, no. 3 (July 1979), 347.
14 Ibid.
15 McDowell, 'Non-cognitivism and Rule-following,' 145. Contrariwise, the degree of conceptual complexity any human mind is capable of grasping is of necessity only finite; and so, if learning a moral concept involves acquiring a grasp, whether conscious or not, of *what it is* that the correctness of the application of the concept is intended to supervene upon, then this *must* be graspable in a finitely complex conception of just the sort which McDowell is at pains to deny need be possible in principle. The same objection applies, I think, to Williams' 'thick ethical concepts,' which are claimed to unite inextricably the evaluative and the non-evaluatively descriptive.

that, tautologically, if belief in the principle is warranted, inferences according to the rule are in order – and vice versa. The rationalist position can equivalently be expressed as backing for synthetic *a priori* principles or for the corresponding rules of inference in ethics.[16]

John McDowell, for his part, thinks that by insisting on the inextricability of empirical reportage from moral evaluation in the relevant cases he is striking a lethal blow against the philosophy of *non-cognitivism*, according to which moral judgments are all truthvalueless. That now venerable viewpoint must surely derive much of its appeal, at least in many non-philosophical educated circles, from the conception scarcely questioned there that the apprehension of truth – or, at any rate, the reliable apprehension of truth – depends upon scientific objectivity, and scientific objectivity requires a stance of strictly neutral detachment. The following quotation from *Ethical Relativity* by Edward Westermarck (1862–1939) could almost have been used as an epigraph to this chapter in place of the Rev. James Martineau's more purple late-Victorian prose.

> I have thus arrived at the conclusion that neither the attempts of moral philosophers or theologians to prove the objective validity of moral judgments, nor the common sense assumption to the same effect, give us any right at all to accept such a validity as a fact. So far, however, I have only tried to show that it has not been proved; now I am prepared to take a step further and assert that it cannot exist. The reason for this is that in my opinion the predicates of all moral judgments, all moral concepts, are ultimately based on emotions, and that, as is very commonly admitted, no objectivity can come from an emotion. It is of course true or not that we in a given moment have a certain emotion; but in no other sense can the antithesis of true and false be applied to it.[17]

'No objectivity can come from an emotion.' Yes, it is indeed commonly admitted that when we become *emotional* our judgment tends to lapse, and we are liable to lose the ability to be objective – the ability, that is, to judge undistortedly. To exercise good judgment, it is apt to be of some importance to be calm and not 'emotional' – that is, not *agitated* mentally. But the kind of 'emotional commitment' which

---

16 But isn't it possible to conceive of a view being taken to the effect that, though the reasoning in question is cogent enough, it is not susceptible of any finitely complex codification? See footnote 14 above.

17 Edward Westermarck, *Ethical Relativity* (Paterson, NJ, 1960), 60.

an honest moral judgment of necessity involves is compatible with remaining quite calm (though, to be sure, some sudden great violation or unexpected fulfillment of what we are committed to can indeed provoke in us a temporary 'emotional arousal,' supplanting our calm).

But does not even the calmest 'emotional commitment' necessarily *bias* the judgment, and in that way militate against objectivity? Of course, any opinion we ever hold on *any* question necessarily 'biases' us in the sense that, in holding it, we are thereby more favourable to one side of the question than any other. But how could *this* show that no opinion can even hope to be more justified objectively than its rivals, or be objectively *true* rather than *false*? Medical researchers and practitioners are *supposed* to be, in *this* sense, 'biased' in favour of health, and judges of law in favour of legality; and those 'biases' are *supposed* to motivate them to be just as objective as they can in their thinking. Why should the emotional commitment adhering to a position involves really have to preclude the position from being itself objectively true or false?

The answer given by noncognitivists, especially in the twentieth century, is that emotional commitments are *desires* (in the generic sense of the word, covering any motivations; see appendix 2). But *desires*, it is argued, cannot be true-or-false because they are not *beliefs*. Not, at any rate, in the sense in which we call people's 'beliefs' about non-ethical matters true and false. But why not? Admittedly, *most* desires are not beliefs, and most beliefs aren't desires. And when any desires *are* beliefs (as is the case with our specifically moral sentiments, according to the claims of this book), it is not *as* desires that they are true-or-false, but only as beliefs. Admittedly, it isn't good English to speak of 'true or false *desires*' (except in the sense of genuine or pretended desires); but a sentence linguistically ill-formed in this way can still make sufficient sense to be entirely true. Consider the following parodies:

- Animals can't be chattels, because animals are healthy or ill, but you can't speak of healthy or ill *chattels*.
- Trees can't be obstacles, because a tree is deciduous or evergreen, but you can't speak of a deciduous or evergreen *obstacle*.
- No auditor can be an organism, because any auditor is either scrupulous or unscrupulous, but it's solecistic to speak of a scrupulous or unscrupulous organism.

- Sounds can't be waves in the air, because a sound is either loud or soft, but it isn't good English to speak of 'a loud or soft wave in the air.'[18]

Of course Rover is not healthy or ill *as* a chattel, but as an animal. An obstacle isn't deciduous or evergreen *as* an obstacle, but as a tree. And so on.

The point is worth emphasizing that to say somebody's psychological state can have certain characteristics *as* a desire and different ones *as* a belief is not the same thing as agreeing with those who have advocated the proposition that moral attitudes are *partly* desires and *partly* beliefs – any more than a pet can be regarded as being *partly* an animal and *partly* a chattel, et cetera. In search of a philosophical argument to make the mutual exclusion of beliefs (insofar as they are beliefs) and desires (insofar as they are desires) seem reasonable, appeal has been made to 'propositional attitude' analysis, which no doubt is altogether defensible, in its way, in saying that *beliefs* and *desires* are 'directed' at the same things, except that what is *believed* (to be so) in the case of the former is *desired* (to be so) in the case of the later. Even then, however, to propose that certain beliefs *are* desires need not imply that *what* is believed is the same thing as *what* is desired. When people *believe mercy (veracity) to be requisite*, this belief of theirs could surely be described as being, at the same time, a desire they have, without it following at all that they *desire mercy (veracity) to be requisite*. Rather, of course, they desire mercy (veracity) to be *practised*. (What would it mean to 'desire mercy [veracity] to be requisite'? *Perhaps*, in a Scotist spirit, one can imagine an angel at the court of the Godhead petitioning the Almighty to *make* mercy [veracity] a moral obligation.[19] Be this as it may, that has nothing to do with what we're concerned with here.)

---

18 Cf. George Berkeley's *First Dialogue between Hylas and Philonous*: 'PHILONOUS. It is then good sense to speak of *motion*, as of a thing that is *loud, sweet, acute*, or *grave*.' From *The Works of George Berkeley, Bishop of Cloyne*, vol. 2, ed. A.A. Luce and T.E. Jessop, (London, 1949), 182.

19 At least, the view is commonly attributed to Duns Scotus that the natural law (morality) owes its content to Divine will. Scotus did credit God with the power to suspend at least the human-related parts of the natural law; and so why not also power to lift the suspension and make something again be morally obligatory? Cf. *Duns Scotus on the Will and Morality*, selected and translated by Allan B. Wolter (Washington, DC, 1986), 272–5. Scotus writes: '... to dispense does not consist in letting the precept stand and permitting one to act against it. To dispense, on the contrary, is to revoke the precept or declare how it is to be understood.' (273), and: '... even if you say that a created will must necessarily be conformed to these truths

Subject to some qualification, then, it has to be admitted that it really wasn't entirely just a flight of poetry on Mark Platts' part in 1979 when he characterized

> a broad distinction between two *kinds* of mental state, factual belief being the prime exemplar of one kind and desire a prime exemplar of the other ... The distinction is in terms of the *direction of fit* of mental states with the world. Beliefs aim at the true, and their being true is their fitting the world; falsity is a decisive failing in a belief, and false beliefs should be discarded; beliefs should be changed to fit with the world, not vice versa. Desires aim at realisation, and their realisation is the world fitting with them; the fact that the indicative content of a desire is not realized in the world is not yet a failing *in the desire*, and not yet any reason to discard the desire; the world, crudely, should be changed to fit with our desires, not vice versa. I wish I could substitute a less picturesque idiom for that of *direction of fit*, but I cannot. [20]

All metaphor aside, though, what sort(s) of 'fit' and what sorts of 'should' are we talking about here? Might we take there allowably to be one generic and literal sense of 'failure' in which false belief and unsatisfied desire do both exemplify *failure*? Even if so, who's to say that a moral claim is not open to 'failure' in *two* distinct ways: the failure of the moral standard it expresses to be realized; and the failure of whatever or whoever it commends or criticizes to be good or bad, right or wrong in actual fact? Corresponding to such a pair of distinct ways of exemplifying failure there would, of course, be two distinct ways in which a reality could be seen to 'fit' a moral claim: proceedings in the world could, in reality, be acceptable by the standard it expressed; and/or whatever or whoever it favourably or unfavourably judged could really be as good or bad, right or wrong as it said.[21]

---

if it is to be right, this still does not say that the divine will wills in accord with them; rather because it wills accordingly, therefore they are true' (275).

20 Mark de Bretton Platts, *Ways of Meaning* (London, 1979), 256–7. Platts apologizes for this conception's being 'difficult to state in non-metaphorical terms'; and, indeed, he raises it, he says, because it poses a serious problem for the moral realism which he still finds 'deeply attractive' (263); it is a problem, though, that he admits he does not see how to resolve decisively (257). Emphasis in original.

21 Cf. David McNaughton, *Moral Vision: An Introduction to Ethics* (Oxford, 1988), 107–10. In opposition to McNaughton's suggestion that a psychological state with 'directions of fit facing both ways' might be possible, Michael Smith cites the

But inertness-of-reason conceptions like James Martineau's, quoted as the epigraph to this chapter, were widespread long before 'propositional attitude' language became philosophically available for formulating any rationalizations of such conceptions. So why is it, then, that this fixed opinion has persisted till now that there is something illogical, or at least 'logically odd' about the idea of *beliefs which motivate*; in other words, *desires* which, by constituting the *moral* sentiments of people, are true-or-false *beliefs* of those people – and, as such, potentially adjudicatable by reason? Why does such an opinion persist? David Hume was putting forward this anti-objectivist opinion already in 1740 (premising his proto-conventionalist doctrine about the subject matter of logico-mathematical knowledge):

> Reason is the discovery of truth or falsehood. Truth or falsehood consists in an agreement or disagreement either to the *real* relations of ideas, or to *real* existence and matter of fact. Whatever, therefore, is not susceptible of this agreement or disagreement, is incapable of being true or false, and can never be an object of our reason. Now 'tis evident our passions, volitions, and actions, are not susceptible of any such agreement or disagreement; being original facts and realities, compleat in themselves, and implying no reference to other passions, volitions, and actions. 'Tis impossible, therefore, they can be pronounced either true or false, and be either contrary or conformable to reason.[22]

But *why* are our passions and volitions 'original facts and realities, compleat in themselves, and implying no reference to other passions, volitions and actions'? Had Hume, perhaps, advanced a *reason* in the preceding year (in terms of his theory of 'impressions' and 'ideas') for asserting the necessary truthvaluelessness of every 'passion'? –

---

differing psychological responses to a perception that something is not the case (a perception that *not p*): 'A state with both directions of fit would ... have to be such that *both*, in the presence of such a perception it tends to go out of existence, *and*, in the presence of such a perception, it tends to endure, disposing the subject that has it to bring it about that *p*.' Michael Smith,' The Humean Theory of Motivation,' *Mind* 96, no. 381 (January 1987), 56. However, as we have seen, to maintain that moral beliefs *are* desires needn't imply that *what* is believed is the same thing as *what* is desired in the case of such a psychological state.

22 David Hume, *Treatise of Human Nature*, Book II, Part I, section I, ed. L.A. Selby-Bigge, 2nd ed., rev. P.H. Nidditch (Oxford, 1978), 458. Emphases in original.

The understanding exerts itself after two different ways, as it judges from demonstration or probability; as it regards the abstract relations of our ideas, or those relations of objects, of which experience only gives us information. I believe it scarce will be asserted, that the first species of reasoning alone is ever the cause of any action. As it's proper province is the world of ideas, and as the will always places us in that of realities, demonstration and volition seem, upon that account, to be totally remov'd, from each other ... Abstract or demonstrative reasoning, therefore, never influences any of our actions, but only as it directs our judgment concerning causes and effects; which leads us to the second operation of the understanding.

'Tis obvious, that when we have the prospect of pain or pleasure from any object, we feel a consequent emotion of aversion or propensity, and are carry'd to avoid or embrace what will give us this uneasiness or satisfaction. 'Tis also obvious, that this emotion rests not here, but making us cast our view on every side, comprehends whatever objects are connected with its original one by the relation of cause and effect. Here then reasoning takes place to discover this relation; and according as our reasoning varies, our actions receive a subsequent variation. But 'tis evident in this case, that the impulse arises not from reason, but is only directed by it. 'Tis from the prospect of pain or pleasure that the aversion or propensity arises towards any object: And these emotions extend themselves to the causes and effects of that object, as they are pointed out to us by reason and experience. It can never in the least concern us to know, that such objects are causes, and such others effects, if both the causes and effects be indifferent to us.[23]

Once again it is possible to observe that in the *present* debate, at any rate, to take Hume's Fork for granted is unacceptably question-begging. And views like Hume's about deductive reasoning are what chapters 3 and 4 were devoted to rebutting.

One further argument of Hume's is worth noting, since something like it seems still to exert some influence even today:

According to the principles of those who maintain an abstract rational difference betwixt moral good and evil, and a natural fitness and unfitness of things, 'tis not only suppose'd, that these relations, being eternal and immutable, are the same, when consider'd by every rational creature, but their *effects* are also suppose'd to be necessarily the same; and 'tis concluded they have no less, or rather a greater, influence in directing the will of the deity,

---

23 Ibid., Book II, Part III, section III, 413–14.

than in governing the rational and virtuous of our own species. These two particulars are evidently distinct. 'Tis one thing to know virtue, and another to conform the will to it. In order, therefore, to prove, that the measures of right and wrong are eternal laws, *obligatory* on every rational mind, 'tis not sufficient to shew the relations upon which they are founded: We must also point out the connexion betwixt the relation and the will; and must prove that this connexion is so necessary, that in every well-disposed mind, it must take place and have its influence; tho' the difference betwixt these minds be in other respects immense and infinite. Now besides what I have already prov'd, that even in human nature no relation can ever alone produce any action; besides this, I say, it has been shewn, in treating of the understanding, that there is no connexion of cause and effect, such as this is suppose'd to be, which is discoverable otherwise than by experience, and of which we can pretend to have any security by the simple consideration of the objects. All beings in the universe, consider'd in themselves, appear entirely loose and independent of each other.[24]

This certainly looks like an ancestor of the now familiar 'logical oddity' argument that a *fact* or quality of something (such as its goodness) could not have the 'magnetic' property of *necessarily attracting* whoever recognized it. Why couldn't it? If an argument like this could succeed, it would not only disprove the possibility of objective rationality as far as answering any basic moral question goes, but equally disprove the possibility of achieving objective rationality in regard to any question at all. From the premise that a mind is truly *well-disposed* it does follow logically that it will, insofar as it is well-disposed, approve of such things as are really good and disapprove of such as are really bad; and furthermore, that it will motivate whoever it is whose mind it is to act accordingly – insofar as it genuinely is a *well-disposed* mind. In like manner, from the premise that a mind is truly *rational*, it follows in the same way that it will agree (provided it understands them sufficiently) with just such ethical precepts as really are rationally well-founded. It is tautological that posing any rationally answerable question to *sufficiently* rational minds desirous of the right answer will tend to cause them all to come up with the *same* answer to the question: that is, the correct answer. To call a mind 'rational' or 'well-disposed' is already saying something by logical implication about what effects on it such stimuli will tend to produce.

---

24 Ibid., Book III, Part I, section I, 465–6. Emphasis in original.

This does not negate Hume's proposition that, logically speaking, 'all beings in the universe, consider'd in themselves, appear entirely loose and independent of each other.' The discussion in chapter 8 gives us no reason to deny that it is always possible so to frame the conjunctive description of any causes and effects operative on a given occasion that, no matter how full this description, if that conjunct is deleted which reports the relevant sequences of type-events occurring in other times and places, what remains will no longer entail any of the causal relationships in operation on the present given occasion.

Accepting that Hume's logical 'looseness' claim (insofar as it's defensible) isn't really violated by the idea of *well-disposed* minds being necessarily attracted to whatever is truly *righteous*, many may still feel, and with some reason, that this is not yet sufficient to discharge ethical rationalism's burden of proof. Just how *do* purely rational considerations *engage the will*, or at least generate volitional *tendencies*, in those to whom they are addressed? This is an issue to which it will be appropriate to return in chapter 26 and chapter 32.

We shall be expressly coming back again to ethical noncognitivism in chapter 24. But even at this initial stage it would probably be a bad idea to pass on without at least briefly dealing with what could be termed the *political* case against ethical rationalism: the charge that it philosophically militates against freedom of thought and discussion. It certainly is true that some notable opponents of free speech (Plato, Torquemada, and the list goes on) have indeed believed firmly in value objectivity. However, other clear opponents of free speech (e.g., Hobbes; e.g., Mussolini: 'Fascism is irrationalism') have, for their part, made an express point of rejecting the rationalist approach to value questions. However, (sceptics aside) before the twentieth century *almost* no one seriously questioned the objectivity of morals. Is that why the classic defences of free speech were apt to be couched in rationalist terms? 'Let her and Falsehood grapple; who ever knew Truth put to the worse in a free and open encounter?' wrote Milton in his *Areopagitica*. And John Stuart Mill argued in *On Liberty*, '... the peculiar evil of silencing the expression of an opinion is, that it is robbing the human race ... If the opinion is right, they are deprived of the opportunity of exchanging error for truth ....'[25] Argumentation along these lines would have to fail,

---

25 John Milton, *The Complete Poetry and Essential Prose of John Milton*, ed. William Kerrigan, John Bumrich, and Stephen M. Fallon (New York, 2007), 961; John Stuart Mill, *Essays on Politics and Society*, ed. J.M. Robson (Toronto, 1977), 229.

of course, when it comes to whatever controversial questions were to be logically *precluded* from having any answers that are true.

Freedom of speech no doubt can still be defended without supposing that there is any real tendency for the truth to triumph, or to be refined, in the process of rational debate. There is still the aesthetic argument, appealing to the attractiveness of diversity as such,[26] the humane objection to suppressing disfavoured outlooks that the persecution of those who embrace them will be *unkind*, and the political consideration that persecution can sometimes provoke socially disruptive resistance. But such reasonings could equally well be countered with aesthetic appeals for harmony, or appeals to prevent any mental *pain* to the opponents of the outlooks being suppressed by shielding their ears from dissentient voices, or appeals to the political advantages of enforced conformity for the sake of national unity.

In the end, there is no evading the point that those to whom it seriously *matters* what moral outlooks people generally embrace, but to whom it does not seem that rational considerations will be at all apt to give any particular advantage to better outlooks over worse ones in the competition of ideas, will find themselves driven in the direction of favouring (insofar as they are feasible) means which are not rational to secure the preferred result: tricks of rhetoric or advertising, rewards and punishments, intimidation, censorship and the like. If there are *even* limits on the moral acceptability of recourse to such methods in dealing with children, criminals and those suffering from severe mental disorders, what possible case might there be for treating the rest of the population in the least way *differently*?

(Nevertheless, there could be this much truth in the relativists' claim that their outlook is an antidote to intolerance. Insofar as we regard the position of those who disagree with us as due to irrationality on their

---

26 Cf. Richard Rorty, *Contingency, Irony and Solidarity* (Cambridge, 1989), 52: '... in respect to words as opposed to deeds, persuasion as opposed to force, anything goes. This openmindedness should not be fostered because, as Scripture teaches, Truth is great and will prevail, nor because, as Milton suggests, Truth will always win in a free and open encounter. It should be fostered for its own sake.' Admittedly, it is not *diversity* but *openmindedness* which Rorty speaks here of valuing for its own sake. And he might well resist classing such a preference as *aesthetic* rather than *moral*. But really, it is not as if there is any upper limit to how strongly felt an aesthetic preference can be. And it will be the upshot of chapter 26 that only a sentiment felt as a preference for something which is preferable objectively – that is, *truly* – could be a conscious *moral* sentiment.

part, we may be somewhat more inclined to hostility towards them than if we were to think them powerless to come over to our position through a process of rational consideration. We may blame them, that is, for insufficient earnestness in honestly examining the question at issue *as well as* for taking a morally objectionable position on it. But the sociological and psychological impediments to rationality on moral questions are so powerful, both as they affect others and as they as they affect ourselves, that justifiable blame for such irrationality can seldom, surely, be very great. By the same token, the overwhelming probability of biological evolution is today a proved fact; but few would blame *very* strongly those who still do sincerely dissent from it.)

20 Sensationalism

The inquiries which have been made by men of leisure, after some general
rule the conformity to, or disagreement from, which should denominate our
actions good or evil, are in many respects of great service. Yet let any plain
honest man, before he engages in any course of action, ask himself, Is this I
am going about right, or is it wrong? Is it good, or is it evil? I do not in the
least doubt but that this question would be answered agreeably to truth and
virtue, by almost any fair man in almost any circumstance. Neither do there
appear any cases which look like exceptions to this, but those of superstition
and of partiality to ourselves. Superstition may perhaps be somewhat of an
exception; but partiality to ourselves is not, this being itself dishonesty.

Joseph Butler (1726)[1]

It is no uncommon thing to observe an action somebody takes and experience instant outrage – 'instant' at any rate, insofar as no conscious
thought processes lie behind the sense of outrage felt. Those who dissent from sensationalism will argue, of course, that *inference* need not
always be conscious, and the conclusion that the action observed here
is outrageous has indeed been *inferred* from (apparent) features of the
total situation experienced more directly – features fully describable,
for their part, in language which is morally neutral. For sensationalism,
on the other hand, the outrageousness of the action observed is included in the *uninferred* experiential data which must serve as the starting
point for any inference that may be drawn.

---

1 *Fifteen Sermons Preached at the Rolls Chapel*, Sermon III (London, 1914), 63–4.

For ethical sensationalists, even if not for Butler himself, thoughts such as his quoted above will point to a methodological insight that the validity of general *rules* of morality can be known only by drawing inferences from the actual experience of concrete individual *examples*. I say 'actual experience' here because in the mere imagining of an example what gets envisaged is of necessity only finitely detailed, and therefore that which gets morally judged is only a *type* of example, so that what is uninferred in such a case is, not the merits of anything completely concrete, but rather just a general rule about the merits of some *sort* of action, inaction, character trait, person or social institution, et cetera.

For sensationalism, though, the validity of any moral rules is known only by drawing inferences from concrete experiences – *inferences* which we may as well call *inductive*, even if not exactly in the sense of part two of this book. The thought does come to mind that it might conceivably be maintained to be possible to experience something's merits directly and then to infer *deductively* from that, that anything sufficiently like it would share the same merits as it, from a moral point of view. But such a conclusion, of necessity, would fall short of grasping any moral *rule*, on account of leaving open, still, the *way* that possessing sufficient similarity to that which had been encountered in experience would result in sharing the same merits as it. Anything actually encountered concretely will possess any number of distinct features, after all, even if it is only possible to learn of a finite set of them in any one encounter (or therefore in any finite number of encounters).

But, if the validity of any moral rules really were knowable only inductively, it is more than just *difficult* to see how the logical possibility could be excluded of two actions, persons, social institutions, or whatever, that were exactly alike otherwise but differed in that one was morally acceptable (say) while other one was not.

Has anybody ever totally embraced 'sensationalism' in the stark terms spelled out here? Maybe yes and maybe no. But the position surely cannot, in any case, be squared with our sense that, of necessity, whatever is *morally objectionable* (say) is so BECAUSE of what it is otherwise, anything whatever that is exactly that way being morally objectionable as well.

21 Naturalism

There cannot be a scientific morality; but neither can there be immoral science. And the reason for this is simple; it is a – purely grammatical reason.

If the premises of a syllogism are both in the indicative, the conclusion will also be in the indicative. For the conclusion to have been stated in the imperative, at least one of the premises must itself have been in the imperative. But scientific principles and geometric postulates are and can be only in the indicative. Experimental truths are again in that same mood, and at the basis of the sciences, there is and there can be nothing else. That being given, the most subtle dialectician can juggle these principles as he may wish, combine them, and pile them up on one another. All that he will derive from this will be in the indicative. He will never obtain a proposition which will state: do this, or, do not do that; that is, a proposition which affirms or which contradicts morality.

Henri Poincaré (1913)[1]

In one form, the theory that an evaluative conclusion of a deductive argument needs evaluative premises is clearly unwarrantable; I mention it only to get it out of the way. We cannot possibly say that at least one of the premises must be evaluative if the conclusion is to be so; for there is nothing to tell us that whatever can truly be said of the conclusion of a deductive argument can truly be said of any one of the premises. It is not necessary that the evaluative element should 'come in whole,' so to speak. If f has to belong to the premises it can only be necessary that it should belong

1 'Ethics and Science,' in *Mathematics and Science: Last Essays*, trans. John W. Bolduc (New York, 1963), 103.

to the premises *together*, and it may be no easy matter to see whether a set of propositions has the property f.

How in any case is it to be proved that if the conclusion is to have the characteristic f the premises taken together must also have it? Can it be said that unless this is so it will always be possible to assert the premises and yet deny the conclusion? I shall try to show that this at least is false ...

Philippa Foot (1958)[2]

In a 1995 lecture, Frank Jackson was bold enough to defend the deducibility of 'ought' from 'is,' putting forward a complex 'descriptivist' account of what an ethical term like 'right' means and commenting (in the subsequent print version of his argument:

> Just as we can sensibly doubt the result of a long complex numerical addition by virtue of its making sense to doubt that the addition was done correctly ..., so we can make sense of doubting the result of the complex story that ... leads from the descriptive to the ethical.[3]

Jackson was in effect prepared to *define* 'rightness' in empirical terms.

> I have spoken as if there will be, at the end of the day, some sort of convergence in moral opinion in the sense that mature folk morality will be a single network of input, output, and internal role clauses accepted by the community as a whole. ... I take it that it is part of current folk morality that convergence will or would occur.[4]

> What is a priori ... is not that rightness is such-and-such a descriptive property, but rather that A is right if and only if A has whatever property it is that plays the rightness role in mature folk morality, and it is an a posteriori matter what that property is.[5]

---

2   Philippa Foot, 'Moral Arguments,' *Mind* 67, no. 268 (October 1958), 507. Emphasis in original. Technically, Foot is correct here. It is indeed a simple, if trivial, matter to deduce a moral judgment from two premises neither of which by itself morally judges anything, whether favourably or unfavourably. Let the 'if' in what follows be taken truth-functionally: 'If anything is wicked, the assassination of Julius Caesar was wicked; it is false that nothing is wicked; therefore, the assassination of Julius Caesar was wicked.'
3   Frank Jackson, *From Metaphysics to Ethics* (Oxford, 1998), 151.
4   Ibid., 137.
5   Ibid., 150–1.

(From what Jackson says, we can read 'analytic' where he writes 'a priori' here.) But surely it is easy to imagine a pessimistic non-conformist who agrees that folk morality will converge – and even that it will do so in (ideally) intelligent, error-free response to empirical information and considerations of coherence – and that as a result some particular property P will play a certain role R in the ensuing 'mature folk morality,' but who nevertheless still regards P as wicked and not what *genuine* rightness is at all. Must such a pessimistic moralist be thinking inconsistently? Yes, Jackson maintains; but, as we have seen, he likens the mistake to overlooking the logical necessity of 'a long, complex numerical addition.'

However, if Jackson is really correct about what 'rightness' means in present-day English, the sentence, 'Whatever property will or would play role R in mature folk morality is the property of rightness' will be, not just analytic, but sufficiently *trivial* that (where 'w' abbreviates that sentence) it will be absolutely impossible to *understand the question* whether or not w without agreeing that w. And so, our imagined nonconformist would be incapable of existence, and not merely less than perfectly able when it comes to reasoning deductively.[6]

As we saw in chapter 19, the language of moral assessment is used by speakers in the first place to express *desires*, of a certain sort, that they (profess to) have. A moral assessment of anything, whether favourable or unfavourable, always M-implies the existence of a specific *desire* on the speaker's part (*for* any sort of thing assessed favourably, for the *prevention or minimization* of any sort of thing assessed unfavourably). Ethical naturalism is the view that at least some moral assessments are validly deducible from premises which do not make any moral assessment. The present antinaturalist case, of course, is going to be that whatever entails a conclusion carrying such a moral commitment will

---

6 Jackson, though, does say, '… to believe that something is right is to believe in part that it is what we would in ideal circumstances desire' (ibid., 159). Might he argue that it is indeed impossible to regard as wicked a pattern of conduct you yourself recognize that in 'ideal' circumstances you *would* desire and consider, even, to be rightness itself? It is important to Jackson's 'descriptivism' that he can declare, 'The relevant facts about your desire profile … that make it rational to desire A can obtain in the absence of even a whiff of current motivation towards A' (ibid., 158). *Perhaps* we could say Odysseus foresaw he would find the sirens' singing irresistibly attractive upon hearing it without even a whiff of motivation that way already in his 'desire profile.' But could we really understand you to regard as 'ideal' circumstances that you foresaw would lead you to desire something towards which you have not even a whiff of motivation currently?

consequently carry such a moral commitment itself and hence be itself a moral assessment.

The first distinction to draw here is that between the sort of statement which M-implies a specific desire on the part of the speaker and the sort of statement which does not. However, whatever entails a proposition, M-implies it, but we are not here interested in statements such as 'I desire coconuts' – though we *are* interested in statements like 'It is a good thing that I desire coconuts,' which does entail 'My desiring coconuts, if I were to do so, would be a good thing.' For our purposes, we can define 'normative' claims – of which the class of moral assessments is a (proper or improper) subset – as follows: Something is a 'normative' claim if and only if it entails a statement which M-implies the existence of a specific desire on the part of the speaker without actually entailing or being entailed by the assertion of such a desire's existence. The argument is then going to be that whatever entails any normative claim will have to make a normative claim itself. (The words 'or being entailed by' in the above formulation are there because, for example, 'I abhor lying' entails the disjunction of 'I abhor lying' and 'Lying is evil,' and this disjunction does M-imply, without entailing, the existence on the part of the speaker of a desire for the prevention or minimization of lying.)

A 'normative' statement, so understood, always M-implies the existence of a specific desire on the part of whoever makes it. But in a broader understanding, a statement can easily be *evaluative* without being 'normative,' as defined here. Such is the case with *instrumental* uses of a word like 'good.' 'Good' in that kind of sense means 'of such a sort as to be relatively likely, in normal circumstances, to preform its function with success.' Here, either the function in question of whatever it is will be the function indicated by the description under which whatever it is gets referred to – as when we speak of a good screwdriver, or a good safe-cracker, or a good farmer, or a good bet, or good tree-roots – or else, if the function intended is not indicated like this, it is to be taken to be the function that most of those concerned would wish items of that type to perform – as when we speak of good concrete, or a good sheaf of wheat, or good weather. In either case, to *evaluate* anything as instrumentally 'good' is *not* to commit yourself to caring one way or another whether the end which you evaluate it as 'good' at furthering does get advanced to any degree or not. When you in fact admit, though, to actually favouring that end's advancement, then there is indeed an M-implication of the existence on your part of an (overridable) desire for recourse to those means should they be both available and necessary.

In yet another broadly *evaluative* sense of 'good,' the word is synonymous with 'pleasing' or 'pleasant,' as when we speak of a good-tasting meal. Presumably, that is 'pleasant' which under normal conditions would (be apt to) *please* such ones as are normal; just as that is 'frightening' which normally would *frighten* the normal, and so on. And, whatever the extension of 'the normal' for these purposes, *the speaker* would always be among those meant to be included, surely. (However, where there is no particular suggestion that conditions are indeed normal, a speaker who calls something 'good-tasting,' say, is not thereby committed to acknowledging even an overridable desire at the moment to taste it, and so to call something good in this hedonic sense is arguably *not* to make a normative statement, strictly speaking.)[7]

A use of words which is neither normative, as defined, nor even evaluative in a broader sense, is the sociological, or 'inverted commas' use of a word like 'good' or 'moral' mentioned already in chapter 19. When we say, for example, 'Although a black cat is a sign of bad luck in America, it is a sign of good luck in England,' what we really mean, of course, is 'Although a black cat is regarded as a sign of bad luck in America, it is regarded as a sign of good luck in England.'

Up to this point, there has been no specific mention of the aesthetic uses of a word like 'good.' If any confusion reigns in aesthetics, it may be related to the fact that more or less all of the previously discussed ways of employing such words as 'good' are to be found there in active use, side-by-side. 'Beauty,' for example, would appear to be primarily a term of hedonic evaluation, as in those applications of the word where it is used interchangeably with 'good looks.' But a 'beautiful' sunset and a 'beautiful' wallpaper pattern equally well mean 'good-looking' ones in a straightforwardly hedonic sense, surely. On the other hand, a work of art can also be evaluated on the basis of how much the artist has accomplished, which will depend not just on how fully the artist's (consciously or otherwise) motivating *artistic intention* has been successfully realized, but, as well, on how ambitious an artistic project it was in the first place. A *good* artist, like a *good* farmer, in this instrumental sense, is an effective

---

7 Thus, for some purposes it can be quite illuminating to speak in terms of such a broad generic category of *evaluative* discourse. Classing the concept of a 'good bet' as (instrumentally) evaluative, for instance, highlights the real parallelism with meta-ethics that an open-eyed examination of the 'problem of induction' discloses. In the next chapter, though, the word 'evaluative,' as employed there, means just *ethically evaluative* (judgmental). And 'value-neutral' is employed in a similarly narrow sense both there and in chapter 6 to mean *ethically neutral.*

or efficient one – one capable of accomplishing much. Lastly, inasmuch as anything anybody does is a fit subject for moral assessment, this has to hold good of artistic productions, too. Hack works which ennoble us (if any do) will certainly deserve moral praise on that account, however inferior they may be artistically.

At first glance, these disparate criteria of evaluation will seem utterly incommensurable. However, an all-things-considered decision does have to be made, for instance, when purchasing art for private or public display. But quite other considerations again, such as expense, will then need to be taken into account as well.

22 Inductivism

Moral theories are often tested in thought experiments, against imagined examples; and, as Harman notes, trained researchers often test scientific theories in the same way. The problem, though, is that scientific theories can also be tested against the world, by observations or real experiments; and, Harman asks, 'can moral principles be tested in the same way, out in the world?' (p. 4)

This would not be a very interesting or impressive challenge, of course, if it were merely a resurrection of standard verificationist worries about whether moral assertions and theories have any testable empirical implications, implications suitable ['statable'?] in some relatively austere 'observational' vocabulary. One problem with that form of the challenge, as Harman points out, is that there are no 'pure' observations, and in consequence no purely observational vocabulary either. But there is also a deeper problem that Harman does not mention, one that remains even if we shelve worries about 'pure' observations and, at least for the sake of argument, grant the verificationist his observational language, pretty much as it was usually conceived: that is, as lacking at the very least any obviously theoretical terminology from any recognized science, and of course as lacking any moral terminology. For then the difficulty is that moral principles fare just as well (or just as badly) against the verificationist challenge as do typical scientific principles. For it is by now a familiar point about scientific principles – principles such as Newton's law of universal gravitation or Darwin's theory of evolution – that they are entirely devoid of empirical implications when considered in isolation. We do of course base observational predictions on such theories and so test them against experience, but that is because we do *not* consider them in isolation. For we can derive these predictions only by relying at the same time on a large

background of additional assumptions, many of which are equally theoretical and equally incapable of being tested in isolation. A less familiar
point, because less often spelled out, is that the relation of moral principles
to observation is similar in *both* these respects.

Nicholas Sturgeon[1]

In stating the case like this, Sturgeon's words advance what would
seem an impressively bold claim. But then Sturgeon goes on to let the
reader down with a thud:

> Candidate moral principles – for example, that an action is wrong just in
> case there is something else the agent could have done that would have
> produced a greater net balance of pleasure over pain – lack empirical impli-
> cations when considered in isolation. But it is easy to derive empirical con-
> sequences from them, and thus to test them against experience, if we allow
> ourselves, as we do in the scientific case, to rely on a background of other
> assumptions of comparable status. Thus, if we conjoin the act-utilitarian
> principle I just cited with the further view, also untestable in isolation, that
> it is always wrong deliberately to kill a human being, we can deduce from
> these two premises together the consequence that deliberately killing a hu-
> man being always produces a lesser balance of pleasure over pain than
> some available alternative act; and this claim is one any positivist would
> have conceded we know, in principle at least, how to test. If we found it to
> be false, moreover, then we would be forced by this empirical test to aban-
> don at least one of the moral claims from which we derived it.[2]

What we would surely want here, though, is some sort of inductive
inference-to-the-best-explanation proceeding from exclusively *value-neutral*
premises which stated observed facts to normative ethical conclusions.

However, there is a general argument which we had better take into
account, directed against the positive or negative ethical merits of any
persons, deeds, developments, or relationships ever *explaining* anything. According to the 'universalizability' constraint, as it has been
called, that we noted in chapter 20, it (given the actual moral and

---

1 'Moral Explanations,' in David Copp and David Zimmerman, eds., *Morality, Reason and
   Truth* (Totowa, NJ, 1985), 50–1. Emphasis in original. The Gilbert Harman quotation
   comes from his book *The Nature of Morality* (New York, 1977).
2 Ibid., 51.

nonmoral truths) would be logically impossible for those merits ever to be different from what they are unless there were differences in facts about their possessors reportable in entirely value-neutral, purely qualitative terms.[3] The ethical merits that are in question can thus be said to 'supervene' upon the actual state of those facts. And so, whatever bond there might be linking those merits to whatever phenomenon was to be explained would likewise be a bond between those *subvening* actual facts and that phenomenon. Those ethical merits would thus appear to be themselves quite redundant as far as explaining that phenomenon goes.

Adolf Hitler, for example, was anti-democratic, deceitful, aggressive, genocidal, contemptuous of the rule of law and, 'in virtue' of those facts, morally depraved. So, if his moral depravity is said to explain, for instance, the widespread reprehension directed at him, this reprehension actually can be accounted for fully by reference just to those facts.

But can Hitler's moral depravity really be distinguished from those facts about him? In common speech we do say both that those facts were what 'made' him depraved, and that that combination of traits is what his depravity specifically 'was.' It is when speaking in the latter way, surely, that we are led to *explain* things by reference to the depravity of the man. Does this mean that Hitler's depravity, considered as something due to, but distinguishable from, those specific traits of his, played no role in explaining whatever observed facts are to be accounted for? Or should we say that it is just thanks to making him depraved that these traits explain those facts? Surely we do *not* mean that the observed facts to be accounted for are in the first place explained by his depravity, while that depravity, in turn, is explained by these specific traits of his character.

Consider a parallel. We say things like 'The possibility of rain today caused many commuters to carry an umbrella.' Does our saying that contradict the proposition, which presumably few would gainsay, that *possibilities* themselves are causally inert? It was surely the actual existence of certain observational evidence that, directly or indirectly, influenced the commuters' behaviour today. Is the existence of the possibility of rain just a matter of rain's occurrence being a good bet at no more than

---

3 And, as we saw in footnote 14 in chapter 19, such ethical merits could not be different unless there were differences in facts of this sort sufficiently uncomplicated for a mind of finite capacity to comprehend. The expression 'purely qualitative terms' is being used here in the sense defined in my paper 'What Are "Purely Qualitative" Terms?' *American Philosophical Quarterly* 23, no. 1 (January 1986), 71–81.

moderately unfavourable odds, or is the existence of the possibility nothing but the existence of the observational evidence *making* rain's occurrence a good bet at no more than moderately unfavourable odds? Surely the difference here is only verbal. In any event, the relevant observations made fully explain the commuters' umbrella-taking behaviour through causal processes involving only concrete actualities: the possibility of rain, as such, does not itself figure as a link in any of the causal chains – except, that is, insofar as what counts as the existence of that possibility just is the existence of that observational evidence for possible rain.

Similarly, is opium's *'virtus dormitiva'* – its soporificity – to be simply identified with the fact that it puts smokers and other ingesters to sleep, or is it to be identified, rather, as that about opium – in fact, specific chemical properties – *thanks to which* opium puts smokers and other ingesters to sleep? In any case, it is notoriously redundant to trace the production of sleep to opium's dispositional property of soporificity, if explanation by reference to its specific chemical properties is available.

When it comes to 'causally relevant and explanatory moral facts,' however, David Brink, writing in 1989, advanced a specific argument to show that their 'causal power ... is neither equivalent to, nor derived from, [the] causal power' of the facts on which they supervene in any particular cases.[4]

> For example, racial oppression in South Africa consists in various particular social, economic, and legal restrictions present in South African society. Now, it seems better to cite racial oppression as a cause of political instability and social protest in South Africa than the particular social, economic, and political restrictions, precisely because there would still have been racial oppression and instability and protest under somewhat different social, economic, and legal restrictions, and the only thing this large set of alternate possible social, economic, and legal bases of oppression have in common is that they realize racial oppression (it is very unlikely that there is a natural – nonmoral – social category that corresponds to this set).[5]

Surely Brink is right at least to insist, as he does, that there are different forms the racial oppression in South Africa might have taken, such that

---

4 David O. Brink, *Moral Realism and the Foundations of Ethics* (Cambridge, 1989). The words quoted first appear on pages 196–7; the words quoted next appear on page 195.

5 Ibid., 195.

under otherwise similar conditions the same result of instability and social protest would still have been produced. But why would Brink think that this tends to show that the moral fact of *racial oppression* – a fact impossible to report except in judgmental language – 'will occupy a distinct and privileged explanatory role'?[6] He lays stress on there probably not being any 'natural social category' of facts subvening *racial oppression* in all those cases where that same result of instability and mass protest would still have been produced. But so what? Why would the supervening *moral* fact, as such, not be explanatorily redundant even so, at any rate, in each particular instance? Brink's answer to that is to cite the 'counterfactual fact' that, *if* the subvening facts had been different in those conceivable ways, but still such as to constitute unconscionable oppression, the same result of instability and social protest *would* have been produced.[7] But how does that counterfactual truth lend support to the conclusion Brink draws?

Consider again the case of possible rain today. Are there not quite different forms the evidence for that possibility might have taken, such that under otherwise similar conditions the observation of large-scale umbrella-taking on the part of commuters would still have resulted? Is the probability of finding a 'natural category' classing together all of those different possible bodies of observations going to be any greater than for finding a 'natural category' classing together all the different possible forms of racial oppression that Brink was speaking of? And yet, do we not remain altogether untempted to endow *possibilities* with any causal powers nonetheless?

Speaking ontologically, we may verbally identify possibilities and moral properties with the natural facts 'constituting' them; and, in doing so, we can verbally attribute to them causal powers. But, secondly, speaking epistemologically, such a possibility or such a moral property, *for us* is going to be something distinct from the facts upon which it supervenes, and so it needs to be inferred from them. To be sure, we might indeed speak of an inductive inference in the former of these two cases. But in neither of these cases is the inference going to be a sort of inference-to-the-best-explanation where the relevant possibility or moral property in question is inferred, as such, on the grounds that its distinct existence best *explains* empirical phenomena. And, however dressed up in contemporary philosophy-of-science language, the 'inductive inference of ethical

---

6 Ibid.
7 Ibid., 195–6.

conclusions' still always does require (to go through) ethically judgmental 'auxiliary hypotheses.'

A century or so ago the inductive justification of ethical precepts could seem much easier. The 'evolutionary ethics' school was prone to see ever increasing *ordered complexity*, or the like, as the empirically revealed natural – not to say divine – law, and so to consider the ethical case for favouring it made. Jean-Marie Guyau (1854–1888) went perhaps further than most in his *Esquisse d'une morale sans obligation ni sanction*:

> We have thus reached our fundamental formula. *Duty* is but an expression detached from the *power* which necessarily tends to pass into action. By duty we do but designate that power which, passing beyond reality, becomes with respect to it an ideal; becomes that which it ought to be, because it is that which it *can* be, because it is the germ of the future already bursting forth in the present. There is no supernatural principle whatever in our morality; it is from life itself, and from the force inherent in life, that it all springs. Life makes its own law by its aspiration towards incessant development; it makes its own obligation to act by its very power of action.[8]

It is easy to see that facts proving (if they do) that a certain sort of result has been and continues to be the overall tendency of the course of biological – or cosmic – evolution can thereby establish the moral desirability of such a developmental tendency only on the supposition that whatever comes *later* in any causal process of this sort is, or is apt to be, *better* than what precedes it. But the supposition itself is not justified by those facts. Such was the thinking behind the stipulation laid down in chapter 6 that evaluative conclusions couldn't be inferred *inductively* from value-neutral premises. In general, from facts about something which can be fully reported in value-neutral statements, it is legitimate to infer a favourable moral judgment of it only on condition that, for *any* x, facts like that about x will reflect well upon x; and it is legitimate to infer an unfavourable moral judgment of it only on condition that, for *any* y, facts like that about y will reflect badly upon y. Philosophers have often called a value judgment like this a 'suppressed premise' of such an inference; and certainly it is more than just difficult to see how the inference could ever succeed in justifying its conclusion unless that ethical judgment, independently of it, were to be in order.

---

8 M. Guyau, *A Sketch of Morality Independent of Obligation or Sanction*, trans. Gertrude Kapteyn (London, 1898), 211. Emphases in original.

Against calling any moral judgment of that kind the 'suppressed premise' of such an inference, however, Stephen Toulmin long ago objected that it is misleading to try to treat all ethical argumentation as really deductive, and that the postulated 'suppressed premise' of such an inference need never actually cross the reasoner's mind.[9] Whatever the merits on its own account of such an ethical 'suppressed premise,' we can agree, the inference which presupposes it will have those merits also whether this presupposed judgment gets invoked explicitly or not. But the inductivist approach here would appear only to substitute the problem of justifying that judgment, or that sort of inference, for the original problem of justifying the moral judgment taken as the inference's conclusion. It is difficult to see how our understanding is advanced as a result of the substitution.

One could imagine a possible response here objecting to this talk about the *problem* of justifying such a sort of inference. To maintain, though, that inferences of such a pattern stand in no need of any further argumentative justification is equivalent to maintaining that the moral judgment which is presupposed stands in no need of argumentative justification. Such a position is recognizably a position of ethical rationalism, not inductivism.

Ought we to classify as inductivists here all those adherents of the 'reflective equilibrium' method in ethics who do not follow John Rawls in departing from moral cognitivism?[10] Can we see them as reaching their 'conclusions' by reflections upon 'premised' facts about what considered moral judgments they (or people generally) endorse (or would endorse) initially, in conjunction with other empirical facts, including facts about just how they (or people generally) are disposed to react when faced with a choice between particular tenets in 'conflict' with

---

9 Stephen Edelston Toulmin, *The Place of Reason in Ethics* (Cambridge, 1950), and *The Uses of Argument* (Cambridge, 1958).

10 '... the idea of approximating to moral truth has no place in a constructivist doctrine: the parties in the original position do not recognize any principles of justice as true or correct ...; their aim is simply to select the conception most rational for them, given their circumstances. This conception is not regarded as a workable approximation to the moral facts: there are no such moral facts to which the principles adopted could approximate.' See John Rawls, 'Kantian Constructivism in Moral Theory,' *The Journal of Philosophy* 77, no. 9 (September 1980), 564. However, rather than alienate theistic and other cognitivists from his liberal political project, Rawls would later 'distinguish, as I should have done in the original of 1980, between moral and political constructivism,' stressing that his 'constructivist conception does not contradict rational intuitionism, since constructivism tries to avoid opposing any comprehensive doctrine.' See John Rawls, *Political Liberalism* (New York, 1993), 90, note 1, and 95.

each other (tenets psychologically impossible to embrace together in full consciousness)? Can we see them as meaning to assimilate the 're-flective' process of which they speak to *inductive reasoning* in some wider sense than Part Two of this book has recognized? In any case, however we were to classify reflective equilibrium, so conceived, as a process of inference, any 'method' based on minimizing deviations from (certain) people's initial set of considered moral judgments, and maximizing acceptance of their belief-reactions-on-reflection – any such method of reasoning can be seen to presuppose those people's presumptive reliability as moral judges. And that presupposition is itself already an ethical position, indeed one no less in need of argumentative justification than any other, if the viewpoint is to be rejected that there are some moral tenets which stand in no need of any argumentative backup.[11]

Richard Boyd is (or in 1988 was) a contemporary realist philosopher disposed to identify both reasoning in the natural sciences and inference to ethical conclusions as cases, where rational, of reflective equilibrium thinking. 'It must be possible,' he acknowledges, though, 'to explain how our moral reasoning *started out* with a stock of relevantly approximately true moral beliefs ...'[12] He writes,

What we need to know is whether it is reasonable to suppose that, for quite some time, we have had background moral beliefs sufficiently near the truth that they could form the basis for subsequent improvement of moral knowledge in the light of further experience and further historical developments ... It is hard to escape the conclusion that this is simply the question 'Has the rational empirical study of human kind proved to be possible?'[13]

Boyd said he found it hard to escape the conclusion that these two questions were the same. Might he, perhaps, with somewhat more

---

11 But Rawls for his part says in *Political Realism* that 'rational intuitionism' must itself 'rely on the idea of reflective equilibrium. Otherwise intuitionism could not bring its perceptions and intuitions to bear on each other and check its account of the order of moral values against our considered judgments on due reflection,' (95–6). In any case, however, if the intuitionists are going to put their intuitions forward as unsupported by arguments, they can at most take reflective equilibrium as a way of clarifying their intuitions, rather than any sort of reasoning (though the reflective process, of course, might well include various particular reasonings within it).

12 Richard N. Boyd, 'How to Be a Moral Realist,' in Geoffrey Sayre-McCord, ed., *Essays on Moral Realism* (Ithaca, NY, 1988), 201.

13 Ibid., 207.

imagination, have succeeded in separating the two questions from each other? He has not actually told us why he thinks a positive answer to the second question will support a positive answer to the first question. Could it be that he is simply *presupposing* the 'optimistic position ... about human potential,' at least as a presumption, upon which he apparently prides himself,[14] and is then content to entertain as the sole objection to this that he can conceive, the argument that 'human nature' is too elusive to be studied scientifically, so that no such optimistic position on it can be warranted? At any rate, the modest outlook according to which, in the absence of evidence to the contrary, it is likelier than not that human beings' heredity and environment tend to endow them with *some* reliability in the making of moral judgments, is an ethical outlook in no less need of argumentative justification than any other, if the viewpoint is to be rejected that there are some moral tenets which stand in no need of any argumentative backup.

---

14 Ibid., 202.

23 Pragmatism

Dream not that men will move their little finger to serve you, unless their advantage in so doing be obvious to them.

Jeremy Bentham (reported by John Bowring)[1]

As often remarked, such a statement as Bentham's here is either false or tautological. It is tautological if it says only that people will never freely do anything unless motivated by something that makes it seem to them a good thing to do, and in just that sense 'advantageous' from their standpoint – apt to be beneficial to what they care about. But the statement is manifestly false if it means that what is morally right, or the welfare of others, is never valued by anybody for its own sake, and never moves anybody to action accordingly. Let us understand considerations of 'self-interest' here as motives for action or inaction exclusive of any concern for that which is right for its own sake or for the welfare of others just for their sakes.

Moral teachers as diverse as Plato, Jesus, and Spinoza have indeed strongly recommended moral action to us on the basis of our own self-interest, and have been sternly rebuked for this by some academic philosophers, unmindful of the obvious point that it is perfectly possible to have more than one motive for the same course of action. It still remains, though, that our moral-type motives – our 'conscientious' motives – for action or inaction are *not the same* as our motives of self-interest.

A manifest difficulty in resting the case for moral action upon an appeal to considerations of self-interest alone is the well-known fact that

1 *Deontology*, vol. 2, ed. John Bowring (London, 1834), 133.

the dictates of morality and the dictates of self-interest frequently do not coincide, even in the long run. In very many cases crime does pay, and foreseeably so, and honesty is not the best policy. A more limited line of reasoning seeks to persuade us that it is in our long-term self-interest to be imbued with an *emotional attachment* to certain moral precepts for their own sake.[2] Even if honesty isn't always the best policy, an honest *predisposition* may indeed pay off in the long run by earning the respect and trust, and even esteem, of those with whom one has dealings. But what moral character traits could be justified this way must vary with the societal and personal circumstances of the individuals concerned. A case like that of the monster Genghis Khan – who presumably died in the robust enjoyment of personal fulfilment, success and power, together with full honour and love from all those who mattered to him – a case like that may well be somewhat rare. Yet it is doubtful if an appeal to our long-term self-interest alone could manage to justify a very extensive conscientiousness in the great majority of us, a conscientiousness extending to *systematic* regard for those weaker than us, for example. Even addressed to a restricted audience, it is perhaps only a fairly skimpy moral code which the appeal to enlightened self-interest can realistically justify.

However that may be, whoever is influenced by any measure of conscientiousness at all feels the dictates of morality as providing cogent reasons for action and inaction distinct from all considerations of self-interest. Whoever isn't conscienceless *feels* the cogency of these reasons to be quite independent of all self-interested considerations. That is an essential characteristic of the human sentiment(s) called *moral concern*. It could not be *moral* concerns of whose validity one were convinced just by self-interested considerations. If arguments are required, they cannot (in that sense) be *pragmatic*.

---

2   David Gauthier, *Morals by Agreement* (Oxford, 1986).

24 Nihilism, Scepticism, and Decisionism

> If Nature encloses within the bounds of her ordinary progress, besides all other things, the beliefs, judgements, and opinions of men; if these beliefs have their revolving seasons, their birth, their death, like cabbages; if heaven moves and rolls them about at its pleasure, what magisterial and permanent authority are we to attribute to them?
>
> Michel de Montaigne'[1]

'What magisterial and permanent authority are we to attribute to them?' the philosopher asks. But (strictly speaking) that is different from a *sceptical* challenge to according them any credence at all, rather than making oneself (if such were possible) completely opinionless. And the reader will not have failed to notice that, in the sentence quoted, Montaigne is speaking of opinions in general, not just our moral sentiments.

Nevertheless, Montaigne's rhetorical question here corresponds to what is surely a principal objection to ethical objectivity claims. The diversity of moral attitudes from society to society, subculture to subculture, and even individual to individual (so the objection runs) in spite of the overall rough similarity of the psychological causation of these attitudes in people, disproves any claims for objective reliability in all those causal processes that originate and sustain these attitudes. And, if, indeed, social science did force objectivists to admit that it could

---

1 'Apology for Raymond Sebond,' Book II, chapter 12 of Montaigne's *Essays*, in *The Essays of Montaigne*, vol. 2, trans. E.J. Trechmann (New York, 1927), 21.

only be, at best, by chance that their moral convictions corresponded to any actual (moral) facts, then they would have to go along philosophically with denying those convictions any particular likelihood of being *true* beliefs of theirs. The position that there is *no telling* whether any of them are true, or at any rate which of them are true, is a sceptical position. And, if none of them are true, then either they are all false – the position of nihilism – or truthvalueless – the position or decisionism. (A nihilist, of course, need not deny the truth of propositions such as the statement that there is nothing morally objectionable about, for instance, lying. But for this very reason *that* cannot count as a *moral belief*, for present purposes. Could there be a view just to the effect that all positive moral claims were *either* false *or* truthvalueless? It is hard to see what could motivate such a view. But, in any event, if the present treatment of nihilism and decisionism in the sequel holds good, that will equally well cover such a view as this.)

To be consistent, a moral nihilist and a moral sceptic alike would have to be conscienceless: completely free of all moral sentiments for or against anything specific, all things considered. A case will be made out in chapters 26 and 27 for the psychological impossibility of such consciencelessness (at any rate, for all those intellectually capable of grasping moral concepts). If successful, that should be enough to satisfy the reader of the untenability, the objective erroneousness, of moral nihilism and scepticism. For to recognize that you yourself are not (and couldn't be) conscienceless in that way is to recognize that you yourself are committed to the rejection of those two positions.[2]

---

2 The argument in chapter 26 will seek to show that, however weak one's moral sentiments are, and however decisively outweighed in practical decision-making, having any conscience at all will be logically sufficient to make one count as subscribing (whether consciously or not) to some moral judgments. Before passing on, though, it is fair to ask just what the psychological difference is between being an ethical sceptic and being an ethical nihilist. And actually there are three different possible positions distinguishable here. For a sceptic, as defined, can be opinionless either about whether anything at all is morally desirable or undesirable or else, in the alternative, only about *what* is morally desirable or undesirable. And sceptics of the second kind are, in a sense, not really *quite* conscienceless, inasmuch as they can be credited with an ethical desire at any rate for righteousness in the abstract: for the realization of whatever (if anything) were to be objectively valuable, satisfying all the formal requirements of morality (see chapter 26). The more extreme sceptics, like the nihilists, will (if consistent) be more *completely* conscienceless; but the nihilists will differ from any sceptics, however, in subscribing to the belief that absolutely all moral convictions are positively erroneous, being either false or cognitively defective,

It is the manifest untenability of moral nihilism and scepticism, no doubt, which has lent attractiveness to the position of decisionism in meta-ethics. The decisionists propose to retain their own moral attitudes while denying any objective truth to moral attitudes in general. But *can* moral attitudes that people have really qualify as being true-or-false *beliefs* of theirs? To classifying any moral attitudes as *beliefs* I have heard the objection suggested that perhaps *beliefs* ought to be (taxonomically) defined by reference to the possibility in principle of a believer's remaining indifferent to the supposed fact which is believed. But why have such a definition? To facilitate conceiving the action-guiding 'practical syllogism' (as Aristotelian scholars call it) to combine together one premise expressing a motivating *desire* with another premise expressing a belief? What will be lost by the amendment of 'belief' here (say) to 'non-normative belief'? In any case, though, whoever believes that genocide is immoral, for instance, need not (whatever this would mean) care one way or another about *genocide's being immoral*, as opposed, rather, to caring about *genocide*.

It is argued in chapter 26 that any (all-things-considered) moral sentiments people have are indeed true-or-false *beliefs* of theirs. If that argument succeeds, it will accordingly refute ethical decisionism.

The social-scientific argument against ethical objectivity, though, most likely ought not to be left just hanging here, completely unrebutted. The main reply must await chapters 26 and 28, but it is possible to raise some pointed questions right away. In the first place, are people's moral sentiments really as completely diverse as the argument seems to suggest? Some precept like the Golden Rule, for instance, is found in many different cultures, it 'makes sense' to people when they hear it, and it would be difficult to suppose that any *mores* whatsoever (any conscience whatsoever?) would seriously sanction a *complete* disregard for the concerns and interests of other people. Cultures do notoriously differ on the score of who fully qualify as *people*, as well as on many other issues. But it doesn't seem that actually existing moral sentiments are *completely* diverse in fact. What do they have in common, and what is the relation of this to whatever the social and psychological causes are

---

but in any case being believed falsely to be true by those who consciously hold them. The nihilists, unlike even the extreme sceptics, will embrace consciencelessness as an attitude, regard it as a presumptively useful attitude for anyone whatever to take, and regard any conscientious commitment as presumptively being just the opposite (see chapter 3).

that are responsible for people's moral sentiments? Must the causation of *all* moral sentiments be seen as so unreliable epistemologically that they could get to be objectively true in any degree only by chance at best? Given the untenability of ethical nihilism, scepticism, and decisionism, and given something like a specific ethic genuinely worthy of credence, we will be in a position in the sequel to answer these questions, I believe, in such a way as to lay the social-scientific argument against ethical objectivity to rest.

25 Ethics and Induction

Yes, there is apt to be more room for disagreement over moral questions than over questions resolvable inductively, if only because answering most moral questions is dependent in large measure on determining inductively some potentially controversial empirical facts, but settling those still could leave the pertinent moral issues unresolved.

26 Mores

Observation seems to indicate that in all human societies there is a basic
moral view that it is good as a general rule to attempt to preserve human
life. Strenuous efforts are normally made to save persons of the community and even outsiders whose life is endangered by accident or sickness.
Devotion in this may even lead individuals to sacrifice their own lives in
the attempt.

Raymond Firth[1]

As social animals, humans are more like bees or wolves than they are
like snails or bears. Human beings, in fact, are genetically adapted to
living in communities. Our *native* endowment is signally skimpy as far
as any means for personal survival in isolation are concerned. But by
way of compensation, our capacities for *learning*, above all, equip us
biologically for successful social life.

Becoming a member of any society, of course, involves learning its
rules. We can trace out a three-way division of these rules into *usages*,
mores, and *laws and regulations*. Usages are rules like fork-on-the-left-
knife-and-spoon-on-the-right or the rules of a language. Observance of
such rules may or may not be of much importance for the life of society.
While in principle what language a community speaks does not matter,
once it has a particular language, general observance of the relevant
linguistic rules will be a precondition of virtually any communication
among its members. But, as with usages generally, there is normally
little motive to break these rules, and so sanctions for breaking them

---

1 *Elements of Social Organization* (London, 1951), 201.

need not be a serious issue. From the breach of some laws (and even more regulations) there is likewise little to be feared as far as any danger to the existing social order goes; but, in contrast to usages, these do involve explicitly formulated criteria of observance and infraction, ways of determining cases of infraction, and specified penalties for such cases. Most mores and laws and many regulations take the form they take because there does exist a considerable motive to violate the norms that they prescribe. In the life of a community, above all, people's interests, desires, and plans regularly come into conflict with one another, and norms are required to adjudicate these conflicts 'on behalf of the community.' If physical combat were the only way to decide whose desires would be satisfied, and how far, and whose would not, the resultant disruption would soon prove fatal to both the community and its members.

But the observance of any society's mores and the sanctions incurred in the case of any breaches depend essentially on the moral sentiments of the people who belong to the society. Insofar as they have 'internalized' the society's mores, their 'consciences' motivate them in the first place against violating these norms. And then censure, including moral self-condemnation, can be a very severe penalty indeed when a violation does occur. Not to mention the further sanctions which a community's censure readily brings in its train.[2]

Why do societies need mores as well as laws and regulations? In the first place, much of what the maintenance of society requires in the way of individual behaviour is difficult or impossible to formulate in precise *dos* and *don'ts*. Explicit rules are possible for special, extreme cases, but a general readiness of society's members to help one another out, for example, is as resistant to any legal definition as it is socially beneficial. Then again, there are kinds of action which it can be in the interests of social stability to motivate people against performing even in those

---

2 The distinction of mores from usages on the one hand and from laws and regulations on the other should not be overdone. For what some mores prescribe is simply lawabidingness as such, just as others prescribe observance as such of whatever usages are socially established. Where 'When in Rome do as the Romans do' is not a prudent recommendation for getting along with the Romans successfully, it is perhaps a moral demand to respect them by following their laws and customs while in Rome. Genuinely *moralistic* sticklers for etiquette could conceivably be as offended by breaches of other societies' usages as their own. But what would prevent this sort of concern from turning those rules into moral norms for them is that this concern would not attach to the specific *content* of the rules in question, but only to the fact of their being established where they are.

cases where detection would be unlikely. Above all, though, mores are sociologically necessary because the naked rule of fear is insufficient by itself to hold a community together for any length of time. Unpopular laws, it is true, can often be enacted and, if detection is not too difficult, it may indeed be possible to enforce them fairly successfully. In fact, an entire legal regime can sometimes continue, in the face of massive unpopularity over an extended time: who can say for just how long a period it is possible to keep a restive conquered people down, given sufficient force? But, if absolutely all the social rules which are required for the life of the community but which are at all onerous to obey could only be enforced by the sanctions of law, social life would soon break down, and there would then be no observance of any of those rules. Human society as we know it could not exist without mores, and the human species itself, of course, can hardly exist in the absence of any society.

However, not quite all who have considered the matter have been convinced by reasoning like this that pure self-interest and fear are bound to be insufficient by themselves to hold any society together. In chapter 27 we will have to consider one apparent twentieth-century attempt to maintain the contrary as a matter of empirical social anthropology. But meanwhile, an opposite sort of challenge suggests itself to the thesis that social life would have to be impossible without mores. We can wonder, would there have to be mores in heaven? Depictions of heaven, of course, even standardly include a monarchial Lawgiver. But, if people's interests, desires, and plans never came into conflict with one another, what need would there be among them for any adjudication, either legal or moral? Coming down to earth to the extent of entertaining the prospect, if not of a Millennium, at least of a radical transcending of economic scarcity of the sort some technological optimists claim could become possible, we may wonder how much need would remain for the force of conscience as well as of the criminal code to keep the members of society interacting harmoniously with one another. On the other hand, it does seem hardly credible that even radical economic abundance, however great, and easeful cooperative living, however habitual, could ever suffice to render people's interests and desires *altogether* mutually harmonious. But any (residual?) conscience that remained could no doubt only find deep gratification in whatever approximation to the full banishing of 'moral evil' were thus attained.

The psychological possibility of total consciencelessness is a question that should be considered in the light of the 'socialization' mechanisms employed by any culture to pass its mores on from generation to generation.

There seems to be near-complete agreement that not only the specific content of these norms is (with more or less success) transmitted afresh 'culturally' to every new generation, but of necessity also even the bare mental disposition to be influenceable at all by considerations which make their appeal in the name of morality.[3] How does this work? How is 'moral sensitivity' generated in the thought processes of a child? Theories about this differ very widely, of course. But, whichever theory is chosen, it is hard to get away from the part played by 'imaginatively taking the role of another.' Your conscience may be developed in childhood, for example, by imitation of one or both of your parents, by imagining what they would say if they were present and then reacting yourself *as if* they were present even when they are not; or it may be developed by modelling yourself similarly on members of your peer group or on some different 'ideal' personality with whom you identify, whose reactions are imagined and in turn reacted to as if they were real. Conditioning processes are no doubt important in building up a child's 'moral' responses, and the aversive meaning for the child of even temporary withdrawal of affection undoubtedly plays a major role here, which also points to the importance of *emotional* imagination in building up a child's moral feelings.

Not untypical is the story told by G.H. Mead, which does in its way stress the essential part played by 'imaginatively taking the role of the other.'

> ... in a game where a number of individuals are involved, ... the child taking one rôle must be ready to take the rôle of everyone else. If he gets in a ball

---

3   The following quotation from Jung's *Psychology of the Unconscious* looks like an exception to this 'near-complete agreement': '... morality ... is a function of the human soul, as old as humanity itself. Morality is not imposed from outside; we have it in ourselves from the start – not the law, but our moral nature without which the collective life of human society would be impossible. That is why morality is found at all levels of society. It is the instinctive regulator of action which also governs the collective life of the herd.' (C.G. Jung, *Two Essays on Analytical Psychology*, trans. R.F.C. Hull [New York, 1953], 26.) It will be observed, though, that in this quotation Jung does commit himself at least to the proposition that 'our moral nature' is part of the 'instinctive' endowment of the human species. How much room would that leave for any psychological possibilities of complete consciencelessness? One other exception to the 'near-complete agreement' mentioned in the text, perhaps, is the speculations of some sociobiologists or evolutionary psychologists; but wouldn't even they agree that what is biologically determined is a greater or lesser innate capability of *learning* to be influenceable by considerations which make their appeal in the name of morality? Indeed, maybe that is all that Jung meant.

nine he must have the responses of each position involved in his own position. He must know what everyone else is going to do in order to carry out his own play. He has to take all of these rôles. They do not all have to be present in consciousness at the same time, but at some moments he has to have three or four individuals present in his own attitude, such as the one who is going to throw the ball, the one who is going to catch it, and so on. These responses must be, in some degree, present in his own make-up.[4]

The attitudes of the other players which the participant assumes organize into a sort of unit, and it is that organization which controls the response of the individual ... Each one of his own acts is determined by his assumption of the action of the others who are playing the game. What he does is controlled by his being everyone else on that team, at least in so far as those attitudes affect his own particular response. We get then an 'other' which is an organization of the attitudes of those involved in the same process.

The organized community or social group which gives to the individual his unity of self may be called 'the generalized other.' The attitude of the generalized other is the attitude of the whole community.[5]

In abstract thought the individual takes the attitude of the generalized other toward himself, without reference to its expression in any particular other individuals ...[6]

... the internal conversation of the individual with himself ... – the conversation which constitutes the process or activity of thinking – is carried on by the individual from the standpoint of the 'generalized other.' And the more abstract that conversation is, the more abstract thinking happens to be, the further removed is the generalized other from any connection with particular individuals.[7]

For sure something has gone wrong here. That 'which gives to the individual his unity of self' *cannot* be simply equated with 'the organized community or social group.' The voice of one's conscience need *not* merely

---

4 George H. Mead, *Mind, Self and Society*, ed. Charles W. Morris (Chicago, 1934), 151.
5 Ibid., 154.
6 Ibid., 155–6.
7 Ibid., 155–6, note 8, attaching to the words 'generalized other' in the preceding quotation.

express 'the attitude of the whole community.'[8] Once an individual has learned to take up the abstract standpoint of the generalized other, the potentiality then exists for this standpoint, in the individual's mind, to come to be mildly or wildly at odds with 'the attitude of the whole community' – with the attitude on anything which is taken by the individual's society, culture, subculture, family, or other social unit – even though it is from them that the individual learned to think in moral terms in the first place. Once implanted in a person's psyche, conscience is capable of taking on a life of its own. Indeed, examples are not all that rare of individuals claiming that the entire society in which they live is profoundly immoral.

Nevertheless, as far as the mechanisms go by which the phenomenon of conscience is initially generated in the individual psyche, surely a story *like* Mead's cannot but have considerable plausibility. Moreover, the importance of imaginatively putting oneself in the place of others in learning to see things from the moral standpoint can help to explain *how* it comes to be that just about any ethic which secures at all widespread support in any society includes some element of at least presumptive concern for the interests of people generally. (By 'presumptive' here I mean that an ethic may put forward the desirability of advancing the interests of people generally as only a derivative or otherwise defeasible moral consideration even though it does favour doing this 'other things being equal.') As far as the social psychology of moral sentiment goes, the utilitarian David Hume may be viewed as an early forerunner of G.H. Mead, even though today it is easy to see that his suggestion regarding moral terms' literal meanings cannot be right:

The more we converse with mankind, and the greater social intercourse we maintain, the more shall we be familiarized to these general preferences

---

8 Just that, however, is apparently what Mead does mean: 'There are certain common responses which each individual has toward certain common things, and in so far as those common responses are awakened in the individual when he is affecting other persons he arouses his own self. The structure, then, on which the self is built is this response which is common to all, for one has to be a member of a community to be a self. Such responses are abstract attitudes, but they constitute just what we term a man's character. They give him what we term his principles, the acknowledged attitudes of all members of the community toward what are the values of that community. He is putting himself in the place of the generalized other, which represents the organized responses of all the members of the group. It is that which guides conduct controlled by principles, and a person who has such an organized group of responses is a man whom we say has character, in the moral sense' (ibid., 162–3).

and distinctions, without which our conversation and discourse could scarcely be rendered intelligible to each other. Every man's interest is peculiar to himself, and the aversions and desires, which result from it, cannot be supposed to affect others in a like degree. General language, therefore, being formed for general use, must be moulded on some more general views, and must affix the epithets of praise or blame, in conformity to sentiments, which arise from the general interests of the community.[9]

I said that just about any ethic which secures widespread support in any society will include some element of concern for people in general. But what about racism, nationalism, and other such particularisms that systematically narrow their adherents' sympathetic horizons? Isn't it observed, though, that people who so deny even the presumptive desirability of benefiting certain others regularly deny those others human status? They deny, I mean, even their zoological humanity. Isn't that connected to an inability on their part to put themselves imaginatively in those people's place? We do not treat non-human animals as moral agents. That is, we do not morally praise or censure them for what they do despite the fact that by 'rewarding' and 'punishing' them we can and do influence their future behaviour.[10] The point is that we cannot *seriously* imagine ourselves in their place – not, at any rate, when we are fully aware of the inherent mental limitation that makes them all of necessity conscienceless. As for the people who do find it possible seriously to imagine themselves in those animals' place, they are the ones – whether on account of personal loneliness or their acceptance of animistic religious doctrines – who do make serious moral appraisals of the animals' behaviour, not recognizing their intellectual limitations.

But what is this mental activity of 'imaginatively putting yourself in another's place'? It isn't the *same thing* as feeling sympathy for the other, though it can *give rise* to sympathy. Adam Smith was perhaps one of the very first academic theorists to put anything like this at the heart of moral psychology. Regarding his cardinal principle of sympathy he writes:

---

9 From David Hume, *Enquiries concerning Human Understanding and concerning the Principles of Morals*, ed. L.A. Selby-Bigge, 3rd ed., rev. P.H. Nidditch (Oxford, 1975), 228. Jeremy Bentham sometimes said that the name of his 'Principle of Utility' was first suggested to him by the writings of Hume, who gave to the very section of his *Inquiry concerning the Principles of Morals* from which this quotation comes the title 'Why Utility Pleases.'

10 A fact noted, for instance, by C.A. Campbell, 'Is "Freewill" a Pseudo-Problem?' *Mind* 60, no. 240 (October 1951), 447.

When I condole with you for the loss of your only son, in order to enter into your grief I do not consider what I, a person of such a character and profession, should suffer, if I had a son, and if that son was unfortunately to die: but I consider what I should suffer if I was really you, and I not only change circumstances with you, but I change persons and characters.[11]

When you sympathetically condole with me and consider what you would suffer if you were really me, just what are you considering? Presumably you are not just contemplating my bereavement. In imagining that you are me you surely are imagining *something* which is contrary-to-fact – not to say impossible – but what? It surely isn't anything impossible to imagine, since you are now imagining it. Presumably you aren't just contemplating what-it-is-like-to-be-me, though such contemplation would certainly be capable of triggering some reflection on what it *would* be like to be me.

Just what is the contrary-to-fact supposition posited in the 'if'clause of 'how you would suffer if you were me'? The supposition of your being me. What is it to suppose that one being is really another? Philosophers have certainly had something to say about *that*. At one extreme there is a philosopher like Leibniz, who held that nothing could be what it is if it were in the slightest way different from the way it is.[12] At the other extreme, a philosopher like Locke would appear to claim it could differ in any or all of its properties and relations and still be just what it is.[13] Saul Kripke appears to hold that the supposition of anything's being something else is *impossible* in a way that would indeed make it unimaginable.[14] None of this would appear to get us very far.

---

11 Adam Smith, *The Theory of Moral Sentiments*, ed. D.D. Raphael and A.L. Macfie (Oxford, 1976), 317.

12 For example, *Discourse on Metaphysics*, 13: '... the concept of an individual substance once and for all includes everything which can ever happen to it and ..., in considering that concept, one can see everything which can truly be predicated of it, ...' See Gottfried Wilhelm Leibniz, *Philosophical Papers and Letters*, vol. 1, trans. and ed. Leroy E. Loemker (Chicago, 1956) 475–6.

13 For example, John Locke, *An Essay concerning Human Understanding*, Book II, chapter 23, 3: '... the substance is supposed always *something besides* the extension, figure, solidity, motion, thinking, or other observable ideas ...' Emphasis in original.

14 Saul A. Kripke, *Naming and Necessity* (Cambridge, MA, 1980), 97–115. Kripke would not, of course, deny the possibility of imagining away whatever contingent facts prevent something from satisfying a particular definite description instead of what does satisfy it as things actually stand. But to imagine Benjamin Franklin as first

For his part, Moscow Art Theatre director Konstantin Stanislavsky, the inspirer of 'method' acting, knew that to recall instances when you have felt grief can help you mightily to understand my grief the better to portray it on stage. Empathic feelings have to be aroused. By the same token, there *has* to be something of you retained in that which you imagine when you imagine being me. What you imagine when you imagine being me does have to be more than a *bare* switch of identity: the individual who now is me being you instead, but without any alteration whatever in the *way* I am; or (if it is not the same thing) the individual who now is you being me instead, but without any alteration whatever in the *way* you are. To talk of 'imagining' that would be to talk quite emptily of a mental act really indistinguishable from contemplating the status quo.

No, *what* you imagine when you sympathetically 'imagine being me' is my 'circumstances, person and character' with at least this much of you added on: your self-reflective emotional sensitivity, reacting as if to grief of your own.

We often can, in this way, empathize and sympathize with the fear, pain, and so on of non-human animals. If we cannot view them in a moral light, that is because we cannot *seriously* imagine them having consciences. There are, of course, fables that tell imaginative stories about animals with consciences like ours: but their divergence from what actual animals are like is too great for us to think seriously that any of *those* are being imagined. To put it another way: animals with a mentality sufficiently like ours to be capable of having a conscience wouldn't find themselves in the situations that real non-human animals are in all the time. What the latter do in those situations is therefore bound to be accounted innocent by us from a moral point of view.

Are there also human beings who lack a mentality sufficient to render them in any way capable of having consciences? Of course there are: young babies, for example, and some victims of extreme brain damage or degeneration. If they had consciences, they wouldn't be who they are. Viewed sociologically, the essential imperviousness to any considerations of conscience which they share with non-human animals makes it no surprise that they are judged unfit for moral appraisal, since the mores' social function is indeed to encourage and discourage different

---

president of the United States, for instance, *isn't* to imagine Benjamin Franklin being George Washington, Kripke would insist.

sorts of behaviour, after all, through the influence of such considerations. Moralizing would simply be wasted on them, as on the animals.

What about psychopaths and sociopaths, whether their disorder is due to biological causes or to inadequate socialization, who are not infrequently described as intelligent, conscienceless adults? To them we will have to turn expressly in chapter 27. This book, of course, is not a work of social science, but must (at least) respect the stated findings of social scientists, insofar as they are generally in agreement at any rate. The preceding discussion offers a good example of the rational bearing that sociological and social-psychological knowledge can have even in relation to basic matters of normative ethics: at the very least such knowledge can serve to back up rather cogent *ad hominem* argumentation. To the extent that we reliably *know ourselves*, we surely are going to be less prone to resist self-deceptively that to which we are committed by what we already unshakeably accept (even if not quite consciously at first). Perhaps censuring such behaviour as manifestly couldn't have been prevented by any considerations of conscience is not among the strongest temptations of misplaced moralism. But, insofar as there were to be any such temptation, the preceding discussion *could* rationally help to dispel it.

It is fair to warn the reader that the imaginative act of 'putting yourself in another's place' is going to occupy a central position in the succeeding discussion. If what you imaginatively transfer to me when you sympathize with me is your self-reflective emotional sensitivity, what you imaginatively transfer to me when you morally judge me is simply your *conscience*, your ensemble of moral pro-attitudes and con-attitudes (all *desires*, in the sense of that word defined in appendix 2). This imaginative transfer is what we cannot seriously manage in the case of animals, infants, and 'human vegetables.' It would be wrong to think, though, that we cannot morally judge people unfavourably for what they do unless we can suppose that we ourselves would behave differently if we were them. After all, we *are* ourselves, and yet we do often morally blame ourselves for what we do – sometimes even right while doing it. Moral judges who cannot truly say they would act any differently in the place of those they condemn must then admit to a moral character defect by their own lights; but who would seriously claim to be free of all character defects? Honestly thinking about it when morally condemning any action, one does of course then *wish*, insofar as one is conscientious, that one would behave differently in the same situation as the actor; but insofar as, like everybody else, one also (according even to one's own principles) truly is a *miserable sinner* – or should we, more diplomatically, just say 'morally imperfect'? – to that extent one is apt to harbour contrary motivations as well, possibly strong enough to outweigh all the promptings of conscience in such a real-life situation.

Every statement-making counterfactual conditional sentence in effect *infers* something hypothetically from an imagined contrary-to-fact condition, considered in conjunction with how things are otherwise. To take 'how things are otherwise' in conjunction with the contrary-to-fact condition imagined, it is always necessary for purposes of the hypothetical inference to imagine certain changes in how things are besides what is actually mentioned in the express formulation of the given contrary-to-fact condition that is being imaginatively laid down; but such imagined changes are to be kept to a minimum.[15] To condole with me sympathetically you indeed must imaginatively take on my relevant non-normative beliefs, such as my belief that my only son has really died. And even my moral prejudices had better be retained in what you imagine when you imaginatively transfer your conscience to me, for otherwise you wouldn't be imagining yourself *in the same situation* I was in when I acted as I did. That doesn't mean, as I'll be arguing shortly, that you have to judge my actions according just to my principles, rather than your own. But you have to take account of my motives for acting the way I did, including my conscientious motives, however misguided. In my situation, could your conscience have overcome *all* contrary motivations, including these, and kept you from acting the way I did? Then only would you be able to claim that in my place you would have behaved different from me.

If the discussion developed up to this point has been at all convincing, I hope you will have found it plausible to conclude (assuming you didn't already think this) that total consciencelessness is not a possibility for you. The psychological impossibility of being completely 'amoral' is not universally accepted, of course, and in chapter 27 the contrary viewpoint will be considered further. But, if the standpoint of the 'generalized other' is learned in a process inseparable from learning how to communicate in language – which certainly for its part involves learning to take on imaginatively the role of others – then it will be easy to see how *complete* consciencelessness, at any rate, won't be possible for anyone with a developed linguistic competence.

---

15 See the discussion in my 'The Truth-conditions of Counterfactual Conditional Sentences,' *Mind* 87, no. 345 (January 1978), 1–21, as described above in note 2 of chapter 12.

Accepting, then, that you have a conscience, must we see it as condemning whatever *I* do contrary to its dictates, even when I am not acting contrary to my own conscience? In a sociological perspective, the affirmative answer to this will be unsurprising in view of mores' social function of discouraging certain courses of action or inaction by censuring them, and encouraging certain other courses by positively praising them, or at least by prescribing them and censuring failure to adopt them. In view of that social function, what would be surprising is an ethic that exculpated breaches of its dictates merely because the violator's own conscience didn't censure them. Indeed, however it is managed, passing any mores on to a new generation cannot but involve, initially, some (even if only mild) censure of these (very young) people for doing things that at the time weren't yet contrary to their conscience. Nevertheless, many a modern intellectual has balked to some degree at the idea of morally judging other persons by any but their own standards. Without embracing such 'moral non-dogmatism' fully, J.D. Mabbott, for example, still felt constrained to declare, 'I am inclined to think ... that we must accept the paradox and award Hitler moral approval.'[16] But what is the problem here? Is it supposed to be *wicked* (because unjust or inhumane, say) to judge people morally by any standards except those they themselves accept? Is this supposed to hold even where such judging is permitted, or indeed required, by the judge's own moral principles? Obviously, if coherent, the 'non-dogmatist' objection to such judgments cannot be a moral objection. It must amount to the charge that they are all somehow *in error*. But where is the error?

To be sure, an honest mistake *can* exculpate. With even the best possible will in the world one would not be unduly negligent, but would rather be led to follow that course of action or inaction which the (non-normative) information available indicated was aptest to further the results which were willed; but all the same, that course, adopted in perfectly good faith, might still operate to frustrate those good results in fact. According to the normative standpoint being urged here, one's ultimate moral obligation really is just to have the best possible will in the world; and it is only for falling short on that score that one can ever truly be faulted. With the best possible will in the world, though, one's

---

16   J.D. Mabbott, *An Introduction to Ethics* (London, 1966), 58. By way of exception, Mabbott held that, on pain of immorality, there is a requirement to take thought carefully and try to determine as rationally as possible how it is best to act whether one's personal moral convictions recognize *this* obligation or do not.

ultimate ends would be morally unobjectionable; and so it would *not* be one's ultimate moral principles which were faulty. According to this conception, ignorance of the *ultimate* moral law is no excuse.

This is not to deny that, like bravery, conscientiousness in pursuit of even a morally objectionable end might well merit some commendation – however outweighed, on balance, by consideration of the depravity of the end pursued. And it should be agreed that we cannot be morally *blameless* when we do act contrary to our own principles. If the principles are in order, we are wrong to violate them. If our ultimate moral principles are not in order, then we are at fault morally on account of that since we do not then have the best possible will in the world. (If it is faulty derivative principles which we have violated, then either these have been adequately or inadequately derived from objectionable first principles, and we are in any case at fault for subscribing to those; or else they have been *shoddily* derived from quite unobjectionable first principles, and we are morally culpable just insofar as the shoddy thinking involved is our fault.)

Here is the logical argument against 'moral non-dogmatism.' Consider the following (expression of a) moral imperative:

(P) 'It is immoral to act contrary to one's own conscience.'

All acts (whether of commission or omission) are plainly either P-violating or not. And all moral imperatives, plainly, either are such as to be breached only by P-violating acts or not. Examples of specific moral imperatives of the former sort can be seen in

'It is immoral to act contrary to one's conscience in cold weather.'

and

'It is immoral to tell lies in opposition to one's own conscience.'

These examples, logically entailed by P, show how it is that P represents the *maximum* that a moral non-dogmatist can censure: for a consistent moral non-dogmatist could not censure any act (of commission or omission) that did not run counter to the actor's own conscience. However, to prescribe any act as being required morally is the same thing as censuring any failure to perform it. Consequently, a conscience restricted to morally censuring only P-violating acts could not consistently subscribe to anything over and above P in the way of moral imperatives.

But a conscience which could not subscribe to anything in the way of moral imperatives over and above P could not subscribe to anything at all in the way of moral imperatives. It could never prescribe any course of action or inaction. It could never tell one to do any act (of commission or omission); it could at most tell one to do it *if* one morally disapproved of failing to do it. But such a conscience could never tell its possessor actually to do or not to do *anything*. It could never say: do this; or, do not do that. It could only ever say: do this *if ...*; or, do not do that *if ...*

In short, there could not be such a conscience. For a conscience which could not ever tell its possessor what to do or not to do would be no conscience at all. If the promptings of your conscience are consistently restricted in accordance with moral non-dogmatism, there are no such promptings, and you are effectively conscienceless – or, rather, you would be were not consciencelessness psychologically impossible.[17]

Accordingly, moral non-dogmatism is untenable. And yet, to those attracted to it, it had presented an air of unavoidability, as a consequence of the tautology that 'ought' implies 'can.' Even that truism has not gone uncontradicted.[18] But it does 'stand to reason,' and it is no mystery why mores will restrict themselves to sanctioning the condemnation of acts (of commission or omission) which the actor *could* have avoided: it is only such acts which conscientious countermotivation and the threat of social censure could ever prevent; and so it is in reducing the incidence only of such acts that mores can function sociologically. The truism that 'ought' implies 'can' must therefore not be rejected, but interpreted in accordance with what the role it actually plays in our moral life requires.

When all is said and done, what does morality require of us, finally, beyond having a good will? To fall short there is to be morally at fault. Otherwise, it is to be innocent. From a moral point of view, therefore, you are morally to blame for something you did only where you would *not* have done it if you had had a better will. Only those acts which a sufficient moral commitment on the actor's part would have prevented are morally culpable. It is only such acts which count for these purposes as acts which the actor 'could' have avoided. And so it is them only which that actor in the relevant sense *ought* to have avoided.[19] Whatever the right (ultimate) moral imperatives are in any situation, to lack sufficient commitment to them is to fall short of having a sufficiently good

---

17 The argument here against 'moral non-dogmatism' summarizes the case advanced in my paper 'Immorality with a Clear Conscience,' *American Philosophical Quarterly* 17, no. 3 (July 1980), 245–50.

18 For example, E.J. Lemmon, 'Moral Dilemmas,' *Philosophical Review* 71, no. 2 (April 1962), 150, note 8.

19 This isn't to say that the clear unavoidability of something which has been done can always be enough to free a decent person from any kind of troubled conscience concerning it. See example (2) at the end of this chapter and in chapter 28.

will. Therefore it is a mistake to excuse any act on the grounds that the actor was motivated by an 'erring conscience' (erring with regard to some non-derivative moral consideration) and accordingly 'couldn't' have done any better. In the relevant sense, the actor really 'could' have done better. With a better will, the actor *would* have done better. Far from exculpating, an inadequate conscience is precisely what, in the final analysis, renders its possessor morally culpable.

Short of full exculpation, however, there certainly are cases where somewhat reduced culpability is imputed to someone on the grounds of 'diminished responsibility.' In cases of specific psychiatric disorder just as in the more general case, acts which only a most exceptionally strong conscientious commitment would have been enough to prevent can hardly count as *very* culpable morally. On the other hand, if a case of kleptomania, say, were to be mild enough that even an only moderately strong conscientious commitment to what is right *would* have been sufficient to overcome any temptation to steal, then the blame which such a thief did incur in consequence would not need to be reduced very greatly.[20]

If, though, when it comes to moral responsibility all that really matters is having or not having a good will, why does a wrongdoer's abusive childhood weigh in the balance as a mitigating – surely not exculpating – circumstance, since undoubtedly the hard-heartedness shown by doing the wrong is just the same regardless of what has caused its development? But, had the hard-heartedness resulted in spite of more favourable childhood experiences, it would have evinced an already bad character earlier on because character development does result from habits built up through the moral choices which are made. Thus, it is not so much that the wrongdoer with the unfortunate childhood is less culpable than some norm for misdeeds of the sort committed, as that the wrongdoer with the more fortunate childhood thereby incurs compounded culpability.

The human condition being what it is, the facts of sociology and psychology are the way they are. Human mores, consequently, being as

---

20 I said above that some human beings, such as infants and certain victims of brain damage, are like non-human animals in being innocent no matter what they do because of lacking all ability to be motivated by conscience. But isn't it the case, trivially, that these individuals *would* be so motivated *if* they had a better will – specifically, *if* they had a conscience (and it were sufficiently strong)? In such a case, though, as argued above, these individuals (like non-human animals) would not then *be* the beings they are, so fundamental (from a moral point of view) is that which differentiates them from genuine moral agents.

they are, moral *concepts* are what they are. This being so, sentences such as the following are analytic: 'To whatever ultimately is morally right it is incumbent on any moral agent to be conscientiously committed, and any act of commission or omission is morally culpable just to the extent that with a stronger conscientious commitment to what is right it would have been avoided.' Such tautologies make up a body of *constraints* upon any ethic that can be considered logically consistent.

But what is an *ethic*? What are *mores*? Which of people's concerns are their *moral* concerns? We already saw in chapter 19 that to hold any moral view about something isn't compatible with complete indifference towards it: so it is, indeed, a question of some specific class of the *concerns* which people have. As often remarked, no concern is a moral concern unless it is 'universalizable': unless, that is, it either is or is instrumentally derived from a concern, as such, for something specifiable entirely in purely qualitative terms.[21] A concern that *your* ox not be gored is only a *moral* concern if derived from considerations telling equally against *my* ox being gored – unless it is possible to cite some specific difference between the two as relevantly distinguishing the cases. And the fact that one ox is *yours* and the other one *mine* cannot in itself count as a difference of the relevant sort here because it isn't a fact specifiable entirely in purely qualitative terms. At any rate, without such a difference being adducible, the concern that your ox not be gored won't be a *moral* concern of yours. But, as very often pointed out, insofar as it is imposed by logic alone this constraint is extremely weak. Nothing in this constraint rules out a moral first principle to the effect that no ox owned by somebody with fingerprints of pattern XYZ is to be gored (where XYZ just happens to be the pattern of *your* fingerprints). To mark off *moral* from other concerns, we need some further constraint(s).

As suggested in chapter 19, the question is one of social-scientific taxonomy. But the answer can guide us in identifying some logical truths. Just what is it that distinguishes *moral* concerns? What more than merely opposing certain behaviour is it to *take a moral stand* in opposition to it? Let us take it that the behaviour in question is a sort of behaviour completely specifiable in terms that are purely qualitative. And let us say that the desire for abstention from such behaviour is a desire for such abstention for its own sake rather than for the sake of anything further. What is added when one is described as taking –

---

21 See my paper 'What Are "Purely Qualitative" Terms?' *American Philosophical Quarterly* 23, no. 1 (January 1996), 71–81.

whether publicly or to oneself – what amounts to a *moral* stand in opposition to such behaviour? What about the mentality of an individual
is it to be *moralistic* regarding such behaviour?

From the preceding, the reader may very well have been able to guess
that the answer I shall want to urge here will in a way be *social* in character, and will specifically tie in with putting oneself imaginatively in
the place of others. What does it come to psychologically to get up on a
moralistic high horse, so to speak, in opposing some sort of behaviour,
whether publicly or not? What is involved in taking such an attitude is
not merely a desire for the incidence of such behaviour to be reduced,
and preferably eliminated. The moralistic attitude likewise involves a
desire that the attitude thus taken be shared by everyone else as well as
oneself. For not only is the behaviour in question censured, but so is the
failure to censure it. (And, likewise, any failure to censure the failure to
censure it; and so on.) But all this flows from a single unitary attitude.
It is not a case of desiring something *and also* desiring that the desire be
shared. It is easy to think of desires we want to see shared because we
believe that will increase the chances of their fulfilment; but, if we
thought the sharing of such a desire would strain limited resources, say,
and so reduce the degree of fulfilment which was going to be likely, we
then might be apt to prefer our desire not to be so widely shared.
However, in this case there is a single psychological state by which
what is desired for its own sake is abstention from the behaviour in
question *and* the desire for such abstention (*and* the desire for such a
desire, and so on).

It is, of course possible to oppose something morally without desiring
on balance – not even just insofar as one is motivated by conscience –
that this desire be shared absolutely universally. Hitler's gigantic vanity
was one of his vices. Towards the end of the Second World War, though,
it led him to pay too little attention to his generals' advice, and this
shortened the war. And so, it is possible to be glad *even for moral reasons*
that he had that vice, and that he didn't mind having it, and so forth.
Nevertheless, from the moral standpoint, his having the vice was still
presumptively undesirable, and the desire that he not have it *presumptively* desirable, and so forth. Presumptive moral desirability and un-
desirability are potentially outweighable even, in given circumstances,
by considerations which themselves are purely moral in character.

The upshot is, I'd urge, that what distinguishes any *moral* concern
from any other concern is the fact that the former either is, or else is
instrumentally derived from, a feeling which (1) is a concern, as such,

for something fully describable in purely qualitative terms, and which, furthermore, (2) involves inherently in itself a (presumptive) concern that it be shared by anybody whatsoever.

This is the right place again to acknowledge authorial planning. It is no accident that the preceding account of what marks off *moral* from other concerns, if successful, will qualify them – and perhaps them alone – to count as *beliefs*, by the criterion of chapter 3. To be sure, the phrase 'true and false desires' is obviously solecistic – bad English – but, as argued in chapter 19, just as with 'deciduous obstacle' or 'scrupulous organism,' that in itself won't stop such a phrase from expressing a completely accurate characterization. The specific 'high horse' of moralists, it turns out, is their claim to objective truth.[22]

Of course that doesn't mean they need to claim complete lack of bias or infallibility, any more than anybody whatever who advances a truth-valuable claim.

If moral concerns alone are objectively truth-valuable,[23] it follows that other desires people have which may or may not conflict with these will not amount to *beliefs* of theirs, no matter how strong such desires are in comparison with the moral concerns with which they may or do conflict. This applies even to expressly *anti-moral* desires – desires which specifically oppose morality as such (and not merely 'morality' as such). The upshot is that whoever has any moral sentiments at all has some moral *beliefs*, whether avowedly or not: that is, subscribes to some true-or-false moral claims, and thus cannot consistently subscribe to moral nihilism, scepticism, or decisionism.

But wait. It certainly is possible to experience what are like moral feelings and have the phenomenological *air* of moral feelings to no small degree, but definitely are not actual moral *beliefs*. Some of these

---

22 This suggestion has been made to me, in opposition to the position advanced in chapter 3, that this conclusion could perhaps be resisted on the grounds that *beliefs* should really be defined (taxonomically) by the possibility in principle of the *believer's* being indifferent to the supposed fact which is believed. Why, though? In any case, whoever believes genocide to be immoral needn't care any particular way about *genocide's being immoral*, as opposed, that is, to caring about *genocide*.

23 Let us say, for present purposes, that a mental state or condition is '*objectively truth-valuable*' if and only if (1) being a *belief*, it is truth-valuable, and (2) neither the proposition so believed nor its negation is a synthetic truth which follows logically from the premise that the believer subscribes to that proposition. (It may be arguable that any belief on your part, however ill founded, that you desire a certain outcome will necessarily have some tendency to lead you to seek that outcome, and thus will itself constitute a *desire*, by the definition of appendix 2.)

feelings fail to represent the overall moral sentiments of the person who has them simply because in the circumstances they are outweighed by some different moral feelings which motivate this person in a contrary sense. In other cases, what keeps people's feelings from amounting to *opinions* of theirs is more complicated. But, in all cases, to say that *moral sentiments* constitute *beliefs* held by whoever has them isn't to say that any moral feelings whatever that people have constitute *beliefs* of theirs. Consider the following five cases.

(1) A French youth under the German occupation has to decide whether to stay at home and care for his frail mother, who without him will die, or leave to join the Free French in England and save his country. Whichever way he decides, even if he considers he has made the right decision, he cannot help having guilt feelings on account of the path not taken.[24]

(2) A subway train driver sees a suicide on the track ahead as the subway train pulls into the station, but it is absolutely impossible to stop the train before it kills this person. The driver afterwards experiences sharp pangs of guilt and needs counselling even though fully convinced nothing could have been done to prevent the fatality.[25]

(3) Through a completely honest mistake, and in spite of taking all reasonable precautions, you have both promised somebody to do something and promised somebody else not to do it. Whichever promise you keep, you *feel* guilty about breaking the other one even though you are sure that you are not morally to blame. And, in spite of also accepting this, the disappointed promisee *feels* a sense of grievance in addition to the sense of being entitled to recompense.

(4) Jane, who had a traditional upbringing, violates a sexual taboo to which she no longer subscribes, but has guilt feelings despite being fully convinced of her innocence. She even feels similar uneasiness about the sexual taboo infractions of others, despite now considering such actions to be altogether licit morally.

---

24 Cf. Jean-Paul Sartre, *Existentialism and Humanism*, trans. Philip Mairet (London, 1948), 35–6.

25 Cf. Bernard Williams, *Moral Luck* (Cambridge, 1981), 28: 'The lorry driver who, through no fault of his, runs over a child, will feel differently from any spectator …' I have altered Williams's example here in order to avoid any (reasonable) lurking suspicion that something the driver could have done might have prevented the tragedy.

(5) Jack, a utilitarian moral philosopher, knows that a whacking sacrifice on his part could produce real benefits far exceeding the loss to him. He makes a smaller sacrifice than that and enjoys a *pretty* clear conscience. He (mostly) *feels* innocent, in spite of in principle considering himself not to be.

What all these examples point out is that a moral *feeling* somebody has amounts to a truth-valuable *belief* only if the feeling is such as to involve inherently in itself a (presumptive) concern that it be shared by anybody whatsoever (or, where the feeling derives from some more general attitude, only if it derives from a general attitude of such a sort as to involve inherently in itself a [presumptive] concern that it be shared by anybody whatsoever).

27 'Consciencelessness'

That which gives to humane Actions the relish of Justice, is a certain Noblenesse or Gallantnesse of courage, (rarely found,) by which a man scorns to be beholding for the contentment of his life, to fraud, or breach of promise.

Thomas Hobbes[1]

Ever the spokesman of self-seeking, Hobbes hates to admit that people can indeed care seriously about truth-telling, say, for its own sake (rather than just for the sake of remaining nobly unbeholden). But Hobbes does not explain how it would happen (if nobody cared about faithfulness for its own sake) that even a 'rarely found' gallant would particularly *mind* owing contentment of life, or even life itself, to fraud and breach of promise, any more than to eating and drinking.

Such rare nobleness aside, in a Hobbesian society the only motivation for obeying the rules (where it isn't otherwise advantageous) is people's fear of the penalties that would be incurred by disobeying. And the only motivation anyone but the sovereign can have for enforcing a penalty (where enforcing it isn't otherwise advantageous) is fear of penalization in case of failing to enforce it. Et cetera. Many writers have commented on the sociological unviability of any such society. But in the second quarter of the twentieth century there was a school of U.S.-based social anthropologists, guessably ill-acquainted with those writings, who liked to contrast 'shame cultures' with 'guilt cultures' in terms like those formulated by Margaret Mead in 1937:

---

1 *Leviathan* (London, 1914), chap. 15, 77.

In societies in which the individual is controlled by fear of being shamed, he is safe if no one knows of his misdeed; he can dismiss his misbehavior from his mind. In societies which are regulated by tabu, the individual who breaks a tabu is safe if he can invoke a stronger magical force. But the individual who feels guilt must repent and *atone* for his *sin*.[2]

When people are emotionally attached to the rules of a society, they will be (at any rate, somewhat) motivated to observe them independently of any thought of the social sanctions attached to infractions. By contrast, wherever a 'shame culture' were to prevail, the members of society would be motivated to toe the line to the detriment of their own interests solely by the fear of being shamed by others if they did not. So A 'behaves' solely out of fear of shaming by B, C, and D. The fear is justified just because B, for instance, is indeed motivated to engage in shaming behaviour should A be caught misbehaving – but all that motivates B in that direction is fear of shaming by C, and D in the event of failing to join in shaming A. And the fear felt by B is justified only because C, in turn, is motivated to join in the shaming solely out of fear of being shamed by B and D in the event of failing to join in shaming A, and by D, at least, in the event of failing to join in shaming B should B fail to join in shaming A. And so on. We have here a pretty pure Hobbesian community, with *tradition* taking the place of the *sovereign* and *shaming* taking the places of the *sword*. Isn't it more plausible to suppose that the members of a community would be unlikely to retain for long the systematic disposition to

---

2 Margaret Mead, ed., *Cooperation and Competition among Primitive Peoples* (New York, 1937), concluding 'Interpretive Statement' by the editor (494). David P. Ausubel, 'Relationships between Shame and Guilt in the Socializing Process,' *Psychological Review* 62, no. 5 (September 1995), 378–90, criticizes a number of these writers for employing an ethnocentrically narrow concept of *guilt feelings* and then on the basis of that concept denying 'guilt feelings' to many other cultures that would not really lack them in a broader sense (which is not, regrettably, kept distinct in these writings). Ausubel's article provides an instructive critique of the theory being contested here, as does *Shame and Guilt: A Psychoanalytic and a Cultural Study*, by Gerhart Piers and Milton B. Singer (Springfield, IL, 1953). The two authors of this book prefer to contrast the sense of 'shame' with the sense of 'guilt' as, respectively, a feeling of having *failed* and a feeling of having *transgressed*.

shame violators of the community's rules unless those violations generally displeased them? But, if such violations of the rules did generally displease people, they then would have a motive for avoiding such violations independent of any thought of social sanctions.

A far more influential case for the occurrence of consciencelessness among not unintelligent adults has been made under the heading of 'psychopathy' or 'sociopathy.' Sometimes, indeed, the term 'psychopathic' or 'sociopathic' is used just to *mean* something like 'conscienceless.' In his classic (thought not uncontroversial) 1941 book, *The Mask of Sanity*, Hervey Cleckley purported to identify a distinct type of personality disorder, marked indeed by failure to experience guilt feelings where others would experience them. In chapter 17 of his book, Cleckley tells an arresting story:

> Eighteen-year-old 'Milt' abandoned his ill mother in a stranded car on a bridge at the edge of town as night was falling. On his way to a nearby garage to get a replacement for the fuse that had blown out, he first spent ten or fifteen minutes checking football scores at a cigar store over the bridge, then decided to look up a girl he knew who lived half a block away, and got into an hour of amiable though not intense conversation there until her date for the evening arrived, at which point 'Milt' exchanged some pleasant courtesies and left. Meanwhile, his mother had with difficulty flagged a passing car down and arrived home very worried and upset. Upon being questioned when he finally showed up, 'he by turns showed vexation at his mother for not having waited until he so belatedly got back and a bland immunity to any recognition that he had behaved irresponsibly or inconsiderately.'[3]

To his mother this young man 'had been, on the whole, thoughtful and attentive ... during the illness'[4] and, in fact, had freely volunteered that day to drive her where she had to go. So what was he thinking that day? A more violent example is the following, cited in Robert D. Hare's popularly written paperback, *Without Conscience*:

> One of our subjects, who scored high on the *Psychopathy Checklist*, said that while walking to a party he decided to buy a case of beer, but realized that he had left his wallet at home six or seven blocks away. Not wanting to

---

3 Hervey Cleckley, *The Mask of Sanity*, 3rd ed. (St Louis, 1955), paraphrased from pages 201–3. The quoted words appear on page 202.
4 Ibid., 201.

walk back, he picked up a heavy piece of wood and robbed the nearest gas station, seriously injuring the attendant.[5]

This book of Hare's on psychopathy is described as 'excellent' by David T. Lykken, who says Dr Hare 'must be regarded as the leading research-er in this area.'[6] On page 34 of his book, Hare has provided a summary of his widely used *Psychopathy Checklist*:

Key Symptoms of Psychopathy

Emotional/Interpersonal

- glib and superficial
- egocentric and grandiose
- lack of remorse or guilt
- lack of empathy
- deceitful and manipulative
- shallow emotions

Social Deviance

- impulsive
- poor behavior controls
- need for excitement
- lack of responsibility
- early behavior problems
- adult antisocial behavior

At the end of *Without Conscience* Hare tells the reader: '... in spite of more than a century of clinical study and speculation and several decades of scientific research, the mystery of the psychopath still remains.'[7]

The uncertainty and debate on the subject has been not just over the causation of psychopathy, but over its definition, and even over whether there really is any such distinct mental condition at all. The American Psychiatric Association does recognize it on pages 645–50 of its *Diagnostic and Statistical Manual of Mental Disorders*, Fourth Edition (*DSM-IV*) un-der the heading '301.7 Antisocial Personality Disorder.' The following diagnostic criteria are given:

Diagnostic criteria for 301.7 Antisocial Personality Disorder

A There is a pervasive pattern of disregard for and violation of the rights of others occurring since age 15 years, as indicated by three (or more) of the following:
   (1) failure to conform to social norms with respect to lawful behaviors as indicated by repeatedly performing acts that are grounds for arrest

---

5 Robert D. Hare, *Without Conscience* (New York, 1993), 58–9.
6 David T. Lykken, *The Antisocial Personalities* (Hillsdale, NJ, 1995), 115, 122.
7 Ibid., 219.

(2) deceitfulness, as indicated by repeated lying, use of aliases, or conning others for personal profit or pleasure

(3) impulsivity or failure to plan ahead

(4) irritability and aggressiveness, as indicated by repeated physical fights or assaults

(5) reckless disregard for safety of self or others

(6) consistent irresponsibility, as indicated by repeated failure to sustain consistent work behavior or financial obligations

(7) lack of remorse as indicated by being indifferent to or rationalizing having hurt, mistreated, or stolen from another

B. The individual is at least age 18 years.

C. There is evidence of Conduct Disorder ... with onset before age 15 years.

D. The occurrence of antisocial behavior is not exclusively during the course of Schizophrenia or a Manic Episode.[8]

It isn't only in popular accounts that psychopaths are often expressly described as being 'without conscience.' This seems to refer especially to their failure to feel conscience pangs for what they have previously done. Does that mean they are altogether devoid of moral-type motivations – that (worthy or misguided) ethical sentiments never have any weight at all with them when they are deciding what to do? Of course, some individuals are highly moralistic indeed, but escape self-blame by believing their own rationalizations. However, this will not apply to psychopaths, who are remarkable for their glib insincerity. They do truly seem not to care at all about things we think people ought to care about.

In chapter 19, footnote 6, above, Hervey Cleckley was quoted already as estimating that 'the so-called psychopath holds no real viewpoint at all and is free of any sincere conviction in what might be called either good or evil.'[9] But, while writing that in a footnote, Cleckley's more qualified statement in the main text on the same page focuses upon

the common substance of emotion or purpose, or whatever else one chooses to call it, from which the various ideologies of various groups and various people are formed. Let us assume that this dimension of experience

8 American Psychiatric Association, *Diagnostic and Statistical Manual of Mental Disorders*, 4th ed. (Washington, DC, 1994), 649–50.

9 *The Mask of Sanity*, 425.

which gives to all experience its substance or reality is one into which the psychopath does not enter. Or, to be more accurate, let us say he enters, but so superficially that his reality is thin or unsubstantial to the point of being insignificant.[10]

So on Cleckley's 'more accurate' account, the psychopath does 'enter the dimension' of moral concern after all. On this preceding page, Cleckley shows the influence of the empathic theory of moral sentiments, shared with this book, when he writes:

The psychopath, however perfectly he mimics man theoretically, that is to say, when he speaks for himself in words, fails altogether when he is put into the practice of actual living. His failure is so complete and so dramatic that it is difficult to see how such a failure could be achieved by anything less than a downright *madman*, or by one totally or almost totally unable to grasp emotionally the major components of meaning or feeling implicit in the thoughts which he expresses or the experiences he appears to go through ...

   Let us then assume, as a hypothesis, that the psychopath's disorder or his difference from the whole or normal or integrated personality consists of an unawareness, and a persistent lack of ability to become aware, of what the most important experiences of life mean to others.[11]

Really? Unawareness? But how could psychopaths be so notoriously successful as con-artists if they were really unable to achieve any awareness of how others felt? To con people successfully it is surely requisite to understand their thoughts and emotions, though not, of course, to share them. And then, as Cleckley stresses, the psychopath is certainly not lacking, either, in the verbal ability to describe emotions.

Despite the extraordinarily poor judgment demonstrated in behavior, in the actual living of his life, the psychopath characteristically demonstrates unimpaired (sometimes excellent) judgment in appraising theoretical situations. In complex matters of judgment involving ethical, emotional, and other evaluational factors, in contrast with matters requiring only (or chiefly) intellectual reasoning ability, in such matters also he shows no evidence

---

10 Ibid.
11 Ibid., 424.

of a defect. So long as the test is verbal or otherwise abstract, so long as he is not a direct participant he shows that he knows his way about.[12]

Is the psychopath's emotional life 'hollow'? Robert G. Kegan objects:

> ... it can only be said to be 'hollow' from some more evolved point of view. It looks hollow to us because we construct a 'bigger' inner world, and when we 'try on' the sociopath's world within ourselves it doesn't fill *us* up; it leaves *us* feeling empty or hollow! So we then attribute hollowness to the sociopath! But this may not be the sociopath's experience of his inner world at all; nor need it be the only perspective for us to take.
>
>   In fact, this is the same world as that of a normal eight- or 10-year-old, and, although most sensitive parents realize their children would be tempted to sell them for a cold drink on a hot day, they do not think of the rather shortsighted self-interestedness of their children as a sign of 'hollowness.'[13]

Robert Hare disagrees:

> These are interesting speculations, but the brain-wave characteristics in question are also associated with drowsiness or boredom in normal adults, and could as well result from the psychopath's sleepy disinterest in the procedure used to measure them as from a delay in brain development. Furthermore, I doubt that the egocentricity or impulsivity of children and psychopaths are really the same. I am certain that few people have difficulty in distinguishing between the personality, motivations, and behavior of a normal ten-year-old and those of an adult psychopath, even after allowing for the difference in age. More important, few parents of a ten-year-old psychopath would confuse him or her with an ordinary ten-year-old.[14]

The phenomenon of psychopathy is the empirical counterevidence, if anything is, to the idea advanced in chapter 26 that first-language learning

---

12 Ibid., 394.
13 Robert G. Kegan, 'The Child behind the Mask: Sociopathy as Developmental Delay,' in William H. Reid, Darwin Dorr, John I. Walker, and Jack W. Bonner, III, eds., *Unmasking the Psychopath, Antisocial Personality and Related Syndromes* (New York, 1986), 69.
14 *Without Conscience*, 169.

involves learning how to put oneself imaginatively in the place of others, which thus gives rise to empathy, sympathy, and, with almost no further intellectual ado, the 'Generalized Other' standpoint of (putative) morality. But is it really accurate to see the psychopath as absolutely without any moral-type motivations whatsoever? In a 1993 paper published by the Royal College of Psychiatrists of London in a volume entitled *Personality Disorder Reviewed*, Herschel Prins speaks of 'curious superego lacunae rather than total lack of conscience.'[15] Cleckley himself conceded:

> The psychopath who causes his parents hardship and humiliation by re-peatedly forging checks and causes his wife anguish by sordid (and per-haps half-hearted) relations with the housemaid, may, in the community, gain a considerable reputation by so often volunteering to cut the grass for the frail old lady across the street, by bringing a bottle of sherry over now and then to bedridden Mr. Blank, by leaving his work to take a neighbor's injured cat to the veterinarian.
>
> ... In these surface aspects of functioning the typical psychopath (unlike the classic hypocrite) often seems to act with undesigning spontaneity, to be prompted by motives of excellent quality though of marvellously at-tenuated substance.[16]

All discussions of the sociopathic personality disorders seem to agree, at any rate, about 'impulsiveness.' In the words of the American Psychiatric Association's *DSM-IV*, 'Decisions are made on the spur of the moment, without forethought, and without consideration for the consequences to self or others ...'[17] Under the heading 'Living for the Moment,' Hare writes:

---

15 Herschel Prins, 'Antisocial (Psychopathic) Personality Disorders and Dangerous-ness: Two Potentially Dangerous Concepts,' in Peter Tyrer and George Stein, eds., *Personality Disorder Reviewed* (London, 1993), 308. In the same volume, Jeremy Coid, citing an earlier article of his own, observes: 'The sheer complexity and range of psychopathology in psychopathic disorder has previously led to the suggestion that these individuals could be considered to suffer from a series of conditions that would best be subsumed under a broad generic term "psychopathic disorders" rather than a single entity.' 'Current Concepts and Classifications of Psychopathic Disorder,' 156. Coid's earlier article was published as 'Psychopathic Disorders,' *Current Opinion in Psychiatry* 2, no. 6 (December 1989), 750–6.

16 *The Mask of Sanity*, 405.

17 *Diagnostic and Statistical Manual of Mental Disorders*, 646.

Although a student of New Age philosophies might shudder at the desecration of sacred principles, much of the psychopath's behavior and motivation makes sense if we think of him or her as a person rooted completely in the present and unable to resist a good opportunity. As an inmate who scored high on the *Psychopathy Checklist* said, 'What's a guy gonna do? She had a nice ass. I helped myself.' He was convicted of rape. Another was picked up by police after he appeared on a television game show in the very city where his victims lived. Five minutes of stardom and two years in prison![18]

The revolution in thought articulated so ably by Thomas Hobbes formed and celebrated the conception of an individual mentality fully actuated by prudent self-interest alone. It took that astute mid-Victorian Henry Sidgwick, in fact quite impressed by egoism personally, to insist nevertheless:

> I do not see why the axiom of Prudence should not be questioned, when it conflicts with present inclination, on a ground similar to that on which Egoists refuse to admit the axiom of Rational Benevolence. If the Utilitarian has to answer the question, 'Why should I sacrifice my own happiness for the greater happiness of another?' it must surely be admissible to ask the Egoist, 'Why should I sacrifice a present pleasure for a greater one in the future? Why should I concern myself about my own future feelings any more than about the feelings of other persons?'[19]

What would we call an individual who voiced this sort of thinking as a serious rhetorical question – or at least thought that way privately – what would we call such an individual if not a psychopath? As Sidgwick envisaged it, the challenge here is that posed by the possibility of restricting all concern *even further* than a prudent egoist would. But it is equally easy to imagine someone's concern being limited narrowly to the 'specious present' – the time right around now – but within such narrow temporal limits by no means being restricted just to selfish or non-moral desires. Is the psychopath really quite indifferent to any and all (putative) moral considerations, however short-range their scope? At any rate, the evidence hardly enforces such a conclusion. Listen to Ted Bundy:

---

18 *Without Conscience*, 88.
19 Henry Sidgwick, *The Methods of Ethics*, 7th ed. (London, 1907), 418.

Before his execution, serial killer Ted Bundy spoke directly of guilt in several interviews with Stephen Michaud and Hugh Aynesworth. '[Whatever] I've done in the past,' he said, 'you know – the emotions of omission or commissions – *doesn't* bother me. Try to touch the past! Try to deal with the past. It's not real. It's just a dream!'[20]

---

20 Hare, *Without Conscience*, 41. The inner quotation comes from Stephen G. Michaud and Hugh Aynesworth, *Ted Bundy: Conversations with a Killer* (New York, 1989), 284. Bundy himself wanted it understood that his attitude resulted from 'studying to some degree, oriental philosophy – Buddhism and Taoism and spiritual-physical traditions of the East,' genially bragging to Aynesworth, 'I've learned to live absolutely and completely and totally in the *here and now*. I don't worry, think or concern myself with the past, or, for that matter, with the future, except only to the extent necessary' (284, 283). Emphasis in original.

28 Utility

Prejudice is of ready application in the emergency; it previously engages the mind in a steady course of wisdom and virtue and does not leave the man hesitating in the moment of decision sceptical, puzzled, and unresolved. Prejudice renders a man's virtue his habit, and not a series of unconnected acts. Through just prejudice, his duty becomes a part of his nature.

Edmund Burke[1]

It is not amidst the hurly-burly of exciting temptations that we can safely look around us for motives to check their promptings. Let the rules be gathered up, let the motives be fixed within us, while the temptations are absent, and it is thus, and thus only, that when the temptations are present, we shall find the arguments at hand for resisting them.

Jeremy Bentham (reported by John Bowring)[2]

Suppose we ask ourselves whether our sense that we ought to pay our debts or to tell the truth arises from our recognition that in doing so we should be originating something good, e.g., material comfort in A or true belief in B, i.e., suppose we ask ourselves whether it is this aspect of the

1 *Reflections on the Revolution in France* (New York, 1955), 99.
2 *Deontology*, vol. 2, ed. John Bowring (London, 1834), 29.

action which leads to our recognition that we ought to do it. We, at once, and without hesitation answer 'No'.

H.A. Prichard'[3]

Whatever the actual specifics of passing a culture on from one generation to the next, according to chapter 26 putting oneself imaginatively in somebody else's place has a key role to play in the whole process of learning to take up the moral point of view. At that rate, it is no surprise that the moral outlook so produced should be apt to involve taking a sympathetic attitude to the interests of people besides oneself. Indeed, is there any ethic that's at all influential which does not give some weight to an imperative enjoining a stance of unprejudiced, humane concern? Wherever certain others are excluded from all direct concern for their interests, that tends to go along with reclassifying these others zoologically as not really *people*.

In any case, when the point of view taken is one of sympathy, there is no reason to distinguish people's interests from their actual *desires* except in the way they do themselves. For we have all learned from pretty early on to take account of the difference between what we do desire and what we *would* desire if we knew enough about what its effects would be. Let us define as being in our genuine 'interests' whatever we would, on balance, desire if sufficiently informed as to its potential effects – sufficiently informed, that is, that no additional information would modify our desires further. It accordingly follows from the definition of 'desire' in appendix 2 that you can be credited right now with a desire in the abstract to further your genuine *interests*, even if you do not know how, since you even now would be moved to take any means to furthering your interests which you did actually know to be effective, necessary, and available. And, even if you do not know concretely how to carry out this desire you have for the furtherance of your interests, it is even now a desire strong enough to outweigh any desires in conflict with it since, by definition, it is your desire to further your *interests* by which you would, on balance, be moved to act if you did know how. So understood, the distinction between what

---

3 'Does Moral Philosophy Rest on a Mistake?' *Mind*, n.s., 21, no. 81 (January 1912), 25.

you on balance actually desire now and what is really in your interests will have to collapse in the final analysis.[4]

Such a result, to be sure, is only secured by turning the word 'interests' away from its most usual meaning – in two ways. In the first place, especially when we speak of your *long-term* 'interests,' we usually have in mind, not just the interests which you, as you are now, have, but also, equally, the interests of your future self for as long as you are going to live. It is only human nature to care already in no small measure about the interests of that future individual even now. But there is no combination of deductive and inductive reasoning that can give you any such directive. Accordingly, there is no contradiction in saying you on balance wish to do something even though you know perfectly well that it runs counter to your long-term 'interests' (in the most usual sense of that word); for instance, by militating significantly against your future health. To the extent that the well-being of the future you does not matter to you now, it can have no bearing on your *interests* now, in that sense of the word which I am here proposing. In that sense, even the long-term *interests* you have now will be affected only by such future contingencies as you care about now, or, rather, would care about if sufficiently informed as to their potential effects.

In this respect, the future you is *like* another person. But, just as you can, and most probably do, take a lively interest in the well-being of that individual destined to 'grow out' of you, likewise there is nothing to stop you from also being concerned to some extent for the interests of anybody else as well. So those interests can form part of what in the present sense count as *your interests*, even aside from any effect they

---

4 These issues are discussed more fully in my paper 'Objective Interests,' reprinted in *Critical Perspectives on Democracy*, ed. Lyman H. Legters, John P. Burke, and Arthur DiQuattro (Lanham, MD, 1994), 147–64, and my paper 'Interests,' *Dialogue* 41, no. 2 (Spring 2002), 241–9. The latter paper makes the point in note 6 on page 247 that a qualification needs to be attached to this definition of what is in your 'interests' as that which you would, on balance, desire if sufficiently informed about what its effects would be. For the possession of such information-or-misinformation affects people's desire in a *regular* way when it is information-or-misinformation concerning what is a good means to what, but an appropriate restrictive proviso is required to exclude other, *irregular* ways that the possession of information can influence people's desires. So, instead of saying simply that something is in your interests if and only if you would desire it on balance if sufficiently informed about the potential effects, let us, for present purposes, limit the relevant *information* about the potential effects of anything, M, to information that would tend to lead you to 'act in furtherance' of something else, E, in the sense given in appendix 2 of this book.

have on what we could call your 'selfish interests.' By the same token, there is nothing to stop you from caring about that which is morally right, or about that which is morally good, for its own sake, so that how the right and the good are going to fare can directly affect your *interests*, in the present sense, quite apart from any effect they have on your 'selfish interests.'[5] The present proposed sense of the word 'interests' is thus something of a departure from a very common way of speaking, in which we are apt to equate people's 'interests' with what I have been calling their 'selfish interests.' But it does seem capricious and unkind to make a point of siding with people as far as everything they care about is concerned, *except* when it comes to their altruistic feelings or their ethical insights or prejudices.[6]

As appendix 2 acknowledges, the sense of the word 'desire' defined there does involve some departure from ordinary usage as well. *Contentment* is perhaps a state free of 'desire' in the most ordinary sense of the word; the same may be true of utter, paralysing depression. But

---

5 To be sure, among the things which it is possible to desire, either instrumentally or for its own sake, is the fulfillment (or the frustration) of the desires of others. Can we consistently conceive of a neighbourhood whose residents all did 'love their neighbours as themselves,' while fully aware of the real interests of each? A, of course, would have to give as much weight to furthering whatever B cared about as to A's 'selfish' concerns. But those values of B's would include not only concerns as strong as C's for everything that C wanted, but also concerns equal to A's for everything which A cared about, including the advancement of each of B's objectives. Should this be seen as objectionable double-counting? After all, upon experiencing any success a neighbour-loving A would indeed be, not just pleased by that, but as well *additionally* pleased by the knowledge that the occurrence of this pleasure would directly please B also. And B's pleasure would then be enhanced additionally in turn by knowing that fact about A. Does this entail the further and further addition of such equal new enhancements of the pleasure of each of them *ad infinitum*? Even if so, what *logical* impossibility can be found in the idea of being (literally) infinitely pleased by developments occurring? Moreover, each such new 'layer' of net pleasure-or-displeasure in prospect (after taking the foreseeable vicissitudes of all the neighbours' projects into account) would only add strength to the motivation for whatever course of action-or-inaction the previous layers were already prompting. So the dictates of pleasure maximization for conduct could be practically unaffected by such infinities. Of course, with imperfect human beings the series of successive enhancements of pleasure at the news that others are pleased by one's own good fortune, and so on, is always a diminishing series. In any case, we know the mutual concern of the members of a real human group does indeed increase their motivation to promote the advancement of their goals.

6 This sentence is taken from page 241 of my paper 'Interests,' cited in footnote 4. See also the discussion in note 3 on pages 246–7 of that paper.

these states do not rid the mind of all 'pro-attitudes' and 'con-attitudes,' as they have been called – 'desires' in the sense relevant here. Still less, in the present sense, does having a 'desire' need to involve any *arousal*, or indeed *consciousness*, as opposed to sleep, even dreamless sleep. The concept of *desire* being employed here is roughly that found in philosophy-of-mind analyses of people's *behaviour* as produced by a 'scissors-action,' so to speak, involving *desire* as one blade and (at any rate, value-neutral) belief as the other blade.[7] This is the sense of the word 'desires' in which it is tautologous that every being that acts always seeks, as far as it is able, to bring about whatever it most 'desires.'

Is it not just the same tautology, put differently, to say every being that acts always seeks, as far as it is able, to bring about whatever it sees as most *pleasing* to itself? Insofar as it is able, in other words, every being that acts does *what it pleases*. In the sole sense of the word 'pleasure' which makes *psychological hedonism*'s claim true that everybody pursues 'pleasure' only, the word does not identify any specific tone-quality of felt experience – or indeed, anything specific at all, but just what-is-desirable in general.

To be sure, the word 'desirable,' as used in the preceding sentence, cannot just *mean* 'pleasure-maximizing,' but the ethic which says that the supreme good and criterion of what's right is simply pleasure or happiness – or, at any rate, *people's* happiness – this *utilitarian* ethic arrives at its basic norm by a process of generalizing from the valuations ('pro-attitudes') of all those in whose place it is possible imaginatively to stand – all 'moral agents,' that is to say. The reasoned case for excluding other animals from *this* sort of consideration will be developed in chapter 32. At the present stage it is enough to note that among the things which even an unbeliever in any afterlife can care about for their own sake are developments of events subsequent to that caring unbeliever's death; and that there is no reason to think such desires would in every case disappear if only that caring individual were better informed about the potential effects of the developments desired. So not only is that *pleasure* or *happiness* which the utilitarian ethic here advocated calls the supreme

---

7 By a 'value-neutral' belief is meant here a belief other than one which evaluates something unconditionally, and not just instrumentally. Moral beliefs, as chapter 19 has argued, fit such a description, and so *are* desires. Are there any other examples? As remarked in footnote 23 of chapter 26, it is arguable that even an ill-founded belief that you desire something might give rise to seeking-behaviour in the way a desire does and so *become* self-fulfilling, as it were.

good not specifically anything experiential; we actually can deny that in the relevant sense people's *happiness* at a particular time even requires their continued existence then.[8] Some may jib at calling *such* a utilitarian philosophy 'hedonistic' at all; but what's in a word?

More to the point is whether such a philosophy is true. The purposed proof of that claim is set out in chapter 32. Chapters 29 and 30, like much of this chapter, are devoted to explaining the *meaning* of the claim which it is proposed to prove in chapter 32. But, as we know, it is not enough to prove a philosophical claim – especially where the proposed proof, however cogent, is by itself as unconvincing as experience has taught most of us to consider *a priori* philosophical arguments in general to be. In short, it is not enough, it is far from being enough, to *prove* such a philosophical claim. It is necessary also, as far as possible, to make the claim *plausible*. And essential to that, without question, is answering the most important objections.

An objection sometimes heard among welfare economists is that the promotion of 'maximum happiness overall' is not just an ethically insufficient undertaking but a logically impossible, not to say meaningless, one, because no coherent meaning can be given to furthering the 'overall happiness' of two or more individuals – except in the special (and infrequent?) case where the happiness of some is enhanced without reducing the happiness of any others. To assess the 'overall utility' of anything which benefits some while affecting others adversely calls for 'interpersonal comparisons of utility,' and these, it is claimed, are impossible in principle. Whatever we think we are up to, for example, when we seek to minimize the 'harm overall' resulting from some foreseen turn of events, it cannot be literally *that* which we ever succeed at all in doing, if this objection is right. For what can it mean to compare the *degree* to which any development furthers the fulfillment of one individual's desires with the *degree* to which it frustrates the fulfillment of another's?

This is the problem to which chapter 29 is devoted: perhaps a theoretical more than a practical problem, since continually in our everyday practice we not only make what, in effect, are 'overall comparisons of utility intrapersonally' whenever we weigh up our preferences as between alternatives which differentially advance and frustrate different desires of ours; but we also undertake what we think is the same thing 'interpersonally' whenever we weigh against each other the conflicting

---

8 See my article 'The Welfare of the Dead,' *Philosophy* 63, no. 243 (January 1988), 111–13.

interests of those we care about. Putting yourself in the place of A and B, you can ask whether A desires something's occurrence as strongly as B desires its nonoccurrence, by considering (other things being equal) which desire would influence *you* more strongly if you had them both. The transfer of A's and B's actual desires to you is mere science fiction, at least at the present time, and it presupposes a non-behavioural reality to desires and to their relative 'strengths' which some philosophies deny. But do not the Principles of Causality and Contiguity discussed in part two, above, require that an organism's desire-manifesting behaviour be caused by something inside it (whenever it is really that organism which is at all desirous of anything)?

The evidence is said to show that the mental causes of memory-exhibiting behaviour are clearly divided into what are called 'short-term memory' and 'long-term memory'; and *desire* might just conceivably turn out in the same way to be composed of distinct psychological realities productive alike or jointly of the organism's seeking-behaviour. That conflicting desires can be weighed against one another in the psyche of a single individual becomes evident in the individual's resulting behaviour. This is not enough to establish that desires' relative strengths can be compared on a 'ratio scale' and assigned cardinal numbers. In the working of an individual's mind, might there not be more than one interconnected cause or set of causes operating in the production of seeking-behaviour in such a way as to fit equally well appendix 2's definition of 'desire'? These different causes' variations in strength would have to be positively correlated, so that when one of them grew 'stronger,' the others did too, for otherwise they would not alike be candidates for the status of *being* what 'desire' is. But would these different causes' variations have to occur in exact quantitative proportion to each other? On the other hand, without an at least approximate proportionality here how could there result the unique ordinal ranking of desires' strengths exhibited in choice behaviour? More precisely: as the intensity of an individual's desires rose or fell to a new level, a particular inner cause's 'candidacy' for *desire*-status could be excluded as a result because of the failure of the relative strengths of different instances of that cause in the individual to correspond – at that level of desire intensity – to the actual ordinal ranking of different desires then resulting within the individual's psyche.

Especially in the nineteenth century a more practical, empirical objection to the long-run goal of 'maximizing happiness overall' was sometimes voiced – but it is still an objection, in principle, to the real possibility of rationally pursuing that goal. The *long-run* consequences of any action or inaction throughout all of future time are incalculable, it was argued, and so no recourse there for the guidance of conduct can in practice be possible. And, in truth, the unproblematic ease of recourse instead to the deontological *do*s and *don't*s of a concrete code of behaviour does compare favourably on this score with what really long-term consequences would often have to require for their serious reliable estimation – which, if not actually impossible, would frequently be too difficult to undertake without an unacceptable sacrifice of the very utility being sought. Accordingly, utilitarianism dictates that rules of thumb favouring practices likely to be most beneficial on the whole ought to guide us on any occasion where it is not readily apparent that some alternative course would have better consequences. In general, when it comes to the balance of resulting benefit and harm, surely the inductive method permits us to regard a deed's relatively short-term consequences as a *prima facie* reliable sample of its consequences overall, since as time progresses the deed's overall effect will most likely tend to be continually weakened by the inevitability of combining with the effects of more and more other causes. Certainly there are exceptions:

For want of a nail, the shoe was lost.
For want of the shoe, the horse was lost.
For want of the horse, the rider was lost.
For want of the rider, the battle was lost.
For want of the battle, the kingdom was lost.

It seems possible to comment that any kingdom brought down so easily must have been in a pretty fragile condition! The Simplicity presumption in favour of a relatively static near-future in any specific respect argues against any hesitation in expecting that the loss of particular single nails will generally *not* cause kingdoms to crumble.

In any case, if it held good, this objection would tell not only against consequentialist ethics such as utilitarianism but against any ethic – any policy – which gave any weight at all to the consideration of really long-term consequences. Sidgwick's terse rejoinder can be quoted:

> ... we may perhaps reduce the calculation within manageable limits, without serious loss of accuracy, by discarding all manifestly imprudent conduct, and neglecting the less probable and less important contingencies; as we do in some of the arts that have more definite ends, such as strategy and medicine.

For if the general in ordering a march, or the physician in recommending a change of abode, took into consideration all the circumstances that were at all relevant to the end sought, their calculations would become impracticable; accordingly they confine themselves to the most important ...[9]

The most prominent objections to utilitarianism, though, have focused mainly on appealing to our common sense moral and other feelings in opposition to it. Common sense, as we have seen, does give some backing to utilitarian considerations as well, but in the end the divergence between common sense and the dictates of utilitarianism is indeed pronounced. Common sense says that besides pleasure, other things, such as understanding or personal affection, are objectively worth promoting for their own sake. Common sense says that it is licit, even obligatory, to care far more about the well-being of those near and dear to you than even of others whose well-being you are able to affect easily by your actions. Common sense says (as Prichard notes in the quotation from him given in his epigraph to this chapter) that promise-keeping, like truth-telling, is an obligation having some force independently of all consequences. And the same thing can equally be said about justice. Legal punishment, for instance, serves the beneficial function of deterring crime; the benefit, however, does not depend upon those punished being really guilty of the crimes they are charged with committing, but only upon their being generally *thought* to be guilty. Et cetera.

To these objections based on common sense, utilitarians have sought to respond by making the co-optive move of showing that their philosophy really supports and indeed justifies (many of) the common sense positions which seem so contrary to it at first sight. They argue that utility is (often) promoted most effectively by adopting an 'indirect' rather than a 'direct' strategy.

It is, of course, a well established fact of human nature that in making change, for instance, people are apt to err, even without meaning to, oftener in their own favour than the other way. In estimating the long-term benefits and disbenefits of an act of commission or omission that we might perform, we are all indeed only too prone to miscalculate and irrationally rationalize taking, in fact, the line of least resistance or greatest advantage to ourselves. So it is obviously of some advantage to society that its members should have 'internalized' an intrinsic abhorrence of lying and cheating, for example, strong enough to be overcome

---

9 Henry Sidgwick, *The Methods of Ethics*, 7th ed. (London, 1907), 131–2.

only by exceptional countermotivation. Individuals so disposed will not be induced to tell a lie by the prospect – however certain – of only modest net benefit from it.

It is well worth emphasizing that this is quite apart from the toil and trouble of figuring out all the probable benefits and disbenefits of taking an action. That toil-and-trouble consideration could at most justify a rule of thumb to tell the truth in cases of doubt since veracity so frequently is for the best. But veracity could not prevail with a conscience *thus* motivated whenever it were readily apparent that even a slight net benefit would result from lying.

Indirect-strategy utilitarianism certainly has its critics, and we will have to turn to their objections shortly, but if those objections succeed they will tell not only against utilitarianism, but against any conscientious position that accords any weight at all to consequence-regarding considerations. For virtually any consequentialist ethical objective will be advanced most effectively under real-world conditions if people on occasion feel a direct emotional attachment not just to it but to other things too, such as telling the truth. And so the empirical fact which Prichard reports and Burke and Bentham in effect applaud in their epigraphs to this chapter must be commended *on consequentialist grounds* not only by supporters of ethical consequentialism as such, but by those supporting any ethical outlook which takes consequences to matter at all. It is not only utilitarianism which leads to 'indirect strategies.'

But utilitarianism does have a specific additional reason for adopting the indirect-strategy approach. Under anything like existing conditions it demands a sacrifice from most of us far beyond what we can seriously be expected to accept. Such are the often horrific conditions of life in the world as it is that sacrifices altogether impossible from any practical standpoint would yet not be so great that making them couldn't readily yield still greater ultimate benefit, and therefore be morally obligatory according to the Principle of Utility. Either far away or close at hand, it is very easy to find cases of misery that would be so markedly alleviated by giving up almost all you have that the overall benefit would clearly outweigh the overall loss. Most of us are far too selfish to countenance such extreme sacrifices, and in existing conditions the effort to change us into fully practising utilitarians, ready to make *any* sacrifice which would foreseeably result in net benefit overall, could not but be effort clearly doomed to failure – and worse. For the more seriously we aligned ourselves with such an effort, the more harrowing the experience would be for us while the effort lasted, and the ultimate end result might well be only to 'cure' us of any disposition whatever to make serious efforts to be unselfish – even otherwise quite feasible efforts. So in the case of most of us, the real-world consequences will be far better if we are not disposed to make the effort to turn ourselves into fully practising utilitarians in our motivations and actions. So far do we fall short of what the Principle of Utility demands of us that the results will be much better if our emotional makeup is such as to let us off with, at any rate, a *relatively* clear conscience, in spite of falling short to the extent we do. From a utilitarian point of view it is far better on this account also that we should not be, or even try to be, wholly utilitarian in our moral feelings, and that these feelings should, at least to some degree, attach instead to a deontological code which we can to that extent avoid feeling guilty by dutifully obeying.[10]

In other words, if utilitarianism is correct and whatever is aptest to cause people happiness in the long run is obligatory, then it is obligatory not even to try to make our moral feelings entirely utilitarian, let alone to make ourselves fully practising utilitarians in everything we do.[11]

If the literal transfer of desires from one individual to another is just science fiction, where shall we turn for depictions of a perfect model utilitarian? Christian churchman R.M. Hare suggests that an archangel is what we should think of here.[12] After all, any such being, if it ever existed, would have to love *everybody* as itself. For any interest it knew you had, it would have to have a desire for the furtherance of that interest as strong as the desire for its furtherance which you yourself would have if you knew you had that interest. Since, as we've discussed above, you can be seen as already having a predominant desire for the furtherance of your interests, whatever they are, there would have to be a place in the model utilitarian's conscience for an equally strong desire for the furtherance of those interests. The model utilitarian's conscience would

---

10 The preceding four paragraphs are mostly taken from my paper, 'The "Two Hats" Problem in Consequentialist Ethics,' *Utilitas* 14, no. 1 (March 2002), 109.

11 According to the philosophy advocated here, any and all of everybody's interests are all alike worth furthering, *prima facie*. But in the real world having a good character involves a certain revulsion at the ascription even only of such presumptive ultimate value to the gratification of people's cruel and malicious desires, for example. This, though, is just as it should be, since the existence of such sentiments operates to maximize the net benefit (as here understood) to society at large in the long run. See Louis Kaplow and Steven Shavell, *Fairness versus Welfare* (Cambridge, MA, 2002), 418–31.

12 R.M. Hare, *Moral Thinking, Its Levels, Method and Point* (Oxford, 1981), 44.

on balance pronounce in favour of fulfilling this last desire, together with any other desires it contained for the same things, as long as that conscience did not also contain contrary desires which, together, were just as strong or stronger. All such desires that anybody ever had or would have, to the best of this being's knowledge, would be matched in the being's conscience, so that it would pronounce in favour of whatever all such desires in the world were on balance in favour of, and it would pronounce against whatever all such desires in the world were on balance against.

Could such a being have any personal preferences other than its conscientious concerns? Could it have food tastes? Could it have friends whose fortunes it cared about independently of the resulting consequences for the good overall? Of course, *every* desire in its conscience for the advancement of somebody's interests would already be a desire for such advancement independently of any further consequences (which doesn't mean, needless to say, that no consideration of further consequences could ethically outweigh that desire in the model utilitarian's judgments). On the other hand, it would be obviously unacceptable double-counting to *add* to a 'nonconscientious' desire that the being had for something a further, utilitarian desire *in its conscience* for the gratification of the first desire. *All* the model utilitarian's desires would be conscientious concerns that this being had, but only because they all would be 'moralized' thanks to the *way* in which this being desired what it desired. Integral to each of these desires would be a desire for the gratification of *any* such desire that anybody would have, or would have had (if sufficiently informed about the consequences of fulfilling it), *and* a presumptive wish for anybody whatever to share this concern for the gratification of any such desire. The model utilitarian wouldn't merely desire something and desire *as well* that such interests of anybody's be served and *also* desire, presumptively, that anybody whatever share the desire for such interests to be served. Instead, it would be one single mental reality which underlay these three distinguishable dispositions to seeking-behaviour on the model utilitarian's part. Being thus invested with moral force, so to speak, *any* desire the model utilitarian possessed would be a conscientious concern that being had: but not because any sort of personal gratification would be off-limits as an object of desire for it.

We can be fairly confident that the model utilitarian, thus described, is not to be found amongst the members of the human race. But, however certain we are that it would be wrong even to try to makes ourselves be just like that, it doesn't follow that we have no obligation to try to make ourselves *more* like that. It doesn't follow that such a being's judgments are not the *criterion* of what, morally speaking, is good and bad, right and wrong. And, for the philosophy of utilitarianism, that is in fact the criterion proposed.

How much like a model utilitarian should we try to be? Hare replies,

> There is no philosophical answer to the question; it depends on what powers of thought and character each one of us, for the time being, thinks he possesses. We have to know ourselves in order to tell how much we can trust ourselves to play the archangel ...[13]

Obviously, young children need a rather firmer emotional attachment to more rigid moral rules. But as they mature they become more and more capable of what Hare calls 'critical moral thinking.' And under differing historical conditions the mores best for different societies or social groups can vary on that score as well as in the concrete content of the moral norms called for. A statement like this reminds Amartya Sen and Bernard Williams of the paternalistic reasoning standardly employed by colonial administrations to justify their behind-closed-doors manipulations. At any rate, Sen and Williams decry 'what might be called "Government House utilitarianism", an outlook favouring social arrangements under which a utilitarian élite controls a society in which the majority may not itself share those beliefs.'[14]

Sen and Williams, of course, are fully aware that present-day indirect-strategy utilitarians favour *direct* emotional attachment to deontological norms not just for others but for themselves also, perceiving their own behaviour as likely to be better than it otherwise would be if they, too, felt that an obligation to tell the truth, for instance, were something holding good in its own right, even if not indefeasibly. To this Williams objects, 'One cannot separate, except by an imposed and illusory dissociation, the theorist in oneself from the self whose dispositions are being theorized.'[15] How *can* one ever bring oneself to feel an emotional attachment in one's heart to veracity, say, while at the same time theorizing that it isn't really justified intrinsically, but is only justified by virtue of

---

13 Ibid., 45.
14 Amartya Sen and Bernard Williams, in the editors' introduction to their anthology, *Utilitarianism and Beyond* (Cambridge, 1982), 16.
15 Bernard Williams, *Ethics and the Limits of Philosophy* (Cambridge, MA, 1995), 110.

the contribution it makes to overall utility in the long run? *Can* one conscientiously wear both of these hats at the same time? Or, at any rate, can one do so comfortably? consistently? honourably?

The criticism of indirect-strategy utilitarianism which Williams is pressing here would appear to suggest at least four distinguishable lines of objection (several of which, of course, might be combined):

(1) The continuing mental effort required to accomplish the 'imposed dissociation' of the ethical theorist in oneself from the conscientious moral agent in oneself is damagingly painful and/or difficult, not to say psychologically impossible.
(2) Such a psychological accomplishment actually is *logically* impossible.
(3) Even if it should be logically possible, it involves thinking *inconsistently*.
(4) Such a mind-set in any case is morally reprehensible, whether because, of necessity, it is *deceptive* – even if only by being *self-deceptive* – or else for some different reason.[16]

On the basis of meta-ethical cognitivism (contrary to Williams' own position), we saw in chapter 26 that it is indeed both logically and psychologically possible, consistently and without self-deception, to *feel* one way and *opine* another way on a moral issue. That leaves the question of the psychic cost of such a mindset, and the possible reprehensibility involved, even if not owing to unavoidable self-deception.

There is no point in trying to wear the two hats jauntily. Since ethical belief necessarily involves *caring* – even if not *caring-on-balance* – when we *feel* one way and *opine* another way on a moral question there is no escaping the lack of psychological robustness that goes with having a mind divided against itself. Such, soberly considered, are simply the facts.

And the facts bearing on the reprehensibility charge are worse still. What requires us to give up the objective of matching our personal way of life to that of the model utilitarian described above? It is just what we know about ourselves and the world we live in. There is nothing to be proud of in our ever-present proneness to be selfish and irresponsible. And the world, we know, continually pits us in opposition to one another by making our interests genuinely conflict. Can this be changed? There arguably has been some real moral progress over the centuries.

---

16 The preceding two paragraphs are based on my paper 'The "Two Hats" Problem in Consequentialist Ethics,' 108–9.

Slavery is disapproved of nowadays, and lip service at least is given to deploring the occurrence of mass killing in warfare. What is certain, though, is that considerable moral turpitude remains both in the world at large and in each one of us. Neither utilitarians nor anti-utilitarians are really entitled to shake off the reprehensibility charge.

However, when it comes to moral progress or its opposite, what better criterion can there truly be than the Principle of Utility? Everybody knows that, as general historical conditions change from one epoch to another, the prevailing spirit-of-the-age tends to change with them. And from the standpoint of the Principle of Utility it *ought* to change with them, though not necessarily in the way that it does. By the spirit-of-the-age prevailing in an epoch I mean both more and less than the moral code which is then generally accepted. More, because the spirit-of-the-age is also reflected in other things, such as tastes in music. Less, because there is some distance between the specific *do*s and *don't*s of a concrete moral code and the general cultural outlook which, with local variations, those are apt to express.

If the Utility Principle is the criterion for ethically evaluating such a general cultural outlook, then that outlook in turn, insofar as it is justified for its time, provides the main standard for assessing the *do*s and *don't*s of a concrete code of behaviour. And it is mostly by reference to whatever the appropriate moral code is that people's particular acts of commission and omission are best judged. This is not to deny that a direct appeal to the Principle of Utility is ever in order to support or oppose a particular moral code. Nor does this mean that it is never ever proper to judge people's doings directly by reference to an appropriate general cultural outlook, or even, indeed, by direct reference right to the Principle of Utility itself. What are the occasions on which a direct appeal to the Principle of Utility is called for? They fall into three classes. First of all, there are cases where a very great deal of benefit or harm is at stake depending on what is done or not done, either in a single instance or as a *rule*. Secondly, there are cases to which no more concrete norm applies than the Principle of Utility itself, although the benefit or harm at stake is significant. Lastly, of course, there are cases of conflict between concrete rules of behaviour which can't be very readily resolved by appealing to a more general ethico-cultural outlook.

I hope the version of indirect-strategy utilitarianism sketched above is defensible. According to it, no norm whatsoever is to be obeyed unconditionally at all times and places and in all circumstances. And certainly the Principle of Utility is, for its part, not to be applied that way.

Nor should the reader be surprised to come across a conclusion like this in the context of a philosophy which disparages as unscientific *metaphysics* even talk of the universal unconditional sway of any finitely complex laws of physics.

Equipped with this way of assessing moral issues, we are in a position to address the common-sense objections to utilitarianism touched on above. There certainly are things worth valuing for their own sake besides people's happiness. And why? Because such valuing does tend to promote and enhance people's happiness overall. Examples include truth-telling, promise-keeping, love, the well-being of family and friends, and kindness to animals. For, unsurprisingly, it is an empirical fact that cruelty towards animals is apt to be accompanied by hard-heartedness and cruelty towards human beings. Justice is another example. Citizens of any community who generally tend to experience a direct passion for justice will usually live more secure and hence more flourishing lives.[17]

Of course, what specific norms of justice are appropriate must vary as historical conditions change. Nowhere is this more evident then when it comes to 'distributive justice.' Were earlier civilizations simply *in error* in considering 'noble blood' to confer special entitlements on those possessing it? They doubtless were in error insofar as they thought this to be an eternal truth of any kind. But the family-tree-based social hierarchies which such conceptions of justice reflected and supported were arguably at the time what stood between settled society and wholesale reversion, with a steep reduction in numbers, to ways of life grounded in primeval nomadism. However, this has long since ceased to hold true. In the words of Epicurus,

> ... where, when circumstances have changed, the same actions which were sanctioned as just no longer lead to advantage, there they were just at the time when they were of advantage for the dealings of fellow-

---

17 Philosophical fashions fluctuate. Eighty years ago it was treating respect for justice as only instrumentally valuable that really exercised so many English-speaking objectors about utilitarianism. Today, what mightily puts white-collar city-dwellers off is perhaps more apt to be identifying *people's* happiness as being that which ultimately matters ethically. But in the case of caring concern for animal welfare just as in that of the disinterested love of justice, the offence so strongly taken will be due to having internalized the very attitude that indirect-strategy utilitarianism recommends.

citizens with one another; but subsequently they are no longer just, when no longer of advantage.[18]

Under today's conditions we rightly consider the birth-based inequality that prevailed in all ancient civilizations to be *unjust*. But *any* systematic inequality, viewed in another way, is also an equality, as Aristotle reminds us.[19] If the reward allotted to each one is in proportion to whatever that one amounts to, then the *ratio* between what an individual receives and what that individual amounts to will be equal for all. And *that* equality would, of necessity, be disrupted by any other distribution of rewards. And so the call just for equality as such is hopelessly indeterminate. If phenomenologically it does not *seem* that way, this is because cultural influences lead us to take for granted certain ways of comparing people as opposed to others.

All this is especially relevant because some have urged that the utilitarian directive to maximize people's welfare should be amended in an egalitarian direction – either by insisting upon equality, or *more* equality, in the distribution of economic resources or consumables; or else (with some) by even favouring something like the equalization of human happiness itself. Equality of the former sort really does get a certain backing from some of our precritical moral feelings. And there is indeed ample utilitarian justification for such feelings in some circumstances – for instance, pretty uncontroversially, in distributing candy to our children. As for equality of the latter sort – the equalization of people's happiness – when it is spelled out, it can receive no backing from our egalitarian or other moral feelings. Indeed, it runs counter to them even more than the unmodified objective of maximizing people's overall happiness does. Some individuals, for instance, are *relatively* uninterested in consumables, and derive their pleasures more from other sources, such as nature, or introspection. A distribution of consumables which was to increase everybody's happiness equally would therefore have to shower greater quantities of consumables upon these individuals than upon those more in a position to benefit from consuming them. There are other, specially fastidious individuals who have expensive 'champagne tastes.' Because they are so hard to please, that much more resources would have to be devoted to gratifying them than others, if the resulting contribution to the happiness of each person had

---

18 Epicurus, *Principal Doctrines*, 38.
19 Aristotle, *Nichomachean Ethics*, Book V, chapter 3.

to be equal. It surely isn't *egalitarians*, as the term is usually understood, who are going to find this attractive.[20]

Of those who have invoked considerations of justice in opposition to the Utility Principle, not all have found responses like the above sufficient to still their objections. They sometimes have been unwilling to follow Burke and Hare in taking an external, 'critical' view of what social consideration often could, after all, vindicate as 'just prejudices' under existing conditions. With some, decisionism acts as a shield against any objective criticism. But, without recourse to decisionism, can a utilitarian concern for people's welfare withstand – any better than deontological theories of justice can – the type of objective critical scrutiny that historical and sociological outlooks are apt to prompt? To this we shall have to return below.

In Victorian times a common criticism brought against utilitarianism and hedonism generally, in effect, was that they seemed to lead to the repugnant conclusion that a happy community of Homeric lotus-eaters would be living more or less ideal lives. And Romantic revulsion was expressed against valuing all equally intense pleasure alike, whether they were animal pleasures or distinctively human ones, whether they were crude or were highly cultivated ones. But were they all equally intense in fact? To suppose that preferring what is 'higher' involves any real sacrifice of happiness, Mill objected, 'confounds the two very different ideas, of happiness, and content. It is indisputable that the being whose capacities of enjoyment are low, has the greatest chance of having them fully satisfied ...[21] However that may be, an indirect strategy for the maximization of long-run utility can, in very many circumstances, justify the preference for an energetic life over a completely passive one and for relishing cultivated enjoyments rather than just brutish ones. Apart from anything else, lotus-eaters and louts are apt to be ill-prepared to cope with crises, or to take advantage of opportunities. Not that it makes sense, as a rule, to cherish a mode of life, on the other hand, devoid of *any* relaxation or 'lower' enjoyments.

In the latter half of the twentieth century an increasing focus for criticism of the Utility Principle derived from arguments about optimum population size. In a number of countries policies aimed at fostering or

---

20 See my paper 'Distributive Justice and Utility,' *The Journal of Value Inquiry* 25, no. 1 (January 1991), 65–71.

21 John Stuart Mill, *Utilitarianism,* chap. 2, from *Essays on Ethics, Religion and Society,* ed. J.M. Robson (Toronto, 1969), 212.

retarding population growth involved truly monstrous encroachments on people's liberty (*and*, often, little in the way of results to show). But that is not to say no public policy on population can ever be justified. So it is quite proper to subject not just any version of the Utility Principle, but any ethic whatever, to critical scrutiny on that specific score. And this is the topic to which chapter 30 will be devoted.

There is, finally, the sceptical *causal* argument against utilitarianism and, indeed, against any ethical truth claim. As remarked above, the argument is often prompted by historical and sociological reflection. Specifically, this is the sceptical argument identified in chapter 24. To be sure, it is only one of four distinguishable arguments that are advanced against ethical objectivity. In the first place, there is the ancient Criterion argument for scepticism in general,[22] depending upon the 'antifoundationalist' presupposition that a belief somebody holds, whether true or false, is always *unjustified* (unwarranted, in error) without a good *argument* to back it up. I hope the discussion in chapter 1 will have been sufficient to satisfy the reader that this line of thinking is untenable. In any case, chapter 4, on the one hand, and part two, on the other hand, were meant to show how incontestable it is that there are both deductive and inductive principles which require no argumentative backup. A second line of argument against ethical objectivity rests on the empiricist principle ('Hume's Fork') that every justified belief is either analytic or else empirically backed up. Both chapter 5 and part two, above, were meant to discredit that claim. Thirdly, there is the argument that, as such, moral pronouncements sincerely or otherwise express *desires* on the part of the speaker and therefore are, in so far, neither true nor false. Chapters 3 and 26 were intended to refute that claim. Lastly, there is the causal argument for scepticism, identified in chapter 24, which maintains that the sociology and psychology of moral belief formation and retention are such that the causes responsible for whatever beliefs we

---

22 '... in order to decide the dispute which has arisen about the criterion, we must possess an accepted criterion by which we shall be able to judge the dispute; and in order to possess an accepted criterion, the dispute about the criterion must first be decided. And when the argument thus reduces itself to a form of circular reasoning the discovery of the criterion becomes impracticable, since we do not allow them to adopt a criterion by assumption, while if they offer to judge the criterion by a criterion we force them to a regress *ad infinitum*. And furthermore, since demonstration requires a demonstrated criterion, while the criterion requires an approved demonstration, they are forced into circular reasoning.' (Sextus Empiricus, *Outlines of Pyrrhonism*, trans. R.G. Bury [Cambridge, MA, 1976], 163–5.)

hold would operate equally well to make us hold those beliefs even if there really were no truth to them. At that rate, if they *were* to be true, that would just be a lucky chance outcome, as there was no particular likelihood (let alone necessity) of the beliefs so caused being true. That (I think) is how the argument should be understood as running.

It is important to note that such a line of sceptical argument, in contrast to the Criterion argument, is not at all based on burden-of-proof considerations. The sceptic here is not challenging those who believe something to *justify* their belief with arguments. The reasoning is, rather, that *even if* the belief that is held were to be true, that would be by chance only. To counter this argument, therefore, it is enough to show that, if the belief were to be true, that would *not* be a chance outcome. The case will be parallel to the case of induction discussed in chapter 11.

Accepting, then, that the Principle of Utility is really true (though the proof to be proposed here will not be set out until chapter 32), what is it that makes the Principle of Utility believed? Are the causes of the belief such that the truth of the belief so caused follows with any reliability from being due to those causes? If the answer is yes, then it is likely to be no accident that the belief so caused is true.

Admittedly, most people have never even heard of the Principle of Utility, let alone decided to subscribe to it expressly. The belief to be defended here against the charge of unreliable causation is therefore something much less definite. By and large without at all being formulated philosophically, there is a widespread disposition among those belonging to our species to consider people, actions, situations, character traits, and so on to be *good*, other things being equal, insofar as they tend to produce happiness for people and *bad*, other things being equal, insofar as they tend to produce the reverse. It is believing *that way* which is to be defended here against the causal objection. Most people, of course, have many moral beliefs in addition to this, but, so long as they have *some* disposition to base moral approval and disapproval on what they perceive to be tendencies to produce happiness and unhappiness for people, what they do believe along these lines will be sufficient for present purposes. It will be enough to defend *that* against the causal objection.

Of course, it isn't only *that* moral belief which people are caused to hold. People's other moral beliefs must have their causes as well, and this includes some beliefs which we nowadays have learned to view with marked disapproval. The once firmly held belief in the rightness of male supremacy, for instance, resulted from, and gave support to, a social order in which men were dominant. But moral beliefs of which we are much more apt to approve, such as the belief in the rightness of promise-keeping, likewise resulted from and contributed to the perpetuation of the overall order of society. Indeed, in causally explaining the prevalence of such beliefs we can cite their contribution to social order, since it is a fair supposition that they would not have survived so long if they had not had that tendency. But it would be a gross oversimplification to see any socially widespread moral beliefs as always contributing to social stability. Sometimes conditions give rise, at least temporarily, to a spirit of revolt, which is liable to be expressed in people's moral sentiments as well as in other ways. What are the conditions which give rise to deep-going, or less deep-going, sentiments of revolt? It is truistic to answer, conditions that produce discontent – an emotional response to a perceived frustration of desire.[23]

The age-long belief in male supremacy and (if some anthropologists are to be believed) the revolt against an earlier acceptance, more or less, of gender equality, were certainly not uncaused. Nor were the operative causes *in fact* any divine decree or genuine masculine superiority in strength of intellect and character. Belief in causes like those would not have to disturb any male chauvinist's tranquillity of mind. But, if it is accepted instead that the actual operative causes actually operated by making it possible for men to *get away with* dominating women, such a realization is bound to be more troubling to the male-chauvinist mentality because it is pretty obvious causes like that would operate equally well to produce male-chauvinist beliefs whether or not there were any truth to them.

Contrast this with the case of promise-keeping, or truth-telling. To be sure, the felt stringency of this obligation, in various different situations, varies from one culture or subculture to another. But, without *some* sense of obligation or other on this, organized society could hardly continue at all. And, without the existence of organized society, human life could not continue, let alone thrive. Causal reflections along these lines need not undermine conscientious support for truth-telling or promise-keeping. Why not? Because that which makes belief in the presumptive propriety of these practices a true belief – their tendency to contribute to human well-being – is just what makes such a belief exist,

---

23 Truistic, but not quite tautologous, owing to the *logical* possibility of a moral reformer whose charismatic personality sweeps all before it and leaves its impress indelibly on the entire age. The 'discontent' such a reformer created *might* conceivably be confined to the sphere of moral values alone.

since moral propriety just is, in the final resort, a matter of contributing to people's well-being. Or, at any rate, moral propriety 'supervenes' upon the causal property of contributing to people's well-being. The important thing for our purposes is that from the tendency of a practice to contribute to people's well-being its moral propriety *follows*. How does it follow? Ethically. At that rate, it is no accident here that what is believed is, in fact, true.

What about the belief in the moral desirability of caring for others as well as ourselves? The prevalence of this belief is obviously due, as a practical matter, to the impossibility of human survival and flourishing without it. Hence this belief, too, is able to pass the causal test: what makes it true is just what makes it believed, since moral desirability, in the last resort, just is a matter of tending to further people's welfare. Or, at least, moral desirability *follows* from that tendency.

It is important to repeat that the foregoing is not a circular argument, because it is no argument for the Principle of Utility at all. It is rather a defence of belief in the Principle against the objection that, *even if* it were to be true, the causes of the belief are such that this would only have come about by a lucky chance.[24]

Except for the explanations to be offered in chapters 29 and 30, this will have to complete, as far as is here possible, utilitarianism's formulation and defence on the score of plausibility.

---

24 See my paper 'A Contribution towards the Development of the Causal Theory of Knowledge,' *Australasian Journal of Philosophy* 50, no. 3 (December 1972), 238–48, especially 243–4; and 'The Causal Argument against Ethical Objectivity,' in Douglas Odegard, ed., *Ethics and Justification* (Edmonton, 1988), 65–74.

29 Comparing Utilities

Of course, we can and must make interpersonal comparisons – we judge, reasonably, that flood victims must occupy the government's attention and receive emergency assistance at the cost of other taxpayers. We decide that the building of a road will serve the general welfare even if it is inconvenient for a few homeowners who are located in its path, and so on.

William J. Baumol[1]

Aggregating utility considerations for comparative purposes is all very well in practice, one is inclined to say, but will it really work in theory? If not – that is, if talk of seeking to maximize people's well-being overall cannot even be given any coherent *meaning* – then the difficulty posed will be fatal not only for utilitarianism but for any ethic at all which recommends the promotion of overall utility as at least one end worth furthering, whether for its own sake or not.

The ethical theory of utilitarianism understands what is beneficial and what is harmful to people ultimately in terms of their pleasure and displeasure, in turn taken – at any rate, here – as a matter of fulfilling or not fulfilling their *desires*: strictly speaking, realizing or not realizing what they *would* most desire if sufficiently informed about its potential effects; but, as was noted in chapter 28, ultimately, this comes to the same thing as simply prescribing the maximum overall realization of people's *actual* desires.

We want to know, however, if the relative intensities of people's positive desires and negative desires – their 'aversions' – really can

---

1 *Economic Theory and Operations Analysis* (Englewood Cliffs, NJ, 1961), 266–7.

meaningfully be compared, even in principle. Consider even the case of physical pain. We may take it (indeed, by definition) that pain is universally aversive – even to pain-seeking masochists, who get a more than compensating sexual thrill from it (or, at any rate, from the fantasized dramas they indulge in which essentially include it). It is said that working anaesthetists used to 'measure' the intensity of a pain by the quantity of analgesic required to extinguish it.[2] But might it not come about that it took twice as much of analgesic X to remove pain P_1 as to remove pain P_2, but took three times as much of analgesic Y? Recourse to such causal correlates of P_1 and P_2 to measure their relative intensities as pains on even a roughly quantitative 'ratio scale' must inevitably be suspect.[3] But it does seem evident, surely, that where some individual is contemplating two prospective future pains and as a result is willing, but only just willing, to trade a completely certain immunity from one of them for a 50 per cent chance of immunity from

---

2 'Pain is measured in terms of its relief. This system is common throughout pharmacology ...,' Henry K. Beecher, *Measurement of Subjective Responses* (New York, 1959), 13.

3 However, it is encouraging to read the empirical case for the quantifiability of pain in *Psychological and Neural Mechanisms of Pain* by Donald D. Price (New York, 1988), 18–75. When experimental subjects are asked to rate the relative intensities of different pains, for instance by pairing these with points spaced out by themselves along a presented line, the results are consistent with a so-called 'power law' of sensory psychophysics, '$\psi=kS^x$,' where ψ is perceived magnitude, k is a constant, S is stimulus magnitude, and x is an exponent that is characteristic for a given sense modality under a standard set of conditions (26). 'The different approaches and methods used to measure pain rely on subjective ratings of different dimensions of pain, behavioral responses indicative of affective-motivational states, or reflexive responses that generally correlate with pain experience. It is of practical and theoretical interest that these different indices of nociception [roughly, *pain perception*] covary, to a great extent and are consistent across different mammalian species.' (46). So-called brain evoked potentials, measured in different ways by electroencephalograph scalp electrodes, are a further pertinent variable. The experimental results of a study reported in 1978 indicated, in the opinion of the researchers, that 'dental evoked responses to electrical stimuli are not only linearly related to stimulus intensity, but also parallel subjective estimates of pain.' See Stephen W. Harkins and C. Richard Chapman, 'Cerebral Evoked Potentials to Noxious Dental Stimulation: Relationship to Subjective Pain Report,' *Psychophysiology* 15, no. 3 (May 1978), 251. A 1984 assessment concluded, '... the EP is not a recorded pain sensation, but it correlates well with the reported experience of pain under controlled conditions.' See C.R. Chapman and R.C. Jacobson, 'Assessment of Analgesic States: Can Evoked Potentials Play a Role?' in *Pain Measurement in Man: Neurophysiological Correlates of Pain*, ed. B. Bromm (Amsterdam, 1984), 239.

the other one (provided the decision is uninfluenced by any particular fondness or aversion for gambling or other extraneous considerations of any sort), that individual can then be regarded as prospectively considering the latter pain, in the circumstances, to be at least twice as 'aversive' overall as the former pain.

In general: where one is sure state of affairs S_1 and state of affairs S_2 cannot both ensue but believes that with equal certainty and ease one can produce either S_1 or S_2, if this belief then causes one to take action so as to increase the chances of S_1 resulting, one's desire for S_1 will be greater than one's desire for S_2.

That part is not difficult. But 'interpersonal comparisons' have been thought to pose a problem. It is easy enough to say that *your* desire for S_1 is greater than *my* desire for S_2 if and only if, were your desire S_1 to be transferred to me in replacement for whatever desires I have already for S_1's realization or non-realization, I would then have a greater desire for S_1 than I would for S_2, other things remaining the same. This is very easy to *say*, but to be fully assured of the pertinent meaningfulness of such talk the reader may feel that reference to some sort of behavioural test (like the behavioural test just proposed for the *intrapersonal* comparison of desires) could genuinely be helpful. The issue here, though, is just the pertinent meaningfulness of such talk, in principle. There is no real requirement that any test proposed be practically feasible at all. *In practice* we have many ways of gleaning the relative depth of people's desires from their verbal and other behaviour and from other things we know about them. Reliance on empathic imagination is indeed no small part of how we do this in practice – in general not at all unsuccessfully, as far as foreseeing people's likely future behaviour goes. The demand here, however, is for a statement of what behavioural difference your desiring something more than I do would ever make in principle – in any circumstances short, that is, of an actual surgical transfer of your desires to me (assuming such an operation to be possible). It will be no objection if the hypothetical conditions proposed for such a behavioural test are slightly, moderately, or extremely far-fetched.

Imagine a sale by auction of something you and I both desire. Who desires it more? The problem is to specify conditions under which your highest bid would exceed mine if and only if you desired the item more. In the first place, of course, we have to stipulate that neither of us is influenced by any extraneous motives, such as the enjoyment of bidding or distaste for it, but only by the desires we each have for money, on the one hand, and for the item being auctioned, on the other hand.[4] That being laid down, two conditions above all suggest themselves right away: (1) the condition that you and I are equal to each other in wealth (financial means); and (2) the condition that we are both of us equally averse to financial sacrifice. Of course, it has to be stipulated that you know for a certainty the extent of your wealth, and I the extent of mine, and that we both are equally confident of really gaining possession of the item on auction in the event of winning out in the bidding. But a couple of further provisos are required as well.

The virtue of money as a measure here obviously lies in the fact that its value stems entirely from its negotiability. On the other hand, you (like me) might possess a non-monetary asset whose *value to you* exceeded its negotiable value (i.e., you would be unwilling to part with it for that price), and this excess has to be considered relevant here, since it could deter you from making bids that would force you to choose between liquidating the asset or giving up something else of relatively high preferential priority. For our purpose, we can consider the auction sale as taking place in circumstances such that you have no asset whose value to you exceeds its negotiable value, and similarly for me. Such a state of affairs could be arrived at either by depriving each of us of any such asset, paying compensation just to the extent necessary to leave the two of us equally wealthy, or else by raising the marketable price of each such asset possessed by either of us just to the point where whoever of us possesses it is no longer unwilling to part with it at that price, at the same time monetarily enriching whoever doesn't possess it to just the degree necessary to keep the two of us equally wealthy. Otherwise, the contribution made by any asset to its owner's wealth can be measured by whatever its negotiable market value is.

There always is the possibility, though, that at lower levels of wealth you would be willing to bid more than I for something I would be willing to bid more than you for at higher levels of wealth because only at higher levels of wealth would you be able to buy instead a comparatively costly

---

4 To say that *only those desires* influence our bidding is to say that any other desire that influences it does so only by giving its possessor a reason for desiring money or the item on auction, or else is itself a desire for something that is wanted only as a means to realize one or both of those desires. The interfering effect of any extraneous desires can in principle be neutralized by credibly informing us that we will each be penalized for acting on them, to just the extent that would be necessary to make us indifferent then as to whether or not to bid, in otherwise identical circumstances, on something for which we do not have any particular desire or aversion.

substitute which you prefer more than I do to the item on auction. This will not apply if we suppose all substitutes for the item on auction to be taken off the market (to everyone's fully confident knowledge) – any uses of such substitutes other than those which made then substitutes for the item on auction being obtainable instead from other goods or services on the market (to everyone's fully confident knowledge). There are some multiple-use products with no known substitutes in respect of some of their uses, so that if they were taken off the market these uses would have to be obtainable from newly invented products placed on the market at the same time. And, on the other hand, absolutely any two consumer products other than 'necessities' *can* conceivably be substitutes for each other – a book and a Ferris-wheel ride, for instance, or a book and a *fourth* Ferris-wheel ride. For purposes of this paragraph, therefore, the word 'substitute' is to be construed narrowly: something, X, is a 'substitute' for something else, Y, if and only if for some level of wealth w (1) one of us would be willing to bid more for Y than the other one at a lower level of wealth than w, and the other would be willing to bid more for Y than the first one at a level of wealth equal to or exceeding w because at this higher level of wealth the first one would choose to buy X rather than pay what the other would be willing to pay for Y, and (2) it is not the case *either* that we would both personally prefer a level of wealth of w, under the conditions envisaged, to our present respective situations or that we would both personally prefer our present respective situations to a level wealth of w, under the conditions envisaged.

So much for the provisos required to ensure that, as rival bidders at the auction, you and I will (in the way that matters here) be on a strictly equal footing when it comes to financial means. There remains the further requirement that the two of us should be equally averse to making financial sacrifices. Unless your desire for money and my desire for money are equal, there need be no reason to deny that the higher bidder actually wants the item on auction less than the lower bidder does but just minds parting with money less still. It is common knowledge that there are some people who care relatively little for money because the things they mostly want in life are not the sort of things that are normally to be found for sale. For, besides any such *marketable commodities*, there are a great many other things which human beings are known to value, often indeed quite highly.

These non-marketable desiderata may be said, speaking generally, to be of three kinds: (1) things which are normally to be had at no sacrifice whatever, such as air to breathe; (2) things which are normally obtainable only through personal exertions on a would-be recipient's part, such as an Olympic medal; and (3) things the possession of which is normally independent of any sacrifice that might be made to obtain them, such as a noble lineage. (Of course, the majority of non-marketable desiderata are mixed cases, such as unfeigned love.) The point to notice here, with all three of these kinds of desiderata, is that, although it is a fact, in each instance, that things like these are normally not for sale, it is in no instance altogether *unimaginable* that they should be. A conceivable objection to this is that such things as an Olympic medal or a noble lineage might not be valued as highly as they now are if they really were to be had in exchange for money. The point, though, is that for desiderata such as these to be available for sale there would be no necessity for them to be actually obtainable in exchange for money, let alone for them to be generally known to be; it would only be required that they should be *thought* to be obtainable in exchange for money by would-be purchasers before making their 'purchase.' In the case of the noble lineage, for instance, it certainly is logically impossible to change that which is past; but it is nonetheless an empirical fact that some persons actually have *thought* that they could pay a sorcerer to turn them into somebody else, somebody with a noble lineage.

Can we specify now a state of affairs in which you and I bidding at the auction would definitely have a just equal desire for money? If conditions can be indicated under which that state of affairs would obtain, such conditions can be laid down in the description of the imagined auction, and your desire for something can then be said to exceed my desire for something if and only if you would bid higher for the realization of your desire than I would bid for the realization of mine in the auction sale under such conditions, given that each of us knew for a certainty that our desires could not both be fulfilled. It is clear that a person's desire for money can be increased to any requisite degree by placing sufficiently high prices on some of the things that person values most. Here is one condition under which there would exist an equal desire for money on your part and on my part: viz., a condition where there were no unpriced desiderata of yours that were not also desiderata of mine and no unpriced desiderata of mine that were not also desiderata of yours; and where absolutely every one of these unpriced desiderata of ours was such that, IF it were to be up for sale at an auction attended by you and me with equal wealth (and you had no assets whose *value to you* exceeded their negotiable value, and I had no assets whose *value to me* exceeded their negotiable value; and, as provided in the last paragraph but two, there was nothing on the market which you or I would prefer to *substitute* for the item on auction given sufficient financial means to make the substitution affordable), THEN at an auction held in just such circumstances the highest bid you would be willing to make for that item would be neither greater nor less than the highest bid I would be willing to make. In that case, you and I would desire money equally. Each one of the *unpriced* desiderata of yours or of mine that did not fit the specified description could always be turned into something with a price instead, until everything that remained unpriced was then something valued equally by you and by me, and consequently, on the other side of the question, the ensemble of things-money-can-buy was likewise valued equally by you and by me, in other words, *money* was valued equally by you and by me.

If all desiderata are either things-money-can-buy or else things-money-cannot-buy, the assumption being made here is simply that, if and only if you and I desire the latter equally, then we desire the former equally. This principle will be plausible on the general presumption that, for any X and Y, your desire for X is as great as my desire for Y if and only if the relation your desire for X bears, in respect of its magnitude, to the ensemble of all your desires, is the same as the relation my desire for Y bears, in respect of its magnitude, to the ensemble of all my desires – that is, in other words, the presumption that your desires, overall, do not exceed my desires, overall, in magnitude, nor mine yours.

It is, of course, common enough in ordinary parlance to speak of one individual having 'weaker desires' overall than another. In this common sense, the word 'desire' indicates a sort of raging of discontent within one, and a 'desire' satisfied is a 'desire' quenched, as it were. Repeated *frustration* or (it is claimed) purposeful spiritual *meditation* can radically reduce one's overall level of 'desire' in this sense, so that one becomes relatively content with a lot that otherwise would leave one comparatively dissatisfied. However, the relatively inert and well-satisfied type of individual to whom this kind of characterization applies will not, by comparison with others, really be short of *desire* overall in the sense in which the term is used here, the sense defined in appendix 2. Such individuals will only have more easily gratified desires than others do. *What* they desire may be less, but their desire for what-they-desire need not be less.

Must we be committed, though, to denying the *logical possibility* of one person's desires, overall, exceeding in magnitude the desires of another person, in the present sense of the word 'desires'? Such a denial would seem to rule out *a priori* (as some modern philosophers have indeed sought to do) the hypostatization both of desire and even, by a very short and natural further step, of *the mind* itself – viz., that in a person or animal of which, specifically, the state of being *desirous* of something is a characteristic state.[5] Any *a priori* ruling against hypostatization here could derive little support from 'ordinary language'; and still less from chapters 15 and 17 and appendix 2. It is accordingly appropriate so to construe 'desire,' for present purposes, as expressly to leave open the logical possibility of one person's 'desire,' overall, exceeding those of another person in magnitude.

It ought to be clear that none of this is to say just what a *desire* actually is. Further investigation is called for, and it is not possible at this point to exclude *a priori* the conceivable contributions that philosophy, psychology, physiology, computer science, and so on will make to such an investigation. It is even perfectly conceivable that the investigation will in time reveal the existence of a plurality of alternative candidates alike fitting (something close to) the concept of *desire* employed here. Such a discovery might call for a revision of the concept, to make it more precise by narrowing down its applicability to one of those 'candidates' only. Our current purposes, however, do not require us to anticipate such possibilities. It is sufficient for us to be concerned here only with 'desires' in the present sense of the word.[6]

---

5 I am using the verb 'hypostatize' here in an extended sense. Strictly speaking, to 'hypostatize' something is to make a *thing* out of it, the way Descartes hypostatized the mind as a 'thinking substance' in its own right, and not just something *about* any thing or things. If there were to be such a *thing* as your mind, your being *desirous* of anything would be a state or condition specifically of that thing (as well as of *you* in general) but would not be another thing on its own. However, the antihypostatizers in the philosophy of mind, along with their denial of substantial thinghood to the human mind, equally reject taking *desire* to be anything over and above a sort of potential; so I have envisaged here a contrary, 'hypostatizing' position, opposed to that denial and that rejection alike, or at least to the latter. According to the 'hypostatizing' position, in my extended sense, if *desirousness* isn't a state or condition of *minds*, it is at least a state or condition of persons and other animals.

6 But what if the range of alternative 'candidates' turns out to be so heterogeneous that, for two particular individuals, A and B, one such narrowing of the concept would make A's 'desires,' overall, exceed B's in magnitude, while another such narrowing of the concept would make B's desires, overall, exceed A's in magnitude? In such an eventuality how could it, in terms of the present concept of *desire*, be said *either* that A's desires, overall, exceeded B's *or* that B's exceeded A's? In the sense of the word 'desires' being employed here, it will be the case unequivocally that A's desires, overall, exceed B's in magnitude only if the psychology of A and the

If we are to say, then, that in the relevant sense one person's 'desires' *can*, after all, exceed those of another in overall magnitude, what justifies our reasoning on the presumption in practice that they do not? From the 'universalizability' requirement discussed in chapters 20 and 26, it does follow that there is no moral obligation to treat two individuals *differently* in the absence of specific evidence indicating any relevant difference between them. Thus, in the absence of any evidence that your desires were unequal in overall magnitude to mine, it could not be morally obligatory to proceed on the basis that they were unequal. Of course, this does not mean there would be any obligation to proceed on a presumption of equality either. There would remain the logical possibility that, in the circumstances, it was neither morally obligatory to proceed (as if) on a supposition of equality nor morally obligatory to proceed (as if) on a supposition of inequality. From a utilitarian standpoint this logical possibility would be realized if and only if either (1) it would make no difference to how much pleasure were going to be produced what supposition was made with respect to the comparative magnitude of your desires overall and mine, or (2) there was no specific evidence bearing on the comparative magnitude of your desires overall and my desires overall. As regards (1), it surely could not be maintained that it would make no difference to how much pleasure were going to be produced what supposition was made with respect to the magnitude of your desires, overall, and mine where the operative end in view was to maximize the overall happiness of the two of us together. But, as for (2), it can scarcely be denied that there actually is evidence available which bears on the question of the comparative magnitude of your desires overall and my desires overall: for the *common humanity* of both of us, together with the awesome success of people's empathic practice, in general, in facilitating human social interaction,[7] is just such evidence. It is this homely empirical fact which

---

psychology of B are such that, for *any* reasonable narrowing of the meaning of 'desire' to apply to one only of the range of alternative 'candidates' alike roughly fitting the concept of 'desire' in use here, A would in the new sense of 'desire' so arrived at have desires which exceeded those of B in overall magnitude. Of course, it is a question for the future specifically to *identify* the member(s) of 'the range of alternative "candidates" alike roughly fitting the concept of "desire" in use,' even though any member of this range discoverable hereafter is undoubtedly already in being right now.

7 It seems that the author of this chapter's epigraph, William J. Baumol, had two children, Ellen and Daniel. 'If Ellen likes marmalade and Daniel likes jam,' he asked,

in the absence of evidence to the contrary underlies the utilitarian maxim, 'Everybody to count for one, nobody for more than one.'[8]

Since from a utilitarian standpoint it *isn't* the case that it is a matter of indifference whether a pair of individuals are treated alike in this regard or not, and since it isn't the case that no evidence is available bearing on the question whether they actually are alike in the relevant way, it follows that judgments about how to act so as to maximize utility should, in the absence of specific evidence to the contrary, proceed on the presumption regarding any two human beings that, in their overall combined magnitude, the desires of each one of them neither exceed significantly nor are exceeded significantly by the desires of the other.[9]

'how do we know what happens to (overall) social utility when we produce more jam and less marmalade?' (*Economic Theory and Operations Analysis*, iv, 253). In producing jam-or-marmalade microcosmically, on the family breakfast table, loving parents must on occasion make real exclusive either-or choices, however subject to compensating measures subsequently in the name of equity. What is it but people's by and large mutually confirming practice of empathy that regularly gets us through such situations with a minimum arousal of ill will? How else does a parent estimate two different children's comparative degree of disappointment, seen or foreseen, knowing that of course disappointment *felt* by a child isn't necessarily measurable by the child's acted-out *display* of disappointment.

8 In *Utilitarianism*, chap. 5, J.S. Mill attributes the maxim to Jeremy Bentham. See John Stuart Mill, *Essays on Ethics, Religion and Society*, vol. 10, ed. J.M. Robson (Toronto, 1969), 257. (The editor of volume 10 of *The Collected Works of J.S. Mill* is forced to admit on p. 515: '*exact wording not located*' in Bentham's writings.)

9 Most of this chapter appeared in an earlier version as 'Assessing Utilities,' *Mind* 80, n.s., no. 320 (October 1971), 531–41.

30 Population

... We are starting to see deep intellectual problems in working out what the ideal population size would be. It is a problem fairly natural to pose in utilitarian terms, but where none of the obvious forms of utilitarianism seems adequate.

Jonathan Glover[1]

'Be fruitful and multiply,' God said to Adam and Eve (Genesis 1: 28); or, as the *New English Bible* has it, 'Be fruitful and increase, fill the earth ... ' But the Bible doesn't say *how full* to fill the earth. In the abstract, it is not hard to imagine a deontological prescription which incorporated a specific limiting formula (or which opposed any limitation whatsoever). But it is harder to imagine a non-consequentialist *rationale* for such a prescription.

It really doesn't seem as if we can get very far with any appeal to people's rights here. How could those who never do come into existence have a grievance on account of that? While those who do actually come into existence could have a grievance (if any) on account of *that* only where their lives were truly not at all worth living. But it surely is altogether implausible to say morality must be *indifferent* as between alternative futures with unequally large and as a result unequally thriving populations, just so long as every member of each

---

1 Editor's introduction to part four of Jonathan Glover, ed., *Utilitarianism and Its Critics* (New York, 1990), 121.

such alternative future population does at least have a life minimally worth living.[2]

What makes it so implausible to say morality must needs be indifferent as between such alternatives is that any sympathetically caring person of conscience will clearly not be indifferent.

A simple quantitative maximization-of-human-happiness ethic would tell us to favour the highest possible value for the product ap, where a is the net lifelong balance of happiness over unhappiness of the average human being of the past, present, and future, and p is the total number of such human beings. The discussion in chapter 28 will encourage suspicion, I hope, of the restriction to the happiness of human beings rather than the happiness of rational beings in general, and likewise to the suggestion that the individual 'happiness' to be maximized depends only on vicissitudes during the lifetime of each individual, or even only on actual subjective states experienced by that individual. Suitable 'friendly amendments' could no doubt meet these two objections, but there would remain what Derek Parfit calls 'The Repugnant Conclusion':

> For any possible population of at least ten billion people, all with a very high quality of life, there must be some much larger imaginable population whose existence, if other things are equal, would be better, even though its members have lives that are barely worth living.[3]

Simple arithmetic makes this conclusion an inescapable consequence of any ethic concerned only to maximize ap. And Parfit surely isn't the only one to find the consequence repugnant. Surely any sympathetically caring person of conscience will find it unacceptable.

These considerations at one time led utilitarians in the direction of *average* utility maximization. And it is, indeed, easy to see why at first it

---

2 This cannot but count against Jan Narveson's interpretation of utilitarianism: 'when we specify the individuals who would be affected by our actions, as we must on the utilitarian view, the characteristic about those people with which we are morally concerned is whether their happiness will be increased or decreased'; against 'the argument that an increase in the general happiness will result from our having a happy child' Narveson insists, '... the question we must ask about *him* is not whether he is happy, but whether he is happier as a result of being born. And if put this way, we see that ... we have a piece of nonsense on our hands if we suppose that the answer is either "yes" or "no".' Jan Narveson, 'Utilitarianism and New Generations,' *Mind* 76, no. 301 (January 1967), 65, 67.

3 Derek Parfit, *Reasons and Persons* (Oxford, 1984), 388.

could well seem as though to envisage alternative future human communities *sympathetically* is to care about their members' happiness on average. But average utility maximization *cannot* be the right ethical standard. Imagine two almost completely disconnected populations (say, on planets too remote from each other for much communication). The members of the first population all live wonderful lives, lives very well worth living. The members of the second population live lives which all are much worse, though still definitely worth living. If the members of the second population were to be aware of this situation and subscribed to an ethic of average utility maximization, they would have to consider themselves duty-bound to minimize their procreation so as to pull down the average utility as little as possible. But this conclusion seems outlandish, and hardly a dictate of human sympathy. Such considerations suggest to Parfit that an outcome cannot be made worse by

> *Mere Addition* when, in one of two outcomes, there exist extra people (1) who have lives worth living, (2) who affect no one else, and (3) whose existence does not involve social injustice.[4]

But is it really a *sympathetic* view to take that the mere addition of extra lives, provided they meet his three conditions, could never make an outcome worse?

On the other hand, Parfit does show that the disconnection between the two coexisting populations in the case just described is not all that makes average utility maximization an unworthy ethical criterion. It will not do even in application just to a self-contained community.

> Consider two possibilities for the last generation in human history ... There are two ways in which history might go, before it is suddenly ended by the explosion of the sun:

> In *Hell One*, the last generation consists of ten innocent people, who each suffer great agony for fifty years. The lives of these people are much worse than nothing. They would all kill themselves if they could. In *Hell Two*, the last generation consists not of ten but of ten million innocent people, who each suffer agony just as great for fifty years minus a day.

---

4 Ibid., 420.

If we assume that we shall certainly exist in one of these two Hells, it would clearly be rational, in self-interested terms, to prefer Hell Two, since we should then suffer for one day less. Should we conclude that Hell Two would be better, in the sense that has moral relevance? Would Satan be acting less badly if this is the Hell that he brought about?[5]

Surely Parfit is right to answer no to both questions. Throughout his now classic discussion in Part IV of his book *Reasons and Persons*, his examples are both ingenious and to the point. Here is one more of them, which draws another absurd conclusion from the proposed ethical criterion of average utility maximization:

Hell Three. Most of us have lives that are much worse than nothing. The exceptions are the sadistic tyrants who make us suffer. The rest of us would kill ourselves if we could; but this is made impossible. The tyrants claim truly that, if we have children, they will make these children suffer slightly less.

On the Average Principle, we ought to have these children. This would raise the average quality of life. It is irrelevant that our children's lives would be much worse than nothing.[6]

From the ethical point of view advocated in this book, the proper ultimate criterion is going to be the informed judgment of a sympathetically caring person of conscience – specifically, the imaginary model utilitarian described in chapter 28. The standard by which such an ethical judge in effect judges is the best interests of all the (past, present and future) people affected, understood as calling for the developments which those people would favour if sufficiently aware of their effects. In chapter 29 we pictured a hypothetical auction sale. Here, let us envisage a system of weighted multiple-preference voting where the voters each vote for as many outcomes as they desire, with each individual vote for any outcome weighted according to *how much* the voter casting it desires that outcome. Individuals do change their preferences over the course of their lives, so we can consider people at each stage of their lives to be distinct voters. As the duration of these 'stages' is progressively shortened, the number of voters in total gets greater and greater,

5   Ibid., 393.
6   Ibid., 422.

until the point is reached where no further shortening of the length of the 'stages' alters the result of the vote significantly.

This is, of course, a completely hypothetical vote, imagined in the mind of our postulated model utilitarian, who is to be conceived as sufficiently well informed (and intelligent) to work out the hypothetical result. Who are the envisaged voters? The hypothetical electorate will take in all those potentially affected by what is being decided, including those who will, in fact, only exist if the decision goes one way rather than another. They are all imagined as casting their votes on the basis of full knowledge of the general effects which different alternative outcomes of the vote would have. But the members of a comparatively large population would each be ignorant as to whether they personally would exist in the event that the result of the vote favoured the existence of a *smaller* population in place of theirs, and they would be ignorant also, with respect to those members of the larger population who still would exist in such an eventuality, of just which individual members of the smaller population they would each be.

Would the vote of a person who had a life barely worth living in a very large population ever exhibit a preference for a population instead, say, of only half the size, and therefore for a personal outcome offering only a fifty percent chance of existing at all, provided that in case of winning existence as a member of the smaller population that existence really would be far preferable to the person's actual existence in the larger population? The answer surely is yes. In real life people do have such wishes, even when certain they cannot be realized.

But how ready are people, in fact, to gamble with their lives? In the real world, not so much, to be sure. Three powerful but for our purposes irrelevant reasons can be mentioned. (1) People often are risk-averse in general. (2) Epicurus notwithstanding,[7] the prospect of death has a strong negative emotional charge for most of us. (3) Another (arguably functional) trait of the human species is to be somewhat more optimistic about one's future than reason, in all strictness, would warrant.

Why do I call these reasons irrelevant? Because (1) it is easy to make an express stipulation that each hypothetical vote in our imaginary referendum be cast in conditions free of all aversion to risk as such (as well,

---

7   Epicurus, Letter to Menoeceus, '... death ... is nothing to us; since when we exist, death is not yet present, and when death is present, then we do not exist.' From Brad Inwood and L.P. Gerson, trans., *Hellenistic Philosophy: Introductory Readings* (Indianapolis, 1988), 23.

of course, as the opposite emotional disposition and, in general, all extra-neous motives; that is, all motivations apart from each individual voter's *interests*). Because (2) in reality no question of death is involved here, but rather just *never living at all*. Some individuals who do consider their lives not worth living and wish they never had been born are still in-clined to recoil from death (even aside from afterlife fears). Similarly, if one considers that one's life is worth living, all in all, though not very much so, one might hypothetically value a fractional chance of a much better life over the life which fate in fact has allotted one. And because (3), as already laid down, our hypothetical voters are each to cast their ballot in full knowledge of every life-history involved, including their own future life-history in the circumstances actually prevailing.

So, under the condition here envisaged, common sense reactions are less to-the-point than might at first be thought. The idea behind the construction here has just been to specify what would be a humane, *sympathetic* attitude towards the population question.[8]

---

8 It is important that the 'referendum' imagined here is not envisaged as being held on a one-voter-one-vote basis, but rather 'with each individual vote for any outcome weighted according to *how much* the voter casting it desires that outcome.' So a member of the much-larger-than-ten-billion-strong population which Parfit envisages in describing his 'Repugnant Conclusion' would be likely to cast only a weak vote, if that, for the high-population outcome and a life 'barely worth living,' as opposed to even a small chance of a far better life in a much smaller population. Let World One and World Two be any two possible worlds in which people's lives are, on average, worth living, though more so in World One. Let U_1 be the degree to which the average value of a life in World One exceeds the cut-off between *worth living* and *not worth living*. Let U_2 be the degree to which the average value of a life in World Two exceeds the cut-off. Let D be the difference separating U_1 and U_2. Let x be the omnitemporal total population of World Two, and let y be the omnitemporal total population of World One. Let the quotient Q be the ratio of x to y.
   If it were possible to leave out of account all motives but the self-interested ones actuating the inhabitants of World One and the inhabitants of World Two in casting their votes, then for any Q there would be a magnitude of D such that for any greater D World One would win the vote as between those two alternatives, and for any lesser D World Two would win the vote. Similarly, for any D there would be a value of Q such that for any higher values World Two would win the vote and for any lower values World One would win. If, in addition to self-interested motives, these hypothetical voters can be seen as actuated by utilitarian concerns as well, the overall outcome of the vote will be unaffected, except that the winning side's margin of victory will end up magnified. The effect on the referendum's outcome of still further motives aside from self-interested ones on the voters' part will have to be more irregular. Such further possible motivations aside, Qs and Ds thus come in

What is hoped is that this chapter has at least served to clarify the ethics of utilitarianism. Beyond that, let us agree with the observation that all the foregoing really is an elaborate theoretical house of cards. Population policy would certainly be doomed as a practical subject if the issues that really come up hinged at all often on considerations like these. It is difficult enough to estimate the actual future resources and technological capabilities available to any country, let alone to the world. And then there is the question of implementation. The known history of various governments' efforts over the past century to increase or decrease birth rates is a history rife with abuses and, in many cases, very little success. Can humanity manage to do better? The answer to that question will admittedly depend very little on the considerations raised in this chapter.

---

pairs such that for each pair World One would win the vote if D were greater or Q less, and World Two would win if Q were greater or D less.

31 'Hypocrisy' Stipulatively Defined

Use every man after his desert, and who should 'scape whipping?

Hamlet, act 2, scene 2

We're all hypocrites. From time to time, we all pretend to be better persons than we are. Occasionally the pretence is even justified. A role model for the younger generation does the future no favour by misbehaving in full view.

But hypocrisy does have a bad name. Especially the hypocritical censure of others. Objectively speaking, though, it cannot really detract from the correctness of any moral criticism someone voices that in the same situation the speaker would really do no better than the individual criticized.

For our purposes, let us call a person's moral condemnation of someone's act of commission or omission 'hypocritical' wherever it isn't the case that that person would behave any differently in the place of the one condemned. This diverges from the ordinary use of the term, because a 'hypocrite' in the sense here defined need not be insincere at all. And we ordinarily wouldn't call people 'hypocritical' – but only 'weak' – when they sincerely condemn acts of their own even as they do them.

If one is sincere, though, it is impossible to condemn any act 'hypocritically,' in the present sense, without being at least somewhat imperfect, morally speaking. For either the first principles on which you are basing your criticism are themselves unsatisfactory, in which case you are at fault in subscribing to them; or else, even if your principles are absolutely perfect, you are not, because it *isn't* the case that you yourself would fully live up to those principles in absolutely any circumstances – including the circumstances of whomever you're condemning.

What sort of 'circumstances' are we talking about? Of course, the 'circumstances' here will include any external facts about the situation of the person morally criticized; but also all the personal characteristics of that individual, both bodily and mentally, including the full range of that individual's feelings, desires, beliefs, memories and experiences. You aren't condemning that individual 'unhypocritically,' in the present sense, unless you really would behave differently in that individual's situation. But, if *everything* about that individual's situation were to be the same, including *all* of the individual's personal traits, what can it mean to say you would behave any differently from that individual in that individual's situation? For present purposes, however, it is *you as a moralist* that is being transferred in imagination to that situation. What is being imagined is just the transfer of *your conscience* to that individual, everything else (including even all of that individual's moral feelings) remaining the same. In that situation, your conscience's attachment to your moral principles has to be sufficient to outweigh any countermotivation in the individual you criticize and produce a course of action in keeping with *them* instead of the course of action actually taken by that individual.

Unless this is the case, you are nothing but a miserable sinner. But then, we already know *that*.

32 Utilitarianism Proved

... rational beings all stand under the *law* that each of them should treat himself and all others, *never merely as a means*, but always *at the same time as an end in himself*.

Immanuel Kant[1]

No, Kant was not a utilitarian. The point of highlighting this quotation from him is his express identification of *moral agents* and *moral ends*. A moral *agent* is a potential wrongdoer, one on whom (breachable) moral obligations fall. From the standpoint of utilitarianism, moral *ends* are those beings for whose sole benefit, ultimately, all moral obligations exist. Someone steeped in Kantian ethics might well regard the identification of the two as self-evident. But, whether it is self-evident or not, this chapter claims to *prove* the equation.

Can an ethic's content be identified with the demands which it makes on people?[2] At any rate, all that is claimed to be proved here is that everybody's conscience, character, and conduct ought to be in accord

---

1 *The Moral Law or Kant's Groundwork of the Metaphysic of Morals*, trans. H.J. Paton (London, 1956), 101. Emphases in original.
2 It apparently cannot, in the view of some, who interpret (a version of) utilitarianism as advocating the *use* of people as vessels for happiness, so to speak, and so just as *means* of furthering the abstraction Utility Maximization. But how, it is asked, can there be an *obligation* owed to nobody? See, for instance, Will Kymlica, *Liberalism, Community and Culture* (Oxford, 1991), 23–9. If, though, the utilitarian ethic were to be construed instead as a demand to *serve people* to the fullest extent possible, that evidently would make no difference to its actual dictates.

with the demands of the Utility Principle.[3] If any theorist wants to say that some 'other' principle, which makes all the same demands and only those demands, is morally preferable to the Utility Principle, nothing proved here will contradict that claim.

The proof offered below is meant to be deductive and take nothing synthetic for granted except on one point. It would admittedly not be inconsistent for someone who really was altogether conscienceless to resist the utilitarian conclusion drawn here. But the empirical evidence reviewed in chapters 26 and 27 was intended to satisfy readers that such a logical possibility at any rate cannot be their own case. Otherwise, the argument will be that certain tautological constraints which any ethic must claim to satisfy can be met, in fact, only by utilitarianism. In other words, if the argument succeeds, it shows that only the uncaring, conscienceless position and the utilitarian position are self-consistent logically.

The argumentation is going to revolve around the model utilitarian envisaged in chapter 28. Let us call this bizarre individual 'U.' If utilitarianism is correct, U and pretty well U alone is morally flawless. For every person in the past, present and future, it will be recalled – and after chapter 30 we can add, for each *stage* in the life of every person – U's conscience is just as keen on the furtherance of that person's interests as that person is. Specifically, for everything that each person desires – or, rather, would desire if sufficiently informed about its effects – U's conscience includes a desire for the realization of that thing which is equal in magnitude to that desire itself. There can be no suggestion that real human beings should try to be like U, for the consequences of really trying this would undoubtedly be worse than an available alternative course. But, just the same, the judgment of U's conscience is the ultimate criterion of morality if utilitarianism is correct. The proof of utilitarianism will be a proof that only somebody like U will be without reproach.

Here are nine indubitable premises, all but the first of which are tautological.
(1) There are moral truths.
(2) If there are moral truths, some of them are propositions, expressible entirely in purely qualitative terms, from which, in conjunction

---

3 Let us say that a person's conscience and character are *in accord* with the Utility Principle if they are such as to motivate the person to act, in any circumstances, in just the way the Utility Principle calls for.

with sufficient non-moral factual information, it would be possible to deduce all the moral duties of anybody in any particular situation. (These propositions may be called true 'moral principles.')

(3) Each formulation of a true moral principle is applicable to any logically possible cases falling within the meaning of its terms.

(4) If there are true moral principles, then insofar as any persons fail to take the attitude of conscientiously opposing the occurrence of that which would violate them more strongly than they desire such occurrences, those persons are derelict in their moral duty.

(5) To desire in one's conscience that something should not occur more than one desires in one's conscience that it should occur is to believe that its occurrence would on the whole be a bad thing from the moral point of view.

(6) If there is such a thing as moral duty, then insofar as one is not prepared to act in full accord with one's moral beliefs, one is derelict in one's moral duty.

(7) One is not prepared to act in full accord with one's moral beliefs if one would ever morally condemn any person's act of commission or omission where it is not the case that one would act any differently oneself in that person's place.

(8) Whatever is morally obligatory is logically possible.

(9) Any desire a person has is a cause *of a certain magnitude* in that person, with the tendency, in suitable conditions, to give rise to action aimed at that which is desired.

Of these nine premises, I asserted that the last eight were tautologies. But to say a proposition is tautological, or even logically impossible to disbelieve or doubt, isn't to say it is uncontroversial. Academic good manners might be thought to militate against attributing self-deception, if not confusion, to those refusing to recognize an alleged truism. (But what else, in practice, are these who *deeply* contradict each other's philosophies most apt to think about each other?) In any event, the case of the Non-contradiction Principle, discussed in chapter 4, surely shows the impossibility of abjuring all such imputations. As remarked in chapter 5, a proposition's *obviousness* need not be disproved by the fact that it remains controversial.

It is to be hoped the consideration advanced in chapters 24, 26, and 27 will be enough to satisfy the reader fully as to the correctness of premise (1). The analyticity of premises (2), (3), (4), (5), and (6) was meant to be established in chapter 26, and that of premise (7) in chapter 31. That leaves premises (8) and (9).

The case for premise (8) does not really rest on the 'Ought implies can' principle.[4] It rests on the consideration that moral truth is consistent, and hence does not call on anybody both to do something and not to do it. Could you, though, have an obligation to do something, and also an obligation not to do it, without having an obligation to both do it and not do it? The argument in the literature for saying you could tended to focus on the demands of disparate but alike legitimate 'allegiances';[5] and, indeed, a family obligation and a legal obligation, for instance, can come into conflict with each other easily enough. But, if it really is a *truth* that, all things considered, you have a MORAL obligation to do something, then surely it is not a truth that, all things considered, you have a MORAL obligation not to do it. In most cases, for instance, people who have made conflicting promises can indeed be faulted morally no matter what they do after that, but is the blame incurred for their indiscriminate promising, or is it for their incomplete fulfillment of all they have promised? It isn't sufficient to justify the second answer, that each promisee has a legitimate *claim* thanks to the promise made, or that it is consequentially a good thing for the promise-maker to feel guilt in connection with the non-fulfillment of that promise. But cases like this were already explored in chapter 26.

As indicated, the essential case for premise (8) depends upon ethical cognitivism. In a philosophical vein, people may speak of 'incommensurable,' equally legitimate moralities, but they cannot seriously *think* that way. The moral truth is consistent and, when all is said and done, only what is licit can be obligatory. Therefore, any conjunctive claim which unqualifiedly both prescribes and forbids the very same thing, directly or by logical implication, cannot be accurately stating the dictates of moral truth.

As for premise (9), here is not the place to develop the case in full for this proposition in the philosophy of mind.[6] But something, at least,

---

4   The *impossibility* of logical impossibility is an epistemic concept. From the certainty that something won't be done, it doesn't even follow that it is a *difficult* thing to do. It may simply be that any will to do it is sure to be lacking. See my 'Could God Make a Contradiction True?,' *Religious Studies* 26, no. 3 (September 1990), 377–87.

5   For example, Bas C. van Frassen, 'Values and the Heart's Command,' *The Journal of Philosophy* 70, no. 1 (11 January 1973), 13: 'The agent is subject to incompatible obligations due to his several allegiances to heaven and earth (sons and lovers, party and fatherland, choose what you will).'

6   See appendix 2 and my paper 'Motivations,' *Philosophy* 75, no. 293 (July 2000), 423–36.

should be said by way of explanation. Just who would ever deny premise (9)? At any rate, computer simulations of mentality have suggested to some that the doings of a genuinely mind-animated system could be governed by a 'lexical ordering' of desiderata rather than by a mutual counteracting of sometimes opposed ultimate desires. Admittedly, the outward, 'behavioural' result of such a simulation *might* be the same, but would it be genuine *mental* functioning which produced that result? The point is this. Regardless of whether a 'computational' model can *map* mental processes, no being that could be credited with possessing a mind would be motivated ultimately just by a determination to follow some particular algorithm – in contradistinction to having a motivational make-up such that, at most, following the algorithm had a certain *attraction* for the being, an attraction possessing some strength, but potentially outweighable, in certain circumstances, by motivations still stronger.

Accordingly, given the nine premises stated, let P be some person of conscience who is without reproach. We are, of course, not yet in a position to say that P = U. In fact, this is not *exactly* what will be said at the end of the argument either. The way we've specified it, U's conscience is as keen on the furtherance of any person's interests as that person is. But imagine instead U_x, whose conscientious desire for the furtherance of each and every other person's interests is fully x times as great as U's (x > 1). U_x is no less utilitarian than U is. The proof developed below shows only that P has to be *either* U or U_x. But, having mentioned this complication, we can now put it aside. The desires combined in U's conscience already compose a gargantuan enough totality. Wherever a person would have, or would still have, a desire for something if sufficiently informed as to its effects, we can call that an "info-immune desire" the person has. With respect to each and every past, present and future info-immune desire, then, U's conscience has to include at least the equivalent of an equal desire for that desire's fulfillment. One really should not expect to meet somebody such as U on the street any time soon.

What about P? P's conscience, we can say, is committed to whatever the true moral principles are, and morally condemns whatever would contravene them. The condemnation need not be vocalized, or even formulated explicitly in P's mind at all. It is enough that P subscribes to principles which forbid the acts of commission or omission condemned. But since P is without reproach, the condemnation must in each instance be non-hypocritical. So it must be the case that in the place of malefactor M, the actor, P, would act differently.

Were malefactor M to be sufficiently informed about the consequences of the act in question, would M still perform it? If the answer is no, the act wouldn't even be one forbidden by P's principles unless the motivations prompting it are evil ones which would, in certain circumstances, issue in decidedly objectionable acts of commission or omission no matter how well informed M were to be about the consequences of those acts. So we can concentrate here on just those objectionable acts prompted by info-immune desires. It is only info-immune desires that motivate acts which P has to be able to condemn non-hypocritically.

But this demand for non-hypocritical condemnation is asking rather a lot. It has to be the case that in M's place P would not perform any act P condemns, however great the temptation. However strong the desires of M's motivating such an act, P's conscientious countermotivation must be stronger, so that in M's place P would not perform that act. But P has to condemn non-hypocritically any actual or *logically possible* contravention of whatever the true moral principles are, and there is no logical upper limit to the strength of the desires which can motivate an act.

Of course, there is, on the other hand, no logical upper limit either to the strength of the conscientious desires which we can attribute to P. But, just as it is impossible to have a positive number that exceeds any negative number in absolute value, so likewise there is an obvious problem about how P's conscientious motivations can be so specified that they would lead P to act morally no matter what the temptation. After all, it is morally obligatory to be without reproach – as P is supposed to be. Therefore, there must be some logically possible style of character which would enable its possessor to live up to all P's obligations.

And there is. If P = U, the problem disappears. No act of M's would violate U's principles unless it ran counter to the balance of all past, present, and future info-immune desires. In that case, the total motivation in U's conscience would be sufficient to outweigh whatever desire prompted M to perform the act. Had M's desire to do the act been sufficiently stronger – strong enough to outweigh U's net conscientious countermotivation, so that in fact U would end up performing the act in M's place after all – in that case, U's utilitarian principles would not oppose the act's performance in such circumstances. So any logically possible act whatsoever which U's utilitarianism does condemn is indeed an act U would not perform in the actor's place.

To remain irreproachable, then, P must be credited at least with conscientious motivations equivalent to those U has. Can we envisage P's conscience as including any non-utilitarian motivations as well? But to motivate some act on P's part, such desires would have to outweigh any contrary balance over all the other desires in P's conscience; and in such a case the Utility Principle would *favour* that act's performance in the circumstances.

If there is any moral truth, we know, it is a duty to accord one's conscience, character and conduct fully to it. However, to the Principle of Utility alone is it logically possible to do this. But all that is morally obligatory is logically possible, we know. Since there is moral truth, it follows that the utilitarian principle is a true moral principle.

It's evidently a truism for any moral consciousness that only beings capable of being influenced by considerations of conscience – only potential *moral judges* – can ever be subject to moral judgment, can ever be considered *moral agents*. And in the last resort it is only these, only potential malefactors, we now see, that can truly be *moral ends*.

This is most assuredly not what Kant meant in proclaiming moral freedom the basis of each person's ultimate worth and dignity. But it is what he should have meant.

33 Conclusion: We Each Sit in Judgment

It was Kant who persuaded philosophy that one can be, simultaneously and without contradiction, an empirical realist and a transcendental idealist. That is, it was Kant who gave us the idea that there is a way of saying the same sort of thing as real live sceptics like Aenesidemus used to say, namely, 'The knowing subject contributes to what is known', which nevertheless does not impugn the objectivity of the judgments in which the knowledge is expressed.

Myles Burnyeat[1]

Diogenes the Cynic is said to have countered Zeno's arguments for the impossibility of motion by simply walking around.[2] Did Diogenes refute Zeno? His action certainly didn't uncover any flaws in Zeno's argumentation. But by showing unmistakably that Zeno's conclusion was false he did show that the argumentation must be flawed. Thus, although we certainly have learned things from Zeno's arguments, what we've learned is *not* that motion is impossible.

Something similar can be said of sceptical arguments in philosophy. Their stated conclusions being untenable, anything we learn from them has to be something else. Kant liked to maintain that Humean 'criticism,' properly understood at any rate, didn't really challenge the necessary

---

1 'The Sceptic in His Place and Time,' in *Philosophy in History: Essays on the Historiography of Philosophy*, ed. Richard Rorty, J.B. Schneewind, and Quentin Skinner (Cambridge, 1984), 250.
2 Diogenes Laertius, *Lives of the Philosophers*, trans. and ed. A. Robert Caponigri (Chicago, 1969), 138.

tenets of good sense. Whatever Hume's own intentions were, though, he does present us with arguments whose direct conclusions are sceptical or nihilistic. Is there some subtle way in which it is possible to accept such propositions 'philosophically' while rejecting them practically? No. What you believe, you believe.

The popularity of Janus-faced approaches like Kant's to deep-seated philosophical issues bespeaks a revealing intellectual evasiveness characteristic of more epochs than his own. The need for illusions of more than individual scope, and for screens of rationalization shielding them from the light of day, will only finally disappear when people's everyday practical relations with one another and with nature are rational and transparent through and through. Until then, philosophy can only hope to dent pervasive unreason, not dispel it.

Appendix 1: 'Tautology'

In this book, the expressions 'tautology,' 'logically necessary truth,' 'analytic proposition,' and 'proposition undeniable without logical contradiction' are used interchangeably, as are the expressions signifying the negations of such propositions: 'logical contradiction,' 'inconsistent proposition,' and 'proposition asserting something which is logically impossible.' It is largely taken for granted that the truth of what a sentence like 'Every bachelor is a bachelor' expresses is no less a matter of the meanings of the linguistic expressions used in formulating it than is the truth of what such a sentence as 'Every bachelor is an unmarried man' expresses. This can be justified on two grounds (though they really are the same at bottom). In the first place, it can be argued that the meaning of a word like 'every' does determine that 'Every ... is a ...' must express something true for any filling of the two blanks here with the same singular count-noun. In the second place, since the two complete sentences quoted do mean the same, they must express the same proposition as each other, and so anything which applies to what either sentence expresses must apply equally to what the other sentence expresses.

A major challenge to this way of thinking and speaking comes from the case brought against the standard conception of meaning by a philosopher like W.V. Quine in his 'Two Dogmas of Empiricism,' and *Word and Object*, chapter 2.[1] In my paper 'Cognitive Synonymy,'[2] I have

---

1 W.V. Quine, 'Two Dogmas of Empiricism,' reprinted in *From a Logical Point of View* (Cambridge, MA, 1961), 20–46; and W.V. Quine, *Word and Object* (Cambridge, MA, 1960), 26–79.

2 D. Goldstick, 'Cognitive Synonymy,' *Dialectica* 34, no. 3 (1980), 183–203.

proposed a rebuttal. The issue hinges on the distinguishability or in-distinguishability of such regularities in the verbal behaviour of the members of a speech community as can be put down to their *linguistic* competence and such as are due rather to their (however habitual) shared *opinions*. Taking it that such a distinction can indeed be drawn, and even drawn in a way that makes a *behavioural* difference (though admitedly not a difference characterizable *altogether* in purely behav-ioural terms), I think it is possible to single out *linguistic* from other so-cial usages, and accordingly call two assertive sentences 'cognitively synonymous' in a language if and only if speakers of the language would not be prevented by their *linguistic* competence in it from inter-changing the sentences wherever their only end in view were to pre-serve the truth-value of what they were asserting or denying. That this will make various different axiomatic logical formulas 'cognitively syn-onymous' with one another does not seem like an objection.

With this laid down, then, we can note the cognitive synonymity of 'That object is red all over,' and 'That object is red all over, and is not green all over,' and use this fact, on the basis of the definition of 'ana-lytic' given below, to explain the analyticity of the biconditional formed from these two sentences. The resistance to calling 'Nothing red all over is green all over' 'analytic' stemmed from the impossibil-ity of *defining* 'red' as '... and not green (all over),' for any filling of that blank, since 'green' would have an equal claim to be defined as '... and not red (all over)', for some filling of *that* blank, and circularity in our definitions is objectionable as defeating their purpose of teaching meanings. But, if a *definition* can be described as a statement of syno-nymity usable to explain a meaning, it does not follow that the state-ment of every genuine synonymity must be so usable. Accordingly, the sort of examples along these lines with which analytic philosophy sometimes dallies as possible 'synthetic *a priori*' assertive sentences are in reality analytic, and for genuine cases of synthetic-apriority it is necessary to turn to altogether bigger philosophical issues, as this book attempts to do.

We may accordingly say that a declarative sentence is *analytic* if and only if

(1) it is a universal closure with respect to all free variables of a theorem of the first-order predicate calculus,

or (2) it is a complete interpretation of a theorem of the first-order predicate calculus,

or (3) it is a universal closure with respect to all free variables of a
     formula which is a partial interpretation of a theorem of the
     first-order predicate calculus
or (4) it is cognitively synonymous with a sentence of the sort
     mentioned in (1), (2), or (3).

Let us understand the phrase 'first-order predicate calculus' here as
abbreviating a completely explicit enumeration of formulas for the
axioms and rules in question. Then, for any sentential formula, abbreviatable as 'f,' which is such that it is provable by means of the first-
order predicate calculus that f, the sentence 'Formula F just states that
f' will provably imply,

> Formula F is cognitively synonymous with a universal closure
> with res-pect to all free variables of a formula of the first-order
> predicate calculus, or with a complete interpretation of a formula
> of the first-order predicate calculus, or with a universal closure
> with respect to all free variables of a formula which is a partial in-
> terpretation of a formula of the first-order predicate calculus.[3]

Hence, by the definition of 'analytic' given above, 'Formula F just states
that f' will logically imply 'Formula F is analytic.'

Accordingly, it will be analytically true that, if a sentence just states
that f, then that sentence is analytic – which is to say, what it states is an
analytic statement. It will be analytically true that *any* statement just to
the effect that it is analytically true that f will itself be an analytic statement. Since it follows from the definition given that every *analytic* sentence is cognitively synonymous with some formula which is such that
what it expresses is provable by means of the first-order predicate calculus, therefore, for any filling of the blank, the sentence 'It is analytic
that ...' will, if true, be analytic itself. Whatever is logically necessarily
so is logically necessarily logically necessarily so.

But what about something which is not a logical necessity? Will its
failure to be logically necessary always itself be a logical necessity? It is

---

3 Owing to the meaning-relation between the expressions 'bachelor' and 'unmarried man,' 'She said something cognitively synonymous with an explicit assertion that the Pope is a bachelor' will be cognitively synonymous with 'She said
something cognitively synonymous with an explicit assertion that the Pope is an
unmarried man.'

easy to answer yes in a case where the logical unprovability in question is logically provable. But there is no reason to assert, and some reason to deny, that every case in logic of unprovability is provably such a case. There are, though, the following reasons for extending the concept of 'logically necessary truth' to include true denials of logical necessity (and hence to include true assertions of logical possibility, since, whenever something is possibly so, it is true to deny that it is necessarily *not* so).

A. If there is anything that determines which propositions are analytic, it will be that which determines also which ones are not analytic. And so, if the analyticity of true propositions is held to consist in there being a particular source of determination for such propositions' truth-value, it will follow that true denials of logical necessity will themselves be logically necessary truths.

B. What a proposition asserts may be conceived as being logically necessary if and only if that proposition is (or would be) true in all logically possible worlds (i.e., under all logically possible conditions or ensembles of conditions). On this account, what a proposition asserts is logically possible if and only if the proposition is true in some logically possible world(s). So that, if and only if it can be said to be true – that is, true in the actual world – that what a particular proposition p asserts is logically possible, then p must itself be true either in the actual world or in some other logically possible world(s). Thus, in general, it will be true in any particular logically possible world w that what p asserts is logically possible, if and only if p itself is true either in w or in some other logically possible world(s) (that is, even where w is not the actual world, it must be the case that p still *would* be true either in w or in some other logically possible world(s) if w *were* the actual world). Accordingly, if it be true, that is, true in the actual world, that what p asserts is logically possible, then it will be true in *all* logically possible worlds that what p asserts is logically possible, and hence the true proposition asserting what p asserts to be logically possible will itself be a logically necessary truth. Hence it follows that all truths which just assert the logical possibility of something must be logically necessary truths.[4]

In order to accommodate these considerations, there is nothing to stop us from adding two further clauses to the above definition. A

---

4 The preceding two paragraphs are based on pages 533–4 of my article 'Analytic A Posteriori Truth?' *Philosophy and Phenomenological Research* 32, no. 4 (June 1972), 531–4.

declarative sentence can be called analytic if and only if it satisfies clauses (1) or (2) or (3) or (4) given above

or (5) it just expresses the true denial of some particular expressed proposition's formulability in a sentence that satisfies any of conditions (1), (2), (3), and (4),

or (6) it is a sentence forming the implicate of a material-implication formula which has a sentence satisfying condition (5) as its implicans and which itself satisfies conditions (1), (2), (3), and (4).

(The work of Alfred Tarski[5] suggests understanding tautologies as statements of maximally general, 'topic-neutral' facts and their applications.)

---

5 Alfred Tarski, 'On the Concept of Logical Consequence,' in *Logic, Semantics, Metamathematics*, ed. Alfred Tarski, trans. J.H. Woodger (Oxford, 1956), 409–20; and Alfred Tarski, 'What Are Logical Notions?' *History and Philosophy of Logic* 7, no. 2 (1986), 143–54.

Appendix 2: 'Desire'

Spinoza has given us a definition:

> *Desire* is the essence itself of man in so far as it is conceived as determined to any action by any one of his affections ... by an affection of the human essence we understand any constitution of that essence ...[1]

Desire, then, is the inner cause of people's *actions*. But what distinguishes people's *actions* from the other things they do, like breathing (most of the time), tripping, or beginning to wake up? In the first place, none of these things is done for any *purpose*, that is, as a means to something else; secondly, none of them is something brought about by the doer's taking means to *it*. Where available, though, means *are* taken to whatever any agent desires, provided that the agent knows how to take them, whenever they seem to the agent, all things considered, to be available, effective, necessary, and not too onerous (not too apt to frustrate the realization of other desires the agent has). And we can say that *means-taking* is in all cases something which is done as a result of holding a belief that doing it will increase something else's chances of realization.

However, we notoriously cannot understand *that to which one takes means* as simply being that, a belief in whose producibility by the doing of something causes one to do *it*. 'Suppose,' R.M. Chisholm writes,

---

1 *Ethics*, Part III, The Affects, Definition 1 and Explanation. These words, translated by W.H. White and A.H. Stirling, come from *Spinoza Selections*, ed. John Wild (New York, 1930), 266–7.

(i) a certain man desires to inherit a fortune; (ii) he believes that, if he kills
his uncle, then he will inherit a fortune; and (iii) this belief and this desire agitate him so severely that he drives excessively fast, with the result that he accidentally runs over and kills a pedestrian who, unknown
to the nephew, was none other than the uncle.[2]

In this example, nothing hinges for our present purposes on the nephew's
desire to inherit a fortune. He might just as well desire the opposite, or
else even be indifferent to the prospective legacy and be agitated simply
by the belief that killing his uncle would make it his and that others
might be tempted to murder in such circumstances. For a perhaps more
plausible type of example, imagine yourself letting go of a valuable vase
because of nervousness resulting from the realization that letting go of it
would cause it to fall and get broken. In such a case, your letting go of the
vase, like the imagined nephew's killing of his uncle, is not something
done as a means to the outcome expected to follow from it, even though
it is, in fact, done as a result of that expectation. The point here is, though,
that precisely because what is done is undesired by the doer in such a case,
the doer does not take any means to it, and would not be motivated to take
any even if means did seem available, effective, necessary, and not too
onerous.[3] Nor need the project of characterizing the relevant conditions
solely in terms of an agent's non-normative beliefs and resultant behavioural dispositions be in principle hopeless.

The general project is still the Spinozan one of understanding *desire*
as whatever it is in an agent that motivates action. This does involve

2 Roderick M. Chisholm, 'Freedom and Action,' in Keith Lehrer, ed., *Freedom and
Determinism* (New York, 1966), 30. Cf. Donald Davidson, 'Freedom to Act,' in Ted
Honderich, ed., *Essays on Freedom of Action* (London, 1973), 153.
3 But what if an individual does desire a certain end and fails to take means to it only
because the shock of realizing that means at hand are indeed necessary, effective,
and not too onerous causes the shocked individual to do involuntarily the very
thing the doing of which *would* be the means to take to bring about that end? 'For
example: a man at a party intends to spill what is in his glass because he wants to
signal his confederates to begin a robbery and he believes, in virtue of their
prearrangements, that spilling what is in his glass will accomplish that; but all this
leads the man to be very anxious, his anxiety makes his hand tremble, and so his
glass spills' (Harry G. Frankfurt, 'The Problem of Action,' in *The Importance of What
We Care About: Philosophical Essays* [Cambridge, 1988], 70). *At the moment*, however,
the man imagined in this example is NOT primed to do whatever actions seem
certain and necessary to make his hand tremble should he know full well that those
actions are alike doable and not too onerous.

some departure from current English usage, in which people are not normally said to 'desire' anything they are sure is absolutely impossible – a change in the past, say – but rather only to *wish* for it (where it is something to which they *would* try to take means, provided they knew how, if the means did seem to them, all things considered, to be available, effective, necessary, and not too onerous). On the present, inclusive understanding of what *desires* are, an agent's ultimate desires, at any rate, are potential inward causes of seeking behaviour, capable of counteracting one another and blocking one another's causation of such behaviour, but each one in principle ranking alternative outcomes in a transitive, asymmetrical 'order of preference' with no absolute last member at the 'high' end, and each one tending to cause just such behaviour as would, if the agent's non-normative beliefs were all true, be aptest for bringing about the realization of the most preferred outcomes available under those conditions.[4]

According to this conception of human (and animal) motivation, which was also that of Thomas Hobbes, voluntary behaviour is apt to be the outcome resulting from a virtual contest of strength among incompatible desires. It is in this spirit that Hobbes formulated his famous definition:

> In *Deliberation*, the last Appetite, or Aversion, immediately adhaering to the action, or to the omission thereof, is that wee call the WILL ...[5]

Deliberation, for Hobbes, was an alternation of occurrent desire-experiences of divergent tendency. We for our part need not identify an agent's conflicting desires, or their contestation against one another in the agent's mind, with any occurrences of which the agent is necessarily conscious. The relevant Hobbesian point is just that the operative *will* of the agent is effectively dictated (as we might put it) by those of the agent's desires that 'win out' in the deliberative contest as a result of their superior strength. Reversing this, we can define the 'desires' into which an agent's motivation is factorable as what the

---

4 See my paper 'Motivations,' *Philosophy* 75, no. 293 (July 2000), 423–36. In that paper, the lack of any such 'best' conceivable alternative, in the case of ultimate desires at any rate, is argued to be the decisive difference distinguishing motivated *agents* from mindless 'algorithmic' automata, which are determined to do what they do in accordance with 'lexical ordering,' rather than what they do resulting from a mutual counteracting of inner causes of differing *strengths*.

5 Thomas Hobbes, *Leviathan* (London, 1914), 28.

agent's eventuating *will* is the resultant of; and the formulation developed below does proceed in that way.

The basic consideration remains that all *means-taking* is something which is done as a result of holding a belief that doing it will increase something else's chances of realization – even though not everything done as a result of such a belief is an instance of means-taking. When something is done as a result of such a belief and it is not a case of means-taking, the difference is that the *intermediate causes* by which the belief results in the doing of whatever it is are not causes of the right kind. But just what kind is that?

Whenever anything is done on purpose, we may say, either the doing of it is accomplished without the taking of any means, or else it is accomplished by means of doing something else, and the doing of that is accomplished without the taking of any means. In short, *something* is done which the agent is able to do, and does, 'just at will.' The doing of this action does *not* result from any belief on the agent's part about what would bring it about, or at least increase its chances of occurrence. But if not-too-onerous means *were*, to the agent's fully confident knowledge, available, effective and necessary for bringing it about, and *it* were judged necessary and sufficient, in the circumstances, for achieving the agent's operative goals, then the action would still get done; whereas, if the agent judged it to be necessary and sufficient, in the circumstance, for *preventing* whatever the agent was most desirous should happen or obtain, this action would then not get done.

To know that something is *not* an action which an agent can perform 'just at will,' it is sufficient to know that true belief on the agent's part about what would increase its chances of occurrence is in the circumstances necessary for it to occur. On the other hand, to know that something is in fact an action which it lies within an agent's power to perform, it is enough to know that its necessity for those results it is necessary for producing, is in the circumstances insufficient to prevent those results. And to know just this about an action is also sufficient for knowing that the action is not, in the agent's judgment, *too onerous* a means to take for the furtherance of whatever ends the agent has in view. Then again, to know that it is necessary for some action to be performed that the agent should believe it to be requisite for a certain result is sufficient for knowing that the other foreseen results of the action are not enough to motivate the agent to perform it. Lastly, to know that doing a particular action has insufficient appeal for an agent to motivate its performance apart from all considerations of its effects, it is enough to know that the agent's holding beliefs about what its effects would be is necessary for the action to be performed.

Accordingly, when and only when some agent A *acts in furtherance of an end* E, there is something M which happens and which is such that

(1) M occurs as a result of a belief on A's part that M's occurrence would increase E's chances of realization;

(2) M's occurrence does not result from any belief on A's part about what would increase M's chances of occurrence;

and (3) (a), *if* an event D were to be conceivable such that A believed correctly that, in the circumstances,

(i) D's occurrence was necessary and sufficient for M's occurrence

and (ii) D's necessity for M was insufficient to prevent the occurrence of M

and (iii) A's believing (i) and (ii) was necessary for D to occur,[6]

and (b), *if* no additional true beliefs on A's part about what would increase D's chances of occurrence[7] were necessary for D to occur, *then* D would not occur if A believed that D were causally necessary and sufficient to prevent the realization of E, but D *would* occur if A believed that D *were* causally necessary and sufficient for the realization of E.

The preceding formulation doubtless deviates a little from the way we normally use the phrase 'acts in furtherance of an end' since, by the criterion given, one 'acts in furtherance' of something even if one *takes no means* to its realization but simply does it (intentionally). For example, it is frequently possible just at will to call to mind, say, what the sum of seven and five is. The present point, though, is that one would be motivated to take means towards that achievement if one saw means as available, effective, necessary and not too onerous.

As the phrase has been defined, it is impossible to 'act in furtherance' of an end without *willing* it; but agents can *will* something, on occasion, without actually doing anything about it, whether because they believe

---

6 Cf. Davidson, 'Freedom to Act,' 151: 'all the conditions may be satisfied, and yet they may fail to ignite an action. It might happen as simply as this: the agent wants φ, and he believes x-ing is the best way to bring about φ, and yet he fails to put these two things together; the practical reasoning that would lead him to conclude that x is worth doing, may simply fail to occur. There is no more reason to suppose that a person who has reasons for acting will always act on them than to suppose that a person who has beliefs which entail a certain conclusion will draw that conclusion.'

7 Let us say that one belief is 'additional' to another if it is logically possible to hold the latter belief without holding the former belief.

it to be unattainable, or attainable without their actually doing anything, or because they expect its attainment or non-attainment to depend on chance, or at any rate forces beyond their control, or because they are paralysed or otherwise unable to take just at will the means which they intend. But even in those cases the agents *would* take means to bring about whatever they *will* if, in full confidence, they knew such means to be available, effective, necessary, and not too onerous. Agents may be said to *will* whatever they *would* bring about if they knew full well that they could bring it about just at will while knowing full well also that it was not something which would come about anyway.

Here, then, is a definition. A being A *wills* something E if and only if it is the case that:

    if an event M were to be conceivable such that A believed correctly that, in the circumstances,

        (i) M's occurrence was necessary and sufficient for the realization of E

    and (ii) the fact of M's necessity for the realization of E was insufficient to prevent the realization of E

    and (iii) A's believing (i) and (ii) was necessary for M to occur,

    and *if* no additional true belief on A's part about what would increase M's chances of occurrence were in the circumstances necessary for M to occur,

    then M would occur.

Necessarily, whatever is willed is desired, but that which is *desired* may fail to be willed because the desire for it may be outweighed or exactly counterbalanced by desires for other things. If it were not for this last, Buridanian sort of case of exact counterbalancing, we could say that a being *desired* something if and only if the being either willed it or would will it but for willing something else. However, it does sometimes happen, apparently, that a human or animal is psychologically paralysed by a virtually exact counterbalancing of incompatible desires. In a case like that, each such desire is an inner cause of the same sort and magnitude and but for the others *would* in itself constitute an instance of willing.

Let us say, then, that a being B *desires* something G if and only if B is in an inner state or condition S of such a sort that B either wills G or *would* will G but for the fact that B wills something else, or but for the fact that, in addition to S, B is also in one or more other inner states or conditions each of which is of the same sort and magnitude as S and each of which *would* be sufficient for B's willing something if it were not for state or condition S and the others.

Index